Opera on Film

Opera on Film

Richard Fawkes

Duckworth

First published in 2000 by
Gerald Duckworth & Co. Ltd.
61 Frith Street, London W1V 5TA
Tel: 0171 434 4242
Fax: 0171 434 4420
Email: enquiries@duckworth-publishers.co.uk

A catalogue record for this book is available
from the British Library

ISBN 0 7156 2943 3

Typeset by Derek Doyle & Associates, Liverpool
Printed in Great Britain by
Redwood Books Ltd, Trowbridge

Contents

Plates between pages 118 and 119

Acknowledgements

The working title for this book was *Opera on Screen*. I was duly horrified, just after I had started writing it, to be asked by Graeme Kay, then editor of *Opera Now* magazine, to review a book called *Opera on Screen*. My immediate thought was that the five years I had spent watching videos and collating my information had been for nothing. Ken Wlaschin's marvellous book turned out to be an encyclopaedia of both opera on film and opera on video. It provided a comprehensive checklist with which I could compare my own lists, gave me details of some films about which I did not know, and allowed me the occasional smile of satisfaction when I discovered a title he had missed. Although I have listed *Opera on Screen* in my bibliography, I would like to acknowledge here my gratitude to Wlaschin. His book is a major reference work which anyone remotely interested in opera, film or television ought to have.

Many of the films mentioned in this book I have watched in the course of reviewing them for *Opera Now* and *BBC Music Magazine*. I must thank Graeme Kay for first asking me to write a regular review column in *Opera Now*, and Ashutosh Khandekar, the present editor, for continuing it. My gratitude, too, to Helen Wallace, who succeeded Graeme as editor of *BBC Music Magazine*, to Keith Clarke, editor of *Classical Music*, who, knowing of my interest in the subject, has commissioned me to interview so many film-makers, and to Antonia Couling, editor of *The Singer*.

Many people have helped me during the course of my research, sometimes with reams of information and rare films to watch, sometimes with a single nugget that has proved invaluable. I would like to thank them all, especially Felix Brenner, the late David Shipman, who was not only a ready source of information and amusing anecdote but a good friend, Stefan Zucker of the Bel Canto Society for sending me tapes and writing such informative blurbs to accompany them, Fritz Curzon, for providing me with information about his mother Maria Cebotari, Marjan and Jane Kiepura for their considerable help, enthusiasm and valued friendship, Marta Eggerth, Charles Osborne, Mary Ellis, Joe Marks, Nigel Douglas, Mark Ricaldone, Harald Henrysson (the curator of the Björling Museum in Borlange), Peter Piccaver, Peter Parker of the Gilbert and Sullivan Society, Valerie Masterson, Gillian Humphreys, Dominik Scherrer, Herbert Wise, Christopher Rawlence, Peter Jaques, Lionel

Salter, Simon Brown, Erich Sargeant, Louise Stein, Brian Large, Trevor Nunn, Willard White, Annette Morreau, Mike Henry, Jane Thorburn, the staff of the BFI Library, Ivan Marinov, Emma Roach, John Steane, Chris Hunt, and the late Nigel Finch.

I am indebted, too, to Deborah Blake, my editor at Duckworth, for her unfailing enthusiasm and encouragement, and to Cherry, Harry, Leo and Caitlin, who have had to put up so frequently over the past few years with having to watch a 1936 black-and-white movie when they would much rather have been watching the latest Bond.

Picture credits

The numbers given below refer to the plate section. The author and publishers are also grateful to the British Film Institute for providing stills.

Lasky-Paramount: 1; Gaumont: 2, 23; Gaumont British: 10; Lasky: 3; MGM: 4, 20, 21, 25; Columbia: 8, 9; RKO: 11; Paramount: 12, 18; Trafalgar: 13; Publicity Picture Productions: 14; ACI Europa: 15, 17; Székely/Intergloria 16; Victoria Films: 19; British Lion/London Films: 22; Rank: 24; Mediascope:26; Artefax: 27; Hell Ltd: 28

Preface

Like millions of my generation, I first experienced opera, not in the opera house, but in the cinema. My mother took me to see Mario Lanza in *The Great Caruso* and I was hooked. As a direct result of seeing the film, I longed to see a live opera and when I did, there was no looking back.

It is easy to be sniffy about filmed opera. It can be off-putting when the lips do not synchronise with the sound; sometimes the performances are ham. But operatic films provide us with the only visual evidence of what many famous singers of former generations looked like in performance, and the visual side of their art is of major importance when assessing the total artistry of any singer. It is only in the twentieth century that sound has become separated from picture. The enormous technical advances that took place in sound reproduction were not matched by similar advances in picture quality. People became accustomed to buying operas on LPs or CDs and 'listening' to them rather than watching them as well. If Mozart were to come back today, he would surely be shocked by this attitude. For him, the visual side of an operatic performance was of equal importance to the aural: you couldn't have one without the other. This is one of the many reasons why filmed opera (and I here include operatic arias in films, not just complete operas) is both so fascinating and so valuable.

Today, the words 'film' and 'video' are often used interchangeably. People talk about an opera transmitted from an opera house as being filmed. It is nothing of the kind. Film is a very specific medium; video is another. This book does not, except in passing, deal with those operas (many available as home videos), which have been recorded electronically, only those that have ended up on celluloid. In the text, I have as a general rule given the original title of a film with an English translation in brackets.

Ever since opera began, towards the close of the sixteenth century, it has had to endure an elitist label. It has always been the most expensive art form there is – 'the most expensive noise known to man', as it was once described. If it is elitist, that is as a result of the places which stage it, not the fault of opera itself. Opera, with its combination of drama, colour and music, has the power to move the human heart in a way no other art form can. Film-makers have always recognised this. From the moment the first movie flickered onto a

ix

screen, they have tried to use the most popular art form of the twentieth century to break down barriers and introduce more and more people to the joys of opera. Making the perfect operatic film has become an obsession. It is that obsession which is charted in this book.

1999   Richard Fawkes

1
Early Days

On 23 April 1915, at the Metropolitan Opera House, New York, Geraldine Farrar sang the title role in *Madama Butterfly*. As was customary whenever she appeared, the house was packed and the applause as she took her final curtain calls, tumultuous.

At the age of 33, Farrar was America's leading prima donna. Born in Melrose, Massachusetts, the daughter of a baseball player, she had studied in Paris and then Berlin where she had made her operatic debut in 1901 singing Marguerite in Gounod's *Faust*. She had made her Met debut five years later as Juliet in the same composer's *Roméo et Juliette*, and had been at the house ever since. She had sung the Met's first Butterfly, was an outstanding interpreter of Puccini (she was later to create the role of Suor Angelica) and a gifted actress. In an age before radio, television or even the cinema, turned people into household names, she was known to millions of Americans thanks to her recordings (especially of arias from *Carmen* which had sold over a million copies) and her frequent appearances in the gossip columns. She was arguably the most famous American woman of her day.

Among those who crowded into her dressing room after the performance was the film producer Jesse Lasky. He had an ulterior motive: he didn't just want to congratulate her, he wanted to offer her the chance to appear in a film. At that time the movie industry had still not created any real stars of its own. Producers, in an attempt to find the next person who might prove popular with a comparatively fickle public, were still turning to Broadway, the stage and vaudeville.

Trying to stay one move ahead of their rivals, Lasky and his partner Sam Goldfish (who was later to change his name to Goldwyn) had formed Famous Players with the principal purpose of filming stage plays. They had not found it difficult to acquire the rights for the latest Broadway successes, but the reluctance of some of the big name actors to recreate their stage roles on film was proving a real obstacle. Film still had more than a whiff of the showground, of being not quite respectable. These actors and actresses felt their reputations as serious artists might suffer if they were to be seen in a film.

Lasky and Goldfish, fed up with meeting this attitude time and again, decided to go for the biggest name then on the stage in America to prove to

1

the others that acting in the movies was respectable. And the biggest star of them all was Geraldine Farrar.

When Goldfish first mentioned his intention to sign her, he was told it would be as easy as getting the Statue of Liberty to walk on water. But, to many people's surprise, following Lasky's appearance in her dressing room after *Madama Butterfly* the diva at least agreed to talk.

The meeting had been set up initially by Morris Gest, a well-known New York theatrical agent. At a party earlier in the year, he had met Farrar and, no doubt with ten per cent of a star's fee in mind, had convinced her that the only way for an artist to live for ever was on the motion picture screen. Farrar had taken the bait and eventually authorised Gest to contact Lasky.

The day after Lasky had accompanied Gest to see *Madama Butterfly*, he and Goldfish met Farrar in her apartment and explained that they wanted her to appear in a film version of Bizet's *Carmen*. The diva was intrigued, not just by the prospect of immortality but by the possibility of appearing as Carmen without actually having to sing. She was also fascinated by the thought that her performance would be seen by thousands more than would ever get to see her in an opera house. According to Gest, Lasky was so keen to sign her that he offered to pay her $2 a minute while in California, whether shooting or not, plus royalties and a share of the profits. In fact, Farrar agreed to a three-picture deal for $20,000.

That summer, after the Met season had finished, Farrar left Grand Central Station on board a train bound for the West Coast. As befitted a prima donna, she had not simply agreed to a fee, but had made other demands. One was that she should travel in a private carriage. Another, that there should be a pianist on board to play her themes from Rimsky-Korsakov's *Scheherazade*. It was rumoured that the pianist, Jimmy Sullivan, a celebrated man-about-town, also provided the star with services not in his contract. Farrar spent most of the journey clad only in a negligée, occasionally climbing onto the lid of the piano to dance, occasionally flying into fits of temper and using language that her mother certainly never taught her.

When the train reached Los Angeles, still little more than a small country town, a red carpet was rolled out to greet her; schoolchildren, given the day off school, sang a greeting; and the mayor of Los Angeles was there to meet her in person and escort her to his waiting car.

The director of *Carmen* was to be Goldfish's young protégé, Cecil B. DeMille. He had already directed some fourteen films in the previous two years since he had made his debut with *The Squaw Man*, but had yet to establish a reputation for being more than competent. DeMille was astute enough to know that it would not be easy for an opera singer, used to filling the great space of an opera house with a grand gesture, to pull back her performance for the more intimate camera, and he suggested they do a try-out film first which would not be released until after *Carmen*.

2

The company already had the rights to *Maria Rosa*, the story of two men's rivalry for a Spanish woman (a plot not totally unlike that of *Carmen*), and Farrar was cast in this opposite Wallace Reid and Pedro de Cordoba. Reid was to play Don José in *Carmen* and DeMille thought it would be useful if the two could get to know one another. He had first noticed the actor playing a small role in *The Birth of a Nation*, and it was as a bit-part player that Reid made his living, supplementing his income by playing mood music for the stars. DeMille decided to take a chance on him. De Cordoba, who was to play Escamillo, was making his film debut. A New Yorker of Cuban extraction, he had started his career as an operatic bass. He was to become one of Hollywood's most distinguished character actors.

Farrar had been given a bungalow in the grounds of DeMille's home. Her contract specified that she would not have to work more than six hours a day, and that those six hours should be broken up into a three-hour session in the morning and a three-hour session in the afternoon, with a two-hour break for lunch. DeMille wasn't at all happy with this arrangement but had to accept it.

Farrar, despite her later memories of calm and co-operation on the set, was far from easy. She had the bungalow redecorated and insisted that her dressing rooms be redesigned; she demanded, and got, endless script rewrites; the servants hired to look after her in the bungalow were almost all fired. She insisted on not being watched while filming and so a covered way was built for her to walk unobserved from her dressing room to the stage. She was blatant about the men she wanted. She also had a legitimate grouse about the make-up she was required to wear. Her face was covered with thick white greasepaint and then heavily powdered. She was given green eye shadow and white lips. Under the heat of the studio lamps, her eyes swelled up and streamed so that she couldn't film.

DeMille was in for a shock, too, when he screened the first rushes of *Maria Rosa*. His cameraman, Alvin Wyckoff, liked strong light, and DeMille had a constant battle with him to include shadows. At the first screening, DeMille was horrified to see that Farrar didn't have any eyes; the film simply hadn't registered them, just as it had failed to register the actors' teeth. The most romantic smile had become a toothless grin.

When he called Farrar in to show her, she screamed with rage and clawed at the screen. DeMille managed to get around the problem by having someone hold a large square of black cloth behind the camera during shooting, and incorporating more cross-lighting.

Having finished *Maria Rosa*, DeMille immediately turned his attention to *Carmen*. The announcement that Farrar was to make the film could hardly have been kept a secret, even if Lasky and Goldfish had wanted it to be, which they certainly did not. They wanted every column inch of publicity they could get. They wanted the world to know they had acquired a class act. The moment their project had become public knowledge, the Bizet estate got in touch to discuss the little matter of rights. They wanted a colossal sum of money and so DeMille simply got his brother William to write the same story from the Merimée novel, which Lasky acquired for significantly less, so that they could legitimately claim they were not making a film of Bizet's opera. There are, in fact, some basic differences between the two, one being that Micaëla does not appear in the film. There is also nothing about Don José's background or why he is in Seville, and his first meeting with Carmen is engineered by her on the instructions of the smugglers well before the fight in the factory.

To get herself in the mood for playing the role of Carmen, Farrar asked DeMille if she could have Bizet's music played on set (musicians on set were to become an enduring image of silent film production in Hollywood). DeMille was terrified that the Bizet estate would somehow find out and demand a royalty, so he engaged a pianist to play other music Farrar liked instead.

DeMille went for a realistic approach to the film. The bullfight, attended by 22,000 people, was staged in Los Angeles with special permission from the mayor, the first bullfight to be permitted in the city for several years. It nearly cost Escamillo's stand-in, a professional matador, his life. The bull caught the matador by surprise and tossed him in the air. It then prepared to gore the prone body, but luckily for the man the bull's horns were set wide apart and instead of killing him, went under him, scooping him up.

For the factory scene and the fight, DeMille decided to cast his script editor Jeannie Macpherson, also an actress, as the girl with whom Carmen fights, knowing that Macpherson loathed the opera singer. During the scene, DeMille got the realism he was hoping for but Farrar certainly got the better of Macpherson who was left bleeding, crying and badly shaken.

DeMille discovered very early on that Farrar was a natural screen actress (it was perhaps ironic that *Maria Rosa*, shot before Carmen as a warm-up, should be reviewed in the *New York Times* as being 'as good if not better than Carmen'). This meant he did not have to impose his view of the character upon Farrar but could discuss a scene with her and her co-stars and then shoot the improvisation.

Two weeks after completing *Carmen*, DeMille and Farrar were back on set filming *Temptation*, the third of the three films she was contracted to make. The release of this, too, was held up until after the opening of *Carmen* which took place in Boston on 1 October 1915. The music accompanying the film had been adapted from Bizet by Hugo Reinfeld, one of Hollywood's earliest film composers. Three singers were engaged to sing the three big numbers – the Habanera, 'La fleur que tu m'avais jetée' and the Toreador song. So much for the studio's vociferous claims that the film had nothing at all to do with Bizet's opera!

That same year Raoul Walsh had made another version of the Carmen story with Theda Bara in the title role. This was premiered on the same night that

Farrar's film opened as part of a deliberate spoiling tactic. But nothing could stop the success of the DeMille version. The audience applauded at the end of scenes, and when the climax came and Don José killed Carmen outside the bullring, strong men were seen to weep. Farrar, who was in the audience, had to stand up to acknowledge the cheers of the crowd.

It was a similar story when the film opened in New York a month later. Sam Goldfish was overjoyed. 'I believe Miss Farrar will supersede any human being ever seen on the screen,' he told a reporter, 'and that she will bring into the picture house people who have never been there before. I am confident she will elevate the moving picture drama to heights never dreamed of.'

When Farrar had returned to New York after filming, she had been asked if she felt appearing in a movie would harm her drawing power in the opera house. 'Watch the box office,' was her reply. She was right. The public flocked to see *Carmen* and she became a role model for countless women. Young girls who copied her style in clothes became known as Gerryflappers.

Filming didn't just bring Farrar to the notice of a much wider public. She learnt a lot about conveying character from her first venture into cinema and was determined to incorporate some of the business from her movie portrayal into her stage persona. When she next sang the role of Carmen at the Met, on 17 February 1916, she suddenly, without warning, slapped Enrico Caruso, her Don José, very hard on the face and then proceeded to have a very realistic fight with a startled chorus girl.

Afterwards she let it be known that if Caruso didn't care for this kind of realism, then the Met could find a new Carmen. The tenor responded that Farrar's departure from the house was quite unnecessary since a repetition of the scene could be avoided by the Met getting a new Don José. A week later the second performance, with both Farrar and Caruso still there, passed without incident.

Carmen not only turned Farrar into a major movie star and established the epic style for which DeMille was to become famous, it is also one of the masterpieces of silent cinema. All the more surprising, then, that it should, despite the denials, be a film of an opera, especially since the most important element of an opera – the sound – is missing. As the critic of the *New York Times* put it at the time: 'It is a curious commentary on the crazy economy of the theatre that a supreme dramatic soprano should give any of her precious time to a form of entertainment, to an art if you will, wherein the chief characteristic is a complete and abysmal silence.'

Of course DeMille's version is not just an operatic video with the sound turned off. It is a dramatic telling of the story in which the characters are seen to speak lines rather than sing them. And unlike opera in the opera house, for which the music is paramount, the score written for playing with the film is an equal partner with the visual images on screen, a way of establishing mood and manipulating emotions.

It was not then so very surprising that Lasky, Goldfish and DeMille had turned their attentions to opera. They had wanted an opera singer to star in one of their films; *Carmen* was a good story and a role for which Farrar was well-known; and opera, in any case, had fascinated film-makers ever since the first flickering films were seen towards the end of the previous century.

No single person was responsible for the birth of the cinema, which was rather an evolution in which many hands took part. The principle of repeating still pictures to give the illusion of movement was well known in ancient times and had been written about extensively by the beginning of the nineteenth century. Magic lantern shows, in which images were thrown or projected onto a wall, were popular forms of entertainment. In the 1860s, William George Horner, an Englishman, and several other inventors, produced the Zoetrope, a drum with a series of pictures mounted inside. When the drum was spun and the pictures viewed through a slot, they appeared to move.

In California in the 1870s, another Englishman, Edward Muybridge, rigged up a series of first twelve then 24 still cameras to record the successive movements of a trotting horse. These pictures, and others like them, were used to illustrate lectures and books, and came as a result of a rail tycoon's determination to find out whether a trotting horse had all four feet off the ground at the same time. They were not intended to be animated or used to produce continuous movement.

It was a German, Ottomar Anschutz, who first devised an apparatus whereby a series of still pictures could be viewed in rapid succession, and a Frenchman, Étienne-Jules Marey, a specialist in animal motion, who devised a single camera capable of recording movement. Fascinated by Muybridge's work, Marey found that his methods were too primitive to record birds in flight, so he developed a photographic gun, based on a device developed by an astronomer for recording Venus crossing the face of the sun, which allowed twelve pictures to be recorded in quick succession on a rotating photographic plate. He also managed to devise a method of projecting the developed images. By 1888 Marey was experimenting with rolls of celluloid film, a new invention originating from America and being successfully exploited by George Eastman, founder of the Eastman Kodak Company.

At the same time, the American inventor Thomas Edison was busy working out how he might harness moving pictures to the phonograph he had recently invented. His initial attempts to build a camera, basing it on the cylinder he used for recording sound, came to nothing and it was not until he visited Marey and saw him using roll film that he realised the way forward. Edison's research assistant, W. Laurie Dickson, duly came up with a film camera, to which they gave the name the Kinetograph, which used film 35mm wide with four sprocket holes to each frame to ensure the smooth advance of the film through the gate which allowed in the light. This was driven by an electric motor that made the camera very unwieldy and bulky. By the time the film industry got going, the lighter and more mobile cameras being used were hand-cranked.

On 6 October 1889, Edison and Dickson gave a public demonstration of their Kinetograph, but Edison was not convinced that projecting the resulting pictures was the right answer. Instead he developed the Kinetoscope, a kind of peepshow machine which contained a loop of film 50 feet long which could only be viewed by one person at a time.

While Marey and Edison were busy with their various experiments, a Frenchman who lived in Leeds in England, Louis Le Prince, patented a sixteen-lens camera and a projector to show the resulting films. By 1889 he was working on a single-lens camera with a claw mechanism for moving the film through the gate that was to become the basis of all later film cameras. Le Prince was clearly destined to become one of the big names of cinema history but the following year, on a visit to France, he disappeared from the train on which he was travelling and was never seen or heard of again.

Many others on both sides of the Atlantic were experimenting with the new medium. There was William Friese-Greene, the man once credited with being the Father of Cinematography, but now considered to have been a very small player within the overall picture, and Wordsworth Donisthorpe, who, in 1889 with W.C. Crofts, built a camera and took a shot of Trafalgar Square which still exists. Nothing seems to have come directly from their experiments, but Donisthorpe is also notable for having written an article in 1878 suggesting that the newly invented phonograph should be combined with some form of moving photography.

In Germany, the brothers Max and Emil Skladanowsky developed the Bioscop, a double projection apparatus which they patented in 1895 and with which they gave the first public presentation of moving pictures in Berlin on 1 November. This consisted of nine short sketches. A second programme of mostly Berlin city views was put together for a demonstration tour of Germany.

Six weeks after the Skladanowsky brothers had given their first show, came the event from which the start of cinema is generally dated. On 28 December 1895 in the converted basement of the Grand Café in the Boulevard des Capucines, Paris, the Lumière brothers, Louis and Auguste, gave what is regarded as the first projected film show to a paying audience. What the public saw for their money were ten short strips of film, none of them lasting more than a minute, showing such events as a train arriving at a station and a ship being unloaded. Two months later the Lumière brothers repeated the performance in London, including in the programme a film of a boy standing on the gardener's hose. When the gardener picks it up to find out what is wrong, the boy lifts his foot with obvious results.

Interest in the Lumières' new invention was sufficient for them to be signed up to give a twenty-minute film programme at the Empire Leicester Square, sandwiched between variety acts. Their movies were considered an interesting novelty and nothing more. But the stage had been set for the birth of the cinema as we know it today.

Four months after the Lumière brothers had given their first show, Edison gave his first public presentation of projected film. By July 1896, the Lumières' shows had reached India and Russia, followed soon afterwards by Australia, China and Japan. Public screenings had become a way of life. But what to show? Edison had always considered the moving picture to be an accompaniment to his sound system rather than the other way round, and his early experiments trying to marry sound and film had led him naturally towards music-based subjects. One of his earliest films, made in 1894 and lasting only 30 seconds, was called *Carmencita* and featured a Spanish dancer who may well have been dancing to a record of Bizet's music.

Other early pioneers felt the same as Edison, that moving pictures should have sound. Songs or operatic arias were the ideal material with which to experiment, especially since they were available on records which could then be synchronised to the screen. In Germany, in 1896, Max Skladanowsky showed a brief film of a duet from an unnamed operetta (possibly Carl Zeller's *Der Vogelhändler* or Karl Millöcker's *Der Bettelstudent*). This featured the Austrian soprano Fritzi Massary, a popular Viennese singer who was then at the beginning of her career, and Josef Gianpetro, and it almost certainly had synchronised sound provided by a record. Two years later, in New York, a two-minute scene from Donizetti's *La Fille du Régiment* was filmed, again to be shown with sound.

Trying to synchronise a recording with the picture was to be the favoured method of reproducing sound for several years. But it had major drawbacks. The first was that in those early days a means of amplifying sound had not been invented so the films could only be shown to very small audiences. The Edison Kinetoscope had something rather like a doctor's stethoscope which was plugged into each ear to make listening possible. Only one person at a time could watch and listen. Indeed most early film shows took place in small booths at fairgrounds, in amusement arcades or in the corner of a drug store on a one-to-one basis. Even if attempts were made to show a film to large audiences in large rooms or spaces such as a tent, those at the back couldn't hear a thing.

Another drawback to any method of sound reproduction was the way early films were shot and projected. Some of the first cameras were driven by electric motors which were so huge and cumbersome that the camera was rooted to the spot and unable to move. In order to introduce mobility, the hand-cranked camera was developed. When filming, the cameraman had to turn a handle, humming something to give himself the correct speed (the Blue Danube was a favourite with many). Similarly the projectionist had to turn a handle to project the film and the chances of him turning his handle at exactly the same speed as the cameraman were not that high. If that speed had to match a phonographic cylinder to get lip synchronisation as well, the problem was there for all to see.

But that did not stop people trying to marry sound and picture. On 8 June 1900, the first public showing of three operatic films took place in Paris. The baritone Victor Maurel, who had created the roles of Iago in Verdi's *Otello* and Canio in *Pagliacci*, sang an aria from *Don Giovanni* and then appeared as Falstaff (another role he had created) while the tenor Emile Cossira sang an aria from *Roméo et Juliette*. All three films lasted for about three minutes and were directed by Clément Maurice. What made them particularly significant is that they were all sound films, with the image on screen being matched to sound from a phonographic cylinder recorded separately.

Also in 1900, another French film using a wax cylinder was made of Polin from La Scala singing an aria from Donizetti's *La Fille du Régiment*. In 1902 Dutch and French film-makers made a number of sound films of arias from *Carmen*, *Faust*, *La Favorita*, Offenbach's *Barbe-Bleue*, *Cendrillon*, *Les Huguenots* and *Clairette's 28 Days*, screened shortly after the operetta by Victor Roger had opened in France.

The following year, French director Georges Méliès appeared as Méphistophélès in a nine-minute, fifteen-scene, tinted version of *The Damnation of Faust* and directed a seven-scene version of *The Barber of Seville*, both with sound from cylinders. Méliès, one of the most important names of early cinema, had made his first musically inspired film in 1898. This was a one-minute film based on Berlioz's *Damnation of Faust*, although whether it had sound or not is uncertain.

Méliès was unlike most other pioneer film-makers. They tended to be inventors looking for an application for their inventions. Méliès was, first and foremost, a showman and a performer. He was a conjuror and magician who, since 1888, had run the Théâtre Robert-Houdin in Paris where he performed his act on stage and showed lantern slides. The cinema seemed to him to be a natural development to what he was doing anyway and he started making films in 1896, producing the usual scenes of everyday life. But what interested him particularly about film was its ability to help illusion. Stopping the camera mid-trick and moving or substituting objects or even people, when projected back, made complex stage illusions appear simple.

Méliès was also interested in opera and in particular the character of Faust. The camera's ability to make Méphistophélès appear from nowhere or the elderly Faust become miraculously young, fascinated him, as did the possibility of creating spectacle on screen. In 1899, the year after his first Faust film, he made a seven-minute film of Massenet's *Cendrillon* with a cast of 35, using special effects. It was shot in twenty scenes and tinted to give the illusion of colour. It was a very ambitious undertaking for its time, although whether Méliès shot it with sound isn't known. Certainly his two operatic productions of 1903 were. He returned to the subject of Faust again in 1904 when he appeared once more as Méphistophélès, in a fourteen-minute film of Gounod's opera.

Another important film pioneer who featured opera was the German, Oskar Messter. A manufacturer of projectors and cameras, he bought his first film theatre in Berlin in 1896. He had started as a film producer principally to provide films for people who had bought his projectors. Among his many patents was one for the Biophon Tonbilder sound-system, which he used from 1903 until 1910 to make many experimental sound films. A large number starred Henny Porten, the daughter of Franz Porten, a former opera singer who became Messter's cameraman and leading director. Henny became the first star of German cinema. In 1907 both she and her father appeared in a three-minute extract from *Lohengrin*, directed by her brother Friedrich, and in Desdemona's death scene from Verdi's *Otello*, with her father singing Otello as well as directing. This time her sister managed to get in on the act as well, appearing as Emilia. The same team went on to produce films featuring arias from *Der Freischütz*, *Il Trovatore*, *Tannhäuser*, Viktor Nessler's *The Trumpeter of Sakkingen* and *Der Bettelstudent* amongst others.

In Britain the first operatic film was a three-minute scene from *The Mikado*, made in 1904 by the Walterdaw company and screened using a British sound system employing a record. Another early British attempt to marry sound and picture came with the Chronophone sound system. In 1906, Arthur Gilbert directed a number of shorts using this system including two of arias from *Il Trovatore* with Edith Albord and Frank Rowe, a scene from *HMS Pinafore*, one from *Lakmé* and a twelve-minute film of *Carmen* featuring arias and scenes from the opera. Gilbert also directed the first operatic film to last over an hour, a sound version of *Faust* (1907) which ran for 66 minutes.

Between 1900 and 1910, there were more than 80 known attempts to make synchronous sound films of operas or operatic arias. Even the great Luisa Tetrazzini appeared in 1909 in a German sound film, now sadly lost, singing an aria from Gounod's *Roméo et Juliette*

Other film-makers, equally attracted to opera as a subject for film, decided on a different method to match sound and pictures. Leopoldo Fregoli, the first Italian film director and a noted quick-change artist, made a six-minute film in 1898 called *Masters of Music* in which he impersonated various composers – Verdi, Rossini, Mascagni and Wagner – conducting. While the images played on the screen, Fregoli stood to one side and sang and talked.

Edison himself made a fifteen-minute version (extremely long for the time) of Flotow's *Martha* in 1900. Directed by Edwin Porter, who made *The Great Train Robbery*, one of the earliest narrative films, this seems to be the first real attempt to film an opera explaining the complete story, rather than just showing scenes or arias. The film was made without sound, and when it came to showing it, Edison suggested that four singers from the local church choir should be hired to stand behind or alongside the screen and sing along. If that proved impossible, Edison informed cinema managers, he would provide the singers himself.

Porter later planned on his own to make a twenty-minute film of *Parsifal* which he intended would be screened with a recording of Wagner's music, but a copyright lawsuit killed the project. *Parsifal* had received its American premiere at the Met in 1903 and, because of hostility from Bayreuth, a lot of publicity. The Edison studio also decided to turn it into an epic film to be screened with recordings, but the Wagner family again sued and the film, although completed, never received wide circulation.

We tend today to think of all films before 1927 as being 'silent'. By that we really mean that they did not have synchronous sound for they were anything but silent. Some films were shown with lecturers standing behind or alongside the screen telling the story, highlighting what to watch out for, and even providing appropriate sound effects. Others would have musical accompaniment. This started originally because the noise of the projectors was so great that something was needed to drown it. The ability of music to sway emotions or set a mood was quickly recognised and music soon became a constituent part of most film shows. Some distributors would send out copies of the appropriate music with the film, and depending on where you lived, you could hear it played by an orchestra, a quartet, or a lone pianist.

Because of the problems there were with synchronisation at a time when equipment was crude, having the music performed live rather than off records became the preferred alternative for most operatic film-makers. Sigmund Lubin's version of Flotow's *Martha*, made in 1902, was intended to be screened with live music from the opera, as was a 1907 Swedish highlights version of *The Merry Widow*. A ten-minute Brazilian comic version of Lehár's operetta, made the following year, had singers behind the screen. In the early days of cinema, one sign of success was if the comic send-ups followed. By 1907, opera was clearly an acceptable target for two films were made exploiting the comic possibilities of singing. In a French film entitled *Le Chanteur Obstiné*, a tenor manages to wreck every place in which he sings with his top notes, while *Sister Mary Jane's Top Note* causes the furniture to shake.

Many film-makers, though not interested in using operatic arias as the basis of experiments with sound systems, gravitated towards operatic plots for their films because composers and librettists had already done a lot of their work for them. With no dialogue to explain who people were or what was going on, film plots needed to be simple and easily understood. Most operas were based on sources already available (novels or plays) and the task of filleting the originals to make them dramatic had already taken place. The film-maker's need to tell a clear story was made that much easier, especially if instantly recognisable music could be added.

In 1908, the year an Italian sound film of arias from *Lucia di Lammermoor* was made, Ernesto Maria Pasquali directed a ten-minute dramatic version of the story. In 1909, Mario Gallo directed *Cavalleria Rusticana* as a silent narrative feature, while in France, Albert Capellani, who had earlier directed a fourteen-minute colour film of *Mary Stuart* based on the *Donizetti* opera, made a version of *Semiramide* starring Stacia Napierkowska and Paul Capellani. D.W. Griffith made a version of *Rigoletto* called *A Fool's Revenge*, starring Owen Moore as the Duke, Marion Leonard as Gilda and Charles Inslee as Rigoletto. This came out at the same time as J. Stuart Blackton's *The Duke's Jester* with Maurice Costello. Both were screened with musical accompaniment taken from Verdi's opera.

Il Trovatore, *Carmen* (to become the most filmed opera), *La Bohème*, *Manon*, *Manon Lescaut*, *Tristan und Isolde*, *Orpheus in the Underworld*, *The Mikado*, *The Bartered Bride*, *Salomé*, *Roméo et Juliette*, a Ring cycle and, from Russia, *The Queen of Spades*, were just a few of the many operas filmed with and without music during the first decade of the cinema as the medium moved out of the circus and fairground to take its place on main street.

2

The Cinema Grows Up

By 1910, the length of the average film had increased to around the fifteen-minute mark and operatic films had settled into a pattern. There were those for which the producers were still experimenting with various sound systems, still trying to find a way to produce 'talkies'; those designed to be accompanied by a pit band, or piano, depending on where the cinema was located, playing a score based on themes from the opera; and those – in the vast majority since mainstream film-making had decided that sound was both unnatural and not worth the effort or expense – in which the story was being used and where the end film might bear only a passing resemblance to the opera.

Experiments with sound in the second decade of the century were largely limited to European companies. In Sweden, Charles Magnusson, using the Messter Biophon system, directed shorts of Oscar Bergstrom singing an aria from *Orpheus in the Underworld* and Carl Barklind singing from *The Dollar Princess*. In Germany, Messter himself filmed an aria from *Der Rosenkavalier* almost as soon as the opera had opened in Dresden, made a short of *Mignon* featuring Mary Runge and a scene from *The Tales of Hoffmann* featuring the barcarole. Other German productions featured two arias from *Pagliacci* sung by Emil Lieben, the Toreador song from *Carmen*, a scene from Nicolai's *The Merry Wives of Windsor*, and a scene from *The Barber of Seville*. While very few of these films have survived, it has been estimated that in Germany alone something like 1,500 operatic shorts with synchronous sound were made before the end of the 1920s, the official arrival of sound.

In Britain, at this time, David Barnett directed a twelve-minute sound version of *Il Trovatore* and one of *Faust* using the Animtophone system which synchronised the on-screen image with records. *Faust* was again the favoured opera for another British attempt to make a sound film in 1911 using the Vivaphone system. The director was Cecil Hepworth who in 1909 had made a sound film of a duet from *The Mikado*.

The majority of film-makers, however, were not interested in sound, which was still associated with the wonders of the peep-show presentation and the nickelodeon. Serious practitioners were trying to develop a cinematic language, which would help take films out of the fairground and raise them to the status of an art form. Sound played no part in that.

Experiments to synchronise sound and picture declined as cinemas showing films to hundreds of people began to open up. Sound films could not be shown in such barns because, without amplification, no one could hear them. Even the pushy Edison, having decided in 1909 to make a series of operatic films, opted to shoot them silent and show them with live music. The first of these was *Faust*, produced by Edwin S. Porter, followed by *La Bohème*, starring Vittoria Lois and directed by Enrico Berriel, and then *Aïda* with popular silent star Mary Fuller in the title role and Radamès played by the actor Mark MacDermott. Shown with Verdi's music accompanying it, *Aïda* was warmly received. The critics generally seemed to like operatic films. They rarely commented on or were disturbed by the fact that the new breed of operatic film did not have synchronous music. Georges Denola's film of *La Favorita* was praised for being a good adaptation of the opera, and when a 1911 French version of scenes from *Don Giovanni*, showing the Don's end and descent to hell, was first screened, one critic noted how nice it was to see opera on film because one could imagine the music.

This was the way most operatic films were made during the period from 1910 to the mid-1920s, and because the music was already there, the stories provided a double attraction to producers. Even when the great French actress Sarah Bernhardt appeared in a film version of the Sardou play, *La Tosca*, and then in *La Dame aux Camélias*, both were screened with music taken from the operas, Puccini's *Tosca* and Verdi's *La Traviata*, respectively.

In 1910, 27 films were made either of scenes from operas or using the story from an opera. These included two versions of *Carmen*, two of *La Bohème* and four of *Faust*, and versions of *Werther*, *La Favorita*, *Orpheus in the Underworld*, *Rigoletto*, *The Ring* (in a twelve-minute Italian version screened with the music), a Russian *Queen of Spades*, *The Dollar Princess*, *Ernani*, *Cavalleria Rusticana*, *The Barber of Seville*, *Manon*, *Manon Lescaut*, *Samson et Dalila*, *Luisa Miller*, *Il Trovatore*, *Tosca*, *Elektra* and *La Muette de Portici* by Auber. With the exception of an aria from *Faust* sung by a bass from the Paris Opéra, none of these films featured opera singers. The American film of *Elektra*, for example, based on the opera and sometimes shown accompanied by Strauss's music, sometimes by other music, featured Mary Fuller.

Twenty similar operatic films were made during 1911, including an Italian *Tristan und Isolde* that was shown with Wagner's music, *Norma*, *The Marriage of Figaro*, a version of *Agrippina* and, in Russia, *A Life for the Tsar* and *Eugene Onegin*, both directed by Vasili Goncharov.

The following year, operatic films took a giant stride forward when Alice Guy-Blaché, the first woman film director, made a film of *Fra Diavolo*. Alice Guy had been a secretary working for the French film equipment pioneer, Léon Gaumont. She became hooked on film and persuaded Gaumont to let her direct some early sketches. He agreed and the first film she made (now lost) was the 1896 *The Cabbage Fairy*, a comic fairy tale which many believe to be the first fiction film ever made.

Like many of his competitors, Gaumont had moved into film production in order to provide something for those buying his projectors to show. Unlike his competitors, Gaumont wasn't that interested in being involved in production himself, so he was happy to let Guy do more and more. She took advantage of the opportunity, turning out more than 200 one-reelers covering every genre from slapstick to historical epics, from melodrama to opera. And she was an important pioneer of film technique for she not only produced and directed these films, she frequently wrote the scripts and acted as wardrobe mistress, all the time experimenting with the possibilities of picture, sound and colour tinting. Several of France's most significant early directors learnt their trade working as her assistant.

In 1902 Guy made her first operatic sound film, a three-minute version of Gounod's *Faust*. Four years later she filmed an aria from *The Queen of Spades* with synchronised sound, following it with a ten-minute adaptation of Gounod's *Mireille*, on which her assistant was Louis Feuillade, himself later to direct a film of Massenet's *Thaïs* (1911).

In 1907 Guy married Herbert Blaché and went with him to the United States where, after the birth of their first child, she founded the Solax Film Company. Of the 200 films put out by Solax, 50 were directed by Guy-Blaché, including *Fra Diavolo* with Billy Quirk, George Paxton and Fanny Simpson, none of them opera singers. Indeed it would appear that the film, although based on Auber's opera, was a silent. Nevertheless it was warmly received by the critics who felt it augured well for opera on the screen.

What made *Fra Diavolo* such an important landmark was not just the skill with which Guy-Blaché directed it, but the fact it lasted 45 minutes. The maximum length of operatic films before that had been around twelve minutes. The expansion of the standard feature film length from a single reel of around ten to twelve minutes to four-reelers of 40 minutes and more meant that film-makers could move away from shooting single scenes or truncated versions of stories and begin to develop plot and character. The infant cinema, now out of its nappies, was about to become a young adult.

Guy-Blaché's next operatic film was a version of *Mignon* with Marian Swayne in the title role, and her last a short version of *The Merry Widow* (1913), again with Swayne. Although Guy-Blaché continued to direct the occasional film until 1920, she and her husband ceased to be a producing partnership in 1917, and she returned to France following their divorce with her two children. She tried unsuccessfully to revive her career at the same time as attempting to correct the impression everyone had that all her films had been directed by male directors. She finally died in New Jersey in 1968.

Those directors interested in opera were quick to utilise the increased lengths now possible. Two long versions of *Carmen* came out in 1913, one with Marion Leonard, the other with Marguerite Snow. In Hungary, Michael Curtiz filmed a 40-minute *Martha*, intending it to be screened with Flotow's music, while Max Urban made a Czech film of Smetana's *The Bartered Bride. Salomé* was given the full-length treatment with Strauss's music played only for the dance, and *Pagliacci* became the first complete opera to be filmed in America when it was shot using the Vi-T-Phone sound system.

As the cinema grew up, various genres began to develop. One form which emerged at this time, due to the ability of film to tell a story (and eventually to develop into a film genre of its own), was the musical biography or biopic as it became known. The first of these appears to have been a French film, *Mozart's Requiem* or *La Mort de Mozart* (1909), the story of the composer's last days, directed by Louis Feuillade. A former wine merchant, poet and journalist before becoming a film-maker, Feuillade had taken over from Alice Guy as artistic director at Gaumont, and like Guy, from whom he learnt much, he covered just about every type of film there was from children's stories to opera.

Feuillade's biopic of Mozart was soon followed by others. In Germany, Carl Froelich directed *The Life of Richard Wagner* (1913), an hour-long feature starring Giuseppe Becce as the composer. Becce, who had been born in Italy, was himself a composer and instrumental in shaping the music of the silent German cinema. He was first employed by Oscar Messter (who produced the Wagner film) and, as well as acting in the film, arranged Wagner's music for the accompaniment. He later became head of music for the German conglomerate Ufa, created in 1917 by the German government through the merger of several small independent companies. The first Italian operatic biopic was the hour-long *Giuseppe Verdi nella Vita e nella Gloria* (Giuseppe Verdi in Life and Glory, 1913) directed by Count Giuseppe de Luguoro-Presicce with Paolo Rosmino as the composer.

In one sense all the experiments with opera were on the fringes of film-making. In another, they were a very important part of an industry that was coming of age and was desperate to be taken seriously. The emergence of the full-length feature meant that, for the first time, actors and actresses were being recognised. Before, they had been members of a company playing out what were often little more than filmed sketches; what was happening on the screen was more important than the person acting it. Now, audiences were beginning to have favourites whom they wanted to see again. The star system was about to be born, and despite its elitist image even then, opera was producing some of the biggest stars around. The exploits of leading opera singers made it into the gossip columns. They were known and talked about by people who did not go to the opera house. More importantly, they were known to millions through their recordings. It was, after all, an opera singer, Enrico Caruso, who had made the gramophone popular, and it was the gramophone that helped turn opera singers into household names. Film producers were always on the lookout for people who might make the transition to film and capture the public imagination. Audiences were fickle. There was still a novelty about cinema-going and producers were having to spend a lot of time wondering which was the best bandwagon to jump on. The presence of an opera singer in a cast was certainly not seen to be a hindrance at the box-office.

In 1913, the famous Czech soprano Emmy Destinn made her one and only appearance in a film. Destinn was a great favourite at the Met where she had created the role of Minnie in Puccini's *La Fanciulla del West*. She had also sung Senta in the first Bayreuth production of *Der Fliegende Holländer* and was a noted interpreter of such roles as Salomé, Butterfly and Tatiana in *Eugene Onegin*. She was a very fine stage actress. Whether this transferred to the screen or not we do not know since *The Lion's Bride* has disappeared totally.

Also in 1914, the Italian soprano Lina Cavalieri, a noted beauty and stalwart of the gossip columns who was as famous for her lifestyle as her voice, appeared in an American version of *Manon Lescaut*, opposite her third husband, the French tenor Lucien Muratore.

Cavalieri, who was publicised as being the most beautiful woman in the world, was born in poverty in the slums of Rome in 1874, began her career singing in cafés, and had even appeared at the Folies Bergère. This enabled her to acquire an aristocratic Russian husband. She then decided to become an opera singer. Confusion surrounds much of her early life. According to some sources she made her operatic debut when she was twenty-six singing Mimi in *La Bohème* at the San Carlo in Naples before going on to appear in Paris, London and other major European cities. According to others, her debut was in Lisbon singing Nedda in *Pagliacci*, in a performance so bad that on the second night the entire company was chased from the stage. She persevered, however, singing successfully in Italy, Poland and Russia.

What there is no doubt about is that, having disposed of husband number one, she arrived in the United States in 1906 to sing at the Met opposite Caruso in Giordano's *Fedora*, having been paid a fee larger than that paid to Farrar. As well as singing in the first Met performance of *Fedora*, she was in first performances of *Adriana Lecouvreur* and *Manon Lescaut* when Puccini, another fervent admirer, was in the audience.

By 1913, the year she married Muratore following a concert tour together (her second marriage, to a member of the Astor family, had lasted only a few weeks), Cavalieri's stage career was virtually over but she was still someone featured on the front page of newspapers and worth trying in films. Her well-known love of jewels and clothes made a part like Manon Lescaut (a simple girl who acquires a love of jewels and fine clothes) the perfect role for her film debut. However, it was claimed (in order, of course, to avoid having to pay for copyright), that the film had nothing to do with the Puccini opera but was based on the novel. Since Cavalieri had sung both Manons on stage, no one believed the denials.

After *Manon Lescaut*, Cavalieri returned to Italy to make her next two films, *La Sposa della Morte* (The Bride of Death, 1915) and *La Rosa di Granata* (The Rose of Granata, 1916), again with husband Lucien Muratore as her co-star. Muratore was the leading French tenor of the day. Born in Marseilles, he had started his career as an actor and been heard by Emma Calvé singing in a play with Sarah Bernhardt. Calvé persuaded him to study singing and he made his operatic debut opposite her in the world premiere of Reynaldo Hahn's *La Carmélite*. Quickly establishing himself as a superlative artist, he went on to create roles in operas by Massenet, Fauré and Henri Février. It was in Henri Février's *Monna Vanna* that he first sang with Mary Garden in Chicago, returning to the opera house there for seven consecutive seasons.

Neither of the films they made in Italy had operatic plots. Cavalieri then returned to America to make a further four films for Famous Players, all with titles designed to cash in on her reputation. *The Eternal Temptress* (1917) was an espionage melodrama in which she played a princess who falls in love with every man she meets. *Love's Conquest* (1918), directed by Edward José who directed her next two films as well, was based on the play *Gismonda* by Sardou, and in *The Two Brides* (1919) she played a sculptor's daughter who loves two men and whose father makes a very lifelike statue of her. Only *A Woman of Impulse* (1918), in which Muratore also had a small part, had anything to do with singing. In this she portrayed an opera singer not unlike herself who rises from rags to riches. Her final film was a melodrama called *Amore che Ritorna* (Love That Returns) made in Italy in 1921 but possibly never completed.

After her retirement from the operatic stage, Cavalieri moved to Paris, where she ran a beauty salon, and then, with her fourth husband, to Florence. During an air raid on the city in 1944 she became anxious about her jewels, left the bomb shelter to return to her villa and collect them, and was killed.

Another opera singer who moved into films was the Romanian soprano Bertha Kalich. Although better known to the general public as an actress than a singer, she had sung Carmen in Bucharest and appeared as Leonora in *Il Trovatore* before emigrating to the United States in 1895 when she was 21. In New York she appeared in productions of Offenbach's *La Belle Hélène* and Strauss's *The Gypsy Baron* before becoming a straight actress. One of the plays in which she appeared was *Marta of the Lowlands* by the Catalan playwright, Angel Guimera. Marta is the mistress of a wealthy Catalan landowner who intends to marry someone else and so arranges for her to marry a shepherd who doesn't know about her past. This was the play on which Eugen d'Albert had based his popular 1903 opera *Tiefland* and it was filmed four times. Kalich appeared in the first, 1914 version for Famous Players, repeating her stage success. Although it was a 70-minute film of the play, screenings were accompanied by music from the opera, as they were for a 1918 Austrian film and for one made in Germany in 1922. D'Albert himself worked on the 1922 film which starred Lil Dagover and featured the eminent bass-baritone Michael Bohnen, a singer who was later to make a number of important operatic films. The fourth and only sound version was again a German production directed by Leni Riefenstahl. After *Marta of the Lowlands*, Kalich was signed up by Fox to make three films in quick succession. She appeared in *Slander* (1916), *Ambition* (1916) and *Love and Hate* (1916). None of them caught on and Kalich's film career came to an end.

Soprano Beatriz Michelena, the daughter of Spanish tenor Ferdinand Michelena, was signed by the California Motion Picture Corporation to become, for a short time, their top star. In 1914 she appeared in *Salomy Jane* and in *Mrs. Wiggs of the Cabbage Patch*, but her most important appearance was in a 75-minute film of Ambroise Thomas's opera, *Mignon* (filmed in 1914 but released in 1915). This was shot on location in the San Francisco area and Michelena was much praised for her performance. At the film's private premiere, she sang her arias live. Offered $5,000 to sing them when the film went on public release, she declined.

It wasn't only in Hollywood that opera singers were going before the cameras. In Russia, the great bass Feodor Chaliapin appeared in *Tsar Ivan Vasilyevich Grozny* (1915), a film based on the Rimsky-Korsakov opera *The Maid of Pskov* or *Ivan the Terrible*, in which he had scored one of his greatest stage triumphs. The film was made to celebrate Chaliapin's 25th year as a singer and he was paid handsomely to appear, but he hated the end result and it was never popular. Eisenstein, however, studied it before making his own 1946 film about Ivan.

The biggest of the stars to make the transition from opera house to screen in those early days was undoubtedly Geraldine Farrar. The American box-office success of 1915 was her appearance in *Carmen*, which was given the supreme accolade of a Charlie Chaplin burlesque with Chaplin as Darn Hosiery and Edna Purviance as Carmen. When *Maria Rosa*, the film Farrar had made as a try-out, was released in May 1916, it confirmed her as a star. *Temptation*, the third of her initial three-film package, had been released four months before *Maria Rosa*. In it she played a poor but talented opera singer who nearly succumbs to the improper suggestions of a villainous impresario (played by Theodore Roberts and dressed not unlike the Met's Giulio Gatti-Casazza) in order to further her struggling composer boyfriend's career (the boyfriend played by Pedro de Cordoba). Although the film failed to get quite such an enthusiastic response as the other two, there was never any doubt that once the next Met season was over, Farrar would be back in Hollywood.

She returned in the summer of 1916 to film *Joan the Woman*, the story of St. Joan of Arc and the first of the DeMille trademark spectaculars which involved personal dramas being played out against historical events. DeMille had decided to shoot the story as a flashback. In a prologue which takes place in the trenches of France during World War I, an English soldier (Wallace

Reid), who has to go on a mission from which he is unlikely to return alive, finds Joan's sword. He is inspired to fulfil his mission in order to expiate the sin he committed against her many centuries earlier in another life. The climax, before returning to an epilogue in the trenches, is Joan's trial and subsequent burning at the stake.

To get the shots he wanted, DeMille developed the largest camera that had been used on a film up until that time, capable of shooting with both foreground and background in focus at the same time. French villages, castles and even Rheims cathedral were built on the Lasky ranch and shooting finally began with hundreds of cowboys dressed in armour as medieval knights. More than 40,000 costumes had to be made or hired.

Filming did not go nearly as smoothly as it had before. For a start Farrar was in a bad mood with DeMille since he had been the person to tell her that Famous Players would not be engaging her new husband, actor Lou Tellegen, as a director. She then asked for a two-week postponement so that she could fulfil some singing engagements, demanding at the same time that she be paid for the missing weeks (she was given $10,000). DeMille himself, up against time, complained to Lasky that Farrar had both put on weight and lost much of the spark that had made her so special the previous year. There were also events off the set which caused anxiety on it since Sam Goldfish was being ousted from the production company by new arrival Adolph Zukor.

For the battle scenes, Farrar was dressed in a suit of armour especially made for her but still so heavy that she had to be lifted onto her horse. Although she had a stunt double for some of the scenes, she took part in the majority, and she hated horses. Every director from the Lasky stable was in the midst of the battle, wearing armour, to help direct the fighting. DeMille communicated with them and the assistant directors by telephone, the first time the instrument had been used for this purpose. The scene of Joan burning at the stake was filmed with Farrar, her dress soaked in a solution to make it fire resistant and her mouth and nose blocked with cotton wool, uncomfortably close to the flames until a dummy was substituted at the last moment for the close-ups. Farrar later said it was a terrifying experience. After she had watched her replacement dummy go up in flames, she went to her dressing room and was sick.

Joan the Woman was a film on an epic scale but, while it more than covered its costs (just over $300,000), it did not do as well as everyone had hoped at the box office, despite the generally glowing reviews and the presence of Farrar and Reid. Lasky and Zukor made DeMille cut the film for general release but it did not pick up, partly because of the hostility of various Christian groups who felt the portrayal of a saint on the screen to be blasphemous, partly because audiences had had their fill of costume dramas.

DeMille also directed Farrar's next two films, made in the late summer of 1917. In *The Woman God Forgot* she played Tecza, daughter of the Aztec king

Montezuma, who falls in love with an officer from Cortez's invading Spanish army, while in *The Devil Stone*, based on a story by DeMille's mother, she was a Breton fishermaid who finds a rare emerald, once the property of a Norse Queen, which is cursed. One critic dismissed the result as 'piffling'.

The Woman God Forgot and *The Devil Stone* were to be Farrar's last two films for Lasky and DeMille. Having been forced out of Famous Players, Sam Goldwyn, as Sam Goldfish had become, had set up his own company and was quick to sign up Farrar among his first half-dozen stars. Her first film for Goldwyn was *The Hell Cat* (1918), in which she played the high-spirited daughter of a ranch owner. This was followed by *The Turn of the Wheel* (1918), set in Monte Carlo with Farrar as a beautiful American who falls in love with a gambler who is arrested for murdering his wife. She tries to find out who really did it.

In 1919 she made four films for Goldwyn, all melodramas. In *The World and Its Women*, she played the part of a famous opera singer and is seen on stage in a scene from Massenet's *Thaïs*. In 1920 she appeared in *The Woman and the Puppet*, based on a novel by Pierre Louys about a girl who works in a Spanish cigarette factory and scorns the love of a nobleman; and then in *The Riddle Woman*, directed by Edward José, the man who had directed three of Lina Cavalieri's films. Farrar loathed him and it was to be her last film. By that time, her star was beginning to wane. Her last few films had failed to make any major impact on the box-office and Goldwyn suggested she should stay off screen for a while. He was, he told her, still prepared to pay her an annual retainer of $125,000 for a further two years. Farrar was livid. She tore up her contract in front of him and walked out of Hollywood never to return.

Farrar's wrath with Goldwyn may have had more to do with his hiring of another opera singer than it was about her own film appearances. Although Farrar was then one of the biggest stars in Hollywood, Goldwyn, hoping to repeat the success he had had when he first engaged her, had signed up her greatest operatic rival at the Met. He had first tried to match Farrar's screen magnetism with Lina Cavalieri but Cavalieri's films had been only moderately successful so he had started looking for someone else. The singer he chose was Mary Garden.

Born in Aberdeen but taken to the States as a child of six, Garden had made her operatic debut in Paris in 1900 singing the title role in the first run of Charpentier's *Louise*. The opera had received its world premiere on 2 February. On 13 February, the soprano singing Louise had fallen ill halfway through the performance and Garden, the official understudy, took over. She became the talk of Paris, going on to create the role of Mélisande in Debussy's *Pelléas et Mélisande*. Massenet wrote *Chérubin* for her. In 1907 she made her American debut at the Manhattan Opera House in *Thaïs* and was hailed as the greatest singing actress in the world, a claim that must have put Farrar's nose out of joint. The two became intense rivals. Garden also caused havoc wherever she sang. Only 5 feet 4 inches tall, everybody thought of her as being tall. They also found her incredibly sexy, so much so that when she sang a performance of *Tosca* in Boston dressed in white satin opposite a Scarpia dressed in black, the women in the audience turned their backs on the stage. When she appeared as Salome in Chicago, police were in attendance and she was informed the opera was sinful.

This was just the sort of person, Goldwyn felt, to make an impact in the movies. With the right publicity, audiences would flock to see her just as they had to see Farrar. In 1917 he hired Garden, at a fee of $10,000 a week, to make two films. Her first, shot at the Goldwyn Studios in Fort Lee, New Jersey, was of her great stage success, *Thaïs*. Unfortunately for her, she did not have a director of stature and Frank H. Crane and Hugo Ballin, who shared a joint directing credit, were content simply to point the cameras at what was essentially a stage performance. While men may have been happy to gaze upon Miss Garden's ample bosom in the opera house while she sang deliciously, in the cinema, without the benefit of sound, it was plain boring. Although *Thaïs* was reputedly the first film ever shown at the Vatican, it did not attract audiences in public cinemas.

Garden's second film, *The Splendid Sinner*, released the following year, was set during the First World War and featured her as a woman who had once loved a German but is now married to an American. Her former German boyfriend shoots her at the front for being a spy. Audiences did not warm to this film any more than they had to *Thaïs*, and Garden returned to the opera stage claiming that film actors deserved every penny they received.

It was not quite a case of putting anyone who could sing in a film, but from 1914 onwards many opera singers certainly had a try. Few lasted for more than one or two pictures. In 1916, Polish soprano Ganne Walska appeared in *Child of Destiny*, directed by William Nigh, playing a supporting role as the heroine's divorced rival who commits suicide at the end of the picture.

Walska is known today, if at all, for almost certainly being the prototype of Susan Alexander in Orson Welles's *Citizen Kane*, her claim being greater than the other name often suggested, Sybil Sanderson. She had made her singing debut in Kiev as Sonia in *The Merry Widow*. In 1915 she appeared in the operetta *Mlle. Nitouche* in New York, acquired a rich New York husband and became friends with Chicago newspaper magnate Harold McCormick. Walska was hugely ambitious but without the talent to support such ambition. McCormick hired the Met soprano Frances Alda to coach her and then persuaded the Chicago Opera, to which he gave significant donations, to let her sing the lead in Leoncavallo's *Zaza*. Like Alexander in the film, Walska left the city before opening night. Welles is supposed to have kept copious notes of the story.

Walska continued to sing, attracting the wrong sort of attention. During a performance of *Fedora* in Havana she was so off-key that she was pelted with vegetables. Married six times, she ended up as a gardener in California and died in 1984 at the age of 93.

Anna Case, the American soprano who sang Sophie in the first Met performance of *Der Rosenkavalier*, starred in the romantic Western, *The Hidden Truth* (1918), and, bearing in mind the success of Farrar, Universal tried casting the ballerina Anna Pavlova in the title role of a version of Auber's opera, *The Dumb Girl of Portici* (1916), directed by Lois Wilson.

As the search for novelty and new talent continued, what could be more natural than to make a film featuring the greatest tenor not just of his day but possibly of all time, Enrico Caruso?

Caruso was born in Naples in 1873. He made his name in Italy and from 1903 appeared in every Met season. The Met became his operatic home and, because of the birth of the gramophone, which made him a household name and which he helped make fashionable, he became the best known operatic singer in the world.

As early as 1908, an attempt had been made using Jules Greenbaum's Synchronoscope to marry a record with film, featuring the voice, though not the image, of Caruso. Shortly afterwards a film of the sextet from *Lucia di Lammermoor* was made which featured actors miming to singers, one of whom was Caruso. Early in 1917, the tenor attended the New York premiere of three films made by George Webb, called Webb's Singing Pictures. In one, an actor, dressed in costume, mimed while Caruso's voice was heard singing 'Vesti la giubba' from *Pagliacci*; in another, Caruso singing 'La donna e mobile' from *Rigoletto* provided the soundtrack. For the third, Giuseppe Campanari had sung the Toreador Song from Bizet's *Carmen*. All these attempts had been made using commercially available recordings. Caruso himself had not been filmed singing.

The man who wanted to change that was Jesse Lasky. In 1918, he persuaded Caruso that appearing on the screen and being seen, if not heard, by millions would help boost his record sales. Caruso's record company, Victor, could also see the benefits of such world-wide exposure and eagerly agreed to help promote the films.

There was talk of Caruso appearing in *Pagliacci*, but eventually he signed for a fee said to have been more than $200,000 to make two romantic comedies over a six-week period in New York. These were filmed at the Artcraft studio on 56th Street between mid-July and the end of September. In *My Cousin*, directed by Edward José, Caruso played two roles: one, a great opera singer, the other his poor but likeable cousin. The film contains scenes at the Metropolitan Opera House and features Caruso singing in *Pagliacci*. Caruso's co-star was a young opera singer named Carolina White.

Caruso was, by all accounts, extremely conscientious. Every day he arrived at the studio early and even though filming took place during a heatwave, his sense of humour never deserted him, nor did his propensity for playing practical jokes on the set.

The opening night of *My Cousin* at the Rivoli was eagerly awaited. The film had received massive publicity and the reviews were, generally, favourable. But the public stayed away in droves. They simply did not want to see Caruso if they could not hear him singing. 'If you cannot hear his marvelous tenor voice you cannot possibly enjoy it much ... You cannot help but wish the star would step through the silversheet and offer just one tiny song,' wrote the critic of *Photoplay Journal*.

Lasky reacted swiftly. He had shot the two comedies back-to-back, ready to release the second on the back of the success of the first. When the first proved such a flop and he had to refund rental money to scores of disgruntled distributors all over the States, he promptly cancelled the release of the second film. *A Splendid Romance*, sometimes referred to as *The Great Romance*, starred Caruso as Prince Cosimo, an Italian piano-playing aristocrat sought out by a young American who wants to become an opera singer. Again directed by Edward José, who seemed to put a curse on any opera singer who ever worked with him, the film was only released in Europe and South America. Caruso, who died three years later, was never invited to make another film.

Operas themselves continued to be filmed throughout the latter half of the decade, although not always without problems. In 1916, Mascagni attempted to prevent two versions of *Cavalleria Rusticana* being made in Italy, failing on both occasions, while in 1917 Puccini successfully objected to his music being used to accompany a 70-minute Italian film of *La Bohème* with Leda Gys as Mimi. It was not so much the idea of filming to which Puccini objected, as the fact that the film was based on the novel, not his opera.

The practice of claiming that a screenplay was based on the original play or novel which a composer and librettist had also used became commonplace, even when not strictly speaking true, in order to avoid having to pay copyright. So when Mary Pickford appeared in *Madame Butterfly* (1915), the screenplay, it was claimed, had been adapted from the story by John Luther Long, not Puccini's opera. Enough differences would be incorporated to show that the book or play had been read, but the accompanying music taken from the opera and the title at least made sure everyone made the connection to the opera.

Not all composers were hostile towards film-makers. When Francesco Bertolini made a film of Leoncavallo's *Pagliacci* (1915), the composer helped choose the actors and design the production. It was screened with live music.

Other operas which formed the basis of feature films at this time were *Maritana* by William Wallace, *Undine* (the Lortzing opera which starred swimming champion Ida Schnall), *Thaïs*, *Miska the Great* directed by Alexander Korda, *Carmen*, *Der Freischütz*, *Rigoletto*, Mascagni's *Iris*, *Pelléas et Mélisande*, and *Halka* (1913) by Stanislaw Moniuszko, one of the earliest films made in Poland.

Hollywood and American producers tended to put opera singers in films which may or may not have had anything to do with opera. In Europe, the

German-speaking countries were already beginning to establish a form of musical cinema in which they would eventually reign supreme: operetta. At first German and Austrian directors stuck to popular operas. Austrian director Richard Oswald, who was to make a number of important operettas after the introduction of sound, began his career in 1914 with, amongst other films, one of scenes from *Pagliacci* and then a *Tales of Hoffmann*.

They then began to look to composers closer to home. In 1914, Lehár's *Die ideal Gattin* (The Ideal Wife) was filmed with Ernst Lubitsch, then an actor, in the cast. Nessler's opera *The Flute Player of Hamelin* was filmed in 1917 to be screened with the music, as was *The House of the Three Girls* (1917), a Schubert pastiche directed by Oswald. Lehár's operetta *Where the Lark Sings* (1918) was filmed in the same year it opened on the stage by Hubert Marischka, who both directed and starred. D'Albert's *Tiefland* was filmed in Austria. The operetta tradition had begun.

Among other celebrated opera films to emerge from Germany during this period was *Carmen* (1919) starring Pola Negri and directed by Ernst Lubitsch. This was one of the major achievements of silent German cinema. Fritz Lang used the Madam Butterfly story as the basis for his film called *Harakiri* and there were full-length versions of *The Magic Flute* and *Manon Lescaut*. Shortly after the end of the First World War in 1919, the German Delog company came up with an interesting solution to the problem of how to stage opera in a war-ravaged country attempting to rebuild itself. They made a series of operatic films, all running about 70 minutes, of such pieces as *Der Fliegende Holländer*, *Martha*, Lortzing's *Der Waffenschmied* and *Undine*, the object being to send them out with soloists, chorus and orchestra to perform live at the screening. It was an attractive novelty and was at least cheaper than sending out full-scale, costumed touring productions.

3

The Coming of Sound

Most attempts to produce synchronised sound pictures had been abandoned by the early twenties. The cinema, it was generally accepted, was a silent medium with the all-important musical ingredient being provided by live accompaniment of some sort. In an attempt to buck the trend, two Italians, Azeglio and Lamberto Pineschi, produced a twenty-minute sound-on-film version of *The Barber of Seville* in 1923 with Gabriella Di Veroli as Rosina and Giovanni Manurita as Almaviva, in order to demonstrate their system. The following year Emilio Zeppieri directed *Fra Diavolo* with opera singers using his Zeppieri Fotocinema system to provide the sound. Apparently neither system worked satisfactorily since both films disappeared without trace soon after their first screenings and the experiments were not repeated.

Operas, however, continued to be filmed, either to have music from the opera performed with them or as the basis for dramatic features. In Britain in 1922, Harry B. Parkinson produced a series of fifteen-minute films entitled *Tense Moments from Opera*. He had already made *Tense Moments from Great Plays* and *Tense Moments with Great Authors*, and his opera series followed a similar format: well-known actors playing the parts in heavily truncated versions of key scenes. The music from the opera, suitably arranged, was played as an accompaniment. The titles Parkinson filmed included *Don Giovanni*, *Martha*, *The Lily of Killarney*, *Samson et Dalila*, *Fra Diavolo*, *Rigoletto*, *Il Trovatore*, *La Traviata*, *Faust*, *Carmen*, *Lucia di Lammermoor* and *Maritana*.

When it came to using operas as the basis for feature films, one that found its way onto the screen was Balfe's *The Bohemian Girl* (1922), about a count's young daughter kidnapped and brought up by gypsies who falls in love with a Polish solider seeking refuge in the camp. The gypsy queen, who also loves the soldier, is furious and plots against the girl. Ivor Novello played the part of the Polish soldier, Gladys Cooper was the heroine and C. Aubrey Smith, who later went to Hollywood and became the archetypal Englishman, wore a huge moustache and hat as the gypsy chief. The great Victorian actress Ellen Terry played the nurse who lost her young charge in the first place. At the time she was making *The Bohemian Girl*, she was also making another film in the same studio. After watching her film one scene, Novello and the rest of the cast were so moved they were in tears. She approached them. 'Can you tell me, my dears,' she enquired, 'which picture am I playing in now?' Even without Balfe's music, *The Bohemian Girl* was an enormous success.

Also in 1922, Ferdinand Hummel, a German composer, wrote what is claimed to be the first opera written directly for the screen, a strange undertaking for the silent era. Berlin-born Hummel wrote seven stage operas, none of them even known by name today. His film opera, *Jenseits des Stromes* (The Other Side of the River), was written to be shown with a live performance by singers and orchestra. Their music cues were shown at the bottom of the screen. How successful Hummel was we shall never know since the film has not survived. It was not well received at the time.

Music had become an integral part of the film industry and was giving employment to thousands of musicians. Ever since Farrar had demanded mood music on set, players had been engaged to accompany the shooting of films. When the film was projected, musicians were required to accompany it. This might in the big cities have been an orchestra, in the towns, a solitary pianist. The music to be played was distributed to cinemas with the film.

The first musical accompaniments, based on music that already existed, had been provided simply as an easy and cheap means of drowning the noise of a whirring projector. It did not take long for film-makers to realise that they had at their disposal a very effective tool for manipulating audience feelings and emotions, and it was not long before original scores began to be written. This spawned a whole sub-industry of film composition.

The attitude of serious classical composers towards the early film industry was largely one of disapproval. Even though in 1908 Camille Saint-Saëns had been invited to write a score for the French film *The Assassination of the Duke of Guise*, a commission that did much to help movies gain credibility as an art form, most composers believed the cinema to be nothing more than popular entertainment. It was the Italians, particularly composers of the verismo school, who were the first to realise what a valuable contribution serious composers could make. Like cinema itself, verismo opera was not considered to be quite high art. Operas such as *Cavalleria Rusticana* by Mascagni or *La Bohème* by Puccini, with their emphasis on reality and low life, were considered by many to be vulgar.

Film-makers were attracted to verismo operas, however, because of this realism, while composers found the process of writing film music very similar to what they were attempting to do on the stage: the building up of character in a few bars, the use of short phrases to establish place or mood, the employment of leitmotifs, and so on. Like the film-makers, they, too, were aiming their work at the masses.

An early pioneer of film music was the Italian composer Giuseppe Becce. Born in Lonigo near Verona in 1877, he had gone to Berlin in 1913 when he was in his mid-thirties and started work in the German film industry. He began by adapting already existing scores such as those for the Wagner biography in which he also acted and Puccini's *La Fanciulla del West*. He became head of music for sound pioneer Oscar Messter and, as well as producing arrangements, began to write original scores which he called *autorenillustrationen* or author's illustrations, for cinema musicians to play. He also produced a book of all-purpose compositions to suit any mood or situation. Becce was one of the most influential and prolific of film composers during the silent era (he became head of music at Ufa in the 1920s), and continued to write when sound was introduced, scoring films for, amongst others, Luis Trenker and Leni Riefenstahl.

Among other composers to work in the German film industry was the Austrian, Robert Stolz. Stolz, who knew Johann Strauss, had conducted the first run of Lehár's *The Merry Widow* and had just started to make a name for himself as a composer of operettas, when he began writing for the cinema in 1913, the year Becce began work in Berlin. His score for the comedy *Der Millionenonkel* (The Millionaire Uncle), starring Alexander Girardi, was the first completely original score to be written for a German language film. Stolz himself conducted the orchestra at the premiere and so began an association with the cinema which was to last for more than sixty years and bring him two Oscars.

One of the first of the established major composers to realise the potential of the screen was Pietro Mascagni, who accepted a commission to write the music for Ninio Oxilia's experimental film, *Rapsodica Satanica* (1915). Collaborating with the scriptwriter Maria Martini, Mascagni wrote what could possibly be considered to be the first opera written directly for the screen, some seven years before Hummel's attempt. They described their work as a cinematic musical poem, and the film, starring leading Italian film actress Lyda Borelli, was certainly sold as if it were an opera.

The year after he had worked on *Rapsodica Satanica*, Mascagni attempted to stop two productions of *Cavalleria Rusticana* being filmed. His objections were certainly not on artistic grounds; he simply wanted to be involved with any filming himself. When his opera *Amica*, which had been given its premiere in Monte Carlo in 1905, was filmed with Leda Gys in 1916, he was on the set. Puccini was another composer who attempted to stop a film, refusing to allow the music of *La Bohème* to be adapted for a film version of the story in 1917. This was because the film was not a film of the opera but a reworking of the Henri Murger novel. Besides he had given permission for his music to be used to accompany Albert Capellani's Parisian film, *La Vie de Bohème*, the previous year.

As producers and directors began casting their nets wider for subjects to be filmed, a number of composers had their works signed up, and frequently went to work on adapting their own scores. Leoncavallo not only worked on the musical side of Francesco Bertolini's film of *Pagliacci* (1915) with Bianca Virginia Camagni and Achille Vitti, he also helped choose the actors and design the production.

Eugèn d'Albert, born in Glasgow despite the name, who had studied with Arthur Sullivan and met Brahms and Liszt, cooperated on the filming of his opera *Tiefland* (1922), the only one of his twenty operas to have survived. First performed in 1903 in Prague, it was seen in 37 other cities before the outbreak of the Second World War and was popular with the British occupying forces in Cologne during the First World War. The film, directed by A.E. Licho, was shown with an accompaniment taken from the opera's themes.

When an Austrian film biography of Franz Lehár was made in 1923, Lehár himself wrote a score based on his operettas to accompany it. He also appeared in person in *Franz Lehár, the Operetta King* (1925), an 80-minute tribute.

The German-speaking countries' preoccupation with operetta continued throughout the 1920s. Hans Steinhoff directed screen versions of *Die Fledermaus* (1923), *Der Bettelstudent* (1922) and *Countess Maritza* (1925). Max Mack also directed a film of *Die Fledermaus* in 1923 with Lya de Putti as Rosalinda, while Max Neufeld directed *The Tales of Hoffmann* (1923). There were films of *The Marriage of Figaro* (1920), Kienzl's opera *Der Evangelimann* (The Evangelist, 1924) with Elizabeth Bergner and Paul Hartman, and Ludwig Berger directed Oscar Straus's *The Waltz Dream* (1925) starring Mady Christians and Willy Fritsch, who was himself to become an important director of musicals. Christians was to star the following year in Fall's operetta *The Divorcee*, directed by Viktor Janson, while Fritsch appeared in *Die keusche Susanne* (Modest Susanne), an operetta by Jean Gilbert set in France with a big finale in the Moulin Rouge and directed by Richard Eichberg. Other operettas to find their way onto the screen included Lehár's *Paganini*, Walter Kollo's *Wie Einst im Mai* (Once in May) and *Casanova* with Nina Koshetz. Ludwig Berger returned to a slightly more serious opera with *Die Meistersinger* (1927), while in Switzerland, the patriotic hero *William Tell* (1925) made it onto the screen accompanied by Rossini's music.

Among biopics from this time were one on Mozart starring Josef Zetenius called *Mozart's Life, Love and Suffering* (1921) and *A Waltz from Strauss* (1925), the first of many screen biographies of Johann Strauss Jnr. Another Johann Strauss, this time the composer's nephew, played his uncle and also conducted the orchestra when the film was premiered in both Vienna and London.

All these films could be shown around the world. Because there were no language barriers for silent films, it did not matter what language the artists were speaking. The art of film-making was universal. There were different and instantly recognisable national styles developing, but film-making had become a highly sophisticated craft with a language and grammar all its own. Many of the silent era European directors now recognised as great established a considerable body of work which frequently incorporated opera or operatic themes. The Hungarian director Alexander Korda made a film in Vienna of *Samson und Dalila* (1922), tying together a modern story with the biblical one by portraying a diva about to sing the role of Delila. Korda went for spectacle, with marvellous sets and hints of sex. The sets were so grand that the film, despite being reasonably successful, bankrupted its backers.

Austrian director Fritz Lang, having discovered that audiences would sit through two successive evenings of *Dr. Mabuse der Spieler*, decided in 1924 to make another epic and for his subject was inspired by the biggest operatic epic of them all, Wagner's *Der Ring der Nibelungen*. Wagner's score was rearranged to accompany Lang's version of the thirteenth-century poem on which both were based. Like Wagner's opera, the film proved an encouragement for the Nazi party, and the stadium the Nazis built in Nuremberg was supposed to have been modelled on the sets Lang used for *Nibelungen* and *Metropolis*.

When the newly formed MGM decided to film Lehár's *The Merry Widow* (1925), they turned to the Austrian actor and director Erich von Stroheim, whose European approach, Irving Thalberg was convinced, would make him the ideal person to direct. As an actor, Stroheim was, according to the publicists, The Man You Love To Hate. His version of *The Merry Widow*, starring Mae Murray and John Gilbert, ran for two hours with Lehár's sparkling score arranged by Victor Léon and Leo Stein. The result was not quite what Thalberg expected. Much of it was set in a brothel and the film is almost two-thirds of the way through before the plot of Lehár's operetta makes an appearance. The earlier part of the film concentrates on the Widow's three suitors, their drunkenness and their lechery. Danilo (Gilbert) is given to looking at rude postcards and seeking comfort with older ladies; the Baron (Tully Marshall) is a foot fetishist; and the Crown Prince enjoys almost every depravity anyone can name.

Stroheim was never over-careful with producers' money and during shooting Thalberg became alarmed at how much he was going over budget. When he reproved Stroheim for wasting film stock on endless shots of a wardrobe full of shoes, Stroheim replied that the character was a foot fetishist. 'And you,' Thalberg is supposed to have retorted, 'have a footage fetish!' The rumours of Stroheim's approach did nothing to harm the film's prospects at the box office and although *The Merry Widow* had been an expensive production, it proved to be both a commercial and artistic success.

Michael Curtiz, who was later to achieve immortality with *Casablanca*, made several operatic films in his native Hungary and in Austria before moving to Hollywood. These included *Martha*, *Lulu*, *The Merry Widow* and a film of Suppé's *Boccaccio* (1920). Howard Hawks, before he became a director, wrote the screenplay for *Tiger Love* (1924), a film based on *El Gato Montes*, the opera by Manuel Penella. Under its English title, *The Wildcat*, *El Gato Montes* had just been a hit on the Broadway stage. Hawks altered the plot considerably but the film was screened with Penella's music being played live.

3. The Coming of Sound

In 1926 King Vidor directed a silent version of *La Bohème*, based on the Murger story, with Lillian Gish and John Gilbert. The costumes were designed by Erté. The *New York Times* described it as virtually flawless and a film that would do its share in bringing the screen to a higher plane. In Germany, F.W. Murnau directed a superbly stylish *Faust* (1926) with Emil Jannings, the first 30 minutes of which are amongst the most triumphant visual achievement of all silent films. It failed to do well in Germany, which was, according to one critic, not then interested in Faustian problems, but was widely appreciated abroad. When it was first shown in Britain it was presented by theatrical showman C.B. Cochran at the Royal Albert Hall with intertitles supplied by the novelist Arnold Bennett. Another German film, *Manon Lescaut* (1926), drawn from both Massenet's opera and the Prévost novel, was notable for the appearance of a young actress in the minor role of Micheline. Her name was Marlene Dietrich. In France, the Belgian-born, former actor Jacques Feyder directed *Carmen* (1926) on location in Spain, coming up with some breathtaking views.

The earlier rush to find opera singers who could appear in films had somewhat abated, and whenever an opera was filmed in the 1920s, it invariably used screen or stage actors. Film stars even began to make the journey in the opposite direction, from the screen to the opera house. Among the first to do so was the American soprano Hope Hampton.

Hampton had been born in Texas and was one of the many young hopefuls who ended up in Hollywood looking for fame and fortune on the silver screen. She had won a beauty contest and on her arrival in Hollywood was immediately taken up by a wealthy businessman who formed a film company to promote her. Her first film was *The Bait* (1920). In *Star Dust* (1921), based on a novel by Fannie Hurst, she played a singer who goes to New York, is discovered and becomes an opera star, making her debut singing in Massenet's *Thaïs*. She then made *A Modern Salome*, a film based on Oscar Wilde's poem, and in 1923 appeared in the first *Gold Diggers* film, based on a play by Avery Hopwood. In 1926, after filming *The Unfair Sex*, her thirteenth film, she gave up the movies to study singing, making her debut in Philadelphia in 1928 singing *Manon*. In 1930 she appeared as Marguerite in *Faust* with the San Francisco Opera, opposite Ezio Pinza as Méphistophélès. She was lured back to Hollywood in 1938 to appear in *The Road to Reno*, singing Musetta's waltz song, and made her last film in 1961.

Another actor to go the Hampton way was the American baritone John Charles Thomas. He had begun his career on Broadway singing in operettas and Gilbert and Sullivan, and in 1915 had appeared opposite Marguerite Namara in Lehár's *Alone at Last*. In 1923, he appeared in the Sam Goldwyn epic *Under the Red Robe* (1923), ordered by Cardinal Richelieu to catch a suspected traitor and falling in love with the man's sister. At the film's premiere he sang the Prologue to *Pagliacci*.

The following year he made his debut with the Washington Opera singing

Amonasro in *Aïda*, then went on to sing in Europe, San Francisco and Chicago before making his Met debut in 1934 as Germont in *La Traviata*. He sang at the Met for the next ten years and became a star of radio. *Under the Red Robe* was his only silent feature.

Thomas's co-star on Broadway in 1915, the soprano Marguerite Namara, also had a limited movie career. Born in Los Angeles, she had made her debut in Genoa singing Marguerite in *Faust*, before appearing in opera in Boston and operetta on Broadway. She joined the Chicago Opera Company where she sang opposite Caruso and made her film debut in 1920 opposite Rudolph Valentino in *Stolen Moments*. This was one of several movies churned out by Valentino before he became a big star. Namara played a woman who falls in love with a South American novelist and after a heated argument over an incriminating letter, thinks she has killed him. Namara did not make another film until 1931 when she appeared in a British sound version of *Carmen*, entitled *Gypsy Blood*.

The most important of the silent operatic films was, without a doubt, that of *Der Rosenkavalier*, made in Vienna in 1926. Richard Strauss, at first reluctant to give his permission for the film to be made, was talked into it by his librettist, Hugo von Hofmannstahl, who had written a number of screenplays. Selected to direct the film was Robert Wiene, director of the 1919 silent classic *The Cabinet of Dr Caligari*. In a letter to Strauss, Hofmannstahl explained why he thought the film was a good idea. 'It is my most seriously considered view that the prospects of the opera on the stage will not suffer in any way; on the contrary I would look upon the film, when it comes out, as a positive fillip and new impetus to the opera's success in the theatre. Why? Please have a look at my sketch for the film scenario or ask someone to read you a little of it. The whole thing is treated in the manner of a novel: it introduces the characters or, for those who know them, tells something new of their old acquaintances. Nowhere (not even in the final scene) are the events of the opera exactly repeated – not in a single scene. If the film appeals, it cannot but arouse great eagerness to see the now familiar characters in the original action on the stage alive, speaking, singing ... it can only whet the appetite for the opera. In this way, too, the project seems to imply value as an advertisement rather than the danger of competition.'

Strauss not only agreed to *Der Rosenkavalier* being filmed, but also agreed that Hofmannstahl could alter the libretto. Sophie meets Octavian before the presentation of the rose, a battle scene was added, together with a masked ball in place of the inn scene and there is a revised ending in which the Marschallin and her husband (who appears quite a lot) are reconciled. Strauss agreed to compose a new march for the film but left the adapting of the score for a cinema orchestra to others. Their work must have met with his approval since he conducted the first screenings of the film in both Dresden and London.

Serious musicians were horrified that Strauss had allowed his high art to be desecrated by the populist cinema. Even today there are some musicologists who disparage the film, usually without having seen it. And of course, it was not the sung opera but the story told with Strauss's music to accompany it. Shot mostly on location (much of it at Schonbrunn), the film starred Huguette Duflos as the Marschallin, Jacques Catelin as Octavian (a role played in the opera by a woman), Elly Felisie Bergen as Sophie and Michael Bohnen as Baron Ochs, a role he had sung many times on the stage. The film was designed by Alfred Roller who had worked on the original stage production in 1911 and was first shown, on 10 January 1926, not in a cinema but at the Dresden State Opera to demonstrate that it was art of the highest quality. In fact it was so lavish that Wiene's company was bankrupted by it.

What few of those who worked on *Der Rosenkavalier* or similar films can have realised is that they were involved with a dying art form. Film as they knew it was about to undergo the most momentous change. The silent era was about to give way to the Talkies.

A major problem with sound had always been that of amplification: how to reproduce a soundtrack that could be heard in a cinema seating over a thousand people. That problem had started to be solved in 1906 when Dr. Lee De Forest invented a valve, or gas-filled tube, which he called an Audion, to help amplify electrical radio signals. The telephone company Western Electric realised the value of this invention and acquired the rights. One of their scientists, Dr. Harold Arnold, discovered that by removing the gas from De Forest's valve and creating a vacuum, the tube could amplify sound by up to 130 times. More importantly, it could do so without distortion.

Although designed to increase the range of telephones, this discovery had obvious applications elsewhere, ushering in the age of electrical gramophone recordings in place of the old acoustic wax cylinders. It also opened up the possibility of developing a satisfactory sound system for the cinema. But no one threw up their hands and cried 'Thank goodness!' Mainstream film-making in Hollywood and elsewhere was quite happy doing things the old way, and when De Forest came up with a method of putting sound on film called Phonofilm, the interest it generated was virtually nil. De Forest's manufacturing laboratory, which he had proudly called The Home of Talking Pictures, soon went bust.

The industry couldn't see the point of sound. It was an interesting gimmick to hear a duck quack or someone speak, but it was only a gimmick and the movie industry had moved beyond that. The general public shared this view. They didn't expect the movies to talk any more than they would expect to go into an art gallery and hear the clip-clop of a horse while looking at an equestrian painting or the chatter of children while viewing a family group.

One person who was interested in these new developments, however, was Sam Warner of the Warner Brothers Studio. The four brothers – Sam, Jack, Albert and Harry – were not among Hollywood's major players. Their small production studio lived from hand-to-mouth, and in order to keep it afloat while avoiding paying their creditors the brothers had begun to look for ways to diversify. As a result they bought a bankrupt radio station in Los Angeles, followed by another station in New York. These acquisitions brought them into contact with Major Nathan Levinson, Western Electric's man on the West Coast. Levinson had seen some experiments in sound film being carried out by his company in New York and felt there was something in it. He invited Sam to see what was going on.

Sam saw a very simple demonstration of somebody dropping something onto a table making a synchronised noise. It wasn't so much the actual demonstration that excited Sam as Levinson's comment that there was now no reason why sound films of such stage hits as Friml's *Rose Marie* couldn't be made.

Sam wanted his brothers to see what he had seen but he knew that Harry wasn't the slightest bit interested in talking pictures and would never agree to attend a demonstration. Instead he told Harry and Abe (Jack was in California) that they were going to a reception. Harry was suitably astonished when he was ushered into a viewing theatre no bigger than a large office. On screen a man sat down at a piano, took off his gloves and began to play. Other musicians joined him and soon a band was performing. And Harry could hear them. He even got up to look behind the screen to see if a band was hidden there.

The amplified sound actually sounded like a real band and was achieved by playing a disc on which the sound had been recorded at the same time as the film was being shot, at the standard revolutions a minute, but from the centre outwards. A series of gears connected the recording apparatus to the camera during filming while a series of similar gears connected the player to the projector during the screening.

With Sam's pushing, Warner Bros. decided to exploit the new process. They knew they had to move fast because other studios were testing other systems, most notably Fox with a sound-on-film process developed by Theodore Case. Warners entered an agreement with Western Electric, the manufacturing arm of the telephone firm, and together they formed a new company, Vitaphone, to develop the system.

Harry took charge of all productions using the Vitaphone system. His first intention was to film more of what he had seen in the demonstration: top vaudeville acts in shorts which could be shown as supporting films to the main (silent) feature. He reopened a studio in Brooklyn that Warner Bros. had used during the war and began shooting.

Within a week, these sound shorts were being shown on Warner programmes, but they made little impact. Cinemagoers were used to seeing variety acts before the main feature and in the biggest New York theatres they even got a symphony orchestra on stage. The Vitaphone shorts were no competition for live acts.

The brothers were worried. They had sunk an awful lot of money into Vitaphone and could not afford for it to fail. Sam decided they had to go for broke and make a sound feature. The film they chose was *Don Juan* with Mary

Astor and John Barrymore. There would be no dialogue but every screen action would be synchronised, and there would be a musical soundtrack composed by Edward Bowes and played by the New York Philharmonic. It was to be Warner Bros.' most expensive film to date, and it's showing would be preceded by Vitaphone shorts. To make these more memorable and to demonstrate the brothers' high artistic motives, Harry decided not to use just vaudevillians, but to feature some of the Met's leading singers. He paid the opera house a fee of $52,000 to be allowed to negotiate directly with individual artists and among those he signed up were the tenor Giovanni Martinelli, who was paid $25,000 to sing one aria, the soprano Marion Talley, who received only $2,000 an aria, and Ernestine Schumann-Heink, whose agreement stipulated a fee of $3,500 for any film lasting longer than seven minutes, $2,000 if it was under that length.

The Brooklyn studio in which Harry was filming the Vitaphone shorts was alongside an elevated railway track. The roof was made of glass. Lining the stage with sound-proofing materials such as old carpets, failed to keep out the noise of passing traffic and every time they went for a take, the pigeons in the rafters would begin to coo. It was an impossible place in which to make sound films and so Warners moved the entire operation to Oscar Hammerstein's Manhattan Opera House. Even there the house was not soundproof and the extraneous noise was so great that at times it jogged the recording stylus. It was decided that filming should take place at night when it was quieter. Only later did they discover that most of the noise was caused by the construction of part of the New York subway.

Don Juan opened at Warners Theatre in New York on 6 August 1926. It was a disappointment. Once again a recorded soundtrack was found to be no substitute for a live orchestra and few in the audience felt that the synchronised sound effects added anything to the movie. The evening was not a total disaster for Warners however.

What did astonish the audience, most of whom had not seen them before, were the Vitaphone shorts. These had started with the New York Philharmonic playing the overture to *Tannhäuser*, while featured in three of the seven remaining shorts on show that night were Marion Talley singing 'Caro nome' from *Rigoletto*, the soprano Anna Case singing 'La Fiesta' with the Met chorus, and Giovanni Martinelli singing 'Vesti la giubba'. They were all billed as from the Metropolitan Opera, a much publicised and prized connection which lent the entire venture an element of class, even though Case, who had sung Sophie in the Met's first production of *Der Rosenkavalier*, had retired from the operatic stage in 1920. She was, however, still giving concerts and was a popular recording star.

Talley was billed as 'the Youthful Prima Donna of the Metropolitan Opera' which she certainly was, being only eighteen. The Kansas City Canary had first come to prominence at the age of fifteen after she had been heard singing in

Thomas's *Mignon* and was offered a Met contract. She made her debut there in 1926 as Gilda in *Rigoletto* and Warner Bros., attempting to cash in on the publicity surrounding her, signed her up to sing 'Caro nome' in a Vitaphone short. After the enormous hype preceding her debut at the Met, her actual appearance there proved to be something of a letdown. Her first film appearance drew even more flak. There were problems with the film's synchronisation, which did not help, but her voice was dismissed as thin – when it could be heard. She also had a tendency to pull faces while singing. 'Her voice,' wrote the critic of Photoplay, 'was far from attractive. As to her face, the producers made the mistake of allowing the camera to come too close … Long shots – and good, long ones – were just invented for that girl.' When the Vitaphone shorts went on the road to cinemas outside New York, Talley's was dropped. Although she continued to appear in major roles at the Met over the next three years and made two more Vitaphone shorts with Gigli, she retired early, a victim of burnout. She attempted several comebacks but none was successful.

Giovanni Martinelli, on the other hand, the leading tenor at the Met, was a true operatic star. Born in Montagnana in 1885, he had made his operatic debut in Milan in 1910. His performance the following year as Dick Johnson in *La Fanciulla del West* brought him international recognition and a contract from the Met. He was loaned out to Philadelphia to make his American debut in *Tosca*, and returned to New York to appear in *La Bohème*. He quickly became a great favourite, making his last appearance in the house in 1945. For the Vitaphone showing on 6 August, 1926, Martinelli performed 'Vesti la giubba' from *Pagliacci*. The sound quality was so good and so realistic that one lady in the audience waited for him outside the stage door afterwards, so certain was she that he had been hidden behind the screen. She was right: Martinelli was there, but in the audience. He had a big voice, recalled one of the engineers responsible for setting up the equipment that night, but he could never have come within a mile of the volume of sound pumped into the auditorium. Martinelli's singing was, indeed, the highlight of the evening. More than a year before Al Jolson sang in *The Jazz Singer*, Martinelli showed just how powerful a combination of voice and image could be on screen.

Finally, when Will Hays, President of the Motion Picture Producers and Distributors of America, who was also sitting in the audience, appeared on screen to congratulate the brothers, everyone sat up and took notice.

A few weeks before that opening night, William Fox of the Fox Film Corporation had acquired the rights to a sound system being developed by Theodore Case and his assistant Earl Sponable. Case had worked with De Forest on Phonofilm and was convinced that the answer to talking pictures lay not in the sound on disc route being taken by Warner Bros. but in sound on film. The first public showing of a Fox Movietone sound film took place in January 1927, followed by a number of trade showings of the usual shorts of musicians. It was not until four months later, in May, that the system's capabilities were really demonstrated effectively. A Movietone news crew had gone to film Charles Lindbergh taking off on his flight to Paris. The film was in the movie theatres the following day but with the addition, on this occasion, of sound. Audiences could hear as well as see Lindbergh's plane rising into the sky. A sound that was thin and rather feeble made an enormous impact on those who heard it. They felt, as they had never felt in a newsreel before, that they were actually there.

These successes didn't mean everyone rushed overnight to make sound pictures. Sound was still a novelty that was not going to have any real impact on real pictures. Almost all producers and directors were convinced there was no need for it. A style and language of movie-making had been developed which was quite sophisticated enough to tell a story without requiring to hear the actors speak. And when Sam Warner had remarked after hearing Hays talk on screen that if he could do it so could actors, Harry's reaction had been, 'Who the hell wants to hear actors talk? The music – that's the big plus about this.'

Sam was determined, however, that Warner Bros. had to enter this particular race and win, or go under. He wanted to make a film that went a step further than a pre-recorded orchestral soundtrack and synchronised sound effects, one that would incorporate musical numbers and really show what the Vitaphone system could do.

The subject chosen was the stage musical, *The Jazz Singer*, which was on Broadway starring George Jessel and for which Warner Bros. had acquired the film rights. Based on a short story, *Day of Atonement* by Samson Raphaelson, it was about a cantor's son who runs away to become a jazz singer rather than confine his singing to the synagogue. It was the ideal property for what Sam had in mind. Jack, jumping the gun slightly, announced that the film would star George Jessel, but Jessel countered that he would not be rushed into a decision: if he was going to risk his career on some new-fangled invention, he told Jack, he felt he ought to be appropriately compensated. They agreed terms, but when Jessel insisted on having the agreement in writing before he would leave for the West Coast, Jack decided to look for his star elsewhere. Eddie Cantor, Jessel's former partner, turned the part down and Al Jolson was asked instead. He was apparently so certain of success that he took shares in Warner Bros. in lieu of payment. More likely he was not offered enough to brag about.

The Jazz Singer was planned as a silent movie with musical extracts. However, Jolson's technique and style of performing was to talk the audience into a song, so when the moment came in the studio for him to film the number 'Toot Toot Tootsie Good Bye', as conductor Lou Silvers raised his baton to cue him, Jolson did what he would have done had he been on stage. 'Wait a minute, wait a minute,' he cried, 'you ain't heard nothin' yet. Wait a minute, I tell yer. You wanna hear Toot Toot Tootsie? All right, hold on ... Lou, listen. You play

Toot Toot Tootsie. Three choruses you understand and in the third chorus I whistle. Now give it to 'em hard and heavy. Go right ahead ...'

It was the moment that was to change cinema history, and it very nearly didn't happen. Jolson was supposed just to sing. The fact that he had spoken as well threw everybody. There were hurried consultations between the producers and director Alan Crosland. They agreed his very personal introduction should be edited out or at the very least the number should be reshot immediately without the speech. But Sam Warner was insistent. It must stay the way Jolson had performed it. He also suggested a new spoken sound sequence should be shot, choosing the scene in which Jolson returns home for his father's birthday. Father is out but Mother welcomes the prodigal son with open arms. Sam wanted to get some dialogue written but Jolson prefered to improvise the scene.

There is not that much dialogue before Jolson breaks into song (Irving Berlin's 'Blue Skies') but it was still extremely difficult to film. The technicians had had little experience of recording sound while cameras were turning. Microphones had to be hidden all over the set, in flower vases, on dresses. Carpets had to be hung on the walls to deaden the sound of passing traffic. Cameras which were not blimped (a blimp being a housing into which cameras were eventually put to deaden the sound of the motor) had to be placed in little booths which became so unbearably hot that the operators fainted or came out in a state of collapse. And there was no means of editing sound and picture together afterwards. The sound recording, being made on a separate piece of wax, and the picture on its celluloid, had to be created together if they were to remain synchronous. A scene could be shot only in its entirety and that was the way it had to stay. If something did go wrong, everything had to be repeated from the beginning. There was simply no way in which a piece could be recorded for dropping in later.

When it came to making *The Jazz Singer*, the non-singing sequences which made up the bulk of the film were shot and edited in the normal way. Where Jolson was due to sing, gaps were left in the film. These gaps were a thousand feet long and the filming had to be timed precisely to fit them. When they were about to film, the set was prepared with the actors and camera crew in position. The preceding silent scenes were projected onto an overhead screen and when the moment came for the song or piece of dialogue to happen, everything had to be timed to start the instant the blank film appeared. The orchestra was on an adjoining set complete with its own sound circuit. It was very complex and another reason why the vast majority of producers were extremely reluctant to commit to all-sound pictures. They felt that having to shoot takes at the rate of 1,000 feet a time without the ability to edit, was an enormous if not impossible restriction.

During the filming of *The Jazz Singer*, costs escalated and the brothers, who were being hounded by creditors, became really concerned they were about to lose everything. The premiere finally took place at the Warner Theatre in New York on 6 October 1927. The audience was overwhelmed, and so too were the critics, although some had reservations; one felt the story dragged in too many places. But whatever the faults of the film, it was the turning point. The irony was that none of the Warner brothers was there to see it. Sam, who had been the one to push for sound, had suffered a stroke in California and the others had rushed to be at his bedside. He died the day before *The Jazz Singer* opened, aged 39.

At the time *The Jazz Singer* was released only 75 cinemas in the whole of the US were wired for sound. Warner Bros. promptly Vitaphoned sequences into most of their movies but few other producers followed suit. Charlie Chaplin was among those who declared sound would never catch on. And when *The Jazz Singer* was shown overseas, it was as a silent. But more and more exhibitors, sensing a novelty on which they could make money, decided to convert their cinemas to show sound films and each one in which *The Jazz Singer* played reported record box-office receipts. The film ran for 35 weeks in New York and even longer in Los Angeles.

Throughout the 1920s, the film industry in the United States had been the largest employer of musicians. Those musicians now saw their jobs under threat. They complained vociferously that their livelihood was being threatened, but they were told not to worry, the new fad wouldn't last. A survey backed up this view: three out of every five Americans, it reported, preferred live musicians.

4

The Sound Effect

Having set a pattern of showing Vitaphone shorts with a main feature, Warner Bros. continued to turn them out, many featuring some of the most notable opera singers of the day.

The immensely popular Giovanni Martinelli, after his first appearance singing 'Vesti la giubba', went on to make a further fourteen shorts over the next three years. He sang 'Celeste Aïda' from *Aïda* and the Flower Song from *Carmen*. He sang arias from *La Juive, Martha, Il Trovatore* and *Faust*, as well as Russian, Mexican and Italian folk songs. For a scene from *Aïda* he was joined by the mezzo Ina Bourskaya (with whom he was to sing at the Met) and by Jeanne Gordon for a scene from *Carmen*.

The Italian tenor Beniamino Gigli, who had made his debut at the Met in 1920 and was considered to be Caruso's successor (even by Caruso himself, who drew a caricature of his young rival when Gigli visited him shortly before Caruso's final, fatal illness), was signed up to sing an aria from *La Gioconda*, then excerpts from *Lucia di Lammermoor* with Marion Talley, from *Cavalleria Rusticana* with Millo Picco and Minnie Egener, and the quartet from *Rigoletto* together with Talley, Jeanne Gordon and Giuseppe de Luca. Talley continued to be berated by the critics. She uttered sounds, wrote the *New Yorker*, 'which could only be duplicated by the twittering of tightly-locked subway brakes'. Also with de Luca, another Met stalwart, Gigli sang the famous duet 'Au Fond du Temple Saint' from Bizet's *The Pearl Fishers*. Separately, de Luca sang Figaro's 'Largo al factotum' from *The Barber of Seville*.

The New Zealand-born soprano Frances Alda had first appeared at the Met in 1908 singing Gilda, an appearance which had attracted more than music critics since it was known she was there only because she was the mistress of Gatti-Casazza, the new general manager. Alda had started her career in Paris, sung in Brussels and London, and then created the title role of *Louise* at La Scala before travelling to New York with Gatti. Despite scathing reviews of her appearances in *Rigoletto*, in the first performance of Puccini's *Le Villi* and in *Manon*, she went on to appear in the house every season until 1930 and was the archetypal prima donna with a quick temper and penchant for public quarrels. For Vitaphone she sang 'The Star Spangled Banner' and 'The Last Rose of

Summer' from *Martha*, together with 'Birth of Morn' and the Ave Maria from Verdi's *Otello*.

Soprano Mary Lewis, from Arkansas, appeared in *Way Down South*, featuring her and a male chorus singing songs by James Bland and Dan Emmett. Lewis had made her name as a Ziegfield Follies girl and appeared in silent comedies before deciding to become an opera singer in her mid-twenties. She had made her debut in Vienna in 1923 singing Marguerite in *Faust*, created the role of Mary in Vaughan Williams's *Hugh the Drover* at Covent Garden and starred in *The Merry Widow* in Paris before returning home to the States where she appeared at the Met in *La Bohème*, *Pagliacci* and *The Tales of Hoffmann*. She was recording her second Vitaphone short, of excerpts from *The Tales of Hoffmann* when Warner Bros. summarily stopped all filming and sued her for breach of contract because of her drinking. It was drink that put paid to her singing career when she appeared on stage at the Met for a performance of *Carmen* in a state of extreme intoxication. She later signed a contract to appear in a film of her life which was never made and worked on a feature about the French Revolution which was not completed, probably due to her drinking. She was only 43 when she died in 1941.

The 66-year-old German contralto Ernestine Schumann-Heink, whose final appearance at the Met was still five years off, went into the studio to make three shorts of songs, including Schubert's 'Der Erlkönig', 'Silent Night' and 'Danny Boy'. But not all Vitaphone operatic artists were on the current Met roster. The American tenor Charles Hackett, although he had appeared at the Met, was a member of the Chicago Opera when he was joined by Rosa Low for a duet from *Roméo et Juliette*. Hackett, who came from Portland, Maine, was noted for the elegance of his singing. He had started his career on the concert platform before going to Italy to study opera. In 1915 he was summoned to a small theatre outside Milan and asked to sing through the role of Faust in *Mefistofele*. Having done so, he was told he would be making his operatic debut singing the role that night. As his stature grew, he received better engagements including sharing tenor roles in Buenos Aires with Caruso, who was best man at his wedding. He first appeared at the Met in 1919 in *The Barber of Seville* and went on to sing in Met premieres of Gounod's *Mireille* and Rossini's *The Italian Girl in Algiers*. For Vitaphone, Hackett also made shorts of arias from *Rigoletto*, *Don Giovanni*, *Faust*, *Sadko* and *L'Africaine*, as well as some songs.

Husband-and-wife team, Rosa Raisa and Giacomo Rimini, were also members of the Chicago Opera when they filmed a duet from *Il Trovatore*. Raisa, considered by many to be the finest soprano of her generation, had fled from her native Poland following a pogrom in 1907, studied in Italy and first appeared in Chicago in 1913 singing Mimi opposite Martinelli. An international career blossomed which included the premiere of *Francesca da Rimini* at La Scala and the title role in the first performance of *Turandot*. Baritone Rimini had also been in the premiere of *Turandot*, singing Pong.

The British baritone John Barclay, who was enjoying a successful recital and recording career in America, made two Vitaphone films. In one, entitled *John Barclay Offering Impersonations of Famous Characters Singing the Prologue from Pagliacci*, he not only sang the Prologue but threw in the Serenade from *Faust*, an aria from *Boris Godunov* and the Toreador Song from *Carmen*. His second featured the aria 'The calf of gold' from *Faust*, plus some songs.

The baritone John Charles Thomas, who was not to appear at the Met until 1934 and had only been singing opera for three years, sang the Prologue from *Pagliacci*, two popular songs and, for his third Vitaphone short, was teamed with musical comedy star Vivienne Segal to sing 'Will you remember?' from Sigmund Romberg's *Maytime*.

Vitaphone may have led the way with these operatic shorts, which were filmed with the artists in costume against an appropriate background, but with very limited camera movement due to the requirement for the artists to stay in the correct relationship with the microphone (which is why modern commentators are so wide of the mark when they look at these films and comment that someone like Gigli clearly could not act). But they were not the only ones. In 1928 Fox-Movietone signed up Met baritone Richard Bonelli (whose real name was Bunn) to sing the *Pagliacci* Prologue and 'Largo al factotum' in their series *Movietone Moments*. The following year, the popular Italian tenor Tito Schipa filmed an aria from *Martha* for Paramount and in 1930 returned to the studio to film *Princesita*, while Tita Ruffo, the baritone described by Tullio Serafin as one of the three singing miracles of the century (the others being Caruso and Ponselle) appeared in three shorts for MGM singing, in costume, arias from *L'Africaine*, *The Barber of Seville* and *Otello*.

An operatic short was even made in Australia by the Italian baritone Apollo Granforte, on tour there with Nellie Melba. Granforte, a favourite at La Scala, had begun his career in Argentina and was noted for his versatility, appearing in operas as varied as Mascagni's *Nerone* and Wagner's *Parsifal*. He was particularly renowned for his interpretations of Verdi and Rossini and his film short, made to demonstrate RCA's Photophone system, was of 'Largo al factotum'.

Despite this burst of activity, sound films did not take over from silents overnight. Many silent films were already in production or about to go into production when first the Vitaphone shorts and then *The Jazz Singer* were shown to the public, and no studio saw any reason to change its plans. Others, believing sound to be nothing more than a passing phase, continued to set up silent productions. It wasn't just producers who did not like the idea of sound. Directors had established a style of film-making, a freedom and fluidity of camera movement, which would be severely compromised by the limitations imposed on them by sound. The addition of words, they felt, would bring nothing worth having to a film.

The first rush of sound films were in fact part-talkies, with snatches of dialogue added to films that had been started as silents. Some features lasting over an hour had only a minute or two of dialogue but would be billed as a talking picture. While such films attracted audiences curious to see and hear them, polls carried out throughout the United States showed that for at least twelve months after *The Jazz Singer*'s first showing, the public still wanted silent films as well.

Among the last of the great silent musicals was Ernst Lubitsch's 1927 film for MGM of Sigmund Romberg's operetta, *The Student Prince*. Renamed *The Student Prince in Old Heidelburg*, it starred Ramon Navarro, Norma Shearer and Jean Hersholt, and was accompanied by a pit orchestra playing selections from the show. MGM also produced in the same year, with money provided by William Randolph Hearst, a lavish version of Victor Herbert's *The Red Mill* starring Hearst's mistress Marion Davies and directed under a pseudonym by Fatty Arbuckle.

Most studios may have been ignoring sound, but having seen the returns for *The Jazz Singer*, Warner Bros. knew they had discovered a gold mine, if only they could exploit it. A few days after *The Jazz Singer*'s premiere in New York, Alan Crosland (now directing *Glorious Betsy*, a cheap costume drama about Napoleon's younger brother Jerome falling in love with an American belle named Betsy Patterson), was told that dialogue scenes were being added to his film. Dolores Costello, the star, was considered to have a good speaking voice. And so *Glorious Betsy* ended up, like *The Jazz Singer*, as a part-talkie, the first to receive its premiere in Hollywood. Although it did not contain a lot of sound, all Hollywood turned out to see it. The film helped convince many in the movie capital that this was the direction in which they should all be going.

The cast of *Glorious Betsy* included the Spanish bass Andrès de Segurola, a popular artist from the Met who was playing the part of a French officer. As well as dialogue being added to the film, De Segurola was asked to sing 'La Marseillaise' and a chorus chipped in with 'Nellie Gray'. Another Met singer, the Italian baritone Pasquale Amato, played the part of Napoleon but did not get to sing. Amato, who had created the role of Jack Rance in the original production of *La Fanciulla del West*, had been the Met's first Prince Igor, La Scala's first Golaud in *Pelléas et Mélisande*, and was Italy's most noted Wagnerian, did, however, sing on film in 1928 when he made a Vitaphone short featuring the Toreodor Song from *Carmen* and 'Torna a Surriento'.

De Segurola had also been in the first night of *La Fanciulla* in 1910, singing Jake, and it was when he was on stage with Caruso again in a performance of *La Bohème* that the famous incident of Caruso singing the bass aria 'Vecchia zimarra' took place. De Segurola lost his voice during the performance and while he mimed singing the farewell to his coat in the final act, Caruso, with his back to the audience, sang the aria for him. After a distinguished career at the Met, where he was noted for being a fine actor, De Segurola's film career had begun in 1927 when he was invited to Hollywood by Gloria Swanson to appear in *The Love of Sunya*, playing the part of an opera impresario who wants her to become a singer (she doesn't, preferring instead to marry her first love). The film was silent and De Segurola didn't get to sing. After *Glorious Betsy*, he went on to appear in several sound films, mostly as a character actor, and also became a well-known Hollywood singing coach, his best-known pupil being Deanna Durbin.

Despite reservations and, in some cases, outright hostility, the other studios soon realised that if they did not follow Warner Bros.' lead and join the sound revolution, they would be left behind. The one thing that showed off sound best was music and so began a rush to make musicals. It has been estimated that between 1927 and 1930, Hollywood alone produced more than 200 musicals. Most of them were so bad that, in what may well be an apochryphal story, at least one theatre manager was reduced to advertising on the marquee outside: 'This film does not have music.'

The first all-singing, all-talking movie to reach the screen was MGM's *The Broadway Melody* (1929), a backstage musical about vaudevillian sisters whose act is broken up by the attentions of a songwriter. Producer Irving Thalberg, who began working on the project in August 1928, originally intended it to be a part-talkie but once he saw the script, full of slang and up-to-date Broadwayese, he decided the audience had to hear it, and so the film became an all-talkie. Warner Bros. already had their first musical in production, a sound version of *The Desert Song* with John Boles, but held up its release, and *The Broadway Melody*, which started filming afterwards, reached cinemas first.

Directed by Harry Beaumont, *The Broadway Melody* took three months to make, the problems of shooting being exacerbated by the fact that MGM had no in-house musicians and every time they needed music, they had to go out and hire players. What was interesting, and pointed the way towards the future, was that they started filming *The Broadway Melody* using the Vitaphone system but by the end of the picture had moved over to sound-on-film. As the talkies (or talkers as they were originally known) had become accepted, the limitations of Vitaphone had been increasingly exposed.

There was the problem of having to have long, unbroken takes. Recording directly onto disc meant there could not be breaks for a retake which could be spliced in afterwards. If an artist made a mistake or went off microphone, it was back to the beginning for everybody. There was also a problem with the discs themselves. They could be broken easily or scratched, and were prone to skipping grooves or sticking when replayed in the cinema. After about ten plays the sound became so bad the disc had to be replaced.

The solution to such problems lay in sound-on-film. With the Movietone process, there were no problems when shooting out of doors, and editing was considerably easier. As long as you had the right projector, it was much easier to show and did not run the risk of going out of synch so badly that the film would have to be stopped, as happened all too frequently with Vitaphone. The projectionist no longer had a box of discs to get in the right order as well as his cans of film. The actual quality of sound may not have been as good as Vitaphone sound initially, but the advantages far outweighed the disadvantages. Although Warners kept going with the Vitaphone system, they gradually began introducing sound-on-film versions as well as Vitaphone films during 1930, and by the beginning of 1931, had dropped Vitaphone completely.

The Broadway Melody was nominated for three Academy Awards, picking up one for best picture, and became a smash hit. It can also lay claim to another first: the first time a sound film used playback. Thalberg wanted to retake the Wedding of the Painted Doll scene. His sound recordist, Douglas Shearer, suggested they should use the first recording with the picture from a later take, which is what they did, although it was not for a few more years before recording songs and arias first and then shooting them to playback was to become the norm.

Once the decision to ditch Vitaphone had been taken, sound filming became much easier. Everybody could do it, and everybody did. Before long each of the major studios (which Warners, thanks to sound, had become) had developed its own particular musical style. Paramount concentrated on operettas, Warner Bros. specialised in the backstage musical, RKO went for elegant, romantic subjects and MGM for the big blockbusters.

Apart from the technical problems brought by the arrival of sound, the studios faced another major headache: none of them had singers under contract. And what would those artists they did have on their books sound like? Famously, the coming of sound killed many careers, most notably John Gilbert, who was discovered to have a high-pitched voice at variance with his suave, romantic screen image (although recent research convincingly suggests that his voice may have been wracked up deliberately to ruin his career in a tussle over a woman). Many foreign artists found they were no longer wanted when audiences couldn't understand what they were saying. Emil Jannings, Vilma Banky and Lya De Putti were among those forced to leave Hollywood. As De Putti, the Hungarian actress who had been brought to America to appear in D.W. Griffith's *The Sorrows of Satan*, told reporters when she left, 'Talkies are the bunk. They will pass and there will be much disappointment over them ... America will realise its folly and the producers will be clamouring for us to come back.'

Neither America nor the rest of the world realised its folly, and the search for suitable performers intensified. Anybody who could sing was rushed into a movie. They came from vaudeville, from Broadway, from revue. It was even discovered that several noted film actors from the silent days possessed good voices, John Boles being a prime example. He turned out to have a very good baritone voice and was immediately cast by Warner Bros. as the Red Shadow opposite Carlotta King in Sigmund Romberg's *The Desert Song* (1929), the first all-singing, all-dancing operetta (and, but for Warners' reluctance to release it, what would have been the first screen musical). The operetta had been a big success on Broadway in 1926 and Warner Bros. acquired the film rights in 1928. It was originally intended that it should be a part-talkie but it was decided to make it as a complete musical. The script kept the outline of the stage musical and most of the original dialogue, but songs were cut (Hollywood never felt any obligation to give its audiences entire stage musicals). Exterior shots of horses and the desert were shot mute. The director was Roy del Ruth and the film was advertised as having a chorus of 132 voices backed by 109 musicians. Del Ruth brought the picture in by early December and on a reasonable budget. But then Warners, who could have made a killing (the film eventually grossed eight times its negative costs), left it on the shelf for five months while they tried to sort out an agreement with a theatrical producer who held the stage rights for *The Desert Song* in certain states and had taken out an injunction to prevent Warners showing the film in her territory.

By the time a court decided that film rights were not the same as theatrical rights, *The Broadway Melody* was playing to packed houses. Still Warners held fire, refusing to alter *The Desert Song*'s release, scheduled for the spring of 1929. By the time they did release it, all the other studios had their first musicals playing. Several critics noted that filming techniques for musicals had already advanced considerably and that *The Desert Song*, being a fairly literal rendering of a Broadway show despite its Technicolor shots of the desert, already looked dated. The public, however, flocked to see it.

In the meantime John Boles had starred with Bebe Daniels in *Rio Rita* (1929), a colour version, shot partly on location, of a musical comedy/operetta written by Harry Tierney for Broadway in 1927, and one of the first films produced by the new RKO company. Set on the Texas border, it contained singing Rangers, a bandit called The Kinkajou and love interest. It had been successful on stage when it opened the new Ziegfield Theatre and ran for a year. On screen, audiences went wild for it, and it helped create a boom for filmed operetta. It was even suggested that Daniels and Boles would make the perfect Carmen and Don José, but RKO baulked at the idea of making a complete opera.

When opera first appeared in a feature, it was not sung by an opera singer but by silent heart-throb Ramon Navarro. According to the publicity hand-outs, Navarro had asked to have time off from filming in order to take singing lessons and was preparing a thrilling operatic voice for a major career in the opera houses of Europe. In fact he sang 'Vesti la giubba' and an aria from *Manon* in *Call of the Flesh* (1930), in which he played a dancer who becomes an opera singer. Neither rendition demonstrated a talent for singing opera. Navarro also directed the Spanish and French versions of the film.

Fox, not to be outdone by its rivals, produced its own operettas, the first being the Marcel Silver-directed, *Married in Hollywood* (1929) with music by the Austrian composer Oscar Straus. This was a typical Ruritanian romance of a prince who falls for a singer, and was the first European operetta to be filmed with sound in Hollywood.

For a short while, operettas became the norm for film musicals, either adapted from existing stage shows or especially written for the screen (it was for one of them, *The Battle of Paris*, starring Gertrude Lawrence, that the term 'floperetta' was coined, despite having songs by Cole Porter). And for every operetta that was made, several were discussed and dropped, among them a *Naughty Marietta* to star Lawrence Tibbett and Grace Moore for MGM, Everett Marshall in Victor Herbert's *Babes in Toyland*, a revamp of *Rose Marie*, and *Danube Love Song*, a screen operetta commissioned by Warners from Oscar Straus which never went into production.

Among those artists brought in from opera to appear in this flood of operettas was the American mezzo Alice Gentle who had made her debut at La Scala in 1916, and went on to appear at the Met as well as on the concert platform. She had sung the role of La Frugola in the 1918 premiere of Puccini's *Il Tabarro*, giving a performance which, wrote one critic, could hardly be improved upon.

Her first film appearance was in *Song of the Flame* (1930), a film based on George Gershwin's only attempt to write a Viennese-style operetta, which had opened on Broadway five years earlier. It tells the story of Aniuta (Bernice Claire), a Russian woman at the time of the Revolution who disguises herself as The Flame in order to incite the downtrodden peasants to rebel against the Czar. Gentle was cast as Natasha, The Flame's rival for the love of the handsome Prince Volodya (Alexander Gray). Only one of Gershwin's original songs remained in the finished film. Bernice Claire was to play the role of Aniuta again in an abridged version of the operetta made for Vitaphone in 1934.

Gentle's second screen appearance was in the operetta *Golden Dawn* composed by Emmerich Kálmán and Herbert Stothart. This is a very strange work about the slave trade in German East Africa during World War I. It has a ludicrous plot which required white members of the cast to black up. Gentle played Mooda, an African who has brought up Dawn (Vivienne Segal), a blonde African princess who doesn't realise she is really white. Dawn falls in love with a British officer (Walter Woolf) who has been captured by the Germans. The villain of the piece is Shep Keyes (played by a blacked-up Noah Beery), a cruel overseer who lusts after Dawn and sings a hymn to his whip ('Listen little whip/While you're in my grip ...'). Lupino Lane sang a number that included such lines as 'Don't propose a limousine/To your dusky jungle queen ...' and Segal had to sing a waltz, 'My Bwana'. Other memorable lines include 'woman gives and remembers; man takes and forgets'. The lyrics, by Otto Harbach and Oscar Hammerstein II, may have been awful but, when the show opened on Broadway, audiences enjoyed the music, even if it was relentlessly Viennese. *Golden Dawn* ran for six months, making it, Warner Bros. felt, the perfect vehicle for a new sound movie.

Unfortunately, on the big screen, the excruciating dialogue seemed even more dire and the film, made in two-colour Technicolor, was given a critical pasting. Some felt it was the worst film of an operetta ever made (although it has now become something of a cult classic) and it virtually finished any chance Alice Gentle might have had of becoming a film star. She made only one more film, four years later, taking a tiny role in the famous RKO *Flying Down to Rio* which launched the screen partnership of Fred Astaire and Ginger Rogers.

In 1930, RKO decided to follow up the successful *Rio Rita* with another musical and chose *Dixiana*, an operetta set in New Orleans. John Boles was not available, and so RKO brought in Everett Marshall, an American baritone who had made his operatic debut in Europe in 1926 and was then at the Met, to play a rich Southerner who falls in love with circus singer Bebe Daniels. Despite family opposition, all ends well. Although Harry Tierney again wrote some of the songs and most of the cast were the same, the film failed to repeat the success of *Rio Rita*, losing the studio money, principally, it was felt, because Marshall was so wooden. Marshall, who later sang in touring musicals, did not make another film until five years later when Warner Bros. cast him in the lead of Busby Berkeley's *I Live for Love*, playing a singer who becomes involved with his rival, Dolores del Rio.

Once talkies had become the norm, Hollywood began churning out Spanish versions of many of its films for distribution in Mexico and among the Spanish-speaking communities of the Southern States. José Mojica, a handsome Mexican tenor who was appearing with the Chicago Opera Company, was cast by Fox in *One Mad Kiss* (1930), hoping that he would appeal to both English-speaking and Spanish-speaking audiences.

Mojica's singing career had started in Mexico City in 1916. He then moved to Chicago where he sang opposite such people as Mary Garden and Amelita Galli-Curci. When Fox signed him up, he left the operatic stage and was heavily promoted as the new Latin lover to succeed Valentino. In *One Mad Kiss*, for which he wrote the title song, Mojica played a Spanish outlaw who fights a corrupt official and finds love with a saloon dancer. It was filmed in both Spanish and English, but failed in a big way to catch on in the English version. The studio felt the English picture was so awful, they considered not releasing it. The Spanish version did well, however, and thereafter Mojica appeared only in Spanish-speaking films. Fox made ten with him between 1930 and 1934, all containing songs or operatic arias, many of them remakes of earlier Fox silents. When Fox decided to stop making Spanish films in 1934, Mojica continued his film career in Argentina and Mexico, where among the films he made was *El Capitan Aventurero*, a version of the opera *Don Gil de Alcala* by the Spanish composer Manuel Penella.

Mojica returned to the operatic stage briefly in 1940, then entered the priesthood and became a missionary, singing occasionally at fund-raising events. His life story was itself made into a film in 1965 with Pedro Geraldo playing Mojica, who provided his own singing voice. The film included excerpts from *Rigoletto*, *Il Trovatore*, *Madama Butterfly*, *La Bohème*, *La Favorita*, *Lucia di Lammermoor*, *L'Elisir d'Amore* and *Faust*.

Another young singer brought in amongst the first wave was the 25-year-old Italian tenor, Nino Martini. Born in Verona, he had made his debut at La Scala in 1927 singing the Duke in *Rigoletto*. Jesse Lasky invited him to Hollywood to add a touch of class to *Paramount on Parade* (1930), a musical revue but Martini wasn't allowed to sing opera, settling instead for 'Torna a Surriento' and 'The Song of the Gondolier', both filmed in colour. It was hardly a memorable appearance; there were no further film offers and Martini returned to the operatic stage to continue his career, appearing with the Philadelphia Opera Company in 1932 and at the Met the following year, again singing the Duke. He was to sing at the Met over the next thirteen seasons and when he did eventually return to Hollywood to make three further films in the mid-1930s it was as a star.

Other singers who made their Hollywood film debuts in 1930 include the popular Irish tenor John McCormack, whose decision to appear in a film was considered quite a coup. Born in Athlone in 1884, 'Count' John McCormack was the son of a labourer who later became foreman in a woollen mill. He had studied in Italy for three months and made his operatic debut there singing the title role in Mascagni's *L'Amico Fritz* under the assumed name of Giovanni Foli. He first appeared at Covent Garden in 1907 as Turiddu, becoming the youngest tenor to sing there in a principal role. He made his Met debut in 1910 as Alfredo in *La Traviata* and sang opera in the States until 1918. After that, he gave up the stage and devoted himself to the concert platform and recordings. He was 46 when he agreed to appear in Fox's *Song O' My Heart* (1930). Fox allocated their top director, Frank Borzage, to the film and gave McCormack a huge bungalow-dressing room.

He was cast as an opera singer who has retired to an Irish village after his girlfriend has gone off with another man. Eventually he is persuaded to sing again and on an American tour meets his former love. She asks him to look after her children if, as she suspects, she should die. Making her screen debut as the girlfriend was the young Irish actress later to find fame as Tarzan's Jane, Maureen O'Sullivan. An entire Irish village had been built on the Fox back lot, but Borzage had taken a unit to Ireland for some location shots and it was while he was there that he found eighteen-year-old O'Sullivan. Playing an old friend from La Scala days who bumps into McCormack in New York was the bass Andrés de Segurola who had been appearing, since *Glorious Betsy*, in Hollywood Spanish-language films with José Mojica.

Song O' My Heart was little more than an excuse for McCormack to sing a dozen songs ranging from 'Then you'll remember me' from Balfe's *The Bohemian Girl* to 'Plaisir d'amour'. It now seems, in many ways, charming, but at the time the film was not a great success, despite McCormack being on tremendous vocal form and proving that although he always claimed to have left the operatic stage because he could not act, he possessed a powerful presence on screen. Even that was not sufficient to keep the tills ringing at the box-office and coupled with McCormack's high fee (he was paid $500,000), Fox decided not to exercise their option with him for a second film. He did not, in fact, return to the screen for another seven years, although in 1933 he did sing the Pies Angelicus on the soundtrack of *The Shepherd of the Seven Hills*, a documentary about the Pope.

In 1933 also, Paramount cast baritone Richard Bonelli in *Enter Madame*, a romantic comedy starring Cary Grant and Elissa Landi. Before his screen career started, Grant had appeared in stage operettas, including one with Jeanette MacDonald, which led to both of them being screen-tested, but nothing came of the tests for either of them. In *Enter Madame*, Landi played a diva (singing voice provided by Nina Koshetz) who marries millionaire Grant. In the opera house scenes, Bonelli sang opposite her in selections from *Cavalleria Rusticana*, *Tosca* and *Il Trovatore*.

Many singers in the early wave disappeared without trace, partly because the vehicles in which they were cast were so awful and there was an audience reaction against musicals, partly because they did not always transfer well to the screen. Broadway musical comedy star Vivienne Segal, who had appeared in one of the early Vitaphone sound shorts and then in three musicals in 1930, including *Golden Dawn* with Alice Gentle, was a formidable presence on the Broadway stage but failed to set the screen alight. J. Harold Murray, who played the romantic lead in *Rio Rita* on Broadway, had, on paper, everything needed for a film star: the looks, the ability, and the voice. He was considered for the lead in *Rio Rita* (a part which eventually went to John Boles), but when he did finally make it to Hollywood, he failed to make the transition. Dennis King, a classically trained actor, had wowed Broadway audiences in *The Vagabond King* and Paramount paid him a great deal of money to repeat his role on film. On screen, in unrelenting close-up, audiences grew tired of him, and after making *The Vagabond King*, his film career was virtually over.

One singer who managed to stay the course was the baritone Lawrence Tibbett. Tibbett was the real all-American opera singer. He was not, as is sometimes claimed, the first American-born, American-trained singer to break the foreign cartel at the Met. There were others, including Rosa Ponselle, who had already done that. But he was, in many ways, the most significant because he took advantage of the new technologies of radio and film to help popularise opera and prove that opera singers were human. He had the appropriate background to go with the image, for his father had been a sheriff. And not just a sheriff, but a sheriff killed in a shoot-out with a bandit.

Born in California in 1896, Tibbett's first ambition had been to become an actor. He came to opera by chance. He had been singing in local concerts in and around Los Angeles, but it was not until he enlisted in the US Navy during

World War I, that he ever considered a singing career. He was heard singing in Nagasaki by someone who immediately assumed he was a member of an operatic troupe then in town. The seeds were sown. Tibbett decided to take singing lessons, auditioned for the Met and was accepted. He made his debut in November 1923 singing the inconsequential part of Lovitsky in *Boris Godunov*, with Chaliapin in the title role. He wore monk's robes over his street clothes and left the opera house as soon as he had finished. He made his name a year later when, on the opening night of the new season, he took over at short notice the role of Ford in Verdi's *Falstaff*. His fine strong voice allied to his acting ability brought him prolonged applause in the house and newspaper headlines the following day.

Tibbett became a regular at the Met and when producer Mack Sennett had an idea for a short about an opera singer who returns to his home town to give a recital accompanied by his childhood teacher, it was Tibbett he wanted for the part. Early in 1929, after the Met season had finished, Tibbett took the train to Hollywood to make a screen test for Sennett. He was also approached by other producers, including big wigs at MGM which wanted him for a film of *Pagliacci*. The MGM producer he got to see thought Tibbett would be ideal for the big number, the 'sob song' as he put it. When Tibbett pointed out that 'Vesti la giubba' was sung by a tenor and he was a baritone, the producer asked him if by any chance he knew any tenors who could do it. The film was never made. *Cyrano de Bergerac* as a specially written operetta was another project that failed to materialise.

Sennett offered Tibbett $3,500 to appear in his film but Tibbett turned him down, signing instead for MGM to appear in *The Rogue Song*, a very free adaptation of Lehár's 1912 operetta *Zigeunerliebe* (Gypsy Love). Since only Tibbett was allowed to sing on screen, only six of the original songs remained, most of the music used in the film being written by Herbert Stothart. The plot itself was changed significantly so that Tibbett became a bandit leader in Imperial Russia who abducts a princess (Catherine Dale Owen) and falls in love with her.

Four weeks into the shoot, MGM got cold feet about the rushes and whether a film starring a singer from the Metropolitan Opera House would appeal to the cinema-going public either in America or overseas. A hurried deal with Hal Roach brought in Laurel and Hardy to play Tibbett's comic sidekicks. They did not, however, make their first appearance until forty minutes into the film and then only briefly with Tibbett or other cast members. Most of their routines were worked out and shot independently, being dropped into the film in editing. The film was directed by the actor Lionel Barrymore, making his directorial debut as a replacement for Robert Z. Leonard, the original choice, who was still on another film. The sequences involving Laurel and Hardy were directed by Hal Roach and took the film ten days over its original shooting schedule.

During filming for *The Rogue Song*, the sound engineers found it very difficult to cope with Tibbett's vocal volume. The process of pre-recording a soundtrack and then getting the singers to mime to it did not start until 1935 although the idea of dubbing in voices had first been mooted in 1930 when MGM cast Greta Garbo as an Italian prima donna in *Romance* and her character was required to sing an excerpt from Flotow's *Martha*. Garbo couldn't sing but still refused to be seen singing with a dubbed voice. Director Clarence Brown had to shoot the scene in a long-shot in which Garbo was replaced by a singing stand-in. But in 1929 when Tibbett made *The Rogue Song*, no one had thought of post-synching and there was no facility to mix sound after a take. What was recorded was what had to be used, and a voice as powerful as Tibbett's put every needle into the red.

Many of Tibbett's colleagues at the Met, and some newspaper pundits, made no secret of the fact that they felt he had prostituted his art by going to Hollywood. In turn most MGM executives, despite having proudly told the world of their acquistion of a big star from the Met, preferred to keep quiet about Tibbett's background. It was felt that being an opera singer was an adverse factor. Moviegoers, Tibbett was told, think opera singers are fat, speak in a foreign language and smell of garlic.

Only in New York was *The Rogue Song* advertised using Tibbett's Met connection. 'Again MGM proves its leadership by being the first to present an operatic genius of such outstanding reputation as Lawrence Tibbett in a full-length motion picture production,' ran the blurb. 'Now you can hear in your favourite theatre the same glorious baritone that has thrilled thousands at the Metropolitan Opera House – that has carried his fame around the world.' Around the States, this publicity was dropped and he was simply billed as the screen's latest singing sensation. On some billboards Laurel and Hardy got top billing.

The Rogue Song opened in New York in January 1930. The film has been lost but according to the reviews, Tibbett looked good and sang well. Audiences were mesmerised, in particular by a scene in which, stripped to the waist and being flogged, he sang 'When I'm looking at you' to Owen. Nothing quite like it had been seen on screen. Tibbett's recording of the title song and of 'The white dove' (which have survived since they were made on a disc separate from the picture) both became hits, and the film, which never quite made its money back largely because people outside metropolitan areas who had gone to see Laurel and Hardy felt cheated, was nominated for an Oscar. MGM offered Tibbett a contract and Louis B. Mayer even suggested he should abandon the Met completely to become a film-star.

As soon as he had completed work on *The Rogue Song*, Tibbett had, in fact, returned to New York for the new Met season, but as soon as it was over he was out west again to begin filming *New Moon*. MGM hoped that the Sigmund Romberg musical, with lyrics by Oscar Hammerstein II, would be a smash follow-up to *The Rogue Song*. Once again, as happened so often when stage musicals were transferred to the screen, the work was totally revamped, with both the story line and even the concept being changed to make it a typical shipboard romance. Tibbett played Lieutenant Michael Petroff, a young Russian cavalry officer, whose singing of gypsy songs on board ship charms the beautiful but arrogant Princess Tanya Strogoff who is engaged to the governor of an outlying province (Adolphe Menjou). The governor sends his rival to the Russian steppes, where he defeats a tribe of nomadic bandits and returns to win the Princess's hand. Playing the part of the Princess was another Met singer, the soprano Grace Moore.

Moore had been born in Del Rio, Tennessee, and educated in Nashville. She began her career in operetta and also appeared in revues. Her move into opera came after she was befriended by Otto Kahn, who paid for her to study in Europe and promoted her in concert. She made her operatic debut at the Opéra Comique in 1928 and in the same year first sang Mimi at the Met.

The success of Tibbett in *The Rogue Song* made MGM look to the operatic stage again for talent and they chose Moore. She was cast as Jenny Lind in *A Lady's Morals*, a film based on the life of the Swedish Nightingale. It was a lavish production, there were new songs by Herbert Stothart, and she was given operatic arias to sing such as 'Casta diva' from *Norma*. Her supporting cast included Wallace Beery as P.T. Barnum. MGM quickly became aware that she did not have the screen charisma of Tibbett and tried to suggest a hidden raciness in a rather dull story by renaming the film. It had started out as *Jenny Lind*, then it became *The Soul Kiss*, and finally *A Lady's Morals*. Even with a new title, the film failed either to excite audiences or to mark Moore out as anything special.

Hoping to succeed better next time around, she was cast opposite Tibbett in *New Moon*. The shoot was not entirely happy. The script was rewritten and rewritten, there was artistic temperament on the set, and the film went way over schedule and budget. However, when *New Moon* opened at the end of 1930, it was generally agreed it was 'the best of screen operettas yet filmed', and Tibbett possessed 'the most effective voice in motion pictures'. At the film's conclusion, audiences would stand up and applaud him. Grace Moore did not receive similar accolades, but their on-screen partnership had clearly worked, which made it all the more surprising that the two were never paired in a film again. But musicals had been suffering a decline at the box-office and, once again, business outside the major cities was poor. Several studios were already cutting music out of films already shot, as well as cancelling operetta projects, some quite well advanced. MGM decided it was not worth risking another operetta and let Moore go.

They did decide to persevere with Tibbett, however, and he was cast in *The Southerner* (1931), a film designed to show off his abilities as an actor while playing down the voice (although the public still expected to hear him sing something). He was cast as a wealthy young southerner who roams the countryside in the company of two tramps (played by Gilbert Young and Cliff 'Ukelele Ike' Edwards). He returns home to the family plantation and falls in love with his brother's wife (silent star Esther Ralston) causing almighty ructions before ending the picture by going off screen singing the hit number, 'Without a song', written by Vincent Youmans. This time Tibbett stuck entirely to popular songs. There was no hint of opera or anything serious. Even so, the film did not do well and MGM withdrew it, shortened it by cutting out two of Tibbett's songs and reissued it as *The Prodigal*. It still lost money.

In the summer of 1931, Tibbett returned to Hollywood to make his fourth film, *Cuban Love Song*, a reworking of the Madame Butterfly theme in which three marines (Tibbett, Ernest Torrence and Jimmy Durante) are sent to Cuba in the early part of the century. Tibbett falls in love with a fiery peanut seller (Lupe Velez, known as the Latin Spitfire) which enables him to sing the hit song 'The peanut vendor', written for the film by Herbert Stothart. Thanks to trick photography he was able to duet the song with himself. *Cuban Love Song* was directed by W.S. Van Dyke, known as 'One Take Woody' for his habit of getting on with the shoot, and it made MGM a small profit. The studio decided, however, that there was no future for musicals starring Tibbett, who had not become the big box-office star they had hoped for. With musicals out of fashion, it was to be another couple of years before he was to make another film.

After her appearance with Tibbett in *New Moon*, and being dropped by MGM, Grace Moore had also returned to the operatic stage and the concert platform. It was her 1932 success on Broadway in Millöcker's operetta *The Dubarry* that made Hollywood decide to take a second look at her. She was in any case keen to resurrect her movie career. When she heard that MGM were planning to make *The Merry Widow*, she contacted the studio and offered to waive her fee if they would let her play the widow opposite Maurice Chevalier's Prince Danilo. MGM was interested but Moore was not prepared to accept second billing and since the studio wanted Chevalier more than they wanted her, she didn't get the part. It was given to Jeanette MacDonald instead. Word got around that Thalberg thought Moore was overweight.

In a fit of pique with MGM, Moore signed a contract with Columbia for $25,000 a picture, but before she had even been cast in anything, Columbia had second thoughts and decided to cancel the contract. Moore threatened to sue, and so the studio pushed her into a real potboiler just to keep her sweet. There was even a rumour that she had partially financed the film herself. It turned out to be one of the most important opera-related films ever made.

In *One Night of Love* (1934), Moore plays a young singer who enters a radio talent contest, first prize a trip to Italy. She doesn't win but goes anyway. There, she rebels against her strict teacher (Tullio Carminati), but eventually makes her debut at the Met, and all ends happily. During the course of the film, Moore not only sang ballads but bits of grand opera including two arias from

Madama Butterfly, the Habanera from *Carmen*, 'Sempre libera' from *La Traviata* and an aria from *Lucia di Lammermoor*. Standards of recording had improved greatly during the previous few years and she was heard to her best advantage. The arias from *Butterfly* were performed uncut. Much to everyone's surprise, not least the executives at Columbia, the public lapped it up, especially the operatic excerpts. The film, directed by Victor Schertzinger, who also co-wrote the title song, won two Oscars, and Moore, nominated for Best Actress, became a big star. For a time, thanks to her screen appearances, she became the best known soprano in the world.

Thalberg was desperate to get her back to MGM and announced that she would appear in two films for him: *Rose Marie* and *Maytime*. But Moore couldn't fit the first into her schedule and the second fell through. Jeanette MacDonald again played both parts.

Moore's next film, written as well as directed by Victor Schertzinger, was again for Columbia and cashed in on all those elements that had made *One Night of Love* such a success. In *Love Me Forever* (1935), a young singer (Moore), talented but poor, is helped by a music-loving gangster (Leo Carrillo) to sing in *La Bohème* at the Met. In the excerpt from the opera, performed in a studio mock-up of the Met, American tenor Michael Bartlett sang Rodolfo. There was also a version of the quartet from *Rigoletto* performed by 40 voices.

Bartlett, who had studied in Milan and appeared with minor opera companies in Europe and America, went on to appear in four more films over the next two years, before returning full time to the stage. While he never became a major star, he did sing in *Madama Butterfly* opposite Jarmila Novotná, and in 1943, when Jeanette MacDonald made her debut on the operatic stage singing Juliette in Gounod's *Roméo et Juliette*, he was her Romeo.

When it made its first two films with Moore, Columbia was still a small studio yet to make its mark. After the success of *One Night of Love*, Moore was treated as befits a prima donna and their biggest star. What she had done was make it acceptable for operatic excerpts to be shown on the screen. Opera, then as now perceived to be an elitist art form, was overnight seen to be something anyone and everyone, no matter how much money they had or where they came from, could enjoy. Whether this upsurge of interest made many people go to the opera house who would not otherwise have gone is a moot point – and one frequently argued over whenever opera is taken to the masses. When Moore appeared at Covent Garden, Thomas Beecham reputedly ignored her while Floral Street, outside the stage door, was a mass of hysterical fans. No one had seen anything like it, not even for Caruso. But opera in films had become fashionable and Moore's part in that was acknowledged when she was given a gold medal in 1935 by the American Society of Arts and Sciences for 'distinctive services in the arts, especially for conspicuous achievement in raising the standard of cinema entertainment'.

Cashing in on Moore

As always happens when someone finds a hit formula, other studios fell over themselves after *One Night of Love* in a scramble to include operatic excerpts in their films and find opera singers who looked good on screen.

Columbia had Moore. RKO promptly went out and signed the French soprano Lily Pons to appear in *I Dream Too Much* (1935), a film to which the novelist Graham Greene, in his capacity as film critic of the *Spectator*, gave the soubriquet, 'I Scream Too Much'. Pons did not scream. Far from it. She was only five foot high but a sensational singer. Born near Cannes, she had made her operatic debut in Mulhouse in 1928 when she was 24, singing in *Lakmé*. She auditioned for Gatti and made her Met debut in January 1931 singing in *Lucia di Lammermoor* with Gigli. De Luca and Ezio Pinza were also in the cast. She took the house by storm and continued to sing at the Met for another 28 years. Many neglected operas such as *Lakmé*, *La Sonnambula*, *Linda di Chamounix* and *La Fille du Régiment*, were staged for her and she sang more Lucias there than any other soprano in Met history. She retired in 1958 after singing, appropriately, Lucia.

The story of *I Dream Too Much* was the familiar one of professional versus private life. Pons is married to a composer (Henry Fonda in his third film) and although she has a wonderful voice, he has to push her into auditioning to sing opera. As her career soars, his declines, something he finds hard to take. Unknown to him, she decides to help him, agreeing to appear in his latest opera which she turns into a smash hit musical comedy. With him at last successful she can do what she really wants, stay at home and have a baby.

RKO put a lot of store in *I Dream Too Much*. John Cromwell was assigned as director, Max Steiner (who wrote the score for *King Kong* amongst many others) became the musical director, Hermes Pan was given the choreography, and Jerome Kern was asked to contribute four new songs with Dorothy Fields as his lyricist. Pons also sang the aria with which everyone associated her, the Bell Song from *Lakmé*, as well as 'Caro nome' from *Rigoletto*. Her real life husband-to-be, André Kostelanetz, was brought in to conduct the operatic sequences, on Pons' insistence it was said. But despite the cast and the care lavished on it, the film was not quite the box-office success RKO hoped for.

5. Cashing in on Moore

The following year RKO tried again, putting Pons in *That Girl From Paris*. A Parisian opera star runs away from an arranged marriage, stows away on a liner to be near the band leader she loves and ends up in the United States as an illegal immigrant. Her co-stars were Gene Raymond and Lucille Ball, and Pons sang an aria from *The Barber of Seville* together with a Strauss waltz, a tarantella and some songs. Again, it failed to take off at the box-office. 'When it's good,' said *Variety*, 'it's very very good, and when it's bad it's pretty awful.'

Pons played a French jazz singer who wants to sing opera in *Hitting a New High* (1937), directed by Raoul Walsh, singing the mad scene from *Lucia* and 'Je suis Titania' from *Mignon*. It was to be her last film. Charming and fascinating though her three films are to watch today, they did not make her a mega-star and she had never enjoyed the process of filming. Disillusioned with Hollywood, she gave up, complaining that the film-makers did not take her singing seriously enough.

Paramount's attempts to find their own Grace Moore were centred on the glamorous American mezzo Gladys Swarthout. She had been born in Deepwater, Missouri, and was engaged by the Chicago Civic Opera before she had a single role in her repertory. She made her debut in 1924 as the off-stage shepherd boy in *Tosca*, and went on to appear at the Met in 1929 singing La Cieca in *La Gioconda*. She was an intelligent artist with striking looks but, until Hollywood had made her famous, she sang only supporting roles such as Siebel in *Faust*, Mrs. Deane in *Peter Ibbetson*, Mallika in *Lakmé* and Frédéric in *Mignon*. After her short film career had made her name better known, she was cast in roles like Mignon, Adalgisa, and, her most famous role of all, Carmen.

Swarthout's first film, opposite John Boles, was *Rose of the Rancho* (1935), a musical western without a note of opera, set in New Mexico, for which Erich Wolfgang Korngold wrote two songs: 'Fight for the right' and 'Without freedom'. The film has been described as *The Mark of Zorro* in drag. Swarthout plays a masked person who leads the ranchers against the villains, sings to alert her followers to assemble, and even gets to dance on Boles' hat. It was not a success. 'One could do very happily without the music altogether,' commented Greene, 'for Miss Swarthout is quite as attractive as any other star dummy.'

She did get to sing opera in her next film, *Give Us This Night* (1936). Her co-star was the Polish tenor Jan Kiepura and Paramount intended the film to be a blockbuster. Kiepura, already a big film star in Europe, plays a fisherman with a voice brought in to show the audience how it should be done when an ageing, temperamental Italian tenor (Alan Mowbray) sings flat in a performance of *Il Trovatore* and is pelted with eggs. Swarthout, the company's prima donna, later refuses to appear with the Italian tenor in a new opera and Kiepura naturally steps in. The opera is a triumph, and he wins Swarthout. Along the way they get to sing a duet from *Tosca*.

The scene from the new opera was especially written for the film by Korngold, who had been in Hollywood working on Max Reinhardt's *A*

Midsummer Night's Dream, arranging Mendelssohn's music and writing some of his own. Korngold was then in the throes of writing his opera, *Die Kathrin*, and had returned to Vienna, but Ernst Lubitsch at Paramount, an old friend, persuaded him to sail back to America for *Give Us This Night*, with the lure of an assignment requiring totally original music. Another attraction for Korngold was the presence in the cast of another friend from Vienna, Jan Kiepura, who had appeared with great success in the Vienna premiere of his opera *Das Wunder der Heliane* (The Miracle of Heliane) in 1927, three weeks after it had opened in Hamburg.

While he was working on the score of *Give Us This Night*, Korngold had quickly written and conducted the songs for Swarthout's first film, *Rose of the Rancho*. He based the original operatic sequence in *Give Us This Night* on the story of Romeo and Juliet so that Kiepura, an ideal Romeo, could appear in a balcony scene. For those scenes in which the composer (Philip Merivale) plays through the scene, Korngold himself dubbed the piano track.

On paper *Give Us This Night* should have been a sparkling example of a popular operatic film. It had Korngold's score, a screenplay and lyrics by Oscar Hammerstein II, plus Kiepura and Swarthout. But things started to go wrong from the beginning. The film was rewritten and rewritten up until the moment of shooting and beyond (one of the reasons Kiepura, who was not at all fluent in English and had to learn his lines parrot-fashion, found it so difficult to deliver them convincingly), and both Korngold and Hammerstein were angered by the interference and rewritten lyrics forced on them by the studio. Korngold, in a fit of exasperation, commented to his wife, 'This thing gets worse, week by week; by the time we start, it will be useless.'

Useless it turned out to be, with its unrealistic and contrived plot, and the uncomfortable acting of Kiepura, which only confirmed he could not then act in English. The sequences that worked best were the musical ones, but neither Korngold's excellent Viennese-style score (which included some beautiful songs for Kiepura and Swarthout, a romantic fishermen's chorus and a Viennese waltz), nor the impassioned singing of Kiepura and Swarthout, could rescue the film. As *Variety* neatly summed it up: 'Music and lyrics are exceptionally good, but of a type too classy to appeal generally.' Certainly Paramount pushed it as a class film, commenting, 'This is the first picture to encourage serious, modern composers toward regarding the screen as a new art form.' Korngold was himself enthusiastic: 'We no longer have to lean on Puccini, Verdi or Mascagni ... we are now conducting a test which will eventually lead to the writing of entire modern operas for the screen. When that day comes, composers will accept the motion picture as a musical form equal to the opera or the symphony.' Sadly, for all concerned, the Alexander Hall-directed *Give Us This Night* did not start the trend.

Swarthout went on to make two further films, *Champagne Waltz* (1937), in which she co-starred with Fred MacMurray as a modern member of the Strauss family who, in flashback, returns to find out what Vienna was like in the days of the Waltz King, and *Romance in the Dark* (1938), in which she played a Hungarian singer who is finally allowed to sing in the Budapest opera house when she pretends to be an Egyptian princess. She was joined by the film's hero, John Boles, in a duet from *Don Giovanni*. Also featured in the film are the Habanera from *Carmen*, the 'Song of India' from *Sadko* and the Berceuse from *Jocelyn*, the only aria from any of the six operas written by French composer Benjamin Godard to have survived.

None of Swarthout's films were particularly good, nor did they turn her into a big star and, like Pons, she returned full-time to the operatic stage, appearing regularly at the Met until 1945. She later sang mostly in concerts before retiring to Florence in 1954.

One singer who used the screen as a stepping stone to the operatic stage was the tenor James Melton. Born in Georgia, he had become a well-known radio singer with the Roxy Gang and the Revelers Quartet. In 1933 he had appeared in a short, singing cowboy songs and performing rope tricks. After the Grace Moore effect hit Hollywood, he was rushed by Warner Bros. into *Stars Over Broadway* (1935), playing a hotel porter with the inevitable brilliant voice who is eventually helped by the hotel's unscrupulous manager (Pat O'Brien) to become a star at the Met. The role gave Melton the opportunity to sing 'Celeste Aïda' and 'M'appari' from *Martha*. In *Sing Me a Love Song* (1936) he again sang, but not opera, and in *Melody For Two* (1937) he played a band-leader who sang 'September in the Rain'.

After his appearance in *Stars Over Broadway*, Melton started studying singing seriously and in 1938 decided to give up films and become an opera singer. He made his debut in Cincinnati in 1938 singing Pinkerton in *Madama Butterfly*, went on to appear in St. Louis and Chicago and then in 1942 made his debut at the Met singing Tamino in *The Magic Flute*. He continued to appear at the Met for the next eight seasons.

As for Moore herself, Columbia had followed *Love Me Forever* by putting her into *The King Steps Out* (1936) with Franchot Tone. Josef von Sternberg directed this adaptation of the Viennese operetta *Sissy* with music by Fritz Kreisler. Moore was on excellent form vocally but, facially reminding many of the comedienne Joan Davis, never managed to look the part of a teenage princess pretending to be a publican's daughter with whom the emperor, also wandering around incognito, falls in love. There was little love lost on set between her and von Sternberg and his direction failed to lift her performance, which showed few light touches. The film failed to ignite the box office and some time later von Sternberg asked for it not to be included in retrospectives of his work.

In an attempt to recapture the winning formula of *One Night of Love* and allow Moore to sing opera, she was cast as an Austrian diva in *When You're in Love* (1937), paying an American (Cary Grant) to marry her so that she can sing in the United States. Written and directed by Robert Riskin, the film featured Moore in arias from *Tosca*, *Madama Butterfly* and *Roméo et Juliette*. She again played an opera diva in *I'll Take Romance* (1937), this time kidnapped by her impresario when she refuses to fulfil an engagement in South America, a role which gave her the opportunity to sing arias from *Madama Butterfly*, *La Traviata*, *Martha* and *Manon*. Melvyn Douglas was her co-star and the title song was written by Oscar Hammerstein II. Neither film attracted huge audiences and Columbia, not enamoured by her temperament (she was becoming a by-word for awkwardness on set), quietly dropped her.

The hunt for opera singers who might make it on the screen was not limited solely to mezzos and sopranos. Lawrence Tibbett, who had not made a film for three years, was signed for a two-picture deal by the independent producer Darryl Zanuck. This time he was required to sing opera. In *Metropolitan* (1935), Tibbett played an American singer cast only in small roles because of the Met's bias towards European artists. An eccentric woman (Alice Brady) forms an American company starring Tibbett, a soprano (Virginia Bruce) and a tenor (Cesar Romero). On tour, their backer pulls out and they are left to their own devices to make sure the season doesn't collapse. During the course of the film Tibbett sang two of his favourite concert pieces – 'De glory road' and 'The road to Mandalay' (a sequence of him singing 'Last night when we were young' was shot but then cut) – together with arias from *Carmen*, *Pagliacci* and *The Barber of Seville*. The film, wrote the critic of the *New York Times*, aimed a 'savage blow at the Metropolitan Opera Association for its treatment of American singers'. It was felt by many to be the best musical of 1935, not least because of Tibbett's presence, and yet it failed to capture the public imagination. Twentieth Century-Fox, with which Zanuck had signed a distribution deal, wanted to cancel the second of the two scheduled pictures and attempted to buy out Tibbett's contract. Tibbett insisted on it being honoured, and so Zanuck did a deal with MGM for *Under Your Spell* (1936).

In *Under Your Spell*, Tibbett plays an exhausted opera singer who has to get away from everything, including a society hostess (Wendy Barrie) who pursues him into the wilderness. They eventually marry. During the course of the film, Tibbett sings 'Largo al factotum' from *The Barber of Seville* and 'Le veau d'or' from Gounod's *Faust*, together with songs by Arthur Schwartz. *Under Your Spell* was directed by Otto Ludwig Preminger, as he was billed, his first film in the United States. MGM decided to release it as the second part of a double-bill with *Give Me Your Heart*, starring Kay Francis and George Brent, a billing which surprised many people but demonstrated what little faith MGM had in it. Tibbett's singing again got good reviews but the film didn't, and Tibbett finally decided he had had enough of Hollywood.

Twentieth Century-Fox may have lost interest in Tibbett, but on the operatic front they had a new star they were anxious to promote, Nino Martini. The Italian tenor had become a star at the Met since his first film appearance in *Paramount on Parade* (1930), and was to sing in the house regularly until 1946, at the same time making guest appearances in Chicago, San Francisco and other North American cities. In 1935, he was whisked back to Hollywood to make *Here's to Romance*, playing a student of Ernestine Schumann-Heink who is convinced he can become a great singer. Sent to study in Paris, his interest in women makes his Paris Opéra debut a disaster, but he finally makes it to the Met in *Tosca*. The film also featured arias from *Manon*, *Cavalleria Rusticana* and *Pagliacci*. *Here's to Romance* was to be Schumann-Heink's only feature film. The 74-year old German contralto, who created the role of Klytämnestra in Strauss's *Elektra*, had become a household name in America through her concerts, radio broadcasts and appearances for the troops during World War I (something which caused her great personal anguish since she had family on both sides). She had sung for fifteen seasons at the Met and made numerous records. She only retired from the operatic stage in 1932 following an appearance as Erda in *Siegfried*, when she was 70. There were plans to turn her life into a film biography with Deanna Durbin playing her as a young singer, but they were dropped when she died the year after making *Here's to Romance*.

In his next film, *The Gay Desperado* (1936), directed by Rouben Mamoulian, Martini played a handsome tenor abducted by a Mexican bandit chief (Leo Carrillo) to become the gang's minstrel. He falls for fellow kidnap victim Ida Lupino, sings some songs in Spanish, a burst of *Aïda* and then the hit song 'The world is mine'. The film was a deft comedy with, according to Graham Greene, some moments of high satire.

Operatic arias were the main feature of *Music for Madame* (1937), an entertaining film in which Martini plays a newly arrived Italian immigrant hired to sing 'Vesti la giubba' in a clown costume at a Hollywood wedding, who discovers he has been a diversion for a robbery. A famous conductor wants to promote him, but Martini is terrified that if he sings again he will be recognised and jailed. Eventually he appears at the Hollywood Bowl and all ends happily, including his winning Joan Fontaine.

A former opera singer who made films at this time was Mary Ellis. The New York-born Ellis had started her career as a performer at the Met when she was eighteen, arriving for work on the same day as another young soprano, Rosa Ponselle. She made her debut playing a novice in the world premiere of *Suor Angelica*, and later took over the role of Lauretta in the first run of *Gianni Schicchi*. She sang in the premiere of Korngold's *Die tote Stadt* with Jeritza and appeared with Chaliapin in *Boris Godunov*. She had also sung Giannetta in Caruso's last run of *L'Elisir d'Amore* at the Met before his death in 1921. After four years there she had given up singing to become an actress, but was lured back to the musical stage when Rudolf Friml wrote *Rose Marie* for her. Although, having moved to England, she continued to work primarily as a straight actress, she also appeared occasionally on the musical stage and this is what most people tend to remember her for, especially the role of the opera singer Militza in Ivor Novello's *Glamorous Night*.

Novello had seen her in a C.B. Cochran production and knew immediately she would be perfect for his new operetta. Ellis had only vaguely heard of Novello and was in any case off to Hollywood to make a film. In 1934, she had appeared in her first film, the British-made *Bella Donna*, directed by Robert Milton with Conrad Veidt and Cedric Hardwicke and adapted from a novel by Robert Hitchens, about an archeologist's wife who tries to poison her husband for love of an Egyptian. Ellis did not sing in it.

The following year the film opera boom led to her being invited to Hollywood by Paramount to appear in *All the King's Horses*, a swashbuckling operetta with music by Edward Horan and a plot not unlike that of *The Prisoner of Zenda*. Ellis played the queen and Carl Brisson the Hollywood actor mistaken for the king. While she was filming in the States, Novello sent Ellis parcels of script and music as they were finished, which she learnt on the sea voyage back.

Glamorous Night, the story of how an opera singer and her gypsy friends save a Ruritanian king from his scheming ministers, opened at Drury Lane on 2 May 1935. Novello himself played the non-singing role of the king, and Trefor Jones and Olive Gilbert, former members of the Carl Rosa Opera Company, were also in the cast.

The show ran until February of the following year and only closed because Ellis was committed to her next Hollywood film, *Fatal Lady* (1936), in which she played a diva who runs away after an accusation of murder. Her co-stars included Walter Pidgeon and she sang music from *William Tell* and two imaginary operas written for the film: *Isabelle*, which had music by Gerard Carbonara, and *Bal Masque*, with music by Carbonara and Victor Young. By this time it had become customary to pre-record the vocal numbers in a film and mime singing to playback during filming. Ellis shocked her director by insisting on doing everything live.

She went on to film *Paris in Spring* (1936), opposite Tullio Carminati, directed by Lewis Milestone, in which four visitors to Paris change partners. She then made the film version of her stage hit, *Glamorous Night*, directed by Irishman Brian Desmond Hurst. Despite Novello's considerable success as a silent screen actor, he did not care for sound films, and the leading role was taken in the film by Barry McKay. Both Trefor Jones and Olive Gilbert from the stage production appeared in the film together with Otto Kruger, Victor Jory and Felix Aylmer.

The next stage show Novello wrote for Ellis was *The Dancing Years* which premiered at Drury Lane in 1939 and was turned into an embarrassingly dull film in 1950 (with Dennis Price and Gisèle Preville). The idea for *The Dancing Years* had come to Novello while at the cinema watching the Polish soprano Miliza Korjus in *The Great Waltz* (1938), a Hollywood biopic based somewhat loosely on the life of Johann Strauss.

Born in Warsaw of Swedish and Estonian parents, Korjus had established a considerable reputation in Berlin, Vienna, Brussels and Stockholm, for her vocal feats in such roles as the Queen of the Night, Lakmé, Lucia and Gilda. In Berlin she had, on several occasions, literally stopped the show. When Louis B. Mayer heard a recording of her, he immediately tried to sign her up, despite the opposition of Jeanette MacDonald. It took him two years to negotiate a contract, which she finally agreed to sign only if she received the same salary as Greta Garbo.

In *The Great Waltz* (1938), directed by Julien Duvivier, who had been brought from France for his Hollywood debut, Korjus plays a prima donna who falls in love with Strauss (Fernand Gravet). Although he reciprocates her love, he marries Luise Rainer instead, but it is Korjus's singing of his waltzes that inspires him to write *Die Fledermaus*.

The musical numbers were staged in an exhilarating style that was extravagent even by MGM standards and the film became one of the studio's biggest successes. Korjus (rhymes with gorgeous, as MGM's publicists pointed out) won an Academy nomination for Best Supporting Actress and cameraman Joseph Ruttenberg won one for his cinematography. Audiences were astonished by her singing, in particular a scene in which she sang 'Tales from the Vienna Woods', high above the orchestra (the violins of which, claimed MGM, were all by Stradavarius!). Although Duvivier is credited with directing *The Great Waltz*, he was reputedly admonished by MGM for making a film about Mrs. Strauss rather than Johann, and Victor Fleming took over towards the end of the shoot with the final sequence being conceived and directed by Josef von Sternberg.

Shortly after making *The Great Waltz*, Korjus was involved in a car crash and moved to Mexico where she made one more film, *The Imperial Cavalry* (1942), shown only in the Spanish-speaking world. The film featured the Mexican tenor Pedro Vargas and in it Korjus sang Strauss again as well as Bellini's 'Casta diva'.

Helen Jepson and Charles Kullman appeared in *The Goldwyn Follies* (1938). Soprano Jepson had just made her debut at the Met in the premiere of John Seymour's *In The Pasha's Garden* in 1935, when she was put under contract by Paramount as a potential star of the opera boom. They never used her. Several projects were mooted including *Something to Sing About* with James Cagney, but it was not until Sam Goldwyn wanted a pretty opera singer to take part in his George Marshall-directed *Follies* that she made her one and only film. Goldwyn was attempting to establish himself in film as the equivalent of Ziegfeld on Broadway, and the movie, set in a film studio, was full of well-known artists including the Ritz Brothers, Edgar Bergen, Kenny Baker and ballerina Vera Zorina in a sequence choreographed by her husband, George Balanchine. The score was written by George Gershwin, who died before he had completed it. In a scene in which film producer Adolphe Menjou is looking to cast a singer in a film he is making, Menjou sees Jepson and Kullman on stage in *La Traviata* performing 'Libiamo' and 'Sempre libera', and hires her.

Tenor Kullman, a stalwart of the Met for 25 seasons, had studied medicine at Yale where he joined the Glee Club and discovered he prefered singing to doctoring. He went on to study at the Juilliard school and made his debut in Philadelphia in 1929 singing Pinkerton. He then went to Europe, where he had appeared in Berlin, Vienna, Salzburg, Florence and at Covent Garden, before returning to America in 1935 to make his debut at the Met in *Faust*. During his time at the Met he sang 34 roles ranging from Cavaradossi and Tamino to Parsifal.

The desire to find photogenic opera singers even extended to giving Marion Talley a second chance. The new Republic studio, to become best known for its Gene Autry cowboy films, had just opened and needed something prestigious to establish its reputation. They felt that Talley, despite the failure of her previous screen appearances, might give them some cultural kudos and cast her in *Follow Your Heart* (1936) opposite Michael Bartlett. He played the customary gifted tenor; she a soprano from an eccentric Kentucky family. When she is first seen singing, she is lying on the floor poking a fire. One day her uncle brings an opera company home and she becomes the star of an operetta composed by the company's tenor (Bartlett). The recording techniques which had made her sound so squeaky in 1926 and 1927 had improved beyond all recognition, and her singing in the film is extremely good. *Follow Your Heart* was not, however, a success.

Norwegian soprano Kirsten Flagstad made her only screen appearance in *The Big Broadcast of 1938*, singing Brünnhilde's battle cry. The film also marked the screen debut of Bob Hope. Enrico Caruso Jnr. appeared as a young tenor from Naples who dreams of singing at La Scala in *El Cantante de Napoles* (The Singer from Naples, 1935), an American-made Spanish language film based very loosely on the early part of his father's life, while the Ukranian soprano Nina Koshetz appeared in a non-singing role in *Algiers* (1938), the film that established Hedy Lamarr as a Hollywood star.

By the end of the 1930s, operatic excerpts had become acceptable and not just for opera singers to sing. In *Broadway Gondolier* (1935), Dick Powell sang 'La donna e mobile' from *Rigoletto* and was featured in the quartet. Young soprano Deanna Durbin, who was trained by Andrès de Segurola but never went on the operatic stage, was expected to sing popular arias in all her films. And opera was awarded the supreme accolade when it was parodied by Laurel and Hardy in their version of Balfe's *The Bohemian Girl* (1936). The duo had earlier parodied Auber's *Fra Diavolo* in *The Devil's Brother* (1933) and made their own special version of Herbert's *Babes in Toyland* (1934). Felix Knight, who played in both *The Bohemian Girl* and *Babes in Toyland*, was on the verge of a stage operatic career, making his debut in a performance of *La Traviata* in the Hollywood Bowl in 1935. In 1946, he made his debut at the Met singing Almaviva and sang regularly at the house until the arrival of Rudolf Bing.

Opera had also become a setting. The thriller *Moonlight Murder* featured Leo Carrillo (voice dubbed) as a tenor murdered during a performance of *Il Trovatore* at the Hollywood Bowl, while Boris Karloff had his voice dubbed for an operatic sequence composed by Oscar Levant for *Charlie Chan at the Opera*. A performance of *The Mikado* was seen in *The Girl Said No* (1937). The most famous film of this period built around opera was the Marx Brothers' *A Night at the Opera* (1935), set at the Met where, in the closing sequences, a performance of *Il Trovatore* is taking place. With the presence of the Marx brothers, it is naturally chaotic and ends with Manrico being kidnapped and replaced by tenor Allan Jones.

A singer who made her film debut at this time, in her only dramatic screen role, was the soprano Beverly Sills. In 1936, at the age of seven, she won a radio talent contest in New York singing 'Caro nome' from *Rigoletto* and was immediately offered a spot on the weekly CBS radio show, *Capitol Family*, as well as a part in an episode of the film series, *Uncle Sol's Problem Court*. These ten-minute films were made in New York and showed Uncle Sol (Willie Howard) solving humorous domestic problems in his courtroom. Sills' episode was entitled 'Uncle Sol Solves It', and she played a little girl with a big voice destined to become an opera star. The domestic dispute was that her parents wanted her to follow the traditional route for American singers and study in Europe while she wanted to study in New York. When Uncle Sol asks her which she prefers, she whips off her hat, belts out 'Il bacio', and is allowed to stay.

That same year another extremely famous singer was invited to make a screen test by MGM. She sang the Habanera from *Carmen* and the 'Chanson bohemienne' as well as talking about her love of *La Traviata* and the effect on her of seeing Greta Garbo in *Camille*, George Cukor's version of the story with a soundtrack by Herbert Stothart based on Verdi. The screen tests have survived; she looks wonderful and sings like an angel; but for some reason, Rosa Ponselle, one of the great sopranos of the century, did not get the part and, in film terms, was never heard of again (Ponselle, like Richard Tauber, had, before their voices were discovered, worked as a cinema pianist).

It wasn't just Ponselle who didn't make it to the screen. Among projected films of the period which did not get made were *The Tales of Hoffmann*,which Max Reinhardt was slated to direct with Richard Tauber, Grace Moore, Jarmila Novotná, Feodor Chaliapin and Charles Laughton in the cast; and *Die Flederamus* which Reinhardt planned to direct with Tauber, Ponselle, Lotte Lehmann and Fernand Gravet.

While the studios were searching for opera singers who might become musical stars, MGM failed for some time to notice that they already had on their books two artists who were to become the biggest film operetta stars not just of their time but probably of all time. One had been an opera singer, the other was to become one for a short time after she had become a film star.

Jeanette MacDonald was born in Philadelphia in 1901 (studio publicity later claimed it to be 1907 which would have made her only thirteen when she made her debut in the chorus of a New York revue in 1920). By 1923 she had progressed to leading roles, appearing in shows such as Gershwin's *Tip Toes* and *Bubbling Over*. Richard Dix saw her in *Angela* and wanted her as his leading lady in his next film. Paramount duly tested her and turned her down. The test was seen, however, by director Ernst Lubitsch, who liked what he saw enough to get on a train and go to see MacDonald on stage in Chicago where she was then playing in *Boom Boom*. He was impressed and she made her film debut in *The Love Parade* (1929), playing opposite Maurice Chevalier. The film was a Ruritanian romantic musical with songs by Victor Schertzinger and Clifford Grey, and it set new standards for the film musical, winning four Academy Awards.

MacDonald's career was well under way. Next she was cast opposite Dennis King, creator of the original Broadway role, in a colour version of *The Vagabond King*. To everyone's surprise, the film did not get a good response. King's stage magnetism failed to transfer to the screen and MacDonald received downbeat reviews. She seemed, according to one critic, to be 'absolutely lost and incapable of rising to the opportunities the part offers'.

Lubitsch had once seen a spark, however, and was determined to recapture it. It certainly didn't reappear in *Monte Carlo* (1930) with Jack Buchanan, in which she sang 'Beyond the blue horizon' and 'Let's go native'. Paramount then dropped her. She moved to Fox and in *Oh, For a Man* (1930) played an opera singer. Only one short extract of an aria made it into the finished film. Musicals were no longer good box-office and Fox, having got cold feet, decided to cut out all opera.

Lubitsch, still believing in her, teamed her with Chevalier again in the musical romance *One Hour With You* (1932), co-directed by George Cukor and a remake of a film Lubitsch had made earlier. Cukor later claimed he had directed it all and had to threaten legal action even to get his name on the credits as assisting Lubitsch. MacDonald and Chevalier then appeared in *Love Me Tonight* (1932), another romantic musical comedy with songs by Rodgers and Hart ('Isn't it romantic', 'Mimi' and others). The director was Rouben Mamoulian, who was to direct the premiere of Gershwin's *Porgy and Bess* on Broadway. He brought style and flair to what on the face of it was a conventional musical, but one that, in his hands, wittily sent up convention. *Love Me Tonight*, sophisticated, often risqué and always imaginative, was one of the finest screen musicals of its time but was not thought much of at the time.

MacDonald looked to be becoming one of those artists who had sung in bad or indifferent film musicals and been forced to give up. But then in 1934, she received her big break. MGM had failed to sign Grace Moore for Lubitsch's sound version of *The Merry Widow*, officially because of a clash of schedules. In reality it probably had more to do with Moore's ballooning figure, her inability to keep weight off and her reputation for being difficult. Lubitsch still had faith in MacDonald and when he was invited from Paramount to MGM to direct *The Merry Widow* and was told Moore would not be appearing, he remembered her.

Lubitsch had been wanting to film *The Merry Widow* for many years, as had MGM boss Irving Thalberg. Lehár's operetta was perennially popular on the stage and Stroheim's 1925 silent version, also for MGM, had made a clear profit of $758,000. MGM had been toying with the idea of remaking the piece with sound for some time. It was to be a lavish production and clearly needed big box-office attractions in the lead roles. But who? MGM did not have any really big musical stars on their books. Ramon Navarro, who had starred in Lubitsch's silent version of Romberg's *The Student Prince* (1927), one of the most expensive films MGM had ever made, was no longer the draw he had once been and there was no one else. So Thalberg signed up Maurice Chevalier who had been released by Paramount as a result of declining box-office returns for the Lubitsch musicals.

Chevalier, so suave and debonair on screen, was a bundle of nerves off. He wanted as his co-star Grace Moore but Thalberg wanted someone 'extraordinary and beautiful and dynamic and unknown'. His first choice was the not entirely unknown Joan Crawford who began taking voice lessons and to whom Chevalier finally gave his approval. Then Thalberg announced, without consultation, that he had signed Jeanette MacDonald rather than Crawford. Chevalier was furious. He had already made three films with MacDonald at Paramount, none of which had been particularly successful, and felt it was time for a new partner. MacDonald was not that pleased to be appearing with him again either. The fastest bottom pincher in Hollywood, she had called him.

However, it was with Chevalier and MacDonald that the film went ahead. Thalberg had the script rewritten so that there was no danger of it seeming like the Stroheim script of 1925 (for which he would have had to pay royalties), and various writers came up with suggestions and outlines, including Anita Loos. He also wanted Lorenz Hart to write the lyrics but since Hart had an agreement with Richard Rodgers that where one went the other went too, Rodgers had to be hired as well. Sitting around doing nothing while being paid for it might seem idyllic, but Hart and Rodgers became increasingly restless and unhappy in Hollywood. Hart hated having to write lyrics for Lehár's music and didn't get on with Lubitsch, whom he found autocratic on the set. The director insisted Hart be punctual for meetings and submit his lyrics on neatly typed sheets, taking personal offence when Hart turned up late and started searching through his pockets for the scraps of paper on which he'd scribbled some words. While this was going on, Rodgers was to be found on the tennis court.

Both men wanted to get back to Broadway as soon as possible but MGM refused to release them from their contract. Rodgers later commented: 'Franz Lehár had written a pretty fine score without any help from me. But because Larry and I had one of those "whither thou goest I will go" contracts with the studio, the lyrics were officially credited to Richard Rodgers and Lorenz Hart.'

The choice of Lubitsch to direct *The Merry Widow* was another irritation for Chevalier. They had worked together on *The Love Parade, One Hour With You* and *Love Me Tonight* but there was no love lost between them. Chevalier was one of the few actors for whom Lubitsch made no attempt to hide his dislike and when Chevalier was later accused of collaborating with the Germans during World War II, Lubitsch said publicly he had no doubt it was true.

The Merry Widow took thirteen weeks to shoot with a separate, French version being produced simultaneously after it was made clear that French audiences would expect Chevalier to be speaking in French. While some people at MGM resented the extra money this cost, Thalberg wondered if it wouldn't be cheaper in the long run to shoot German and Spanish versions at the same time as well. The editing took Lubitsch longer than expected and he came to an agreement with Thalberg which was unheard of in the big studios at the time: he completed the editing free on the understanding that Thalberg did not let Paramount know.

When the film was finally finished, the publicity drive got under way. A trailer was shot with Lehár extoling the film's virtues, but then the censors of the Production Code and The Legion of Decency stepped in. Production Code member Martin Quigley, the right-wing publisher of the *Motion Picture Herald*, castigated Thalberg for deliberately introducing filth into the operetta. The film was, Quigley maintained, an industry double-cross with several offensive and suggestive scenes. The administrator who had passed it was hauled over the coals and was forced to admit publicly that the film was 'typical French farce that is definitely bawdy and offensively – in spots – suggestive'.

What upset these guardians of public morality was the character Danilo's attitude towards his philandering. He displayed no remorse for actions which were deemed to be immoral and therefore unacceptable. Thirteen cuts were proposed to modify the character, to soften the impression that Maxim's was simply a brothel, and to cover up a scene in which Sonia was partially undressed. Thalberg had to agree to the cuts even though the final prints had been made. In all just over three minutes were removed, although the original negative remained untouched.

The Merry Widow can with some justification be claimed to be Lubitsch's masterpiece, but it was to be the last musical he would direct. The teaming of Chevalier and MacDonald did not pack the cinemas and financially *The Merry Widow* was not an enormous success. It cost over $1.5 million to make and lost $115,000, despite winning an Oscar for its design.

MacDonald had, however, impressed MGM sufficiently for them to offer her a five-year contract. The first film made under this new deal was Victor Herbert's 1910 operetta, *Naughty Marietta*, an idea which MGM had suggested to MacDonald a year earlier but which had never got off the ground because the studio could not find a suitable leading man. This time they cast a former opera singer on the fringes of a film career, Nelson Eddy.

Baritone Eddy had been born in Providence, Rhode Island, where he sang in church choirs. He moved to Philadelphia in his teens, and while working as a switchboard operator, shipping clerk and then a journalist on the local paper, became involved in amateur musicals, especially Gilbert and Sullivan. He won a competition to sing with the Philadelphia Civic Opera and made his debut there in 1924 as Amonasro in *Aïda*. He turned professional and went on to appear in *Elektra, Madama Butterfly, Lohengrin, Tannhäuser* and the 1928 American premiere of *Ariadne auf Naxos*. It was with the Philadelphia Civic Opera that he made his debut at the Met, singing Tonio in *Pagliacci* when the company played there in 1924. In November 1931 he returned to the Met with the Civic Opera to sing the role of the Drum Major in a performance of *Wozzeck* conducted by Stokowski, apparently taking over at the last moment, despite it being a tenor role. Under Stokowski's baton he took part in 1933 in what appears to have been the first radio broadcast of *Parsifal*, singing the role of Gurnemanz and receiving very favourable reviews.

Maybe he realised he was never going to become a great opera singer, but whatever the reason, at the beginning of the 1930s, Eddy decided to concentrate on concerts and recitals rather than the operatic stage. Together with his appearances on radio, he became quite well-known and, after he had appeared in concert in Los Angeles, MGM offered him a contract. For a couple of years he appeared in such films as *Broadway to Hollywood* (1933), *Dancing Lady* (1934) and *Student Tour* (1934) doing a guest spot, singing a single song. Quite obviously, the studio didn't know what to do with him. It was even suggested at one stage that he be cast opposite Jeanette MacDonald in a straight remake of *The Prisoner of Zenda*.

It was Louis B. Mayer who insisted that Eddy be given his chance in *Naughty Marietta*, one of Mayer's pet projects. Eddy was cast as a lecherous rake and MacDonald as a much maligned loose woman in Herbert's fizzing operetta which contained the hit number 'Ah, sweet mystery of life'. Directed by Woody Van Dyke, the film, its setting transferred to Louisiana, had a good script, was played to the hilt by everyone and with its excellent score, was adored by the public. As a result Eddy was immediately cast opposite Grace Moore in the Rudolf Friml musical, *Rose Marie* (for reasons no one has ever satisfactorily worked out, the film is sometimes given a hyphen which the stage show does not have).

Rose Marie had been a huge hit on Broadway starring Mary Ellis, but Ellis was never considered for the film role. Instead MGM wanted Grace Moore who again proved elusive, being unavailable until after Eddy was due to have left on a concert tour. Since, after *Naughty Marietta*, Eddy was considered to be the bigger draw, the studio did not want to wait for her, so Moore (who was still rumoured to be having weight problems) had to be replaced. What could be more obvious than for Eddy to be teamed once more with MacDonald?

Naughty Marietta may have done well at the box-office but *Rose Marie* (1936), directed once more by Van Dyke and shot mostly on location, far outstripped it. MacDonald played an opera singer in Canada looking for her outlaw brother (James Stewart) at the same time as Mountie Eddy. The Mountie gets his man, and his woman. Also in the cast were Allan Jones and a young David Niven, playing one of a crowd of MacDonald's admirers.

Most of the numbers from the original show were dropped from the film and replaced by the songs 'Dinah', 'Some of these days', two extra songs written by the film's music director, Herbert Stothart, and operatic arias from *Tosca* and *Roméo et Juliette*, put in originally for Moore to sing. MacDonald coped with them well, but it was for 'The Indian love call' from the Friml original, that *Rose Marie* became famous. MacDonald and Eddy sing it on a lake in the Rockies, she sings it as he leads her captured brother away, they sing it when they are reunited at the end and, in one of the film's most memorable moments, MacDonald, singing in a performance of *Tosca*, hears him crooning, 'When I'm calling youooooo.'

Rose Marie was a hit, but although the MacDonald/Eddy partnership had established itself in the public consciousness it had not registered as far as MGM was concerned. MacDonald, who had become Louis B. Mayer's special protégé (there were unsubstantiated rumours they were having an affair), was next cast in *San Francisco* (1936) with Clark Gable and Spencer Tracy, while Eddy was teamed with Moore for Sigmund Romberg's *Maytime*. It was only when Moore failed to materialise, that MacDonald was brought in to rescue the film.

Set in Paris, *Maytime* tells the story of a prima donna who falls in love with a penniless singer who is subsequently shot by her jealous impresario husband (John Barrymore). At the end the lovers are reunited in death while their ghosts sing 'Will you remember?', the only Romberg number to survive the transition to screen. The film also contains a scene from Meyerbeer's *Les Huguenots*.

Maytime was a pet project of Thalberg. When he died just after the film had gone into production, Louis B. Mayer ordered an immediate rewrite of the script to remove any hint of immorality and recast several supporting roles, including bringing in Barrymore for Paul Lukas as the Svengali-like impresario. Footage already shot by director Edmund Goulding was scrapped and Goulding himself was replaced by Robert Z. Leonard.

Maytime was a sentimental, mawkish film and Eddy's acting is, at best, rudimentary. Yet *Maytime* did incredibly good business around the world, confirming MacDonald and Eddy as America's and the world's singing sweethearts.

Their voices may have blended on the screen but that didn't mean every-thing was harmonious between them when the cameras weren't rolling. They didn't particularly like one another and there was often animosity between them. And they didn't always work well together. But as a team they went on to make *The Girl of the Golden West* (1938), which was not the Puccini opera but the Belasco play on which it was based with a new score by Romberg. They then appeared in *Sweethearts* (1938), MGM's first Technicolor film and one of the year's top money-spinners, playing a husband-and-wife team on Broadway who never stop fighting each other while singing the music of Victor Herbert. With its excellent script and supporting cast, this is often considered to be the best of the MacDonald/Eddy musicals, winning an Oscar for cameraman Oliver Marsh and a nomination for music director Herbert Stothart.

New Moon (1940) was a remake of the Romberg operetta in which Grace Moore and Lawrence Tibbett had starred in 1930 and much closer to the orig-inal, with Eddy as a freedom fighter in old Louisiana and MacDonald as a French countess. This is the film in which Eddy and the chorus give a rousing version of 'Give me some men who are stout hearted men' as they tramp through a swamp.

They then went on to make a chocolate-box version of Noel Coward's *Bitter Sweet* (1940), produced by Victor Saville and directed by Van Dyke, with George Sanders playing the baron who duels with Eddy. Lavish the production may have been, winning an Academy nomination for the photography, but this was one of the poorest of their films, with Eddy's wooden acting emphasised, MacDonald being arch, and a general air of people being in the wrong film. The public didn't seem to mind but Coward loathed it. It was so dreadful, he felt, that he could never revive the stage show. 'A pity,' he commented, 'I was saving it up as an investment for my old age.'

After *Bitter Sweet*, MGM planned to star MacDonald and Eddy in new versions of *The Vagabond King* and *Show Boat*, but neither project reached the studio. Their last appearance together came in *I Married an Angel* (1942), the Rodgers and Hart musical. Added to the Broadway score was an aria from *Faust* for MacDonald and some *Carmen*. Soaring costs, changing styles and the advent of World War II made the studio hesitant about continuing to take chances on old-style operettas even though there was still a significant public for them. The differences between MacDonald and Eddy made both of them reluctant to continue their association, and since the producer responsible for most of their films was leaving MGM, their contracts, which were almost up, were allowed to lapse. *I Married an Angel* was announced as being their last appearance together even before the film went into production.

Eddy's career went slowly downhill afterwards. In 1943 he appeared in *The Phantom of the Opera* with hair dyed black and a pencil-thin moustache, singing with Susanna Foster from Flotow's *Martha*. *Phantom* was an enormous success, winning two Oscars, but it took Eddy a year to land another part, this time in Kurt Weill's *Knickerbocker Holiday*. His last major film as a singer came when he provided all the voices for the classic Disney cartoon, *Make Mine Music* (1946), including Willie the Whale and the chorus for which his voice was dubbed and redubbed to make it sound like a hundred people.

Meanwhile MacDonald, who had always longed to become an opera singer, on finding that her screen appeal was fading took the opportunity to do something she had always wanted to do: appear on the operatic stage. Coached by Lotte Lehmann, she made her debut in Montreal on 8 May 1943, singing Juliette in Gounod's *Roméo et Juliette*. She got rave reviews. In 1944 she repeated the role with the Chicago Civic Opera and also appeared in *Faust* with a cast that included Ezio Pinza. The reviews were only lukewarm, and she did not appear on the operatic stage again.

In the mid-1940s there was talk at RKO of reteaming her with Eddy, and despite their past frictions both were agreeable to the idea, but when the studio executive who proposed it died, the project was shelved.

6

Sound in Europe

One might have thought that with the interest in opera and operatic stories shown by Hollywood throughout the silent era, the advent of sound would have been welcomed as the opportunity at last to make a full-blown opera. Not a bit of it. With the exception of a film of *Pagliacci*, made in New York in 1931 and hardly a mainstream production, American producers turned their backs on opera, perhaps sensing that a film of a complete opera might not have the impact on the box-office that a lone aria had.

Only Fortuno Gallo welcomed the potential of sound. He ran the San Carlo Grand Opera Company, which had nothing to do with the famous San Carlo opera house in Naples but was a small-scale touring outfit comprised largely of Italian-American performers taking productions to those parts of America where major companies did not go. As soon as it became obvious that the new sound systems were going to last, Gallo engaged director Joe W. Coffmann to film the company's production of *Pagliacci* starring Fernando Bertini as Canio, Alba Novella as Nedda, Mario Valle as Tonio and Giuseppe Interranti as Silvio. The film was shot in a studio on Long Island and received warm reviews for the singing but less favourable comment about the direction. Coffmann had done little more than point cameras at the action on stage. He had certainly not attempted to make a cinematic film.

Gallo claimed on the credits that his *Pagliacci* was the world's first sound picture of a grand opera. That depends how you define grand opera. The previous year, 1930, Auber's comic opera *Fra Diavolo*, one of the most popular of the last century, had been filmed in Italy starring the Croatian tenor Tino Pattiera as Diavolo. What was even more remarkable about this version was that, unlike Coffmann's *Pagliacci*, it was conceived by director Mario Bonnard as a film, not simply a visual record of a stage show.

Bonnard did not just point his cameras at the cast singing (of which Pattiera, who had sung in Chicago in the early 1920s, was the only one with an operatic background); he included spoken dialogue which, following the custom that had emerged once actors started to speak, was filmed in Italian, French and English. He also introduced action scenes, many involving Diavolo's two clumsy sidekicks, Giacomo and Beppo. These two inspired Laurel and Hardy to make their own version of the opera three years later, with Dennis King in the title role and Hal Roach directing.

Fra Diavolo, which had Auber's music arranged by Giuseppe Becce, marked the beginning of a fascination in Europe with filmed opera, for it was in Europe, in Italy and in the German-speaking countries in particular, that the vast majority of operatic films with sound were made. The arrival of the talkies marked, for the first time, a clear difference between films made in English-speaking countries and those made elsewhere. In the silent era it did not matter where a film had been made. It could be watched with equal enjoyment anywhere in the world, and if explanations were required, it was a simple job to include an inter-title in the language of the audience. Being able to hear the dialogue meant that films in a language not understood by the audience stood little chance of getting a world-wide release, and even Hollywood relied on overseas sales to put pictures into profit. The answer, certainly in the decade after sound had arrived, was to make each film in several languages. Some Hollywood studios opened European studios to make these, others took European film-makers to the States.

It had taken some time for European producers to turn to sound. Independents, of which there were many, were reluctant to embrace a system which would cause costs to spiral and was felt might not even last. There was also the question of which system to adopt. As well as Vitaphone and Movietone, there were a number of European systems under development and the German Tri-Ergon company, with its sound-on-film process, was deter-mined not to be overtaken by the Americans. A short, sharp patent war ensued during which producers adapted an approach of wait-and-see. In 1929 only three out of every hundred pictures made in Germany had sound. The following year, once the patent problems had been sorted out, 84 out of a hundred were sound films.

The German-speaking countries had already established a genre of operetta in silent pictures. The coming of sound was welcomed as an opportunity to make film musicals properly. The first German sound film was a part-talkie with music, *Dich hab' ich geliebt* (Because I Loved You, 1929). This was well-received abroad, but the first German film to enjoy a major international success and convince producers that there was a future in sound was the all-singing, all-speaking, *Zwei Herzen im Dreivierteltakt* (Two Hearts in Three Quarter Time, 1930).

While operetta was a natural and obvious genre for early German sound pictures, *Zwei Herzen* was unusual in that it was not a well-known stage show but was written expressly for the screen. The last ingredient to be added was the music. Julius Heimann, a millionaire shoe-manufacturer in Berlin, had two daughters who were avid fans of the new talkies, so to indulge them he decided to put up the money for a film. They wanted a musical so he invited writers Walter Reisch and Franz Schulz to come up with a script. It was only when the script was finished that he approached Robert Stolz, whose connection with the cinema went back almost twenty years, to provide the music, including a waltz to match the film's title. At his initial meeting with Heimann, Stolz was asked how long it would take for him to compose a waltz. Stolz took the script to read over lunch and find out what the film was about. By the end of his lunch, the waltz was written on the back of a menu.

Stolz himself conducted the orchestra on set while the singers were recorded live. Each set had a different acoustic and there were problems with trains rumbling past during the takes so that scenes had to be shot around the train timetable. When the film opened in Berlin on 13 March 1930, it was well received by a star-studded audience. The only criticism came from one reviewer who described Stolz's title waltz as a failure since he found it impossible to remember. The sheet music went on to sell over seven million copies, doing especially well in China and Japan! *Zwei Herzen* ran for almost a year in New York and Stolz later turned it into a stage musical, possibly the first operetta to make the journey from screen to stage rather than the other way round.

Zwei Herzen starred Willi Forst and the soprano Irene Eisinger. Eisinger, one of nine children, had been born in Austria and had made her debut with the Basle Opera when she was 22. She was immediately snapped up by the Berlin State Opera to become the company's youngest member. Her best known role was as Susanna in *The Marriage of Figaro* and it was in that opera that she made her Salzburg debut not as Susanna but as Cherubino. She was later to become a great favourite at Glyndebourne. Eisinger's good looks and vivacious personality made her a natural for films and after *Zwei Herzen* she appeared in a film of Stolz's stage operetta, *The Merry Wives of Vienna* (which Stolz had written to a libretto intended originally for Johann Strauss).

The Merry Wives of Vienna, like *Zwei Herzen*, co-starred Forst and was directed by Geza von Bolvary. Bolvary was a Hungarian who had worked in Germany and Austria during the silent era directing mostly melodramas and comedies. *Zwei Herzen* was his first sound film and established him both as a hot property and the founding father of Viennese operettas filmed with sound. The form, for which many composers wrote directly, was dominated by Hungarians and Austrians, whether working in Berlin or Vienna, which became an important centre for German language film-making not just because so much talent resided there but because the Viennese accent became very fashionable for actors.

One of those Austrians making a big impact in Germany was Georg Wilhelm Pabst who was asked to direct the screen version of the Weill/Brecht hit, *Die Dreigroschenoper* (The Threepenny Opera) in 1931. Although this was not made in an English version, it was co-produced by Warner Bros. in an attempt to break into the lucrative German market.

Kurt Weill and Bertolt Brecht's adaptation of John Gay's *The Beggar's Opera* had opened in Berlin in 1928 with Lotte Lenya, Weill's wife, as Jenny. It was a smash hit and Nero Films, backed by Warner Bros., quickly acquired the film rights and engaged Pabst to direct.

Brecht and Weill were paid a lump sum and put on retainers to rework the script and music. Brecht began collaborating on the screenplay with Caspar Neher and, without telling anyone, not even Weill, radically altered the framework and plot of the stage show. When Nero Films found out, they were horrified. They had paid for a hit opera and that was what they wanted to see on the screen. They attempted to buy off Brecht so he would keep out of the way, but he refused to go. Both he and Weill had it written into their contracts that they would have the last word on all matters concerning words and music, and he was determined to exercise that right. He refused to do any more work and when the producers opted to go ahead without him, decided to sue.

Pabst had just started shooting the film when the show opened in Paris to such acclaim that it was decided a French version should be made simultaneously with the German one. Weill was far from pleased with the changes Brecht had made to the plot and the words of *The Threepenny Opera*. He was even less happy when he discovered that Pabst, in an attempt to turn the stage show into a film, was not only using Brecht's altered script but had changed the order of the songs, dropping some and allocating others to different characters. Most of Weill's haunting score had gone, only the ballad of Mack the Knife (sung by Ernst Busch) and some songs for Lotte Lenya being kept.

Weill was furious. He took out a separate injunction to stop the filming and the two cases came to court in October 1930 while Pabst was still shooting. Judgement was delivered the following month. Brecht lost, the court deeming that by refusing to work on the script any further, he had broken his contract. He was ordered to pay costs, but the production company, not wanting any more aggravation, agreed to waive the payment provided that he agreed to stay away from the film. They also paid him an additional fee.

Weill, on the other hand, won his argument that the producers had adapted his score without permission and in so doing had destroyed the spirit of the original. They had, in Weill's words, taken liberties. Weill did not want damages. Instead he got an assurance that he would be commissioned to write the music for three major films over which he would have complete artistic control. He began work on the first of these but because of the rise of Nazism and his subsequent decision to leave Germany, none was ever made.

Pabst's film of *The Threepenny Opera* sticks closely to Brecht's revised screenplay, but although a left-of-centre liberal, he softened much of the original social criticism by concentrating upon the relationships between the principal characters. With Rudolph Forster as Mackie Messer and Lotte Lenya a compelling screen presence as Jenny, the German version has a much harder edge than the French film even though the camera movements are identical and only the cast is different. Set in a stylised London with pools of light and deep shadows, the German film has a much more sinister feel to it.

6. Sound in Europe

Once sound reached Europe, the rush to make operatic films began in earnest. Louis Ganne's 1899 comic opera *Les Saltimbanques* (1930), about a troupe of circus performers, was made in three different languages with Käthe von Nagy starring in all three as the heroine who eventually runs away from the circus for love. *Amours Viennoises* (Viennese Loves, 1930) featured a score by Lehár, *The Czardas Baroness* (1930) was an operetta by Hungarian composer Georg Jarno whose *Die Försterchristl* (The Forester's Daughter) was filmed in 1931 with Irene Eisinger. *Der Grosse Tenor* (1930) featured Emil Jannings as an opera singer (his voice being dubbed), and *Zwei Kravaten* (Two Ties, 1930) was an attempt by Mischa Spoliansky to write a film opera set in America, featuring the bass Michael Bohnen as a waiter who swaps his white tie for a black tie when he becomes a gentleman crook. Bohnen also appeared in Paul Abraham's operetta, *Viktoria und ihr Hussar* (1931), directed by Richard Oswald.

André Messager's *Coups de Roulis* (1931) and *Passionnement* (1932) were filmed in France where the first sound version of *Die Fledermaus* was made in 1931 with Czech actress Anny Ondra starring in both French and German versions. Richard Heuberger's *Der Opernball* and Hervé's *Mam'zelle Nitouche* also made it to the screen in 1931.

In Germany, *Rigoletto* (1931) was filmed with Lina Pagliughi as Gilda, Carlo Galeffi in the title role, Primo Montanari as the Duke and Maria Castagna-Fullin as Maddelena, while in Italy, *Figaro's Great Day* (1931) featured Gianfranco Giachetti as a singing teacher who steps in to save a performance of *The Barber of Seville* when the baritone singing Figaro walks out. Rossini's opera, together with Mozart's *The Marriage of Figaro*, later provided the music for *Le Barbier de Séville* (1933), a French film combining the two operas. Also in Italy, Guido Brignone directed a version of *La Wally* (1932) which had a score based on Catalani's opera but retained only two of the arias, dubbed by Giannina Arangi Lombardi.

It was't just those who had worked in the silent cinema who were attracted to sound. In Berlin, many of those who had gathered around Otto Klemperer at the opera house and Max Reinhardt at the Deutsche Theater Berlin became fascinated by the creative possibilities offered by sound. Max Ophuls, who had established a reputation for innovation in the theatre and on radio, joined Ufa, the German studio, in 1931. Among the five films he made before being thrown out of the industry in 1933 for being a Jew was one of Smetana's *The Bartered Bride* (1932), starring Jarmila Novotná and Willi Domgraf-Fassbaender.

Novotná, born in 1907 in Prague, where she had studied with Emmy Destinn, had made her debut in 1926 singing Rosina in a provincial Czech theatre. The following year she sang her first Mařenka in *The Bartered Bride* at the Prague Opera. It was to become one of her trademark roles. In 1929, when she was 22, she joined the Berlin State Opera and it was in Berlin that she first met Max Reinhardt. He invited her to sing in his production of *La Belle Hélène* and later to take the role of Antonia in his staging of *The Tales of Hoffmann*.

Novotná had made her first film while still a teenager in Prague. Her first film in Berlin was as one of the singers on stage in *Brand in der Opera* (Fire at the Opera, 1930), the story of a rich man putting on a production for his girl-friend in the chorus to sing the lead. The opera house burns down on opening night. The film was made in two versions, the German one being directed by Carl Froelich, the French by Henry Roussell.

She followed this by taking the lead in the first sound film of Karl Millöcker's *Der Bettelstudent* (The Beggar Student, 1931), which had already been filmed three times during the silent era. The setting is Cracow during an occupation in 1704. Novotná plays the aristocratic Laura, who spurns the advances of the governor and is forced to marry a poor student disguised as a rich count, only to discover that he really is a rich count. The part of the student was taken by the baritone Hans Heinz Bollmann, and Viktor Janson directed. An English version of the film was made at the same time, directed by John Harvel and Victor Hansbury, with Shirley Dale replacing Novotnà as Laura, Margaret Halstan as her mother and Lance Fairfax, the original Australian Red Shadow, as the student.

Then came *Die verkaufte Braut* (The Bartered Bride, 1932), a cinema classic in its own right, which showed what could be done with opera on the screen in the hands of a master craftsman such as Ophuls. His direction, with its use of flowing camera movements, building of character through detail and his keen eye for the telling frame, turned Smetana's rustic comedy into a distin-guished and poetic piece of cinema. Novotná is radiant as Mařenka, and Willi Domgraf-Fassbaender superb as Jenik. Also a member of the Berlin State Opera, he was the father of mezzo Brigitte and later became a stalwart at Glyndebourne where he sang Figaro on the opening night.

In 1933, with the advent of Nazi rule, Novotná left Berlin and moved to Vienna where she became a member of the State Opera and continued her film career starring opposite Gustav Fröhlich in *Die Nacht der grossen Liebe* (The Night of Great Love, 1933) an operetta written for the screen by Robert Stolz and directed by Geza von Bolvary. In 1934 she appeared in *Frasquita*, a film of Lehar's Spanish operetta about the entangled love-life of a gypsy girl in which her co-star was again Hans Heinz Bollmann.

Throughout the 1930s, Novotná was a regular at the Salzburg Festival and it was there, on the suggestion of Max Reinhardt, that Louis B. Mayer of MGM went to offer her a $1,000 a week contract to go to Hollywood. She turned him down. But in 1938 Novotná decided she could remain in Europe no longer and emigrated to the States, where she appeared at the Met for sixteen seasons. Her last German-language film was *Der Kosak und die Nachtigall* (The Cossack and the Nightingale, 1935), a spy thriller with music by Lehár in which she played an opera singer. She was then asked to film the popular Oscar Straus operetta,

Der letzte Walzer (The Last Waltz, 1936). This had already been filmed in Germany in 1934 with Camille Horn as Countess Vera and Ivan Petrovich as Count Dmitri, directed by George Jacoby, another stalwart of the silent era who turned to operetta and was later to direct *Eine Nacht im Mai* (1938), the first German attempt to ape the Hollywood production number musical. His film of *The Last Waltz* was sufficiently successful for the producers to decide it was worth refilming in different languages, and Novotná was hired to star in English and French versions which were shot simultaneously with different supporting casts and different directors. Her Count Dmitri in the English version was the popular star of British musicals, Harry Welchman.

Novotná's final film in Europe was *Song of the Lark* (1937), a Czech film about a glamorous opera singer returning to her home village. A young boy studying for the priesthood falls in love with her but she decides not to pursue the relationship for the sake of his dying mother. Novotná sang Czech folk music and also arias from *Carmen*. The film was directed by Svatopluk Inneman who had earlier been one of three co-directors on a Czech film of *The Bartered Bride* (1933), made in Prague with Ota Horakova as Mařenka as a riposte to the Ophuls film, which many Czechs felt was not the authentic Smetana opera.

Novotná was one of many European operatic stars who found their way onto the screen in the early 1930s. Like their Hollywood counterparts, producers in Europe wanted star names and were on constant look-out for artists who could make the transition to the screen and bring in the public. When it came to musicals and operettas, many films were conceived as star vehicles.

The Hungarian soprano Gitta Alpar, a great favourite in Munich and Vienna in such roles as the Queen of the Night and Violetta, and a member of the Berlin Opera since 1927, appeared in two films in 1932, both directed by her husband, the actor Gustav Fröhlich. In *Die oder Keine* (She or Nobody), she played a prima donna seen singing in a production of *La Traviata*, who wins the love of a young prince and helps him see off the rivals to his throne. *Gitta Entdeckt ihr Herz* (Gitta Discovers her Heart) saw her as Gitta, a famous Hungarian singer and big star in Berlin (there were intended parallels with her own life), who helps a young composer (played by Fröhlich) to become a success. The music was written by Nikolaus Brodszky.

The tenor Alfred Piccaver, who, despite the name (which may have had a Spanish origin, the family never quite knew), was born in England, had been a great favourite in Vienna for over twenty years when the sound movies began. Brought up in the United States and trained at the Met's Opera School, he began his career in Prague, quickly becoming a sell-out draw. He first appeared at the Vienna State Opera in 1910 when he was 26 and went on to partner such artists as Selma Kurz, Maria Jeritza (with whom he had a famous row) and Lotte Lehmann. He was short and fat, and yet his appearances still drew full houses, so it was natural for film producers to try to cash in on that popularity.

He appeared in his first film in 1932 and then, in 1933, in *Abenteuer am Lido* (Adventure at the Lido), a film written for him and made on location in Venice, in which he played, rather unsurprisingly, a singer.

As a young music student, Richard Tauber had played the piano for the movies and knew what an impact films could have. He had made his screen debut in 1923, in a short promotional film to help sell his records. It was intended that they would be played along with the film, although no attempt was made to synchronise the sound with his lip movements.

When sound first reached Germany in 1929, one of the earliest films to use it was *Ich küsse ihre Hand, Madame* (I Kiss Your Hand, Madame) with Marlene Dietrich and Harry Liedtke, who was seen singing the film's title song with a voice provided by Tauber. Tauber's singing helped the film become an international hit and he was immediately cast in a film himself, opposite Maria Solveig. In *Das Dirnenlied* (later retitled *Ich glaub' nicht mehr an eine Frau*/Never Trust a Woman), he played a wise old sailor who helps a young friend win a music hall artist. He wrote the title song himself and throughout the film sang popular songs. Suffering at the time with arthritis, he found the experience of filming much more enjoyable than appearing on stage. He enjoyed it so much he decided to form his own production company.

The Tauber company's first venture, directed by Max Reichmann, who had directed *Das Dirnenlied*, was *Das lockende Ziel* with Lucie Englisch as Tauber's co-star. He played a Bavarian singer who becomes a big star at the Berlin Opera appearing in a production of *Martha*. The film was shot simultaneously in English (as *The End of the Rainbow*) and French (*La Marche à la Gloire*) as well as German.

He then went on to make a film version of *The Land of Smiles*, the Lehár operetta he had sung in the Berlin premiere of 1929, which contained the song with which his name will eternally be associated, 'You are my heart's delight'. For the film, which was again directed by Reichmann, the plot was altered so that Tauber played a Prince being entertained by a performance of the operetta in which he also appeared.

Tauber's company made two more films, *Die grosse Attraktion* (The Great Attraction, 1931), which contained some new songs by Lehár including a tango, together with songs by Bronislaw Kaper, Paul Dessau and Franz Grothe; and *Wie werde ich reich und glücklich* (How to Become Rich and Happy). Neither helped Tauber become rich for both failed at the box office and Tauber's company folded having lost the tenor thousands.

In Italy, Giacomo Lauri-Volpi, one of the many fine tenors of the period, able to sing a D above top C with ease, appeared as himself in *La Canzone del Sole* (Song of the Sun, 1933) which had an original score by Pietro Mascagni. In addition to singing Mascagni's title song, Lauri-Volpi is seen in recital performing arias from *I Puritani* and, in the film's closing sequence shot at the Verona Arena, taking part in a scene from Meyerbeer's *Les Huguenots* with the mezzo Gianna Pederzina. Directed by Max Neufeld and made in German and Italian versions, the film also starred Vittorio De Sica as Lauri-Volpi's lawyer.

Tito Schipa, one of the most lyrical of Italian tenors, was lionized around the world and adored by women. His antics drove his first wife to drink and after their separation, he married a woman 35 years his junior. He earned a great deal of money, which he managed, without difficulty, to spend. After the war he, like Gigli, was tarred with having sung for Mussolini.

Schipa was a natural for the screen, first appearing in two Paramount shorts. In 1932, in Italy, he began his career in feature films, his first being *Tre Uomini in frac* (1932) which became *Trois Hommes in Habit* in the French version and *I Sing For You Alone* in the English. Schipa played a tenor who cracks on a top note and has to leave town. When shooting different language versions of a film, it was customary for songs to be sung in their original language no matter what language was being spoken. In *I Sing For You Alone*, Schipa sings everything in the language of the film, even throwing in a song in Spanish.

The film did well, but it was *Vivere* (1936), directed by Guido Brignone, which established Schipa as a film star as well as an opera singer. He played the inevitable singer, this time working in a nightclub, who is discovered and becomes a star at the opera. His daughter (played by Caterina Boratto who was to appear in Fellini's *8½* and *Juliet of the Spirits*) falls in love with an unsuitable man of whom he disapproves but by the end the two are reconciled. During the course of the film he sang an aria by Donizetti and Federico's Lament from *L'Arlesiana* together with some songs written for the film by C.A. Bixio.

The film was so popular that Schipa and Boratto were cast together again in *Chi e piu felice di me?* (Who is Happier than Me? 1938) with Brignone again their director. Schipa plays a middle-aged tenor (he was almost 50) who has an affair with a younger woman. He marries her when he discovers she has had his child while he's been away on tour. As well as popular songs, the film included Schipa singing an aria from *Andrea Chénier*. He played a tenor again in *Terra di Fuoco* (Land of Fire, 1938), this time killing the man he thinks is having an affair with his wife. She admits to the affair in the hope his sentence will be reduced. After his release, he learns that she was really innocent. The featured aria was from Massenet's *Werther*. Schipa went on to make a further four features over the next twelve years.

Another tenor who was to make an even more successful career in film was Leo Slezak. The father of Walter (who became a famous film actor himself and later appeared in musicals and at the Met in *The Gypsy Baron*), Leo had been a stalwart of the Vienna Opera for many years, noted for such roles as Canio, Radamès, Otello, Walther, Tannhäuser and Lohengrin. It was Slezak who is supposed to have delivered the immortal line, when the swan meant to carry Lohengrin off disappeared without him, 'What time is the next swan?' He retired from the operatic stage in 1932 when he was in his late fifties, and went on to appear in more than 40 films. The majority were dramas in which he was a supporting actor, but many did have a musical element or were operettas in which Slezak was required to sing. He was in *Grand Duchess Alexandra* (1933) with Maria Jeritza; he played an old farmer in *Die ganze Welt dreht sich um Liebe* (1935) a film of Lehár's operetta *Clo-Clo*; and he was Falstaff in a German adaptation of *The Merry Wives of Windsor* (1935). He was in the Robert Stolz operettas, *Das Frauenparadies* and *Liebe im Dreivierteltak*.

Slezak had made his film debut in *Die Frauendiplomat* (1932), a musical comedy set in the world of diplomacy, opposite the young Hungarian soprano, Marta Eggerth. Eggerth had made her film debut in 1930, when she was eighteen, in *The Bridegroom's Widow* which, even though Eggerth could not then speak a word of English, was filmed in England. Born in Budapest, she had made her professional stage debut at the age of eleven singing in the operetta *Mannequin*, and shortly afterwards gave her first public recital. When she was fourteen she went on a tour of Scandinavia, and was offered a recording contract. Brought to Vienna by Emmerich Kálmán to understudy Adele Kern in his operetta *Das Veilchen von Montmartre*, she took over the role, transferring with the production to Hamburg. She was still only eighteen when she appeared in the celebrated Max Reinhardt/Erich Korngold version of *Die Fledermaus* as Adele.

Eggerth possessed good looks and an excellent voice. The fact that she was equally at home in opera or operetta made her perfect for German musical films. After *The Bridegroom's Widow*, she appeared in almost 40 films over the next twenty years, many of them written for her by such composers as Emmerich Kálmán, Franz Lehár, Robert Stolz, Paul Abraham and Oscar Straus.

Such a hectic filming schedule did not leave Eggerth much time for the stage and she was forced to turn down an engagement to sing Zerbinetta in *Ariadne auf Naxos*, a role she had learnt at the request of Richard Strauss himself, as well as an appearance in Max Reinhardt's production of *The Tales of Hoffmann* in Berlin.

At the time that Eggerth was making her film debut, another opera singer was appearing in a film for the first time, the popular Polish tenor, Jan Kiepura. Kiepura, the son of a baker, had been born in the coal mining village of Sosnowiec. Although it soon became clear he had a voice, his parents insisted he become a lawyer and sent him to the University of Warsaw. But he continued singing, making his operatic debut in Lvov in the title role of *Faust* when he was still only 22. At the age of 24 he auditioned for the Vienna State Opera. Franz Schalk, the Opera's director, listened, then commented 'an impertinent voice', before asking Kiepura if he was free the following Tuesday to sing Cavaradossi opposite Jeritza in *Tosca*. Kiepura was free and his appearance got him noted, but it was when he sang Calaf in *Turandot* with Maria Nemeth that everyone realised a new star tenor had arrived.

Engagements followed at La Scala, Covent Garden, Paris, Berlin and other major European houses. Korngold asked him to sing the role of the Stranger in the Vienna premiere of his opera *Das Wunder der Heliane*. Kiepura was one of the brightest stars in the European operatic firmament.

The arrival of sound launched Kiepura onto a second career. His voice, his looks and his personality had won him a loyal following in the opera house. His transfer to the screen was to make him a household name throughout Europe, creating a Kiepura cult. Just as Geraldine Farrar had had her devoted Gerryflappers, so Kiepura was followed everywhere by his Kiepura Mädchen, the Kiepura Girls. Every stage door was crowded with them, and Kiepura's party trick became, wherever crowds gathered for him, whether in Vienna's Ringstrasse or outside the stage door at Covent Garden, to jump onto the bonnet of a car and sing a song.

It wasn't just adulation Kiepura wanted. He was passionate about opera and knew that a film would be seen by more people in a week than would see him in the opera house in a year. He saw films as a way to share his passion. His first was *Die singende Stadt* (City of Song, 1930) in which he was cast as a Neapolitan singer brought to London. The film was shot in both German and English, and the director was Carmine Gallone, one of the most important names in the story of opera on film.

Gallone had started his long directing career in 1914, when he was 28, making melodramas which frequently starred his wife Soave. In the 1920s, the Italian film industry had gone into recession and Gallone moved to Germany. It was there, with the coming of sound, that he began to make films either of operas or containing operatic excerpts. In a career lasting until the 1960s, he made more operatic films than any other director.

City of Song was an immediate hit. Kiepura followed it up with the *Das Lied einer Nacht* (Tell Me Tonight, 1932) in which, as an Italian tenor who changes places with a fugitive and falls in love with the mayor's daughter, he sings arias from *La Bohème*, *Rigoletto*, *La Traviata* and *Martha*, as well as songs by Mischa Spoliansky. He was also a famous tenor in *My Song For You* (1934). In Vienna to star in a production of *Aïda*, he becomes involved with a young woman who is trying to get her composer boyfriend a job. Like all Kiepura's early films, this was made in dual language versions. The cast of the English film included Patricia Roc as the young woman, Emlyn Williams as the composer and Sonnie Hale as Kiepura's secretary. The director was Maurice Elvey. Elvey had started his career in 1913 directing silents and worked in Hollywood and Europe as well as in Britain. He made his last film in 1957, and has the distinction of having directed more films than any other British director, over 300 of them.

Kiepura was now recognised throughout Germany and Austria, and to a lesser extent in Britain, by the person in the street. His box-office pull was such that he could pick and choose his projects, and he always insisted every one of his films had to contain opera. His next had a score especially written for him by Robert Stolz, which included excerpts from *Tosca*. *My Heart is Calling You*

(1934) tells the story of an opera company stranded in France, trying to get an engagement at the Monte Carlo Opera House. Kiepura, the company's leading tenor, and his leading lady, the woman he loves, perform *Tosca* on the steps outside the opera house while the resident company plays the same opera inside. Needless to say, the alfresco performance is much better than the one going on in the opera house, and the audience rushes out to listen to Kiepura. The film was made in English, French and German, and Carmine Gallone was the director of all three. Danielle Darrieux was Kiepura's co-star in the French version, Marta Eggerth in the German and English versions.

The way alternative language versions were shot varied. In some cases the film would be made in its entirety in one language. The producers would wait to see how the public reacted. If the reaction was favourable, a different language version would be shot, sometimes in a different studio, sometimes even in a different country. Usable scenes from the original would be incorporated into the second or, if there was one, the third version. Gigli's concert hall sequences filmed for *Non Ti Scordar di Me* (Forget Me Not, 1935) appear not just in the English and Italian versions, but in other Gigli films as well. For *My Heart is Calling You*, the producers obviously thought they were on to a winner from the outset and decided to make the film in German, French and English simultaneously. All three casts were at the studio at the same time, dressed and made up. Gallone would shoot a scene in German, then clear the set, bring on the next cast and shoot again in French, repeating the same process for the English film. Kiepura was the only one of the principals who stayed on set for each scene.

Eggerth found it extremely difficult having to deliver her lines in German, including repeats for close-ups, then wait behind the set re-learning them in English ready to go back on again at a moment's notice. 'It was very difficult to build up any sort of atmosphere,' she recalled, 'because the moment we got a mood going, we would have to break it for the other cast to come on.'

As well as the dialogue, all the arias and songs had to be repeated since they were sung live. Kiepura refused to film to playback since he felt that miming did not communicate the music's emotion. 'Singing nicely was important to him,' Eggerth says, 'but singing with the soul was more important.'

What Kiepura didn't know when they began working together was that Eggerth had idolised him ever since she had first seen him on stage in Budapest singing Calaf opposite Jeritza. He, however, was much more interested in Danielle Darrieux, his co-star in the French version. Eggerth's disappointment showed in the rushes. 'Come on – you're supposed to be in love,' Gallone kept chiding her.

One night, after shooting had gone on well into the evening, Kiepura offered to walk Eggerth home. It was, she felt, too late to invite him in but he clearly wasn't ready to go home. Although it was snowing heavily, they walked up and down the street outside her apartment and Eggerth started to tell him how jealous she felt seeing him flirting with other people. Kiepura rushed over to a flower seller, took her basket and handed it to Eggerth. It was only when he came to pay that he discovered he didn't have any money. Eggerth ending up paying for the flowers herself.

My Heart is Calling You was an enormous success and shortly afterwards Kiepura and Eggerth married. Sometimes referred to as Europe's answer to MacDonald and Eddy, they made surprisingly few films together, both continuing to have successful independent careers. After *My Heart is Calling You* they did not appear together again for another couple of years.

Kiepura was, yet again, a singer in *I Love All Women* (1935), another musical written by Robert Stolz, and in *Opernring* (1936) he played a singing taxi driver who becomes a successful tenor at the Vienna State Opera singing in a production of *Turandot*. Directed by Gallone, this won a prize at the 1936 Venice Film Festival.

Eggerth, meanwhile, had appeared in *The Unfinished Symphony*, an Anglo-Austrian biopic of Schubert, directed by Willi Forst, in which she sang Schubert's Ave Maria; in *Die Blonde Carmen* (The Blonde Carmen, 1935), as an operetta star who sets out to convince a composer that not all women in the theatre have loose morals; and in Gallone's *Casta Diva* (1935), a biopic of Bellini in which she played the singer who inspired him. This won the prize for the Best Italian Film of 1935 in Venice.

When Kiepura sailed to the States to make *Give Us This Night* with Gladys Swarthout, Eggerth accompanied him. She, too, had been offered a film contract. Universal wanted her to make three films, the first to be directed by Preston Sturges. Before shooting could start, the studio ran into financial difficulties and all its films were cancelled. When the studio eventually reopened, Eggerth was back in Europe and the roles she had been asked to play were given to Deanna Durbin.

The second film Kiepura and Eggerth made together was *Zauber der Bohème* (The Charm of La Bohème). This was one of a type of operatic film which was to become extremely popular, in which the events of the opera are mirrored by similar events in the lives of the 'real' people playing them. Kiepura and Eggerth are singers who are in love. When she discovers she has an incurable disease, she leaves him so that she will not hold back his career. Fate brings them together again for a performance of *La Bohème* at the end of which not only does Mimi die but the character singing her does also. The director was Geza von Bolvary, and Puccini's music was adapted by Robert Stolz who, for good measure, also threw in a couple of his own songs for his stars to sing. Some of the sentiment may be over the top but the singing of Kiepura and Eggerth is electrifying. Kiepura was paid $150,000 for *Zauber der Bohème*, an enormous sum for the time.

It was not only tenors and sopranos that movie directors were after. G.W. Pabst set up a film of *Don Quixote* to star the great Russian bass Feodor Chaliapin. This was not the Massenet opera in which Chaliapin had created the title role in 1910, but a reworking of the Cervantes novel with music written especially for it by the young French composer, Jacques Ibert. Pabst, having considered such composers as Manuel de Falla and Darius Milhaud, eventually asked Maurice Ravel to provide some songs for Chaliapin. Ravel failed to meet the deadline and Ibert, who had been playing piano for silent movies and writing both popular songs and dance music under the pseudonym William Berty, was asked to step in. Included in the score were four songs for Chaliapin, who also sang 'Sierra Nevada' by Alexander Dragomizhsky.

Chaliapin was regarded as one of the finest actors on the operatic stage and was an influence on Stanislavsky. He was 60 when he accepted Pabst's offer. On screen he offers a powerful portrayal of the posturing Cervantes' hero, his shuffling gait being particularly effective. The film was made in two versions, French and English (with George Robey playing Sancho Panza in the English version), both shot on location in Spain. Now acknowledged as a classic, *Don Quixote* did not get a particularly favourable reaction on its release. *Variety* felt it was strictly for an arty clientele and that the general public would find it tedious and dull.

When it came to complete operas, one of the earliest to be filmed with sound was *Carmen*, in England in 1931. Director Cecil Lewis took the opportunity of the fact that the American soprano Marguerite Namara was in Britain following a tour of Europe playing Carmen, to invite her to film the opera. Namara, who had appeared in a silent film opposite Rudolf Valentino and was then married to playwright Guy Bolton, accepted and filmed *Gypsy Blood*, as it was titled, in English with Thomas Burke singing Don José and Lance Fairfax, Escamillo. Sir Malcolm Sargent conducted the orchestra.

British film-makers had, like their American and European counterparts, tended to gravitate towards operetta and musicals with the coming of sound and were just as much on the lookout for talent which could make the transition from stage to screen. In a direct attempt to ape the Hollywood biopic, Joseph Hislop, the Scottish-born principal tenor at the Royal Opera in Stockholm, who had sung with Melba, Selma Kurtz, Claudia Muzio and Galli-Curci and appeared at Covent Garden and La Scala, was cast as the Scots poet Robert Burns opposite Eve Graty in *The Loves of Robert Burns* (1930). He sang some of Burns' songs arranged by Leslie Heward, the conductor of the City of Birmingham Symphony Orchestra.

It was Margaret Namara's husband, Guy Bolton, who wrote the screenplay for Alfred Hitchcock's only foray into musicals. *Waltzes from Vienna* (1933) was an adaptation of a stage musical created by Erich Korngold before he went to Hollywood, from music by the elder and the younger Johann Strauss. Later to become better known as *The Great Waltz*, it was one of Korngold's biggest stage successes. A romantic comedy based on the friction between Strauss senior and Strauss junior as father tries to discourage son from becoming a musician, *Waltzes from Vienna* had opened to great acclaim in Vienna in 1930 and in London the following year. In 1933 Hitchcock, who had made the first talkie in Britain, was asked to film it with Esmond Knight as the younger Strauss, and Jessie Matthews and Fay Compton as Resi and the Countess, the two women who help the younger Strauss become famous.

Gaumont-British claimed it could not afford the rights to the Korngold score and dropped most of it, using, in its place, new arrangements by Herbert Bath. Hitchcock was not pleased with the result. 'I hate this sort of thing,' he said. 'Melodrama is the only thing I can do.' In later years he disowned the film and refused ever to talk about it.

The music of Johann Strauss featured as well in *Waltz Time* (1933), a very free adaptation of *Die Fledermaus* by A.P. Herbert, directed by William Thiele. Among a cast led by Evelyn Laye and Fritz Schultz, was the Welsh tenor Parry Jones as Alfred. Jones, considered by many to be the finest tenor ever to come out of Wales, was born in Monmouthshire and had studied in London, Italy and Germany. He made his debut in the States in 1914 and at Covent Garden in 1921 singing Turiddu, before becoming the leading tenor of Beecham's British National Opera Company.

The year after making *Waltz Time*, Evelyn Laye appeared in one of the best British films of the period to utilise opera, *Evensong* (1934). Directed by Victor Saville, this was based on a novella by Beverley Nichols who, as a young man, had been Dame Nellie Melba's private secretary. Their relationship was far from close and with *Evensong*, Nichols got his revenge on his former employer by writing a story about an ageing diva who simply doesn't know when to give up.

Irela (Evelyn Laye) is a young Irish girl with a voice who turns into the most famous diva in the world, having sacrificed true love for the sake of her singing. As her career slides towards its close, a fact recognised by everyone except her, she is forced to watch a new young star being born. She at last realises the time has come for her to give way gracefully.

Laye, one of the West End's leading musical actresses, is by no stretch of the imagination an opera singer but she copes more than adequately with the singing she is asked to do. She certainly holds the screen by virtue of her looks and presence. Singing Alfredo to her Violetta is Browning Mummery, an Australian tenor who had made his debut at Covent Garden singing Rodolfo opposite none other than Melba herself in the great diva's farewell to the house. He made a name for himself in London singing on BBC radio and also sang in the States. In *Evensong*, his only film, he makes a second appearance as a gondolier serenading Laye.

The undoubted vocal star of *Evensong*, however, is the Spanish mezzo Conchita Supervia who appears at the end of the film as the young singer about to supercede the Laye/Melba character. Supervia was born in Barcelona and began her career with a Spanish touring company in Argentina, two months before her fifteenth birthday. A short time after her return to Europe, she sang Carmen for the first time in Bari from where she was snapped up by the Rome

Opera House to appear as Octavian in *Der Rosenkavalier* in the opera's Italian premiere. She was sixteen, a year younger than Octavian is supposed to be in the libretto, casting which cannot have happened on many other occasions, if ever. Seventeen years later she was to sing the same role at La Scala with Strauss himself conducting.

Supervia became a notable Carmen and Rosina, and was instrumental in making managements look again at what were then some of the more obscure Rossini operas. In 1931 she married a wealthy English timber broker who was an orchid specialist with a shop near the Wigmore Hall in London. London became her home together with a country retreat in Rustington on the Sussex coast. In 1934 she was invited to Covent Garden for the first time to sing three performances each of *Carmen* and *La Cenerentola*. Geoffrey Toye and Sir Thomas Beecham, who ran the Covent Garden company, wanted her to sing Carmen first since they did not believe *Cenerentola*, which hadn't been performed in London for 40 years and at Covent Garden since 1848, would be a success at the box-office. Even in Italy, it was hardly considered an opera worth performing.

Supervia told them she would not consider appearing as Carmen until she had got the three *Cenerentola* performances out of the way. Faced with this ultimatum, Toye agreed to replace two Carmen performances with *Cenerentola*. He then announced that he was dropping *Carmen* altogether. Supervia, suitably indignant, informed the world she would not be appearing at Covent Garden after all.

Victor Saville, meanwhile, was setting up his production of *Evensong* and as soon as he read in the papers that Supervia had withdrawn from her contract, offered her the role of the ingenue, Baba L'Etoile (widely considered to be modelled on Toti dal Monte). Supervia was delighted to accept since it kept her in London in case there was a resolution of her impasse with the Opera House, and made up for the fees she had lost.

She did eventually give two performances of *Cenerentola* at Covent Garden and was so successful she was immediately re-engaged to sing Carmen the following season, together with *Cenerentola* and Isabella in *L'Italiana in Algeri*, another Rossini opera she had been largely responsible for rescuing from neglect. In *Evensong*, she sang Musetta's waltz song from *La Bohème*, an excerpt from *Cenerentola*, and three Spanish songs.

Two years after she had made the film, Supervia became pregnant for the second time. For reasons we do not know (although she was an inveterate dieter which may have caused complications), things went horribly wrong. She was rushed to hospital and died after delivering a stillborn daughter. She was buried, her baby in her arms, in north-west London. She was 40. *Evensong* is the only visual record we have of her singing, another reason why such films are invaluable.

7

War Clouds Gather

Just as sound was establishing itself in the cinema, the film indu try was to change again, this time not as the result of a technical innovation, but because of the 1933 election in Germany of the National Socialist Party. The tremors from that election were to be felt around the world before too long, but the changes it brought to the German cinema were immediate.

Between 1930 and 1933, the German film industry, the largest in Europe, produced more than 500 feature films. In addition to having its own distinguished film-makers, it attracted major talents from Austria, Italy and France. Joseph Goebbels, the Nazi's new Information Minister, saw films as a major platform in the propaganda war to win the hearts and minds of the German people. He was far too clever to want to make simple, crude propaganda. Rather he preferred wholesome entertainment that would show the regime's ideology as an attainable goal, and so he made no radical changes to the way the industry was run, letting it continue much as it had before, with one major exception. In April 1933 the Nazis issued a promulgation that no Jew could take part in German public life, especially in the entertainment industry. The result for the film industry was an immediate exodus of talent from behind and in front of the camera of those known to be Jews. Overnight the German film industry lost a third of its personnel as directors, art directors, cameramen and technicians, found themselves out of work. Many moved back to Austria, went to France or to England, or crossed the borders into neighbouring countries. Others emigrated to the United States. Five years later most of those who stayed in Europe were forced to uproot again as the political situation deteriorated and war became inevitable.

Those 'Aryan' directors, technicians and artists who continued working in Germany and won Party approval were sure of getting all the necessary support. One of the first to be picked out as a Party favourite was Leni Riefenstahl, a former dancer and film actress who had appeared in 'mountain films' opposite Luis Trenker, and had just directed *The Blue Light*, her first feature. Hitler was so impressed by *The Blue Light*, that he personally invited her to make a film of the 1933 Nazi rally in Nuremburg.

Riefenstahl did not consider herself to be a documentary maker, however, and as soon as she had completed the 1933 rally film, began to set up her second feature, a film of Eugen d'Albert's opera, *Tiefland* (The Lowlands). She was attracted to the story because of the opportunities it would give her to use the mountains as a symbol of good and the lowlands as a symbol of evil. She planned not a film of the actual opera but a film based on the libretto using d'Albert's music as the score.

She wrote the script herself, cast herself as the female lead and went to Spain to find locations. Having found them, she sent for the crew. Her problems then started. The money to finance the project, promised by her studio, failed to materialise. No crew turned up, nor did any of the film stock. Riefenstahl had a breakdown and woke up to find herself in a Madrid hospital. Her studio reacted by cancelling the film and claiming on insurance while Reifenstahl, asked for again by Hitler, was ordered to return to Berlin and work on the film of the 1934 Nuremberg rally, a film which was given the title, *The Triumph of the Will*.

Among the most eminent of those many film-makers forced out of Germany in 1933 were Fritz Lang, Max Ophuls, G.W. Pabst, Anatole Litvak and Robert Siodmak. And it was not just film-makers whose careers were peremptorily ended. Many of Germany's favourite opera singers were Jews or had Jewish blood.

All the German engagements of soprano Irene Eisinger, on the stage as well as in the film studio, came to a sudden end in 1933. To keep working she had to take a job with the German Opera in Prague and it was there that Rudolf Bing went to persuade her to appear as Despina in *Cosi fan tutte* during the first Glyndebourne Festival of 1934. Eisinger accepted the invitation and was an immediate success, returning to Glyndebourne the following season to sing Papagena and Blonde. She was seen in *The Magic Flute* by the impresario C.B. Cochran who signed her up to appear in his revue *Follow the Sun* at the Adelphi, where she sang 'Love is a Dancing Thing'. Back at Glyndebourne in 1937, she alternated the roles of Susanna and Barbarina with Audrey Mildmay.

The 1940 Glyndebourne season was cancelled because of the threat of imminent invasion by Germany. To keep Glyndebourne's name before the public, a production of Frederic Austin's arrangement of John Gay's *The Beggar's Opera* was staged by John Gielgud. Michael Redgrave played Macheath, Mildmay was Polly Peachum. The production opened in Brighton then toured for six weeks to Cardiff, Liverpool, Manchester, Glasgow and Edinburgh before going into London's Haymarket. When Mildmay went down with German measles less than a week after the London opening, Eisinger took over as Polly. She was then living in London where she was to remain resolutely throughout the war, even at the height of the Blitz.

Gitta Alpar, despite her popularity in Munich, was another soprano forced out of Germany in 1933. She went firstly to Austria, then, in 1936, to America.

On her way there, she stopped off in Britain to make *Guilty Melody*, a musical espionage thriller, in which she played a singer, this time singing Gounod and Verdi, whose manager husband sends out coded messages on her records, causing her to be suspected of being a spy. The film was shot in both English and French, with different supporting casts. Richard Potter directed both.

Among the tenors most affected by the arrival in power of the Nazis was the Romanian, Josef Schmidt. Schmidt had been born in Bucovina in 1904 and first came to notice as a treble in the choir of his local synagogue. He made his operatic debut while still a treble. When his voice broke, and it was obvious he possessed an adult voice that was special, he was sent, at the age of twenty, to music school in Berlin. His singing impressed everybody who heard him and there was no dispute over the quality of the voice. There was equally no dispute over whether he would succeed on the operatic stage: he wouldn't. Every time he auditioned he received the same response: he was too short. Schmidt was officially only five feet tall. In reality, he was almost certainly shorter. But he was determined to sing professionally, and when he finally auditioned for radio in Berlin in 1929, he at last found his route to international stardom.

One month after his audition, Schmidt appeared on Berlin radio singing the role of Vasco da Gama in *L'Africaine*. The public reaction to the broadcast was phenomenal. Further broadcasts in Smetana's *The Bartered Bride* and in *Martha* confirmed the discovery of an exciting talent. Schmidt was offered recording contracts and concert tours. He became known as either the German Caruso or the Pocket Caruso.

Although he was desperate to appear on the operatic stage (he did, in fact, appear in 1939 in a production of *La Bohème* in Brussels and on tour in Belgium and Holland, and in the operetta *The Three Musketeers* by Ralph Benatzsky), a stage career was never really a feasible option and Schmidt had to be content with being a star on radio (he sang in some 42 broadcast operas), on the concert platform, and being a very successful recording artist.

Schmidt may not have been suitable for the stage but he could appear in films where clever photography, giving him lifts or standing him on a box, would help disguise his lack of height, although nothing could disguise the fact that he looked like a twelve-year-old schoolboy. In 1931, to cash in on his enormous popularity, he was featured singing in a scene in the musical comedy *Der Liebesexpress* (The Love Express), directed by Robert Wiene, director of the silent *Der Rosenkavalier*, who was another German film-maker about to be exiled by the Nazis. The following year Schmidt was again a featured singer in *Gehertzte Menschen*, a crime drama set in the south of France.

Schmidt received his first top billing when he appeared in *Ein Lied geht um die Welt* (My Song Goes Round the World, 1933), a semi-autobiographical film set in Venice which tells how a short tenor who wants to sing opera becomes a star on radio but loses the girl he loves (Charlotte Ander) to a better-looking man (Victor De Kowa). The film was shot in both German and English versions with John Loder taking over as his rival for the English film. Schmidt almost didn't make *My Song Goes Round the World*. He was not at all happy with a plot which laid such emphasis on his height and physical appearance (he complained that De Kowa was not exactly handsome), but director Richard Oswald (another who eventually fled Germany) persuaded him to go ahead.

During the course of *My Song Goes Round the World*, Schmidt sang the title song, written by Hans May, the aria 'O paradiso', and several songs including the Neapolitan songs 'O sole mio' and 'Santa Lucia'. When the film opened in Berlin in May 1933, it was a roaring success. The audience demanded that Schmidt, who was present, should sing for them, and he did. Even Goebbels applauded enthusiastically and declared he would have Schmidt made an honorary Aryan. The adulation did not last. The original title of *My Song Goes Round the World* had been *The People's Singer* but the censors had refused to allow it to be called that because Schmidt was Jewish.

While the public flocked to see him on screen, Schmidt's contract with Berlin radio was terminated and his concert appearances cancelled, because he was a Jew. Friends and colleagues such as Richard Tauber arranged for him to tour overseas and he went on a concert tour of America appearing with Grace Moore, Maria Jeritza, Jussi Björling and Tauber himself, as well as giving a concert in Carnegie Hall. When word reached him that anti-Jewish sentiment in Germany, far from lessening had actually increased, he realised it would not be safe to go back. Instead he went to Austria where he appeared in *Ein Stern falt vom Himmel* (A Star Fell From Heaven, 1936) playing a singer who dubs the voice of another tenor who has lost his voice drinking cologne instead of cognac, and who loses the woman he loves when she falls for the right voice but the wrong man. An Austrian-British co-production, it was again shot in both English and German with separate casts, Paul Merzbach directing the English version, Max Neufeld, the German. The highlight of the film was Schmidt singing 'Una furtiva lagrima'.

In 1937, the Nazis finally banned *My Song Goes Round the World* and when the war started, the tenor fled first to France and then in 1942 to Switzerland. Having entered Switzerland illegally, he was interned in a labour camp, fell ill with chest pains and was taken to a hospital in Zurich. They thought he was a malingerer and sent him back to the internment camp before he had properly recovered. He died there of heart failure on 16 November 1942. He was 38, and an hour before his death, was still singing.

Schmidt was not the only opera singer to have his films banned. The same fate befell his friend Richard Tauber. After the collapse of his own company in 1931, Tauber had made one more film in Germany, *Melodie der Liebe* (Melody of Love, 1932), directed by George Jacoby, who stayed in Germany to became the most successful director of musicals during the Nazi era. Tauber played the inevitable opera singer, in love with a girl who is not interested in him, only in his money (Alice Treff). When he discovers the truth, he is heartbroken but finds consolation in the arms of Lien Deyers. Although filmed in 1932, hostility was already being stirred up against Jewish artists and Tauber was part-Jewish. Like so many musicians, he was not political but he could hardly be unaware of the hostility towards Jews, especially when he was set upon outside his Berlin hotel one night and beaten up.

Unlike Schmidt, Tauber had the perfect out. He immediately left Germany to tour Austria and Switzerland with the Vienna company of *Das Dreimäderlhaus* (The House of the Three Girls), an operetta originally cobbled together by Heinrich Berte from melodies by Schubert. This had already been filmed as a silent in 1917, a year after its premiere, by Richard Oswald, and had been rewritten by Sigmund Romberg and then by George Clutsam. The production starring Tauber as the composer was so successful that it went on to Sweden, Belgium and Holland, and then to London where it opened at the Aldwych Theatre in 1933 as *Lilac Time*.

Set in Vienna in 1820, *Lilac Time* tells the story of Schubert's love for Vicki, the daughter of a dancing master who occupies the apartment below him. Vicki, fond though she is of the portly, cherubic-faced Schubert, is in love with a soldier who happens to be a count. Poor Schubert, realising he will get nowhere with her, goes to see the Archduchess to obtain permission for the young lovers to marry, and is left to sing his own songs.

Such was the success of *Lilac Time* on the stage that British International Pictures promptly acquired the film rights, signed up Tauber, and cast Jane Baxter in the role of Vicki, Carl Esmond as the Count and Athene Seyler as the Archduchess. Filming, with Paul Stein as director, began using a mixture of all three stage versions and the title was changed to *Blossom Time* (*April Romance* in America). Although shot in England, four days were spent on location in Vienna during which Tauber slipped in a quick opera house performance of *Giuditta* opposite Jarmila Novotná.

Few of even his most ardent admirers would claim that Tauber is a good screen actor. Round and cherubic, he remains resolutely Tauber, and yet in *Blossom Time*, the casting worked because this is how we imagine Franz Schubert to have been. It is perfectly acceptable that Baxter should be oblivious to his feelings and prefer the soldier. And then there is Tauber's glorious singing.

Blossom Time made him an enormous star in the English-speaking world, so much so that the general public thought of him as a film star who happened to sing rather than as an opera singer who appeared in films. There was the most enormous surprise when Sir Thomas Beecham offered him a serious singing role at Covent Garden.

Blossom Time was never shown in Germany. It was banned on the grounds that Tauber was an immigrant and the film did not fulfil the necessary conditions for a foreign film to be shown there. Knowing that Austrian-born Tauber was a Jew, the censor refused even to view it. Tauber decided not to return to Germany but to make his home in England.

On the back of the success of *Blossom Time*, he was signed to make *Heart's Desire*, a romantic comedy in which he played a humble Austrian beer-garden singer plucked from obscurity by Frances (Leonora Corbett), sister of an impresario, to star in a new opera in London. He falls in love with her only to discover that she is in love with the opera's composer. He returns to Vienna and the arms of his waiting sweetheart. Tauber wrote two of the songs he sang in the film: 'My world is gold because you love me' and 'I shall awaken your heart'. He also sang songs by Schumann, and the hit number of the film, 'Vienna city of my dreams'.

Shortly before filming on *Heart's Desire* was due to begin at Elstree Studios in May 1935, Tauber attended the premiere of *Mimi*, a drama based on *La Vie de Bohème* starring Douglas Fairbanks Jnr. and Gertrude Lawrence. Playing the small role of Sidonie was a young actress named Diana Napier. Tauber, who had a reputation for his offscreen romances, was sitting close to Napier in the cinema and liked the look of her. Since the director of *Mimi* was his old friend from Berlin, Paul Stein, who had directed *Blossom Time* and was also directing *Heart's Delight*, he insisted Stein find a part in his new film for her. Napier was duly cast as a lady of means who meets the young singer in London and falls for him.

During the course of filming, Tauber and Napier announced their engagement and it was hardly surprising that she should be cast in his next film, *Land Without Music*, in which he played (what else?) a world famous tenor whose Ruritanian song-loving homeland, has, on the orders of the Queen (Napier), had singing proscribed until the people start to work and repay the national debt. Tauber slips into the country to give a concert, his voice captivates the Queen and the law is repealed. Jimmy Durante provided the comic relief in a slight tale which was really only a vehicle for the public to hear Tauber in full flow.

Napier again appeared in the next Tauber film, *Pagliacci* (1936), directed by Karl Grune. This was filmed as a story within a story with Tauber as a member of a travelling group of players performing the Leoncavallo opera, who discovers that his wife (Hungarian actress Steffi Duna), who sings Nedda, is having an affair, with the inevitable tragic consequences. The film was in black and white, apart from the Prologue and Epilogue which were shot in an early colour process called Chemicolour, a process which didn't last long. *Pagliacci* was again a vehicle for Tauber, who not only sang the role of Canio but delivered the Prologue as well as the music of Silvio and Beppe. The poet John Drinkwater provided new English lyrics.

While artists such as Tauber had left Germany and opted to settle in places such as London, the German film industry was still proving to be a magnet for many singers who were not Jewish. The Italian tenor generally acknowledged to be Caruso's successor, Beniamino Gigli, had appeared in Vitaphone shorts, but did not make his first feature film until 1935 when he travelled to Berlin to make *Vergiss mein nicht* which was filmed in both German and Italian (as *Non Ti Scordar di Me*). Gigli played a world famous Italian opera singer who happens to be a widower with a small child. He meets his agent's secretary, who has just had a shipboard romance with a ship's officer, she gets on with his son, he proposes, she accepts. They are blissfully happy until the ship's officer comes back into her life. They arrange to elope while Gigli is giving a concert, but at the last moment she finds she cannot leave him.

During the course of the film Gigli sang 'Di quella pira', arias from *Rigoletto*, *L'Africaine*, *Mignon*, *La Favorita*, *Martha* and *L'Elisir d'amore*, a lullaby, some Neapolitan songs, and the title song, composed by one of his accompanists, Ernesto de Curtis. This became a hit record and Gigli discovered very quickly that a successful career in the cinema was a great help in selling records.

The Hungarian brothers, Alexander and Zoltan Korda, who had decided to leave Austria while they could and had moved their base to London, were sufficiently impressed with the film to invite Gigli to film an English version which was given the title *Forget Me Not*. This is often erroneously claimed to be Gigli's first feature film but he filmed the German and Italian versions in May and June and did not arrive in England until December. He stayed, as was his custom when in London, at the Savoy Hotel throughout his two weeks of filming, when only those scenes in which he appeared with new cast members were shot (directed by Zoltan Korda). Scenes which did not involve Gigli were filmed without him even being in the country. His concert appearances and the scenes from his round-the-world operatic tour were simply taken wholesale from the German version. The climax of the English version, when his wife (Joan Gardner) is in a box waiting for the clock to tick round to the time she has arranged to meet her lover while Gigli sings 'Non ti scordar di me' on stage, was filmed with Gardner in London and Gigli in Berlin (the same shots of him were to appear in other Gigli films).

The following year Gigli was back in Berlin for *Ave Maria* with Käthe von Nagy and Erna Berger. Soprano Berger had made her debut as First Boy in *The Magic Flute* in Dresden in 1925. She became one of the foremost interpreters of the role of Queen of the Night, and the year after her film with Gigli was invited to Glyndebourne to sing the part and that of Constanze. The Berlin Opera agreed she could have leave of absence but Goering, who had the last word on who did what at the Berlin Opera, would not agree that her salary should be paid while she was in England. Glyndebourne could not afford to increase her fee, she refused to sign her contract and Glyndebourne had to find another soprano.

In *Ave Maria* Berger sang Violetta to Gigli's Alfredo in a scene from *La Traviata*. In the film's story, Gigli, an opera singer, has just discovered that von

Nagy, a nightclub singer with whom he has fallen in love, is part of a plot to blackmail him. He directs his aria from Act 3, when Alfredo condemns Violetta for being unfaithful, towards von Nagy sitting in her box, a very powerful and emotional piece of singing even if it goes to prove that Gigli was no great shakes as an actor. He also sang 'Di quella pira' from *Il Trovatore*.

As long as he was cast as an Italian opera singer, which he was in almost all the eighteen features he made, Gigli's dramatic shortcomings could be disguised by the warmth of the personality that came from the screen, and by that glorious voice. Gigli had been born in Recanati in the Marche region of Italy where his father was a cobbler making shoes for local peasants. He had learnt his singing in the cathedral choir, creeping up the bell tower whenever he could to sing to the world below. As a young man it looked as though lack of money would prevent him from becoming a singer but he won a competition in Parma, and began his life as a professional singing in *La Gioconda* in the provincial city of Rovigo. Within two years he had appeared in most of the major Italian houses. In 1920 he made his debut at the Met, where he was considered to be Caruso's natural successor, in *Andrea Chénier*. He was a great favourite in the house until, in 1932, as a result of the Depression, all Met personnel were required to take a salary cut. Gigli, alone of the star singers, refused and returned to Italy where he began his film career proper.

He appeared as an opera singer again in the two films released in 1937. In *Die Stimme des Herzens* (Voice of the Heart), he sang arias from *Martha* and *Lohengrin* together with songs by Giuseppe Becce and Ernesto De Curtis. In *Mutterlied* (directed by Carmine Gallone and also shot in Italian as *Solo Per Te*) he played a member of an opera company, seen singing in the role of Faust in Boito's *Mefistofele*, in a scene from *Andrea Chénier*, and in a performance of *Un Ballo in Maschera* during which a backstage murder takes place. There is also a fascinating glimpse of him as a female impersonator when he duets with himself singing Don Giovanni and Zerlina. Playing his wife, the woman with a secret past, was the young Bessarabian soprano, Maria Cebotari. The villain of the piece, the man from her past who joins the company and ends up dead, was Michael Bohnen.

Cebotari had been born in 1910 and started her career as a teenage actress/singer with a touring Russian theatrical company. She married the company's actor-manager and ended up with him in Paris where she sang in cafes to supplement their meagre income. Unable to make enough to live on, they left for Berlin where her husband hoped to land a film part. There Cebotari was heard singing by a professor at the Berlin Music School, given three months intensive training and signed up by Fritz Busch for the Dresden Opera where she made her debut in April 1931 as Mimi.

Versatile and beautiful, Cebotari's operatic career blossomed. She was engaged by Bruno Walter to sing in Salzburg, created the role of Aminta in Strauss's *Die schweigsame Frau*, and brought the house down in Berlin when she sang Mimi opposite Gigli. She sang in Vienna and at Covent Garden, and her repertoire embraced not only Mimi and Sophie but Salome, Turandot and Carmen.

In 1936 she appeared in her first film, *Mädchen in Weiss* (The Girl in White), playing a young girl with a voice in pre-revolutionary St Petersburg, whose aristocratic fiancé does not want her to sing. She goes ahead anyway. She was then cast in *Stark Herzen* (1937), a powerful film directed by Herbert Maisch, in which her co-star was the popular German film actor, Gustav Diessl. The film is another example of the operatic film in which events onstage are either mirrored by or mirror, events offstage. Cebotari and Diessl play members of a company putting on *Tosca* during a communist uprising in Hungary in 1918. There is one masterly sequence of intercutting between the property master handing out rifles backstage to the firing squad for the last scene of the opera, and the insurgents handing out guns prior to invading the elitist opera house. Cebotari's Tosca is mesmeric.

During the course of making *Stark Herzen*, Cebotari and Diessl fell in love. As soon as Cebotari could obtain a divorce from her first husband, they were married. The film did not have such a happy outcome. Although Cebotari had become one of the Nazi leadership's favourite singers, *Stark Herzen* did not meet with official approval. The subject, of ordinary people rising against their leaders, proved to be too uncomfortable, and the film was banned.

After *Mutterlied*, Cebotari and Gigli went on to make *Divine Armonie* together, again with Gallone as director. Filmed in Italy, this was an epic biopic of Verdi (played by Fosco Giachetti) with Cebotari as Teresina Stolz, the soprano who became Verdi's love towards the end of his life, and Gigli as Raffaele Mirate, the tenor who created the role of the Duke in *Rigoletto*. The film included excerpts from many Verdi operas including *Un Giorno di Regno*, *Nabucco*, *I Lombardi*, *La Battaglia di Legnano*, *La Traviata* and *Simon Boccanegra*. The operatic scenes were filmed on the stage of the opera house in Rome and the film ends with the first night of *Aïda* performed by, amongst others, Tito Gobbi, Pia Tassinari, Gabrielle Gatti and Apollo Granforte. The conductor was Tullio Serafin. The film was an enormous success at the box-office, offering the escape to a certain past that audiences with an uncertain future craved, for by 1938 few people in Europe remained unaware of the political tensions that were about to erupt into war.

If Gigli had a rival for his crown amongst tenors, it was surely the Swedish tenor Jussi Björling. Born in Borlange in 1911, Björling had toured as a child with his father and brothers as the Björling Quartet. When his voice broke it was soon evident that he had the potential to become a very fine singer indeed and by the time he was in his early twenties he was being entrusted with leading roles at the Stockholm Royal Opera. He quickly became an international star and received several invitations to appear in films, invitations he always turned down.

As the war approached and travel overseas became increasingly uncertain, Björling, against the advice of his manager who felt he should wait to be contacted by Hollywood, decided to appear in a film in Sweden. *Fram för Framgang* (Head for Success, 1938) was written as a vehicle for him by the director Gunnar Skoglund. Björling was cast as Tore Nilsson, a tenor who can't get on radio. During an educational programme he forces his way into the studio and sings 'La danza'. The schoolchildren listening to the broadcast are filled with wonder. Björling makes his escape from the studio when the police are called, and goes into hiding while the police hunt for him and the whole of Sweden is trying to find out the identity of the mysterious Mr X. He is finally cornered in Grona Lund, the Stockholm pleasure gardens, is hoisted up on a mobile platform where the police can't get him, and sings to the vast crowds below, much as Björling did annually in real life. The film company had no need to hire extras for the scene: it was estimated that 20,000 people packed the park to hear him.

Björling, like Gigli, was not a great actor, but having to deliver his lines, and the occasional song, in Swedish, appearing on a boat singing the rollocking evocation of the sea, 'Di tu se fedele', from *Un Ballo in Maschera* (Björling was never happier than when he was boating), enabled him to be as relaxed as he ever could have been when performing. Certainly Swedish critics and audiences thought his acting was more than passable, and allied to his singing, they didn't much care if it wasn't. *Fram för Framgang* was a great success in Sweden.

In November 1937, Björling made his Met debut in *La Bohème*, and the opportunity was taken to release the film in New York where it played to enthusiastic if modest houses. Despite the warm reception *Fram för Framgang* received, Björling was not to make another film for ten years. He found the filming process interesting but had no wish to make another movie until he was persuaded to play the supporting role of an opera singer in *En Svensk Tiger* (A Swedish Tiger, 1948).

During the final three years before the Second World War, the number of films of operas and operettas, or those containing operatic arias, filmed on both sides of the Atlantic, fell significantly. In 1936 45 films were made, in 1937 the number had reduced to 34 and, by 1938 it was down to 21. A changing mood meant that old-style operettas, set in their Ruritanian worlds, were out of fashion, especially in Germany and Austria where most of them had been directed by Jews who had subsequently been forced to flee their homelands.

Audiences still wanted escapism, of course, but it had to be escapism based more in the real world or, as in the case of a film such as *Divine Armonie*, in a recognisable past. And they still wanted to hear good singing on the screen. When John McCormack agreed to appear in *Wings of the Morning* (1937), a story about a racehorse of that name which ran in the Epsom Derby, he did so as himself singing Irish songs to an audience of what look like retired lieutenant-colonels and their wives in an Irish stately home. *Wings of the Morning*, starring Henry Fonda and the stunning French actress Annabella, was the first British feature film to be shot in Technicolor.

There were still attempts being made to film complete operas or operettas but even they had to have a harder edge to them than most of those filmed in the days after the introduction of sound. The Danish tenor Helge Roswaenge starred in a German production of *Martha* (1936), Adam's opera *The Coachman of Longjumeau* was filmed in Austria, George Jacoby directed Marika Rokk in *Der Bettelstudent* and the Millöcker operetta *Gasparone*, while Jean Gilbert's operetta *Die keusche Susanne* was filmed in England as *The Girl in the Taxi* with Frances Day. The Polish folk opera *Halka*, written by Stanislaw Moniuszko (generally regarded as the creator of Polish national opera), was filmed by Jules Gardan with Wladislaw Ladis-Kiepura, brother of Jan and a tenor with the Hamburg State Opera. The film began as an Anglo-Polish production but became totally Polish when the British producers pulled out. Set in the countryside near the Tatra Mountains during the early part of the nineteenth century, *Halka* reflected the social conflicts and injustices of the time, and appealed to audiences who felt threatened by what was happening in Germany during the 1930s. It was an enormous success.

Grace Moore, looking to resurrect her ailing film career, agreed to appear with Georges Thill in a film of Charpentier's opera *Louise*, to be directed in Paris by the great silent director Abel Gance. Thill was probably the greatest French tenor of the century, singing 40 such roles as Parsifal, Tannhäuser and Samson as well as the more lyric roles of the French repertory in the Parisian opera houses for over 40 years.

Moore was coached in the role by Charpentier himself, who was on the set throughout the shoot. Despite some fine singing by Moore, Thill and the bass André Pernet, who plays Louise's father, the film was not entirely successful in its transition to the screen. Gance's adaptation turned the opera into a musical without good tunes.

Louise was to be Moore's last film. After the shoot, she returned to the United States, continuing to sing at the Met until 1944. She was discussing the possibility of appearing in an operetta to be directed by Ernst Lubitsch, when she was killed in a plane crash in Denmark while on a concert tour in 1947.

One of Britain's contributions to filmed opera at this time was an hour-long version of Gounod's *Faust* (1936). This was shot at Bushey Studios on the outskirts of London and was produced and directed by Albert Hopkins. It was one of the earliest colour films made in Britain (using the Spectracolour system), but not even that distinction could save it from being dire. *Faust* has gone down as being the worst operatic film ever made. The singing is quite acceptable. Webster Booth, a former member of the D'Oyly Carte Opera Company, is a smooth-voiced Faust and Anne Zeigler, whom he met on the set and was later to become his third wife, is an attractive Marguerite, but Dennis

Hoey plays Méphistophélès as a pantomime villain, the production is cheap and looks it, and the direction is almost non-existent. The camera is often high to disguise the fact that there is virtually no set. Most scenes are shot against a wall, although there is a risible duel scene filmed in a wood. The final scene when Méphistophélès and Faust visit the condemned Marguerite in her cell (she has murdered her baby) is a gem of dreadful acting and unimaginative film-making.

In 1939 Geoffrey Toye, who had been running Covent Garden with Thomas Beecham, saw what he thought was a gap in the market and formed a company to film the entire Gilbert and Sullivan canon. His first production was of *The Mikado*, filmed at Pinewood with such stalwarts of the D'Oyly Carte company as Martyn Green, Jean Colin and Constance Willis. To increase the film's appeal in the States, Kenny Baker was brought over to play Nanki-Poo and Hollywood veteran Victor Schertzinger was engaged to direct. Toye was convinced he would have an English *Wizard of Oz* on his hands. He had also done considerable research in order to make sure that the sound system used on the film would provide the best sound then currently available. *The Mikado* got a warm press when it was released but failed at the box office, and the outbreak of World War II ended Toye's attempts to continue the series. The last word must surely go to the critic who wrote after watching *The Mikado*, that 'as for film opera, there is, it is reasonably safe to say, no future for it'.

8

The War Years

In 1939, Leni Riefenstahl was sent into Poland with the invading German troops as a war reporter. On her first day, she witnessed a massacre of Polish civilians and was so sickened by what she had seen that she immediately returned home. To help her forget the experience she decided to resurrect her film of D'Albert's *Tiefland*. She went to the mountains of Austria to work on the script and finished it within six weeks. In the lead, she cast Franz Eichberger, an Austrian army ski instructor she had met on the slopes (a decision that bemused everybody), but could not find the right actress to play opposite him. Although she had not intended to appear in the film herself this second time around, she eventually decided to cast herself, with one proviso: she wanted another director to direct her scenes in front of the camera. The man she asked was the veteran G.W. Pabst, who had recently returned to Europe from Hollywood. She was horrified to discover that his spark had gone, so was not the slightest bit unhappy when she received a message from Goebbels that Pabst would have to leave the picture because he was required for a project in Prague. She chose as his replacement Mathias Wieman.

Having friends in high places, Riefenstahl was given permission to take her crew to Spain even though there was a war on. She had completed shooting her lowland exteriors and was planning on moving to the Pyrenees for the mountain scenes when she and the crew were ordered back to Germany as a safety precaution. She made her base in Bavaria but since Goebbels-approved propaganda films took priority, found it hard to get on with her own film. At one point Goebbels commandeered her studio and she was unable to shoot anything on *Tiefland* for two years.

She faced other problems. For one scene she used 60 gypsies from a local holding camp as extras. What she did not know, so she afterwards claimed, was that that particular camp was to become a holding camp for Auschwitz, but it led to the accusation, from which she was never able to escape, that she had employed slave labour on *Tiefland*.

Not allowed to film in the Pyrenees, she moved to the Dolomites, but trouble continued to dog her there. Heavy snowfalls held up shooting, sets were built incorrectly and had to be rebuilt, a wolf with which the hero was supposed to

101

wrestle died of over-eating and its replacement from the local zoo escaped and had to be shot. A lake had to be constructed and hand-filled with water. The sheep, which firstly refused to browse contentedly by the water's edge and then refused to take fright on cue at the wolf's approach despite crew members shouting and banging pots and pans, drank all the water. Twice the lake had to be refilled. Goebbels noted in his diary in December 1942 that five million marks had already been wasted on a film which would take another year to finish.

Riefenstahl continued to work on *Tiefland* intermittently throughout the war including visiting Barcelona to film a bullfight, but when the war was over it was seized, first by the Americans and then by the French, who decided to edit it themslves. Riefenstahl, eventually cleared of being a Nazi but never quite able to remove the stain of her association with Hitler, managed to get back most of the film and re-edit. *Tiefland* finally received its first public showing in February 1954 in Stuttgart with a soundtrack played by the Vienna Symphony Orchestra. It had taken Riefenstahl twenty years to get it onto the screen.

The outbreak of the war in Europe had surpringly little effect on film-making, either in Europe or America. The value of the cinema as a means of entertaining and encouraging the civilian population was recognised immediately by both sides, and even though the personnel changed as technicians and actors went off to war, most of the films being made were similar in content to those from the years before hostilities started. Big-budget epics no longer went into production, but most of the established genres continued to be made, including operatic films. A well-known and familiar star singing arias everyone loved was safe and uplifting. Certainly film-makers had to be careful to ensure the correct attitudes were being portrayed, for although not every film became direct propaganda, they were all expected to reflect the nation's hopes and ideals, whether filmed in Germany, Italy, Britain or the United States. The majority of the films made during the first year of the war had, in any case, gone into production well before the outbreak of war.

Tiana Lemnitz, who had become the leading soprano at the Berlin State Opera in 1936, the year she appeared at Covent Garden as Octavian in *Der Rosenkavalier* and Eva in *Die Meistersinger* with Beecham conducting, appeared in a scene in *Altes Herz wird wieder Jung* (An Old Heart Becomes You, 1939) singing with the Berlin State Opera tenor, Max Lorenz. The film was a comedy starring Emil Jannings and Maria Landrock, directed by Erich Engel, a close friend of Brecht (and one of the playwright's favourite theatre directors), who managed to keep a subversive element in his films without ever upsetting the Party.

One German singer who made his film debut at this time was the bass-baritone, Hans Hotter. Hotter's family came from Bavaria, although he was born in Offenbach-am-Main, where his father had accepted a post teaching architectural drawing. When his father died, the family moved back to Munich where Hotter attended the university, intending to become a music teacher. Although people told him he had a voice, he wasn't sure that he wanted to become a singer. Even when, at the age of 21, he was offered a contract at the Troppau Opera company to sing Wolfram in *Tannhäuser*, the Wanderer in *Siegfried*, Tonio, the Speaker in *The Magic Flute*, and Hans Sachs, he wasn't sure his future lay in opera. While he sang all the other roles, his planned appearance as Hans Sachs was postponed when the production was cancelled to save money.

From Troppau, Hotter moved to Breslau, Prague and then Hamburg where his reputation as one of the finest young basses around, and a Wagner singer of international potential, was confirmed. Although he was to remain on contract in Hamburg until 1945, Hotter was allowed to make guest appearances elsewhere. In 1937 he made his debut with the Bavarian State Opera in Munich, where he later sang the leading role of the Commandant in the world premiere of Richard Strauss' anti-war opera, *Friedenstag*. In June 1939 he made his debut at the Vienna State Opera singing Jokanaan in *Salomé* and, two days later, appeared there with the Hamburg company in the title role of Handel's *Julius Caesar*. Three days after that, he sang in the Austrian premiere of *Friedenstag*. It was a gala occasion, celebrating the 75th birthday of the composer and in the audience were Hitler and Goebbels. Hotter became one of Hitler's favourite singers, but as a Catholic, with a brother who was a priest, he was officially considered politically suspect. During his days in Prague, he had been watched by the Gestapo. In his file was written, 'No action to be taken – he is under the personal custody of the Führer.'

Certainly Hotter's first film appearance came about not because he was a good opera singer, but because, as a tall, blue-eyed, handsome man, he personified the German ideal. A scriptwriter in Vienna read a review of his appearance as Julius Caesar and called director Gustav Ucicky to say Hotter seemed to be just the person they were looking for to play the role of the young country boy opposite Käthe Dorsch in *Mutterliebe* (Mother Love, 1939).

Ucicky, a cameraman as well as director, made films that were both beautiful and intense in atmosphere. Born in Austria, he had become one of the leading directors in pre-war Germany, making musicals, operettas, historical dramas and comedies, but there was a streak of nationalism in many of his early films which appealed to the Nazis and he became one of the principal directors of Nazi propaganda films. For *Mutterliebe*, a family film, he wanted an actor with a southern accent and assumed that, because Hotter was a member of the Hamburg company, he was from the north. When it was pointed out that Hotter was from Bavaria, Ucicky invited him for a screen test.

The test consisted of a love scene with Dorsch, an actress considerably older than Hotter. It was not a success and Hotter was convinced he had not got the part. To his great surprise he was asked to repeat the scene with a younger actress, then offered the role. He found out later that it was Dorsch herself who had persuaded Ucicky to give him a second chance. When it came to the actual take, she whispered to him to imagine he was with the younger girl.

103

Hotter spent most of the war in Austria singing at the Vienna State Opera, and it was there that his film career continued when he appeared in *Bruderlien fein* (1942), a biography of the Viennese poet Ferdinand Raimun, with Marte Harell. He got his first starring role in *Seine beste Rolle* (His Best Role, 1943), a German-Czech co-production, shot in Prague. This was a musical designed to lift German spirits during the darkest days of the war.

Also in 1943, Hotter travelled to Berlin to appear in the Italian-German co-production, *Lache Bajazzo* (Laugh Pagliacci), the story of how the opera came to be written by Leoncavallo. The real Canio (played by Paolo Horbiger) has been released from prison twenty years after he killed his unfaithful wife, Nedda. He tries to find his daughter to ask for her forgiveness, meets Leoncavallo (Carlo Romano) and tells him his story. Leoncavallo then writes the opera.

Laugh Pagliacci was shot in both German and Italian with a different director for each version. Appearing in both as the singer who creates the role of Canio was Gigli, on marvellous form. Adrianna Perris was Nedda, Leone Pacci, Tonio. In the Italian version, Gigli, who also sings other snatches of opera, sings the Prologue. In the German version, it is sung by Hotter.

In addition to recognising the propaganda value of films, authorities everywhere knew that the cinema had a vital role to play in maintaining morale. In Germany, while the various genre pictures such as melodrama, historical, thrillers and biopics continued to be made, 50 per cent of the output under Goebbels consisted of musicals and comedies. These were what audiences wanted, these were what was provided. All films, Goebbels was fond of saying, are political, most especially those which claim not to be. He also believed in the power of popular films which did not contain obvious, heavy, political messages and were not overtly intellectual. But, he was adamant, such films had to be technically and artistically competent.

The film with operatic excerpts, the parallel stories, operas themselves (as long as they were popular operas), fitted Goebbels' criteria. Geza von Bolvary filmed Heuberger's operetta *Der Opernball* with Marte Harell, and *Rosen in Tirol*, a version of Zeller's operetta *Der Vogelhändler*, with Harell and Leo Slezak. Slezak appeared in *Operette* with Willi Forst, who also directed. Forst directed a film of Johann Strauss's *Wiener Blut. One Night in Venice* made it to the screen, and Michael Bohnen appeared in *Der Liebe Augustin*, a biography of a famous Austrian singer of the nineteenth century. Bohnen and Leo Slezak were in the cast of one of the most important films made during the war in Germany, the fantastic *Baron Münchhausen*. Theo Lingen directed *Frau Luna*, an operetta by Paul Lincke. A biopic of the composer Karl Millöcker was being filmed towards the end of the war but shooting was halted by the Allied advance and it had to be completed later.

Carmine Gallone cast Maria Cebotari in *Premiere der Butterfly* (1939), another of his films in which stage and real life form a parallel story. Cebotari plays a young singer who falls in love with an American musician who returns to the States leaving her pregnant. Four years later, just as she is about to go on stage in *Madama Butterfly* (a role Cebotari had actually sung in the opera house), he returns with his new wife. With Cebotari on top form vocally, the film did very well at the box office.

Although *The Dream of Butterfly* was filmed in German and Italian, the dual-language film as a matter of course was coming to an end. The war meant that Hollywood could no longer distribute films in Europe in any country other than an English-speaking country and they could hardly continue to be co-production partners with German producers or producers in Vichy France. So they pulled out of involvement in multi-language productions. As for the Germans, having got rid of American competition and having physically taken over most of Europe, they suddenly had the cinematic dominance they had always craved. They continued to make dual-language versions in German and Italian because the Italians were, after all, their allies. And just as Goebbels controlled the German industry, so Mussolini's son ran the Italian one. There was a constant flow of talent between the two countries.

Directors such as Gallone and Guido Brignone moved freely between the studios of Berlin and Rome. So too did artists like Gigli or Cebotari. Cebotari appeared in Gallone's next film, *Amami, Alfredo!*, another parallel film, this time of *La Traviata*. He then went on to make a version of *Manon Lescaut* which used Puccini's music and had Alida Valli and Vittorio de Sica in the leads. The voice of Maria Caniglia is heard on the soundtrack.

Gallone next directed Cebotari in *Odessa in Flames* (1942), in which she played a Romanian opera singer during the war whose search for her young son takes her to Odessa. A co-production with Romania, *Odessa in Flames* was also shot in a Romanian version and was shown at the 1942 Venice Film Festival.

Cebotari then went to Italy for *Maria Malibran* (1943), a romantic version of the life of the celebrated soprano, directed by Guido Brignone. As Malibran, Cebotari sang arias by Rossini and Bellini. Playing the part of Charles de Bleriot, the Belgian violinist who became her lover and then second husband, was a young Italian actor named Rossano Brazzi.

Malibran was also the subject of a French film made in 1943 by Sacha Guitry, who wrote the script, directed, and appeared as her first husband, Eugene Malibran. Jean Cocteau played the part of the poet Alfred de Musset and Malibran herself was played by Geori Boué.

Appearing with Cebotari in *Premiere der Butterfly* had been a young Italian baritone who had just started his film career before the outbreak of war, Tito Gobbi. Born in 1913 in Bassano del Grappa, where his parents were well-off shopkeepers, Gobbi had made his debut singing the Count in *La Sonnambula* in a town called Gubbio in 1936. It was a bass role, he was a baritone, and everyone who saw him thought he was dreadful. His singing teacher simply commented that if he felt he needed more lessons, Gobbi knew where to find him. Shortly afterwards, Gobbi stepped in at the last moment to sing one line in the world premiere of Pizzetti's *Orseolo* at La Scala, Milan. Once more he failed to cover himself with glory: he came in at the wrong time. He went back to see his teacher.

The following year, he won an international singing competition in Vienna and, on the strength of the prize money, decided to become engaged. The money didn't last long, he still did not have a career, and so, in an attempt to help him, his singing teacher showed him an announcement in the paper that Luis Trenker, well-known star of popular mountain films turned director (and former lover of Leni Riefenstahl), was looking to cast a young man who could not only sing but leap about athletically.

The 23-year-old Gobbi duly turned up for a screen test only to find himself in a long queue. By the time he got into the studio, late in the day, the man directing the tests was clearly bored out of his mind. He gave Gobbi his instructions, to enter from the back, jump over a group of sitting men, take hold of a guitar and sing something, anything. Gobbi, realising he had to do something very different to be noticed, ran in from the back and turned a somersault over the seated men before seizing the guitar and bursting into song. He got the part.

I Condottieri was a romantic medieval epic about Giovanni de Medici and his sixteenth-century Blackshirts which twisted history to make it acceptable to Mussolini's Fascists. Trenker himself played the lead and Gobbi the part of Nino, a troubador who roams Europe looking for the heroine on behalf of the hero. The film was shot in Rome and Berlin and on location. Gobbi, suitably disguised, played two more small roles which actors had refused to play because they were dangerous. Dressed in armour and riding a horse, he led a troop across a river, then, wearing a moustache and beard as a soldier, he climbed the castle walls and leapt over the battlements.

Despite its political correctness (Trenker, eyes and teeth agleam, preaches nationalism and love of the Fatherland, betraying the film's willingness to toe the Party line), *I Condottieri* did not find favour with the Nazis. Not long before the film's release, the Pope had issued an encyclical which had been taken (as intended) as criticism of the Nazi regime, so when, in the film, Trenker was blessed by the then Pope, Goebbels took it to be an endorsement of the encyclical. He ordered the scene to be cut from the film. After only a week's run in Berlin the film was withdrawn.

Gobbi was then cast by Carmine Gallone in his epic life of *Giuseppe Verdi* (1938) featuring Maria Cebotari, as one of the singers in the operatic excerpts, a role he was to repeat in the same director's *Premiere der Butterfly*. The first time Gobbi got his name above the title was in *Musica Proibita* (1943). By then he was no longer a young hopeful without a career but a singer with a burgeoning reputation, having already sung the role which was to make him world famous, Baron Scarpia, first in Rieti in 1940, then in Rome in 1941. Shortly after singing Scarpia in Rieti, Gobbi had been approached by talent scouts from MGM who wanted him for a film they were planning about the life of a singer. Gobbi, more anxious about his operatic career than becoming a film star, held out for terms he felt were ludicrous and would kill the offer. His demands were eventually agreed upon but the day he signed his contract, Italy joined the war on the side of Germany, and his chance of working in Hollywood vanished.

Musica Proibita was a taut, realistic drama in which Gobbi played an opera singer whose son falls in love with the niece of the woman he once loved but had to leave after he was accused of murdering her brother. Many films with opera singers in the lead were simply vehicles for the singer to sing. Not *Musica Proibita*. The drama comes first with Gobbi excellent as the father and as a young man seen in flashback. The singing is an integral part of the story. After making *Musica Proibita*, Gobbi returned to the operatic stage and did not film again until the war was over.

One artist who continued to make films in both Italy and Germany throughout the war years was Gigli. As always, Gigli's shortcomings as an actor were hidden in plots in which he invariably played a famous opera singer, giving his personality an opportunity to emerge and the audience a chance to hear the honeyed voice for which they had bought their tickets.

In *Casa Lontana* (1939), filmed in Rome and made in Italian and German, he is an opera singer whose ballerina wife leaves him for another man. He meets her again in South America and kills her lover in self-defence. He sings arias from *L'Arlesiana*, *Lucia di Lammermoor*, Zandonai's *Giulietta e Romeo*, *Fedora* and *Pagliacci*, with Liva Caloni as his soprano.

In *Ritorno* (1940), a film directed by Geza von Bolvary (another director who worked in both Germany and Italy during the war years), Gigli played himself. He is invited by diva Marte Harell to sing the role of Ulysses in *Penelope*, a new opera based on the story from *The Odyssey*, written for Harell by her boyfriend composer (Rossano Brazzi). The music for this opera was actually composed by Riccardo Zandonai, who also appears in the film. Zandonai, who had come to prominence in 1908 with an opera based on the Charles Dickens novel, *The Cricket on the Hearth*, was considered by many to be the natural successor to Puccini. He had studied with Mascagni and become world famous after the first performance of his stage opera, *Francesca da Rimini*, in 1914. This was composed to a libretto by Tito Ricordi based on a play by Gabriele D'Annunzio that had been filmed several times in the silent era. Zandonai finished his last opera, *La Farsa Amorosa*, in 1933 and died in 1944, aged 60. In addition to singing the excerpts from *Penelope*, Gigli is seen with Harell in a scene from *La Bohème* (with Harell's voice provided by Mafalda Tavero).

That same year Gigli appeared in the film which was to become his most well-known and popular. In *Mamma*, he is again a famous opera singer, this time with an ancient mother who hurries through the rain-swept streets, to prevent his wife from running off with another man, while her son is on stage singing an impassioned Otello. The parallels between Gigli in tears on stage and the rain outside are obvious. Mamma (played by Emma Gramatica) succeeds in her quest, but the exertion is too great for her and she dies, happy in the knowledge her son's marriage is saved. Directed by Guido Brignone, and filmed in Rome, *Mamma* had them crying in the aisles. The title song, written by Cesare Andrea Bixio, became a smash hit sung by Italian soldiers and prisoners of war everywhere.

Brignone directed Gigli's next film, *Vertigine* (1942), in which he was an opera singer who loses his true love because of an infatuation with another woman. All comes right in the end. Filmed in Venice, Rome and San Remo, the film featured music by Wagner, Giordano, Cilea and Puccini. Appearing with Gigli in a scene from *La Bohème* were Tito Gobbi as Marcello, Liva Caloni as Mimi, Tatiana Menotti as Musetta and Gino Conti as Colline.

Gigli travelled to Berlin to make *Lache Bajazzo* (Laugh Pagliacci, 1942), the film based on the story of the true Canio which had Hans Hotter singing the Prologue in the German version, then back to Rome for *Achtung! Aufnahme* (1943), playing the inevitable opera singer, this time obtaining a part in the film he is making for a young girl he fancies and becoming jealous when she prefers a younger man.

Among other Italian singers who made films during the war was the lyric soprano Toti Dal Monte. She was considered to be the last of the line of coloratura sopranos that had included Melba and Tetrazzini. She had made her debut in 1916 at La Scala singing a secondary role in an opera by Zandonai, before appearing as Lola in *Cavalleria Rusticana* with Mascagni himself conducting. When the 1922 season opened at La Scala with a production of *Rigoletto*, she was chosen by Toscanini to sing Gilda, the role with which she was most associated during the early part of her career. Her success in the part took her to the major opera houses of Europe and then to North America, but her success at the Met was short-lived, due, she always felt, to the jealous intervention of Amelita Galli-Curci.

In 1940 Dal Monte appeared in her first film, *Il Carnevale di Venezia*, directed by Giacomo Gentilomo and Giuseppe Adami, playing the part of a retired opera singer whose daughter is due to sing during Carnival. When daughter suffers from stage fright, mother goes on instead, sings arias from *Lucia di Lammermoor* and *La Sonnambula* (both of which were in Dal Monte's stage repertoire), and enjoys enormous success.

Venice was again the setting for her second film, *Fiori d'Arancio* (Orange Blossoms, 1944). This was made towards the end of the war, after the Allied invasion of Southern Italy had been countered by a German invasion of the north, and the two sides were locked in some of the bitterest fighting of the conflict. Cinema-going in Italy was at its lowest ebb, film distribution was non-existent, and *Fiori d'Arancio* languished on the shelves, hardly seen by anybody.

8. The War Years

The exodus of so many eminent film-makers from Germany and Austria during the thirties had left the German industry seriously denuded of talent, one reason why Italian directors were made so welcome. One of the few native-born directors of note who continued to work under the Nazis was Werner Hochbaum. A former dancer, actor and journalist, he had started his film career at the end of the silent era, coming to notice with *Brüder* (Brother, 1929) about a strike in the Hamburg docks. The films he made during the war years were not particularly distinguished but they did demonstrate an individuality which worried Goebbels. In 1939 Goebbels ordered Hochbaum to make a film which which would prove uplifting to German troops and reinforce the Nazi view of life. The result was *Die Drei Unteroffizieren* (The Three NCOs), a study of life in a small garrison town in which three NCOs put loyalty to each other above everything except their regiment. Both these loyalties are severely tested by the arrival on the scene of an actress.

In one scene of *Die Drei Unteroffizieren*, one of the NCOs takes his girlfriend to a performance of *Carmen*. Singing the role of Carmen opposite tenor Gunther Treptow, was the 24-year-old soprano, Elisabeth Schwarzkopf. It was her first film appearance. She had arrived in Berlin to start her career in 1938, full of ambition to succeed, and made her debut at the State Opera as a Flowermaiden. She was a more than competent actress and was immediately attracted to the cinema, which still played a vital part in Berlin's artistic life.

Die Drei Unteroffizieren was to be Hochbaum's last film. Although he had done all that was asked of him and the film received its official seal of approval (but not the grant which usually went with it), he was then banned from working in the film industry on the trumped-up grounds that he had in 1923 offered his services to France as a spy. He died in 1946, just as *Die Drei Unteroffizieren* was itself being banned by the Allies as Nazi propaganda.

Schwarzkopf's sympathies for the Nazis have been the subject of much debate in recent years, particularly since she has always refused to talk about that period of her career. However, since at that time film was such an important cog in the Nazi propaganda machine, no one could have got a part in any film without the approval of Goebbels. He controlled everything to do with the German film industry and there's no doubt that Schwarzkopf did receive official approval because after *Die Drei Unteroffizieren*, she made at least four more films in Ufa's Berlin studios before 1944, all of which appear to have been lost. These included the 1943 *Nacht ohne Abschied* (Night Without Parting), in which she was seen on stage in a production of *La Traviata* singing Violetta opposite Peter Anders (another film later banned by the Allies for being propaganda), and *Der Verteidiger hat das Wort* (Counsel For the Defence May Speak), a crime thriller filmed in 1944 in which she played the piano in a party scene and sang the song 'Mona'.

Just as audiences could escape the tribulations of every day life by watching a costume drama, so the biographical film could take them back to a time when life was more settled. *Falstaff in Wien* (1940) was a film about Otto Nicolai, the composer best remembered for *The Merry Wives of Windsor*, which tells in a fanciful way the story of how he came to write the opera. Among the singers performing scenes from *The Merry Wives* were Erna Berger and Carla Spletter.

Berger was seen on screen in her most famous role, The Queen of the Night, in *Wen die Gotter lieben* (Whom the Gods Love, 1942), an Austrian biography of Mozart which had the Vienna Philharmonic providing the accompaniment. Mozart had also been the subject of *Melodie Eterne* (Eternal Melodies, 1940), an Italian biopic directed by Carmine Gallone which concentrated on the composer's relationship with the Weber sisters and had arias sung on the soundtrack by Margherita Carosio.

Bellini was featured in *La Sonnambula* (1942), an Italian film directed by Piero Ballerini which dealt with events that led him to write the opera. According to the film, Bellini was recovering from illness at Lake Como when he had an affair with a sleepwalker which gave him the inspiration for the opera.

It was also in Italy, that one of the best musical biographies of all time was made. *Rossini* (1943) follows the composer's career from 1815 when he was 23 to 1829 when he completed *William Tell*, his last opera. Nino Besozzi plays Rossini, Paola Barbara plays Isabella Colbran, the singer who was to become his wife. This was a well-crafted, visually gripping film which had the considerable bonus of generous excerpts from many of Rossini's operas performed by some of the leading Italian singers of the time. The La Scala tenor Pietro Pauli is seen as Otello with Gabriella Gatti, a regular at the Rome Opera as well as La Scala, as Desdemona. Tancredi Pasero, a leading bass at La Scala from 1918, who sang in London, Paris, and at the Met and was in the premiere of Mascagni's *Nerone*, sings Don Basilio in a scene from *The Barber of Seville* with the baritone Mariano Stabile, another La Scala favourite who sang in Chicago, Buenos Aries and at Salzburg, singing Figaro. The mezzo Gianna Pederzini, who was noted for her acting and later appeared in the premiere of Poulenc's *Les Dialogues des Carmélites* at La Scala, sings Rosina, and the tenor Enzo De Muro Lomanto, who appeared regularly at La Scala where he created the title role in Giordano's *Il Re*, sings Count Almaviva. De Muro Lomanto, who was married for a time to Toti Dal Monte, sang throughout Europe and in Japan, China and Australia. Vito de Taranto sings Dr. Bartolo and the conductor is Vittorio Gui, who had conducted at Covent Garden and was, after the war, to appear at Glyndebourne.

Among rising singers who appeared in films for the first time during the war was the tenor Ferruccio Tagliavini. He was born near Reggio Emilia and trained as an engineer before making a name for himself singing operetta. Nicknamed 'Little Caruso', he made his professional operatic debut in Florence in 1939 when he was 26, singing Rodolfo, and quickly established himself as one of Italy's leading lyric tenors. He worked in Italy throughout the war and his first involvement with films came when he provided the voice of Cavaradossi for the film Jean Renoir was making of *La Tosca* in 1940. Renoir had left France at the beginning of the war to work in Italy on the film, with Luchino Visconti as his assistant. His screenplay was a mixture of the opera together with the Sardou play, with Rossano Brazzi as Cavaradossi, Imperio Argentina as Tosca (singing voice, Mafalda Tavero) and Michel Simon as Scarpia. Once it became clear that the war was not going to be a short, sharp action, Renoir left Italy for Hollywood and the film had to be completed by Carl Koch.

Tagliavini also provided one of the voices for a version of *L'Elisir d'Amore* (1941) and for *The King's Jester* (1941), a retelling of the Rigoletto story based on the Hugo play and using Verdi's music (Dal Monte sang for the screen Gilda). He finally made his on-screen film debut in *Voglio Vivere Cosi* (1941), playing a schoolteacher who is desperate to sing opera and is tricked by his colleagues into attending an audition at the local opera house. He gets a job as a stagehand and when the tenor falls ill he just happens to be there, ready to take over.

He was again a schoolteacher with a voice in *La Donna e Mobile*, singing arias from *La Bohème*, *La Sonnambula*, *Lohengrin* and *L'Elisir d'Amore*, and then appeared in *Ho Tanta Voglia di Cantare*! (Anything For a Song, 1944), one of the few films made in Italy directly after Mussolini's overthrow.

Tenor Giuseppe Lugo, although in his forties, had made his first film just before the outbreak of war. Lugo's career had started in Paris in 1931 with Cavaradossi. He returned to Italy in 1936 and became one of the leading lyric tenors in Milan, Rome and throughout the country. In *La Mia Canzone al Vento* (My Song in the Wind, 1939), directed by Guido Brignone, he played an Italian singer offered as a prize in a charity raffle. When he's won by a village girl, he decides, before going to see her officially, to find out unofficially what she is like. He was again a famous singer in *Cantante Con Me* (Sing With Me, 1940) this time followed to Rome by an infatuated housewife who is desperate to see him in *Tosca*.

He became a millionaire in *Miliardi, Che Follia*! (1942), albeit a millionaire with a voice who hides from kidnappers by becoming a member of a theatrical company where he sings a lot (critics noted that his films seemed to consist of nothing but Lugo singing) and falls in love. He was rich again in *Senza una Donna* (Without a Woman, 1943), this time as a duke who hates women but begins to change his mind when a group of stranded dancers arrives at his castle.

Gino Bechi, who listed 'film actor' alongside 'baritone' as his profession in all his directory entries, made the first of his two dozen films in 1943 when he appeared in *Fuga a Due Voce* (Fugue for Two Voices), a musical comedy about a film company looking for a suitable vehicle for its baritone and finding it in an event that happened to him when he ended up in jail for a night with a girl who had missed the same train.

Bechi had been born in Florence in 1913 and made his debut singing Germont in *La Traviata* in 1936. He was to become a regular in Rome and Milan, and also appeared at Covent Garden, Barcelona and in Germany and

South America. Just as the war was coming to an end, he appeared in *Pronto, Chi Parla?*, a love story about a famous singer (he gets to sing the Prologue from *Pagliacci* amongst other arias) who changes places with his butler in order to woo a woman.

Tito Schipa appeared in three wartime films. In *In Cerca di Felicità* (In Search of Happiness, 1943), directed by Giacomo Gentilomo, he plays an opera singer who adopts a young woman because she reminds him of his daughter and disapproves of the young man she loves. His two other films, *Rosalba* and *Vivere Ancora* were both made in 1944 as the war in Italy was coming to an end.

Plots didn't matter in this type of film. They were vehicles for star singers to sing. The first Russian sound film to incorporate arias in this way was made at this time with the tenor Serge Lemeshev. A member of the Bolshoi company from 1931 until the 1950s, and a noted interpreter of both the Russian and Italian repertoire, he appeared in *A Musical Story* (1940), playing a chauffeur sent by his fellow workers to music college where he falls in love and wins the girl while singing lots of opera, including arias from *Eugene Onegin*. Lemeshev also appeared in *Kino-Concert 1941*, a morale-boosting film of a variety concert, in which he sang arias from *Rigoletto* and *Martha*.

Film production in France had ground to a halt during the first few months of the war with several films being abandoned. But during the German occupation, film production returned to near normal, with one major exception: the Hollywood studios that had pulled out of France had been replaced by German studios. The Vichy government also made sure that no Jews could work in the industry. The number of operatic films fell dramatically. Jean-Louis Barrault played Berlioz in *La Symphonie Fantastique* (1941), a film which contained operatic sequences, Sacha Guitry made his film about Maria Malibran, and there was a lavish film of *Carmen* made as a co-production with Italy in 1943 by Christian-Jaque with Viviane Romance as Carmen and Jean Marais as Don José. The Italian version was dubbed. And that was it. *Carmen* also featured in an Argentinian comedy in 1943 in which a dressmaker at the opera house is hit on the head and hallucinates that she is singing the title role on stage.

British interest in filmed opera was virtually non-existent during the war years. Richard Tauber returned to the studio only towards the end of the war, in the autumn of 1945, to play a cameo role in *Waltz Time*, directed by his old friend Paul Stein. A variation on themes from *Die Fledermaus* (an empress poses as her masked friend in order to win a philandering count), the film also had Webster Booth and Anne Ziegler in the cast.

Soprano Margaret Ritchie, who had appeared in the 1936 premiere of Vaughan Williams's *The Poisoned Kiss* and was later to create the roles of Lucia in Britten's *The Rape of Lucretia* and Miss Wordsworth in *Albert Herring*, appeared in the Ealing film *Pink String and Sealing Wax* (1945), starring Googie Withers and Mervyn Johns. Ralph Hamer both directed and co-wrote the screenplay about a publican's wife who plans to have her husband poisoned in Brighton in 1880. Ritchie played the soprano Adelina Patti and sang the James Hook song 'Hush, every breeze', which became a best-selling record.

The only other British film of the time to feature operatic excerpts was a biopic, ironically about a German. Just before the war, wealthy flour miller J. Arthur Rank, had decided to enter the film industry. He started by buying up such studios as Pinewood, Denham and Amalgamated at Elstree, and taking over the Odeon cinema chain. In 1942, the Rank Organisation produced its first major film, *The Great Mr. Handel* with Wilfrid Lawson as the composer. Rank had wanted to make a religious film but did not want to lose money, so he chose to adapt a radio play for children about the German composer Handel who had made his home in London. The film centred on Handel's feud with the Prince of Wales and his acceptance back into royal favour following the composition of *Messiah*. Apart from excerpts from *Messiah*, arias from the opera *Xerxes* were sung by Mrs. Cibber (Elizabeth Allen with a singing voice provided by Gladys Ripley). Shot in Technicolor and directed by Norman Walker, with Jack Cardiff and Claude Friese-Greene, son of film pioneer William, as his cameramen, the film was popular in Britain and also did respectable business in the States, although not as much as Rank had hoped.

If British directors were reluctant to employ opera singers on screen during the war years, Hollywood recognised the need to continue offering audiences the traditional entertainment they craved to help keep up their spirits and take their minds off the war. That meant musicals done the way they'd always been done, with the best singers around. Production of every kind operated at full throttle to keep up with demand.

Marta Eggerth had moved to America in 1938 when her husband, Jan Kiepura, had been offered a five-year contract at the Met. While Kiepura did not make any more films until the war was over, Eggerth was signed by MGM to appear in the Busby Berkeley musical romance, *For Me and My Gal* (1942), playing a glamorous member of a vaudeville troupe just before World War I, who nearly gets fellow troupe member Gene Kelly ahead of Judy Garland. She sang 'Do I Love You?' but no opera. Considered little more than routine escapism at the time, despite winning an Academy nomination for the music, the film is now recognised as being amongst Berkeley's best work.

Eggerth was again cast opposite Judy Garland in *Presenting Lily Mars* (1943), a musical directed by Norman Taurog about a girl who dreams of becoming big on Broadway. She played Garland's rival whose high notes, amply demonstrated in three songs, were parodied by Garland, complete with her singing style and Hungarian accent. Despite the cruelty of the parody, Eggerth and Garland became good friends off screen.

Another Hungarian soprano who ended up in Hollywood during the war was Gitta Alpar, who appeared in René Clair's comedy romance, *The Flame of New Orleans* (1941). In the opening scene, she is seen on stage with Anthony

Marlowe, as Edgardo, in a production of *Lucia di Lammermoor*, while in the audience Marlene Dietrich, a European adventuress, sets out to ensnare a rich man.

The Kiev-born Nina Koshetz, who had retired from the operatic stage to open a restaurant in Hollywood, provided the voice for Binnie Barnes, playing the part of a diva, in *Wife, Husband and Friend*. Koshetz returned to the screen herself as a diva in *Our Hearts Were Young and Gay* (1944), a film based on a biography by Cornelia Otis Skinner and Emily Kimbrough about two wealthy flappers in the twenties who found fun and romance in Paris. The same year she was again a singer in *Summer Storm*, set in 1912 Russia and based on *The Shooting Party*, a short story by Anton Chekhov. The stars were George Sanders and Linda Darnell.

Baritone Leonard Warren, a popular stalwart of the Met from 1939 until 1960, when he died on stage singing Don Carlo in *La Forza del Destino*, made his only screen appearance in *Irish Eyes are Smiling* (1944), a biopic about nineties songwriter Ernest R. Ball (played by Dick Haymes). Warren was a singer at the Met seen on stage with his real-life Met colleague, Blanche Thebom. The film was produced by Damon Runyon and one of Ball's friends was played by Anthony Quinn.

As the war entered its closing stages, another singer who made it to Hollywood was the Danish tenor, Lauritz Melchior. Melchior was considered by many to be the finest heldentenor of all time. He had made his debut singing in *Pagliacci* at the Royal Opera in Copenhagen and sang his first Wagner role in 1918. He sang Parsifal at Bayreuth in 1924 and made his Met debut in *Tannhäuser* two years later. He continued singing there until 1950 when he left following disagreements with Rudolf Bing. Melchior celebrated his 70th birthday by singing Siegmund on radio.

Melchior was in his mid-fifties when he made his first feature, cast in a singing character role. This was *Thrill of a Romance* (1945), a vehicle for Esther Williams to wear her swimsuit and fall for a returning serviceman, Van Johnson. In the only memorable parts of a film described as an empty musical with nothing memorable about it except the waste of time and money, Melchior played a Danish singer who got to sing 'Vesti la giubba', Schubert's Serenade and a song. Just in case the operatic excerpts should alienate audiences, MGM hedged its bets and included Tommy Dorsey as well.

Throughout the war years, Hollywood encouraged its singing stars, even if they had never sung on the operatic stage, to include at least one popular aria in their films. The reason was the phenomenal success just before the war of Universal's new singing sensation, the Canadian soprano Deanna Durbin. Durbin had been signed originally by MGM while still at school to portray Ernestine Schumann-Heink as a child in a biographical film, but when Schumann-Heink fell ill the film was cancelled. She did appear in a short with Judy Garland but was then dropped, moving to Universal, where she was coached by the eminent bass Andrés de Segurola. In 1936, at the age of fourteen, she appeared in her first feature, *Three Smart Girls*, directed by Henry Koster. It was an instant hit, took $2 million at the box office and turned Durbin into a major star. In most of the remaining two dozen films she made until her retirement in 1949 at the age of 27, Durbin sang at least one aria: Musetta's Waltz Song, 'Vissi d'arte', 'The last rose of summer' from *Martha*, an aria from *Roméo et Juliette*, 'Libiamo' from *La Traviata* – Durbin even sang the tenor aria 'Nessun dorma' and a comic version of Figaro's 'Largo al factotum'. In *Something in the Wind* (1947), she dueted with Jan Peerce, the first American singer to appear at the Bolshoi after the war, who had himself made a couple of American propaganda films during it.

Like Grace Moore before her, Durbin was responsible for introducing millions of cinemagoers to the joys of opera, and as with Moore, all the studios were desperate to acquire her equivalent. MGM already had Jeanette MacDonald, who usually included something operatic if she was not in an operetta with Nelson Eddy, but her star had begun to wane, and the studio needed to find a more Durbin-like replacement. They discovered her at a school in North Carolina. Her name was Kathryn Grayson.

Grayson had always wanted to be an opera singer. According to the MGM handouts, she used to wander onto the deserted stage of the St. Louis Opera House and just sing. Her voice was light but she looked good on screen and in her first film for MGM, *Andy Hardy's Private Secretary* (1941), she sang the Mad Scene from *Lucia di Lammermoor*. In *Thousands Cheer* (1943) with Gene Kelly, the film which made her name, she sang 'Sempre libera' from *La Traviata*, and in *It Happened in Brooklyn* (1947), opposite Frank Sinatra, an aria from *Lakmé*. She went on to appear in many films including such operettas as *Rio Rita* (a remake with Abbott and Costello of the 1929 Bebe Daniels/John Boles vehicle), *The Desert Song*, the 1951 remake of *Show Boat*, and *Kiss Me Kate* with Howard Keel. In 1956, after appearing in *The Vagabond King*, Grayson, who was then in her mid-thirties, retired from the screen and, like MacDonald before her, used her position to go on the operatic stage. She appeared in *Madama Butterfly*, *La Bohème* and *La Traviata* in Phoenix, Arizona, as well as productions of *The Merry Widow*, *Die Fledermaus* and *Naughty Marietta*.

Susanna Foster was another singer brought in to rival Durbin who used her fame as a film star to tread the boards later, though in her case it was in operetta rather than opera. Foster had been born in Chicago and as a child was recognised as having an incredible voice reaching well above top C. She was first signed by MGM when she was eleven but, although her family moved to Hollywood, the film planned for her, was never made. Paramount picked her up instead and cast her in *The Great Victor Herbert* (1939), a biopic which contained little in the way of fact, being mainly a vehicle for Mary Martin and Allan Jones to sing Herbert melodies. Foster played their daughter, singing 'Kiss Me Again' in a revival of *The Fortune Teller*.

In the entertaining *Glamour Boy* (1941), with Jackie Cooper as a former child star having to tutor his successor, Foster played his girlfriend and sang the 'Sempre libera' from *La Traviata*. She then joined with many of Paramount's other stars in *Star Spangled Rhythm* (1942), directed by George Marshall. A doorman at the Paramount studios pretends to his son in the US Navy that he is a big producer. Eventually, as their way of contributing to the war effort, the studio's stars rescue him from his lie by putting on an impromptu concert for the navy.

Foster then moved to Universal to star opposite Donald O'Connor in another musical with a war-time setting, *Top Man* (1943). Lillian Gish played Foster's mother and the film made a star of O'Connor. Foster played an opera singer in *The Climax* (1944), a sequel to *Phantom of the Opera*, reminding Boris Karloff, an eye-rolling, mad doctor, of the murdered mistress he has kept embalmed for ten years. She sang in *Bowery to Broadway*, and then appeared as herself in *Follow the Boys* (1944), another Hollywood tribute to the boys in uniform with such stars as Orson Welles, Jeanette MacDonald, Marlene Dietrich, W.C. Fields and Artur Rubinstein. She was teamed with O'Connor again in *This is the Life*, appeared in the musical Western, *Frisco Sal*, and then, *That Night With You* (1945), which used Tchaikovsky's music as the basis for its songs. Foster then decided to leave films at the age of 21 for a career on stage, appearing in such operettas as *Naughty Marietta*, *The Merry Widow*, *Brigadoon* and *Show Boat*.

The desire to have operatic arias in features led to the American mezzo Risë Stevens (who had appeared at the beginning of the war with Nelson Eddy in *The Chocolate Soldier*) being cast in *Going My Way* (1944), one of the most successful of all the films made in Hollywood during the war. Stevens, from New York, had made her stage debut in Prague in 1936 and joined the Met in 1938. She was cast in *Going My Way* as a former girlfriend of Father O'Malley (Bing Crosby), a young priest sent to take over a tough New York slum parish. In an attempt to raise funds for his church and youth club, he enlists the support of Stevens who is a big star at the Met. He visits her there and watches her perform the Habanera from *Carmen*. She naturally agrees to help by giving a concert with his choir, sings Schubert's Ave Maria and duets with Crosby on the title song.

Going My Way was the smash hit of 1944, winning seven Oscars, including Best Picture, Best Actor, Best Supporting Actor (for Barry Fitzgerald as the irascible but lovable old Irish priest from whom Crosby takes over) and Best Director (Leo McCarey). It became the most successful film, after *Gone With the Wind*, yet made. Risë Stevens became the best known Carmen in the world even though she had not, up until that point, sung the role on stage.

9

Picking Up the Pieces

After World War II, the most serious sustained attempt ever made to film opera began in Italy. The Italian film industry had been devastated towards the close of hostilities. In 1943 the Allies had invaded southern Italy, Mussolini, in Rome, had been arrested and his successor government negotiated a surrender. Germany promptly invaded from the north, reached Rome and released Mussolini. Bitter fighting then racked the country for two years as the Allies inched their way up Italy. Film making became the last thing on most people's minds. Those films that were in production had to be shot on locations away from the fighting, without full facilities, and did not get a proper release until the fighting was over. By April 1945, the Allies had succeeded in driving the German troops out of Italy, and Mussolini and his mistress had been captured by the partisans and executed before being hung upside-down in a Milan square. The Cinnecita studios in Rome became a temporary refugee camp and when an Allied committee met in Rome to discuss how the Italian industry could get back on its feet, an American admiral declared that as a former fascist country, Italy did not need a film industry and should not have one.

Nevertheless, film-making, which had never entirely stopped, did pick itself up and in the desire to distance themselves from fascism and take part in a renewal of traditional values in Italian culture, several film-makers turned to the art form which, above all others, had been at the heart of Italian culture for 300 years – opera. It was no coincidence either that at that time there were a number of young Italian singers who were both photogenic and the possessors of extremely good voices, chief among them, Tito Gobbi.

Gobbi's first film after the war was *The Barber of Seville*, the first full-length version of the opera ever filmed. Directed by Mario Costa, this was a record of a production at the Rome Opera House, taken into the studio to film. Despite Gobbi's presence in the title role, his name went below that of Ferruccio Tagliavini (Almaviva) when the film was shown in the United States, since Tagliavini was a big name at the Met and the producers hoped to cash in on his popularity there. Nelly Corradi sang Rosina, Vito de Taranto appeared as Dr. Bartolo and Italo Tajo, Don Basilio. Tajo, who had made his debut in 1935, was still singing almost 60 years later.

As a piece of cinema, *The Barber of Seville* is hampered by limited camera-work and poor post-synching. It resembles an early black-and-white television production. But it proved to be a great success and Gobbi was immediately engaged to sing and act Baron Scarpia in a film of *Tosca*. This, too, was based on a Rome Opera production but, since the director was Carmine Gallone, it became a 'parallel' action film renamed *The Man Before Whom All Rome Trembled* with the action updated to the German occupation of Rome. The diva starring in the production of *Tosca* was Anna Magnani, one of the leading actresses in Italian neo-realist films and described by Gobbi as 'magnificent though rather difficult'. She has a lover (played by Gino Sinimberghi, who sings Cavaradossi) who has helped a British soldier hide from the Germans. She is suspicious that he is having an affair.

Magnagni's singing voice was dubbed by Elisabetta Barbato. Hiring actresses to play singing roles in opera which were then dubbed by real singers was to become commonplace, both in Italy and elsewhere. The demand to have faces on screen which looked right rather than because they simply possessed fine voices, eventually became standard practice.

In Gallone's next film, *Rigoletto* (1946), the role of Gilda was acted by Marcella Govoni and sung by Lina Pagliughi, the Brooklyn-born soprano who made Tettrazzini look undernourished. The film was shot on the stage of Rome's Opera House, with Mario Filippeschi as the Duke, Giulio Neri as Sparafucile, Anna Maria Canali as Maddelena and magnificent in the title role Tito Gobbi. Gobbi then went on to appear as Sergeant Belcore in Mario Costa's film of *L'Elisir d'Amore* (1947) with Nelly Corradi as Adina, Gino Sinimberghi as Nemorino and Italo Tajo, wearing a costume he had designed himself, as the quack doctor Dulcamara.

As Italy began to recover from the ravages of war, directors were quick to take advantage of the greater freedom this gave them to shoot their films. The first few operatic films had been shot in the studio as if they were stage productions. By the time Costa came to shoot *L'Elisir*, he was able to combine filming in the studio with filming on location, which gave him the opportunity to treat the opera much more cinematically than had been possible earlier.

In the cast of *L'Elisir d'Amore*, playing a friend of Adina, was the Italian actress destined to become the first of Italy's post-war sex-symbols, Gina Lollobrigida. Eighteen-year-old Lollobrigida, who was studying in Rome to become a commercial artist, had been stopped in the street by Costa and asked to do a screen test. The director had to suffer a tirade of abuse against men who accost respectable young women on the streets, but eventually managed to persuade her that he was genuine. She made the screen test, got the part, and spent her fee on a new coat and an umbrella.

Lollobrigida also made a fleeting appearance as little more than an extra in Piero Ballerini's film of *Lucia di Lammermoor* (1946) with Nelly Corradi singing Lucia, Mario Filippeschi as Edgardo, Afro Poli as Lord Ashton and Italo

1. Cecil B. DeMille rehearses Wallace Reid and Geraldine Farrar for a scene in *Carmen* (1915).

2. Seventy years later, Francesco Rosi rehearses Julia Migenes and Placido Domingo for a scene in his *Carmen* (1984).

3. Enrico Caruso in a scene from *My Cousin* (1918), in which he played two roles: an opera singer and the cousin he visits in New York.

4. Czech soprano Jarmila Novotná in Max Ophuls' *The Bartered Bride* (1932), the first opera filmed in Germany after the arrival of the Talkies.

5. Lawrence Tibbett doesn't seem to have much to sing about in *The Rogue Song* (1930), but that didn't stop him. He even managed a song while tied up.

6. The great Russian bass Feodor Chaliapin in Pabst's *Don Quixote* (1933). In the English language version Sancho was played by George Robey.

7. Josef Schmidt, known as the Pocket Caruso, in *My Song Goes Round the World* (1933), later banned by the Nazis because Schmidt was a Jew.

8. Grace Moore and Tullio Carminati in *One Night of Love* (1934), the most influential opera film of its time.

9. Grace Moore on the set of *One Night of Love* (1934).

10. Spanish mezzo Conchita Supervia sings a Spanish song in Victor Saville's *Evensong* (1934), her only appearance on film.

11. Lily Pons, the French soprano signed by RKO to rival Grace Moore, with Henry Fonda in *I Dream Too Much* (1935).

12. Met mezzo Gladys Swarthout, Paramount's answer to Grace Moore and Lily Pons, in *Give Us This Night* (1936) with Polish tenor Jan Kiepura.

13. Richard Tauber on the set of *Pagliacci* (1936).

14. *Faust* (1936), with Webster Booth as Faust, Anne Ziegler as Marguerite and Denis Hoey as Mephistopheles. This has been described as the worst operatic film ever made.

15. Hungarian soprano Marta Eggerth in *Casta Diva* (1935), Carmine Gallone's lavish biography of the composer Bellini.

16. Marta Eggerth and her husband, Jan Kiepura, in *The Charm of La Bohème* (1937), a 'parallel' film directed by Geza von Bolvary.

17. Maria Cebotari and Rossano Brazzi in a scene from *Maria Malibran* (1943), Cebotari's last film. The leading coloratura soprano in Nazi Germany, she died aged only thirty-nine.

18. *Going My Way* (1944), the biggest box-office hit of the year with mezzo Risë Stevens, Bing Crosby and Barry Fitzgerald.

19. Michael Denison and Tito Gobbi in *The Glass Mountain* (1949), the film that made them both stars.

20. Jarmila Novotná confronts Mario Lanza in *The Great Caruso* (1951).

21. Met soprano Dorothy Kirsten, whose study in Italy was paid for by Grace Moore, and Mario Lanza in *The Great Caruso* (1951).

22. Robert Helpmann watches Robert Rounseville in Powell and Pressburger's *The Tales of Hoffman* (1951). Helpmann's singing voice was provided by Welsh baritone Bruce Dargavel.

23. José Van Dam as Leporello and Ruggero Raimondi as Giovanni in Joseph Losey's *Don Giovanni* (1978).

24. The opening scene of Paul Czinner's film of *Der Rosenkavalier* (1960), the Salzburg Festival production with Elisabeth Schwarzkopf as the Marschallin and Sena Jurinac as Octavian.

25. Luciano Pavarotti in his only feature film, *Yes Giorgio* (1982). With Kathryn Harrold as the love interest.

26. American baritone Thomas Hampson as the Dark Fiddler in Peter Weigl's film of Delius' *A Village Romeo and Juliet* (1989). Hampson was the only singer in the cast.

27. *M is for Man, Music and Mozart* (1991), Peter Greenaway's contribution to the BBC's *Not Mozart* series.

28. Richard Duployen as the Priest in Dominik Scherrer's *Hell for Leather* (1998).

Tajo as Raimondo. She was an extra again in *Il Segreto di Don Giovanni* (1947) with Gino Bechi playing a lecherous singer who loses his voice and hires killers to end his life, deciding, too late, he wants to live. Directed by Camillo Mastrocinque, the film was, wrote the critic of the New York Times, 'eminently qualified to discourage the average moviegoer from ever wanting to see another Italian film'.

Having used Lollobrigida in *L'Elisir d'Amore*, Costa decided to put her into his next operatic venture, *Follie per l'Opera* (Mad About Opera, 1948), a romantic comedy set in London's Italian community. An Italian journalist is helped by an English secretary, who is in love with him, to organise a fund-raising gala to rebuild a bombed Italian church in Soho. When she discovers that he is already engaged to Dora (Lollobrigida), she does her best to ruin the concert but it goes ahead anyway and is a great success. Among the singers who appeared in the concert, as themselves, were Tito Gobbi, Beniamino Gigli, Gino Bechi, Tito Schipa and Maria Caniglia. *Follie per l'Opera* the first Italian film to be shown in the USSR after the war was Lollobrigida's first picture to be released in the United States, where she was billed as Lollo Brigida.

Lollobrigida was still only twenty when Costa offered her her first starring role, as Nedda, in the production of *Pagliacci* he was setting up to film after *Follie per l'Opera*. Like his previous *L'Elisir*, Costa planned to shoot much of *Pagliacci* on location. His version opens with Leoncavallo seen composing the opera; Gobbi, who plays both Tonio and Silvio, then sings the Prologue at La Scala before the scene changes to a naturalistic Sicilian setting.

Lollobrigida turned Costa down, not thinking she could play the part. He screen-tested several other actresses and a week later went back to Lollobrigida. She finally agreed, provided he paid her a million lire a day. She had always wanted to be an opera singer and had been taking singing lessons, but she did not sing in *Pagliacci*. Her voice was dubbed by Onella Fineschi. But the post-synchronisation is extremely good, she looks right on screen, and it is quite obvious why all the men fight over her.

With the exception of Gobbi, who cunningly differentiates physically and vocally between the two characters he is playing, the other principals are also dubbed. Galliano Masini provided the voice for Afro Poli's Canio and Gino Sinimberghi the voice for Filippo Morucci (Beppe).

Pagliacci was warmly received in Italy and around the world, and the offers immediately began to come in for Lollobrigida. She did not make any more operatic films until 1951 when she appeared in *Enrico Caruso, Leggende di una Voce*, as Caruso's first great love, Stella. Ermanno Randi, his voice dubbed by Mario del Monaco, played Caruso. Her singing voice was dubbed by Dhia Cristiani. She finally got to sing on screen herself when she portrayed the soprano Lina Cavalieri in the 1955 biopic, *The Most Beautiful Woman in the the World*, directed by Robert Z. Leonard.

If Lollobrigida was becoming a household name around the world, so too was the man who had been the star in some of her early films, Tito Gobbi. Gobbi was much in demand to star in opera films but it wasn't only opera that lured him into the studio. In 1946 he appeared in *O Sole Mio*, a feature film directed by Giacomo Gentiluomo, playing an anti-Nazi spy parachuted into Naples, who transmits military information during radio recitals until he is betrayed by a girl. The same year he was in *Les Beaux Jours du Roi Murat*, a French-Italian co-production, playing a revolutionary in the old kingdom of Naples who sings his way into the palace and is almost executed.

Then came the film that was to make him an international star, and it wasn't an opera. It was a low-budget British film, one of many being churned out which harked back to the heroic days of the Second World War. *The Glass Mountain* was also to make a star of its leading man, Michael Denison.

Denison plays a composer whose plane had crashed during the war in northern Italy. There he had fallen in love with an Italian partisan (Valentina Cortese) despite having a very English wife back home (Dulcie Gray), and met Gobbi, an opera-singing Partisan. On his return to Italy after the war, he completes an opera about his experiences, called *The Legend of the Glass Mountain*, sung at its premiere by Gobbi and Elena Rizzieri with the orchestra and chorus of La Fenice, Venice. Denison waved the baton in the film, Franco Ferrara conducted for real. The music for this imaginery opera was composed by Nino Rota and thanks largely to the score and to Gobbi's warm screen presence and marvellous singing, *The Glass Mountain* became one of the biggest UK box-office successes of 1948.

Gobbi's frequent film appearances (he appeared in more than twenty) did not endear him to his colleagues in the opera house who used to refer to him rather snidely as 'the singing film star'. But he found, much as Farrar had many years earlier, that filming helped his stagecraft. Although the techniques required for acting in front of a camera are different from those needed on the stage, the way films are shot out of sequence taught Gobbi how to get into character instantly without a long musical build up. He also learnt not to rely on audience reaction.

Among others films in which Gobbi appeared were five highlights films produced in 1948 by George Richfield as part of a series entitled The Festival of Film Opera. These were each 25 minutes long, based on Rome Opera House productions and shown with a voice-over to explain the plots. In most of them Gobbi was the only person both to sing and act his role. The other parts, almost without exception, were played by dubbed actors or even dubbed singers. The confusion this sometimes caused is illustrated by Richfield's film of *The Marriage of Figaro* in which the role of Almaviva was sung by Luciano Neroni but acted by Giulio Tomei who sang the role of Dr. Bartolo which was acted by Gino Conti! As for Gobbi, he appeared as Figaro in *The Barber of Seville*, Malatesta in *Don Pasquale*, Escamillo in *Carmen*, in the title role of *William Tell*, and as Lord Ashton in *Lucia di Lammermoor*.

9. Picking Up the Pieces

But even Gobbi wasn't always required to act. He provided the voice for Germont in Carmine Gallone's full-length feature of *La Traviata* entitled *La Signora delle Camelie*, with the on-screen acting being done by Manfredi Polverosi. Nelly Corradi (again dubbed by Ornella Fineschi) appeared as Violetta, and Gino Mattera both sang and acted Alfredo.

Corradi was dubbed again when she appeared as Leonora in Gallone's *La Forza del Destino* (1949), shot on location outside Rome. Gino Sinimberghi was also dubbed as Alvaro but Gobbi both sang and acted the role of Don Carlo. Sinimberghi was again dubbed (by Antonio Salvarezza) when he appeared in Gallone's feature of *Il Trovatore*, as was Corradi (by Fineschi) when she appeared as Marguerite in Gallone's *La Leggenda di Faust*, an American-Italian co-production of the opera starring Italo Tajo as Méphistophélès and Gino Mattera as Faust. Cesare Berlacchi's film of *La Sonnambula* mostly used actors miming to singers from the Rome Opera, and the singing voice of Elsa in a film of *Lohengrin* (1947), directed by Max Calandri, was that of Renata Tebaldi.

In this rush to film opera – almost twenty in the three years immediately after the war – not only the well-known operas made it to the screen. Rossini's *La Cenerentola* was hardly ever staged, even in Italy, when Fernando Cerchio filmed it on location in palaces outside Milan with Fedora Barbieri providing the voice for Lori Randi's Cinderella.

In the aftermath of war, Allied censors carefully vetted the kinds of film being made throughout the occupied territories. In Italy itself, a law was passed in 1949 which permitted the government to censor scripts, withhold grants from productions deemed controversial and refuse to grant an export licence to any film considered to be slandering Italy.

Opera was clearly acceptable since it embodied a cultural past of which the country was proud. So too were undemanding operettas or films with operatic arias, especially when the singers were internationally known and popular and the film might get distribution abroad. A film that did well overseas could help a country's balance of payments.

Gigli's first film after the war was *Voglio Bene Soltanto a Te*, a virtual remake of *Achtung! Aufnahme*, the film he had made two years earlier which had not been widely shown because of the fighting. As a tenor making a film who gets a part in it for the girl he fancies, only to find she loves another man, he got to sing arias from *La Favorita*, *Tannhäuser*, *Martha*, *Die Walküre*, *Lohengrin*, *L'Africaine* and *L'Elisir d'Amore*. Some clips of him were recycled from his film *Mamma*.

Gigli had been accused during the war of having Fascist sympathies. Certainly he had done nothing to condemn Mussolini and had even made public pronouncements supporting him. Appearing in popular films was a good way to rehabilitate himself while at the same time testing the waters of public opinion. No one threw bottles at the screen or tore up seats when he appeared in *Follie per L'Opera* (1948), nor when he appeared, again as himself, with Tito Schipa and Gino Bechi in *Una Voce nel Tuo Cuore* (One Voice in Your Heart, 1950), a film about a war correspondent (Vittorio Gassman) who loves a nightclub singer who wants to be in opera.

Tito Schipa's first film after the war had been a Donizetti biopic, *Il Cavaliere del Sogno* (1946), in which he played the French tenor Gilbert Duprez, creator of the role of Edgardo in *Lucia di Lammermoor*. He also sang arias from *L'Elisir d'Amore* and *Don Pasquale*.

Another famous tenor to go in front of the cameras at this time was Giacomo Lauri-Volpi. Fifty-eight years old and still singing (he made his last public appearance at a concert in Spain when he was 85 and still hit a high C), Lauri-Volpi appeared in *Il Caimano del Piave* (1950), playing a captain in the Italian army during the First World War. It is Christmas time in the trenches and Lauri-Volpi is asked by his men to sing for them. As his voice floats across No Man's Land to the German trenches, the fighting stops while both sides listen. The incident was apparently based on Lauri-Volpi's own experience.

Jan Kiepura and Marta Eggerth had spent the war years in the United States with Kiepura singing at the Met and then appearing together with Eggerth on Broadway in a production of *The Merry Widow*. Carmine Gallone brought back them back to Europe for *Her Wonderful Lie*, a remake of their extremely successful *The Charm of La Bohème*, made ten years earlier, in which the dying Eggerth gives up the unknown tenor Kiepura for the sake of his career. They are reunited in a production of *La Bohème*, and just as Mimi dies at the end, so, too, does Eggerth. This was shot in Italy, in English, and aimed very much at the international market.

The national film industry most affected by the war was inevitably that of Germany. So many talented people had left the country or been forced to leave by virtue of being Jewish, and the moment the surrender was signed in 1945, the Allies set about dismantling the German film industry. Ufa was closed down and, because of the split between the communist East and capitalist West, two parallel industries began to develop, neither of which was ever to be as powerful as under the old system. The vast propaganda machine of Goebbels became a cottage industry of independent producers.

It took time for German producers to get into production. A biopic of operetta composer Karl Millöcker, directed by Theo Lingen, which had remained unfinished at the end of the war, was eventually completed, while Geza von Bolvary's film of *Die Fledermaus* starring Marte Harell, which he was shooting in Prague as the war came to an end, was seized by the advancing Russians and first shown in East Berlin in 1946.

The Allies, just as they did in Italy, governed what could be filmed or shown in Germany and Austria. Light musicals with no political undertones were acceptable. In 1950, Hans Hotter sang some arias in the Austrian musical *Grosstadtnacht* (Night in the Big City) and then went to Germany to make

Sehnsucht des Herzens (Yearnings of the Heart) playing a singer who falls in love with the already married Linda Caroll.

If ever a country wanted to forget the immediate past and think only of the good times exemplified by its cultural history, it was postwar Germany. And there were few higher pinnacles of German-language achievement than the operas of Mozart whose *Marriage of Figaro* became the first opera to be filmed in Germany after the war.

Directed by Georg Wildhagen, *Figaros Hochzeit* (1949), had Willi Domgraf-Fassbaender as Figaro and Mathieu Ahlersmeyer as the Count. All other roles were dubbed, with Berlin favourite Tiana Lemnitz providing the voice of the Countess, Erna Berger the voice of Susanna and Anneliese Müller the voice for Cherubino. Bartolo was acted by the director Viktor Janson. Wildhagen followed up *Figaro's Wedding* with a film of Nicolai's *The Merry Wives of Windsor*, again shooting with actors miming to playback. Among those providing the voices were Martha Mödl and Rita Streich.

Elsewhere in Europe, studios and producers were trying to pick up where they had left off in 1939. Jan Kiepura and Marta Eggerth returned to their home in Paris and were asked to make *La Valse Brillante* (1949), with Kiepura as a bodyguard with a voice hired to mind a singer who has been receiving threatening letters. They end up as singing partners.

In Sweden, Jussi Björling went before the cameras for the first time in ten years to make *En Svensk Tiger* (A Swedish Tiger, 1948), appearing in a supporting role as a tenor who is seen singing arias from *The Tales of Hoffmann*, *Don Giovanni* and *L'Africaine*. The film was not particularly successful.

The film industry in the Soviet Union cut itself off from what was taking place in the West but there, too, opera crept into films intended to inspire audiences from Leningrad to Siberia. Lev Arnshtam directed *The Great Glinka* (1946), an account of the composer's attempts to found a native Russian operatic idiom, which included excerpts from *Ivan Susanin* sung by members of the Bolshoi. Modest Mussorgsky, another important figure in the history of Russian nationalist music, also ended up as the subject of a biopic directed, in 1950, by Grigory Roshal. Concerned with Mussorgsky's struggle for recognition, the film contained sequences of *Boris Godunov* and won a prize at the Cannes Film Festival.

Britain's contribution to filmed opera in the years immediately after the war was left to two tenors. Richard Tauber appeared in a supporting role in *The Lisbon Story* (1946), again for his friend, Paul Stein. This was a spy story starring Patricia Burke and David Farrar, about a Parisian prima donna who succumbs to Nazi pressure to return to the stage but only so that she can help a French scientist with an atomic secret to escape. This had been a great success on the London stage with the number, 'Pedro the Fisherman', devised originally to cover the bangs and crashes of the scene changes, becoming one of the most popular songs of the war. Tauber, who sang the song in the film, was one of several guest artists to appear in the film. Others included Harry Welchman and Stéphane Grappelli.

Nino Martini, who had not appeared in a film for over ten years, was brought to England in 1948 to appear in *One Night With You*, an English remake of a 1943 Italian film starring Gino Bechi. Martini played an Italian tenor and movie star stranded by a train breakdown with an English girl (Patricia Roc). They are taken to be a pair of forgers and spend the night in jail. Directing this frantic and at times amusing comedy, was Terence Young, later to become director of the Bond films. In the cast supporting Martini were Bonar Colleano, Guy Middleton, Stanley Holloway and Irene Worth.

One Night With You was a comedy which harked back to the innocence of the thirties. Hollywood, too, tried to turn back the clock, making the kind of films they had made before the war, still looking for that magic ingredient, such as a Deanna Durbin, which would turn an otherwise ordinary picture into a hit. Musicals were high on the list. The success of Risë Stevens in *Going My Way* meant that, for a time, operas, or rather opera singers who could deliver a good aria, were very much back in fashion.

Stevens was cast in *Carnegie Hall* (1947), a vehicle for a number of mostly classical musicians to perform their party pieces. The son of the caretaker at Carnegie Hall is encouraged to practise by hearing such performers as Bruno Walter conduct Wagner, Gregor Piatigorsky play from *The Carnival of the Animals*, Artur Rubinstein play Chopin and Jascha Heifetz perform part of the Tchaikovsky Violin Concerto. On the operatic front, Stevens sang arias from *Carmen* and *Samson et Dalila*, Ezio Pinza sang arias from *Don Giovanni* and *Simon Boccanegra*, Lily Pons the 'Vocalise' by Rachmaninoff together with the Bell Song from *Lakmé*, and Jan Peerce, 'O sole mio'.

Carnegie Hall was directed with very little style by Edgar G.Ulmer and the story was woodenly acted, especially by the musicians coming in to give their homely advice to the caretaker's son. That the film was little more than an excuse to sling together the performances was demonstrated by the fact that it was released in several versions with some items omitted or heavily edited.

The powerful singing and impressive screen presence of Lauritz Melchior in the Esther Williams' vehicle *Thrill of a Romance* had marked him out as a distinctive supporting artist, and he was cast in *Two Sisters from Boston* (1946), in which June Allyson and Kathryn Grayson arrive in New York at the turn of the century looking for work and end up in Jimmy Durante's Bowery saloon. Grayson wants to sing opera, which her family thinks she does already, so she sneaks on stage at the Met to sing a scene with Melchior from an imaginary opera based on themes from Mendelssohn. The film's finale is a scene from *Marie Antoinette*, another imaginary opera written especially for the film using the music of Liszt. Both pieces were arranged by Charles Previn. In *Marie Antoinette*, Melchior played the King, Grayson the Queen, and the sequence, with extras everywhere, was shot on a 500-foot wide reproduction of the interior of the Met.

While many of these films from the end of the forties have a certain charm, a large number were witless and formulaic. When Melchior returned to the screen with Williams in *This Time For Keeps* (1947), directed by Richard Thorpe, the result was described as dim and a waste of money. The son of a famous opera singer prefers modern music and falls for a swimming star. Melchior, as the father, sings arias from *Rigoletto*, *Martha* and *Otello*, and a song by Cole Porter. 'The money spent on this production might easily have kept Mozart and Schubert alive and busy to the age of 60, with enough left over to finance five of the best movies ever made,' wrote James Agee. 'It might even have been invested in a good musical.'

In the shipboard musical *Luxury Liner* (1948), Melchior again played an operatic tenor, this time opposite Jane Powell as the captain's stowaway teenage daughter. He and Powell got to sing a duet from *Aïda*, and on his own he sang an aria from *Die Walküre*. Also on board were Xavier Cugat and his orchestra, and Marina Koshetz, daughter of Nina and herself an opera singer.

Looking to start a new career in films was Lotte Lehmann, the German-born soprano who had settled in America. The most famous Marschallin of her generation, she had just retired from the operatic stage when she was offered a seven-year contract by MGM. In *Big City*, she played Margaret O'Brien's grandmother and sang – Brahms' 'Cradle song', 'The Kerry dance' and 'God bless America' – but they were hardly representative of her art and after *Big City* her contract was allowed to lapse.

Charles Kullman, the Met tenor who had appeared with Helen Jepson in the 1938 *Goldwyn Follies*, appeared in Universal's *Song of Scheherazade* (1947), a kitschy biopic of Rimsky-Korsakov with Jean-Pierre Aumont as the composer. In 1865, when Rimsky is a 21-year-old naval cadet in St. Petersburg, he falls for a girl working in a dance hall (Yvonne de Carlo) and is inspired by her to compose. Kullman sang Rimsky's 'Song of India' from his opera, *Sadko*.

Another opera singer from the Met appeared in MGM's attempt to recreate the successful all-star *Goldwyn Follies*, the Vincente Minnelli-directed, *Ziegfeld Follies*. MGM had the rights to the Ziegfeld name, which they had wanted to use for some time, and they came up with a plot in which Ziegfeld (William Powell), in heaven, looks down at the many wonderful acts still on earth. The film, the first revue since the thirties, was started in 1943 and cost $3.25 million. The sequence involving cowboy singer turned tenor James Melton singing the 'Libiamo' from *La Traviata* with Marion Bell was filmed in 1944, but the film was not released until 1946 since it was thought that its ostentation would not look good during the austerity of wartime.

The Czech soprano Jarmila Novotná, who had made her home in America following the outbreak of war in Europe, resumed her film career with a non-singing role in Fred Zinnemann's *The Search* (1948), playing a mother desperately searching for her lost son in war-ravaged Europe. He has been interviewed by an American woman trying to reunite lost children with their families, panicked and run away. He is befriended by GI Montgomery Clift, making his screen debut. The film, a co-production between MGM and a Swiss company, contains some striking images and moving performances, and it was nominated for four Oscars. Audiences left it in floods of tears.

Outstanding films at this time tended to be the exception rather than the rule, particularly as far as musicals were concerned. Most musicals being made at the end of the 1940s were uninspired. The singing was largely irrelevant, holding up the action, and if the star wasn't big enough, the public didn't want to sit through an hour of tedium for a song, or have an aria break whatever dramatic tension may have been built up. Films of operas themselves, outside Italy, were not good box-office except in the art cinemas where audiences were limited. Cinema audiences everywhere, even in the States, were declining markedly. Hollywood was under threat, not from film industries in other lands, which were themselves under threat, but from a rival within the home – television.

10

Mario Lanza

In November 1943, *Winged Victory*, Moss Hart's patriotic musical play starring such American servicemen as Karl Malden, Lee J. Cobb and Edmond O'Brien, opened in New York. It was a spectacular production, designed to beat the drum and raise funds for the Army Emergency Relief Fund. It ran for six months and handed over more than $25,000 a week to the fund. Singing in its 50-strong chorus was a young Italian-American tenor in the US Army. When Twentieth Century Fox bought the rights to the stage show and handed it to George Cukor to direct, they shipped the entire cast, including the chorus, out to Hollywood.

This was the first screen appearance of the man who was to become the most influential of all screen tenors, and the person who was to spearhead Hollywood's fight back against television, although no one was aware of it at the time. Mario Lanza may not have had much of a part in *Winged Victory* (even knowing he's in it, you can't spot him) but it gave him a definite taste for the movies. According to Jack Warner, he was so keen to become a movie star that he sent a recording of himself to Warner's maid, Maria, who persuaded Mrs Warner to play it for her husband. Warner listened, and commented that the singer sounded a lot like Caruso. He was, he said, right. It was Caruso. Lanza had pasted his own label over the correct one. Warner agreed to see the singer, but although impressed by the voice, did not think much of Lanza's looks. He appeared far too fond of his food and so Warner didn't even offer him a screen test. 'Sorry', Warner recalled saying, 'I don't think the movies are for you.'

While it is true that Warner turned down Lanza, the rest of the story as Warner told it is simply not true, for the pasting of Lanza's name over the name of another singer had happened while Lanza was stationed with the US Army Air Corps at Marfa in Texas, and it wasn't a recording of Caruso. Lanza was due to audition for a role in a musical written by then-Sergeant Peter Lind Hayes and Frank Loesser, but had such a bad throat he couldn't possibly sing. A fellow serviceman, Johnny Silver, who had been in burlesque before his call-up and was later to appear in *Guys and Dolls*, pasted Lanza's name over a 78 recording of an aria from *Tosca* sung by the Brooklyn-born but Italian-trained

Met tenor Frederick Jagel (who had made his debut in the house singing Radames in 1927). Silver played it for Hayes. According to legend, when Hayes eventually heard Lanza, he commented that he sounded much better live. It was a story Lanza himself was happy to repeat.

Lanza had been born Alfred Cocozza in South Philadelphia in 1921 and took his stage name from his mother, Maria Lanza Cocozza. As a child he sang in choirs and when his voice broke, it was apparent at once he had an instrument of remarkable potential. His first break came when Serge Koussevitsky was conducting the Boston Symphony Orchestra in a concert in Philadelphia. The concert manager, William K. Huff, had heard Lanza at the studio of his singing teacher and been impressed. After the performance, Huff took the young tenor backstage to meet the conductor. Koussevitsky was by then having a post-concert massage and told Huff to take Lanza across the hall to a room with a piano where an accompanist would play for him. Lanza sang 'Vesti la giubba'. Koussevitsky was sufficiently impressed to stop his massage, cross over the hall and offer Lanza a summer at Tanglewood.

At Tanglewood, Lanza worked with Koussevitsky's young protégé, Leonard Bernstein, sang Rodolfo in a workshop performance of excerpts from *La Bohème* and the role of Fenton in the end-of-term production of Nicolai's *The Merry Wives of Windsor*. While everyone was impressed by the quality of the voice, most were exasperated by Lanza's refusal to learn to read music properly. He had to learn his roles either by listening to them or by having them drummed into him. In later years he gained a reputation for doing all his recordings in one take. It was often said that that was the only way he could record, that he didn't know how to vary his interpretation.

Before he could capitalise on his Tanglewood experiences, war intervened and Lanza received his call-up papers. He spent a miserable two years in uniform and after his discharge in 1945, went to New York to continue his studies. There he was taken under the wing of a fellow student, a businessman and amateur music lover named Sam Weiler, who was so impressed by Lanza's voice that he gave up singing himself and agreed to pay for Lanza's lessons in return for a slice of any fees he might get.

While at Tanglewood, Lanza had signed a contract with Columbia Artists and in 1946 the tenor began a series of concerts across North America as a member of the Bel Canto trio with soprano Frances Yeend and baritone George London. They got rave reviews everywhere, especially Lanza, and before long had clocked up some 200 performances. Lanza was also beginning to appear in concert on his own.

At the time he had been in Hollywood as a member of the chorale in *Winged Victory*, Lanza had signed a contract with RCA Victor and made some test recordings. One of these demonstration discs found it's way to Louis B. Mayer's secretary, Ida Koverman, who was desperately trying to find a replacement for Ferruccio Tagliavini at a Hollywood Bowl subscription concert on 28

August 1947. She played the Lanza recording for her boss and Mayer straight-away arranged for him to be booked. It was Lanza's most important engagement and he rose to the occasion. George London later recalled: 'He sang that night like he had never sung before or has sung since.'

It was to be the turning point in his career for that night Hollywood discovered Lanza and the operatic stage lost the singer who might well have become the greatest tenor since Caruso. Two days after his Bowl concert, Lanza was invited by Mayer to the MGM lot in Culver City. There, in Studio One, Mayer had assembled all his producers, executives and directors. Aware that Lanza's appearance might prejudice people – he had a shock of wild hair and, although only 26, was already beginning to have problems with his weight – Mayer hid Lanza behind a curtain from where he sang two arias, 'Che gelida manina' and 'Thine alone' from Victor Herbert's *Eileen*. When Lanza then walked out to meet them, all the producers except Joe Pasternak shook their heads. Pasternak, who had been brought to MGM from Universal and was the man who made Deanna Durbin into a star, recalled that he looked like a caveman. But Pasternak had been bowled over by the voice and was determined to do something with Lanza. 'I like him very much,' he told Mayer. 'He's all yours,' was the reply.

Despite the misgivings of most MGM executives who couldn't see this portly singer ever becoming a hit, Mayer offered Lanza a seven-year contract, with a salary increase as each picture was made. The contract also included a clause allowing him six months off each year in order to fulfil his concert engagements and recording contracts. He was, Mayer told him, going to become MGM's singing Clark Gable, although opinion within the studio was divided as to whether he should be developed as a new talent in his own right or whether he should be groomed as a replacement for Nelson Eddy.

Lanza's first screen tests were not encouraging. He was badly dressed, his hair looked, according to Pasternak, like a horsehair mattress that had burst its seams, and he was very much overweight. Pasternak made him get a haircut, go on a diet and wear suits that emphasised his height rather than his width, then put him into *That Midnight Kiss* (1949), opposite the experienced Kathryn Grayson. The story was supposed to be based on Lanza's own life but owed more to the MGM publicity department's inventiveness than it did to fact. Lanza is a barrel-chested van-driver with a glorious voice who is heard singing while delivering a piano to the home of a wealthy patron of the arts. She has just formed a new opera company in Philadelphia for her grand daughter (played by Grayson) to sing leading roles, and it turns out that Lanza is just what the company needs.

While waiting for the script of *That Midnight Kiss* to be written, Lanza made his professional stage debut in New Orleans singing Pinkerton in *Madama Butterfly*. Tomiko Kanazawa sang the title role, and Jess Walters, the role of the American consul, Sharpless. Lanza sang two performances and was sufficiently well received to be offered a contract to sing in *La Traviata* the following season. Although he signed the contract, the appearances never took place. His two performances as Pinkerton were, despite periodic announcements that, for example, he had signed to sing opposite Renata Tebaldi, the only two professional stage performances he ever gave. After them he returned to Hollywood to begin work on *That Midnight Kiss*.

A strong supporting cast had been assembled, including Ethel Barrymore as the wealthy grandmother, Keenan Wynn, J. Carroll Naish and the Spanish pianist José Iturbi, who played the musical director of the new opera company and got a billing above Lanza. The Oscar-winning director Norman Taurog was assigned to the project and Charles Previn, cousin of André's father, was appointed musical director. Lanza was given songs to sing ranging from Jerome Kern's 'They didn't believe me' to the Neapolitan Caruso favourite, 'Mama mia, che vo' sape'. A new song, 'I know, I know, I know,' was especially written for the film and there was a duet with Grayson, 'Love is music'. Had *That Midnight Kiss* contained only these songs, it would probably not have attracted that much attention since, although it was pleasant enough, the film rarely rose above the level of a sentimental pot-boiler. But Lanza was also given the arias 'Una furtiva lagrima' from *L'Elisir d'Amore* and 'Celeste Aïda' to sing, though without the introductory recitative which studio bosses felt would be asking too much from the audience. It was these brief moments that excited preview audiences during the tryout, and were ultimately to determine the direction of Lanza's career.

Although Grayson and Lanza were sent on a nationwide concert tour to drum up business for *That Midnight Kiss*, it did not exactly set the box-office alight when it opened in September 1949, but it did do respectable business and there was general agreement that Lanza was an exciting new star. He had, it was admitted at the studio, come into his own in the operatic arias. Audiences who had heard other tenors in the cinema, suddenly found one with whom they could identify totally. Not only did Lanza possess a fine voice, he also possessed an earthy realism which touched those who knew nothing about opera. MGM decided to press ahead with plans to turn him and Grayson, whose career had not been going that well, into the new MacDonald and Eddy, and the following month they were rushed into a film with the working title *Kiss of Fire*. Renamed *The Toast of New Orleans*, it had a conventional story of a local fisherman with a voice who becomes a renowned opera singer. Norman Taurog was again the director and the supporting cast included J. Carroll Naish, Rita Moreno and David Niven.

During the filming of *That Midnight Kiss*, Lanza had begun to show signs of becoming difficult. He had accused the 70-year-old Ethel Barrymore of trying to upstage him, and he upset the film crew with some crude exhibitionism which included urinating in a bucket within view of Kathryn Grayson while she was trying to film her close-ups.

By the time he got on set for *The Toast of New Orleans*, he was deliberately being difficult, arriving late and drinking and eating to excess, which meant his weight fluctuated alarmingly. The studio was naturally concerned and a deep mistrust developed between MGM and its new star which was to have important repercussions later.

Special songs were written for *The Toast of New Orleans* by Nicholas Brodszky and Sammy Cahn, one of which, 'Be my love', was to become Lanza's signature tune. The amount of opera he was permitted to sing was increased significantly. He sang the Flower Song from *Carmen*, 'O Paradiso' from *L'Africaine*, 'M'appari' from *Martha*, 'Libiamo' from *La Traviata* and 'Stolta paura l'amor' from *Madama Butterfly*.

Contractually, Kathryn Grayson had top billing but there's no doubt that the film, just as *That Midnight Kiss* had been, was a vehicle for Lanza, and for Lanza to sing opera. Despite all the reservations at MGM, audiences around the world didn't just suffer the operatic excerpts while waiting for the more popular stuff, they lapped it up and wanted more. Lanza's fresh voice, his committed singing and the power of his personality, opened people's ears to the glories of opera in a way no other singer on screen before or since has quite managed to do. He became a pop star, mobbed by women and autograph hunters wherever he went. Within six months of *The Toast of New Orleans* being released, 'Be my love' was at the top of the charts. Lanza albums outsold all others. Not since Frank Sinatra a decade earlier had a singer taken the public by storm in such a manner. And, whatever the critics might have said about his ability or inability to sustain an operatic role or, another frequent charge, that he was only in films because he couldn't sing properly, Lanza was not a pop singer but an opera singer.

Before *The Toast of New Orleans* even opened, Lanza was at work on his next picture. Louis B. Mayer used to refer to him as his Caruso, and it was with Enrico Caruso that Lanza was most often compared. It was not entirely coincidence, Lanza was certain, that Caruso had died the same year that he was born and it was, he felt, inevitable that when the biopic of the great tenor was made, it should be Lanza playing him.

The project to make a film about Caruso had been brought to MGM by the legendary producer Jesse Lasky, then in his seventies and in semi-retirement. Lasky, many years earlier, had lost a small fortune producing Caruso's two silent films, *My Cousin* and *A Splendid Romance*. In 1945, he was at a performance of Gershwin's *Rhapsody in Blue* when he met Caruso's widow, Dorothy. He mentioned that he had always wanted to make a film of her husband's life but had not yet started research for the screenplay. Dorothy told him not to bother since she had just written her book, *Enrico Caruso: His Life and Death*. She sent him a copy, Lasky bought the rights for $100,000 (the amount he is supposed to have lost on his Caruso films in 1918) and set about finding a studio interested in the project. His intention was to cast an unknown in the leading role who would mime to Caruso's recordings. Dorothy wanted herself to be played by Joan Fontaine.

Lasky could not get anyone interested. But the arrival on the scene of Lanza convinced Lasky (who had been at his Hollywood Bowl debut) that the project was once again viable with Lanza himself singing, not miming to Caruso's records. He went to see Mayer at MGM, offering to co-produce the film. Mayer was enthusiastic and in December 1949 the film was announced for production. But Mayer's colleagues, in particular producer Dore Schary, did not share Mayer's enthusiasm. Schary, an urbane New Yorker whom Mayer had originally pulled out of MGM's scriptwriting pool, was about to oust Mayer and become MGM's head of production. He did all he could to oppose the film. He disliked Lanza with an intensity bordering on hatred (no one seems to know quite why), considering his films to be worthless. *The Toast of New Orleans*, he stated publicly, had bombed. In fact it was MGM's most profitable film of 1950. He felt, in any case, that Lanza was too young to play Caruso. And television was beginning to hit the film industry hard. MGM's profits were down alarmingly, and Schary could not see any financial justification for an expensive film which would, by its very nature, have to contain an awful lot of opera. It was not, he felt, the way to revive flagging public interest in the cinema.

Mayer, however, got his way and a screenplay was ordered based on Dorothy's biography. Lanza was immediately put on a diet and sent on a rigorous six-week training programme at Ginger Rogers' ranch in Oregon. He lost 40 pounds.

Lanza didn't just play the role of Caruso. He studied film footage of the singer, he listened to his recordings again and again, and he even dressed like Caruso. The press began to wonder if he had gone off his head. 'Is Mario Lanza Looney?' asked one headline.

The Great Caruso, directed by Richard Thorpe, was a highly romanticised account of the singer's life with no mention of previous children, affairs or any other facts that might get in the way of sanitised storytelling. Despite the fact that he met and married Dorothy Benjamin only four years before he died, their marriage, against the wishes of her wealthy father, formed the basis of most of the film. Dorothy (played in the film by Ann Blyth) disliked the end result and was scathing about Lanza. In Italy the Caruso family took out an injunction against the film and MGM was ordered to withdraw all copies in Italy and pay the family five million lire in damages. The critics, especially music critics, were very sniffy about Lanza's attempts to fill Caruso's shoes. But the film was to do more to popularise opera than any single film before or since.

During the course of the film, Lanza sang some 21 arias and songs. He had demanded that the operatic sequences be staged by Peter Herman Adler, who was later to take charge of NBC's televised operas, and it was Adler who persuaded Joe Pasternak that the soloists and singers in the operatic excerpts had to be first-rate. If they were second-rate or not really opera singers, he said, the film itself would end up being third-rate. Pasternak accepted his argument and so Metropolitan Opera artists Dorothy Kirsten, Blanche Thebom and Nicola Moscona, together with Giuseppe Valdengo, Gilbert Russell and members of the Met's chorus, were signed up to appear with Lanza.

Kirsten was a protégé of that influential film singer, Grace Moore. She had been working as a telephonist, singing the occasional radio date, when a columnist heard her and mentioned her to Moore. Moore paid for her to study in Italy with Gigli's teacher, and on her return from Italy, Kirsten made her debut in Chicago in 1940 singing Pousette in *Manon*. She was soon singing roles such as Nedda, Micaela and Musetta. She then moved to the New York City Opera, making guest appearances in San Francisco, Mexico City, New Orleans and Montreal. She made her Met debut in 1945 singing Mimi, the start of a 30-year association with the house which included such roles as Violetta, Marguerite, Butterfly and Tosca. She always vowed she would never sing the part of Louise while Moore was still alive. Moore died in January 1947. In December Kirsten sang the role for the first time at the Met, dedicating the performance to her mentor. In 1950, she had made her first film appearance in *Mr. Music*, a remake of the 1935 *Accent on Youth* about a college girl falling for a middle-aged songwriter. Kirsten was in one scene playing herself and singing 'Accidents will happen' with the film's star, Bing Crosby.

Blanche Thebom was another stalwart of the Met. She had been born in Pennsylvania and started singing with the company on tour. She first appeared in New York in 1944 singing Fricka and became a well-known Carmen. Her overseas engagements included Covent Garden and Glyndebourne where she sang Dorabella in 1950. She, too, had made one previous film appearance, singing with Leonard Warren in an operatic sequence in *Irish Eyes Are Smiling* (1944). Nicola Moscona was one of the Met's principal basses singing everything from Ramfis in *Aïda* to Sparafucile in *Rigoletto*, while the baritone Guiseppe Valdengo was another Italian to have made his main career in the States. He had made his debut in Parma singing Figaro in 1936, made his debut at La Scala in 1939 and then spent the war playing the oboe in an army band. After the war, he returned to La Scala where he was spotted by Toscanini, who took him to New York for a television production of *Otello*. He stayed and began to sing in the American houses, making his Met debut in 1947 as Tonio.

During the course of *The Great Caruso*, Lanza was joined by Kirsten and Thebom for 'O terra addio' from *Aïda*, and by Kirsten and Thebom again for the finale from *Martha* (with Moscona). He sang arias such as 'Vesti la giubba', 'Cielo e mar' from *La Gioconda*, 'La donna e mobile', 'Che gelida manina', 'E lucevan le stelle', the quartet from *Rigoletto* (with Thebom, Olive Mae Beach and Valdengo), a duet from *Il Trovatore* (with Lucine Amara, who had just made her debut at the Met and was later to appear at Glyndebourne as

Ariadne) and the Sextet from *Lucia* (with Kirsten, Thebom, Gilbert Russell, Valdengo and Moscona). In an excerpt from *Cavalleria Rusticana*, he was partnered by Marina Koshetz, daughter of Nina. The Czech soprano Jarmila Novotná was also in the film playing a diva, though, sadly, she did not get to sing.

The Great Caruso was given a star-studded Hollywood preview in April 1951, before it opened in May at Radio City Music Hall, New York, to break all box-office records. When it was released around the world, in the process introducing millions of people to opera, it was equally successful. It was MGM's biggest earner in 1951 and the studio's twelfth most profitable film of all time. The LP of the soundtrack became the first classical album to sell a million copies.

The film genre of the musical containing operatic arias, which was supposedly dying if not actually dead, had been brought back to life in a spectacular fashion by a comparatively low-budget movie. In Italy, *Enrico Caruso: La Leggenda di Una Voce* (released as *The Young Caruso*) was rushed into production with the voice of Mario del Monaco being used for Caruso. Based on a novel, Giacomo Gentilomo's film purported to tell the story of Caruso's early life in Naples and how he got his first chance. The actor Ermanno Randi, who was killed by his jealous boyfriend a few months after finishing the film, played Caruso, while the part of Stella, the girl he loves, was played by Gina Lollobrigida (with her singing voice dubbed by Dhia Cristiani). The film was no more true to Caruso's life than *The Great Caruso* had been and the Caruso family took out an injunction against it as well. Both injunctions were eventually lifted, and *The Young Caruso* with Gina Lollobrigida oustanding, was among Italy's top ten box-office draws of the year.

Lanza's next film, first suggested to him by Pasternak during the filming of *The Great Caruso*, was due to be Sigmund Romberg's *The Student Prince*, a choice, everyone agreed, that would be the perfect follow-up to *The Great Caruso*. It overflowed with lovely melodies, it was 'serious', it was a good story, it would showcase Lanza's talents to their best advantage. It took longer than anticipated to get the production moving and Lanza was asked to knock off another pot-boiler instead. In *Because You're Mine*, he played a famous opera singer drafted into the army, who falls in love with his sergeant's sister and sings a lot.

Lanza felt that for someone who had just played Caruso the film was a retrograde step and he let everyone know just how he felt. The story and everything about it, he said repeatedly, was junk. Pasternak justified his decision to put Lanza into *Because You're Mine* by saying that he didn't want him to become fixed in the public's mind as just an opera singer.

There had also been changes in MGM's top management: Louis B. Mayer, who had first signed Lanza and supported him against all comers had finally lost his battle with Dore Schary and left the company. Lanza knew Schary did not think much of him and did what he always did in times of stress, went on almighty binges. His weight ballooned and filming on *Because You're Mine* had to be postponed while he was ordered to go on yet another diet.

Weight was always a problem for Lanza and there is a scene in the film in which he goes from outside a barrack-room looking quite thin, to emerge inside looking as though he has been padded. Throughout filming, the wardrobe department had its work cut out remaking his clothes. Nor was Lanza's temper helped by the fact that he took a great dislike to his co-star, Doretta Morrow.

In the film, Lanza sang the title song written for him by Brodszky and Cahn (nominated for an Oscar but beaten to it by the theme song from *High Noon*), the song 'Granada', which he was the first to popularise, and a Lord's Prayer which Lanza himself insisted on including. The operatic arias came from *Rigoletto, Cavalleria Rusticana* and *L'Africaine*.

By the time *Because You're Mine* was released, *The Student Prince* was ready to go into production. As a sop to Lanza, Brodszky, who had written 'Be my love', was allowed to interpolate new songs into the score, a job he did so well that many people think 'Summertime in Heidelberg' and 'Beloved' were actually written by Romberg. Ann Blyth, Lanza's co-star in *The Great Caruso*, was engaged to recreate their successful partnership.

Lanza had, as usual, pre-recorded the songs and duly appeared at the first rehearsal. The director, Curtis Bernhardt, working with Lanza for the first time, made the great mistake of criticising the way he sang 'Beloved'. Lanza's immediate reaction was to walk off the set. So began a locked-horns struggle between MGM and their star. Lanza was determined, come what may, he would not return until Bernhardt was sacked. He began to eat again and when, under the threat of legal action if he didn't go back, he suddenly reappeared on the set, he was considerably fatter than when anyone had last seen him. No filming could take place, there was one final row between Lanza and Schary, and Lanza left the studio never to return. *The Student Prince* was cancelled and MGM took legal steps to ensure that Lanza could not work anywhere else until the fifteen months left on his contract had run out.

Joe Pasternak never lost hope that one day he would film *The Student Prince* and MGM finally called off its lawsuit against Lanza when the singer agreed that his pre-recordings could be used in any new film even though he would not be appearing on screen. The man chosen to replace Lanza and mime to the recordings was the British actor Edmund Purdom, who had been spotted on stage with Laurence Olivier in a production of *Antony and Cleopatra*. The final irony was that by the time everything was sorted out and the cameras were ready to roll, Curtis Bernhardt, whose comments had sparked the crisis in the first place, was no longer available. The director brought in to replace him was Richard Thorpe, who had directed Lanza so successfully in *The Great Caruso*. Lanza refused to go and see the film, which only did moderate business at the box-office, and until the day he died it was a taboo subject in front of him.

Lanza's relationship with MGM may have ended acrimoniously, but other studios were still interested in him and as soon as his contract with MGM had expired he was signed by Warner Bros. to appear in *Serenade* (1956), an adaptation of the James M. Cain novel about homosexuality between a poor peasant boy with a voice and his impresario. There was absolutely no hint of this in the film, of course, which simply became another vehicle for one Lanza song after another. The impresario became a woman (Joan Fontaine) and the Cain plot was reduced to an eternal triangle between her and her rival for his affections, Sarita Montiel. Vincent Price was also in the cast as was the soprano Licia Albanese who had appeared with Caruso and was a regular partner at the Met of Gigli. Together, she and Lanza sang a fifteen-minute excerpt from Act Three of *Otello*. Albanese was very impressed by Lanza's voice and Lanza always said that he hoped one day to sing *Otello* with her on stage.

Serenade included generous chunks of opera: 'Amor ti vieta' from *Fedora*, 'O soave fanciulla' from *La Bohème* (sung with soprano Jean Fenn), 'O Paradiso' from *L'Africaine*, 'Di quella pira' from *Il Trovatore*, 'Di rigori armato' from *Der Rosenkavalier*, and 'Nessun dorma'. Lanza also sang 'Torna a Surriento', 'La danza', Schubert's Ave Maria, 'My destiny' and the film's title song, 'Serenade'.

Filming took place on location in Mexico but Lanza, still under stress from his battle with MGM, was drinking heavily. His weight battles and a poor script, combined to produce a mediocre film, and while it was agreed that Lanza was in fine voice, fashions were changing so fast that the film did not do as well as hoped for at the box-office. Younger filmgoers in particular did not enjoy the sentimentality of plots which were simply vehicles for stars from a previous generation to sing songs, even if those songs did include an excellent rendering from *Otello*. Interest in the film quickly tailed off and a couple of other film projects Lanza was discussing were quietly shelved.

Shortly after he had finished *Serenade*, however, Lanza was offered a film in Italy. He jumped at the opportunity to visit the land of his forefathers and, as he told the press, study opera in the great opera houses of Europe prior to his own return to the legitimate stage. When he arrived by ship in Naples several thousand people turned out to welcome him, including Caruso's son. Lanza made a pilgrimage to see Caruso's grave on the hillside above the poor part of Naples in which the great tenor had been born before travelling on to Rome to begin filming.

The Seven Hills of Rome was another undemanding Lanza vehicle in which he was cast as a world-famous tenor down on his luck in Rome following heavy gambling losses in Monte Carlo. His co-stars included Renato Rascel, Peggie Castle and Marisa Allasio, known as the Brigitte Bardot of Italy, an epithet which led to Lanza thinking he was going to be working with Bardot herself. He was not over-pleased when he discovered his mistake.

The film was low-budget and shot with old equipment by inexperienced technicians. His co-stars could not speak English and the script was rewritten every day. Lanza began to drink heavily and over-eat, the producers accused him of being too drunk to film and the production was cancelled. Lanza's manager flew to Rome, Lanza agreed to give up alcohol, and production recommenced. Although there were still alarms, filming was completed and the film opened at the beginning of 1958 to surprisingly warm reviews.

With the exception of the aria from *Rigoletto*, 'Questo quella', during the recording of which he broke down so that the finished film had to use a recording made in 1950, Lanza sang only popular numbers such as 'Arrivederci, Roma'. Even though 'Arrivederci Roma' got into the singles charts, Lanza was aware that he was slipping as a performer. The producers said they wanted to show a more casual side to him but Lanza dismissed his performance as terrible and the film as lousy.

Lanza's final film was also made in Rome when he signed to appear in *For the First Time* (1959). The producer, Alex Gruter, realised he had taken on a problem the moment he met his new leading man. Lanza was bloated, nervous and withdrawn. Gruter suggested he go to a clinic in Austria but the tenor refused. Instead, in a mood of deep depression, he drank even harder. Finally Gruter did persuade him to go to the clinic where, although he cheated by sneaking out for a drink, he did lose weight and emerged refreshed and ready to commence pre-recording. This took place at the Rome Opera House and he sang the aria 'Nium mi tema' from *Otello*, the triumphal scene from *Aïda*, 'Vesti la giubba' and the trio from *Cosi Fan Tutte*. Chorus members, prepared to scoff at this Hollywood-created singer, marvelled instead at the voice they actually heard. Lanza, it was said, so impressed all who heard him that he was asked about his availability for operatic engagements. It was even rumoured that he had accepted to sing Cavaradossi in the Rome Opera's production of *Tosca* due to open the 1960 season.

In *For the First Time*, directed by Rudy Maté who had earned five Oscar nominations as a cinematographer, Lanza played a hard-drinking, temperamental opera singer who misses a performance and goes to Capri to hide. There he falls in love with a deaf girl who regains her hearing and returns his love. The story was the usual banal fare of such films but Lanza's singing and acting were back to their best.

The film was shot in Austria and Germany and on Capri. It opened in the middle of 1959 to goodish reviews but failed to attract a sizeable audience. Of all Lanza's films, it took the least at the box-office. A few months later, Lanza was dead. He died following a heart attack in Rome on 7 October 1959. He was 38. His career had lasted barely ten years during which time he had appeared in seven films (discounting *Winged Victory*), made innumerable recordings and brought pleasure to millions. In Spain, one seven-year-old boy watching *The Great Caruso* on the silver screen was determined to become an opera singer like Lanza. His name: José Carreras. Pavarotti, Domingo, even the baritone Thomas Allen have all testified to the enormous influence Lanza had in shaping their lives and musical tastes.

Lanza had something that was thrilling. He had an animal passion and, despite his constant weight problems, Italianate good looks. He looked like a singer. More than that, he clearly enjoyed singing and could communicate that enjoyment whether singing an operatic aria or a popular song. He never differentiated between the two. He took often banal lyrics and sugar-sweet tunes and made them memorable in a way few other singers have managed. He, and his voice, came off the screen and, quite simply, touched people's hearts.

Lanza rarely found favour with music critics. It was often said, as a putdown, that he could never sustain a complete stage role. That was not true, for he sang those two performances of *Madama Butterfly* at the beginning of his career. What is true is that he was a phenomenal tenor who became lost to the operatic stage. Part of his personal angst seems to have been that he was aware that he should have been on the stage. A planned appearance with the San Francisco Opera in *Andrea Chénier* with Renata Tebaldi in 1951 was put on hold because he had to go on a film promotional tour (his place was taken by a young Italian tenor making his American debut, Mario del Monaco). He had been invited to return to New Orleans and had agreed, but somehow could never quite manage to fix a date. When interviewed and asked about future stage engagements, he was always about to accept an offer to sing the following year at La Scala, the Met, at Covent Garden, wherever. But the following year never came.

Mario Lanza may have been a loss to the stage and it was a great shame that none of the plans for him to record a complete opera ever came to fruition. But he will live on as one of the greatest and most influential of all tenors simply by virtue of what he gave on the screen.

11

The Fifties

The Great Caruso is, arguably, the most influential opera film ever made. Not only did it inspire singers such as Domingo, Pavarotti and Carreras, it also introduced millions worldwide to opera. Attendances at opera houses in America, and at the Met in particular, rose as a direct result of the film. It also spawned a rash of operatic biopics as producers everywhere, not just in Hollywood, tried to cash in on the Lanza effect.

Hot on the heels of *The Great Caruso* came Italy's *The Young Caruso* with Mario Del Monaco and Gina Lollobrigida, followed by a biography of Puccini directed by Carmine Gallone, and one of Mascagni directed by Giacomo Gentilomo. Both contained operatic sequences performed by actors and dubbed by singers. In the USSR, there was a biopic of Rimsky-Korsakov featuring the bass Alexander Ognivtsev as Chaliapin and members of the Kirov performing excerpts from *Sadko*, *The Tale of Tsar Sultan*, *The Snow Maiden* and *The Golden Cockerel*. Also in the Soviet Union, a biopic of Glinka contained sequences from *Ivan Susanin* and *Ruslan and Ludmilla* plus an appearance as Liszt by the eminent Soviet pianist, Sviatoslav Richter.

Britain's response to *The Great Caruso* was to cast Patrice Munsel in *Melba*, a biopic of the great Australian diva who had died in 1931. Born Helen Porter Mitchell, Melba had arrived in London to audition for Sir Arthur Sullivan. He told her she could have a part in one of his operas if she studied, so she went to Paris to do just that and nine months later made her operatic debut in Brussels singing Gilda. She was an immediate success, going on to become one of the most famous people in the world, an extraordinary woman as well as an extraordinary singer.

Patrice Munsel was an American soprano, born and bred in Spokane, Washington, who had made her Met debut, after winning a competition, in 1943 singing Philine in *Mignon*. Risë Stevens sang the title role, James Melton was Wilhelm and Beecham conducted. Munsel was eighteen and had never been on stage before, having only made her debut with a professional orchestra a few months earlier. The press, irritated by the hype that surrounded her debut, went after her in a big way. She was not put off, however, and went on to appear at the Met for fifteen consecutive seasons appearing in a repertoire that spanned Lucia, Olympia in *The Tales of Hoffmann*, and Juliette, to *The Golden Cockerel*, *The Barber of Seville*, *Die Fledermaus* and *La Périchole*. During the course of *Melba*, she sang many of the arias associated with the diva, especially from *La Bohème*. The film was directed by Lewis Milestone (*All Quiet on the Western Front*), and Munsel's co-stars were Sybil Thorndyke as Queen Victoria, Martita Hunt as her teacher Mathilde Marchesi, and Robert Morley as the impresario Oscar Hammerstein.

Morley was in the next British operatic biopic, *The Story of Gilbert and Sullivan*, playing Gilbert to Maurice Evans' Sullivan. The film was produced and directed by Frank Launder and Sidney Gilliat, two film-makers noted for their gentle comedies of English life and manners such as *The Happiest Days of Your Life*, *The Belles of St Trinians* and *Lady Godiva Rides Again*. Their company, London Films, was about to celebrate its 21st anniversary in 1953, and they persuaded Alexander Korda to back the film. It was an odd choice for Korda, who loathed Gilbert and Sullivan and disliked musicals generally, but the success of *The Great Caruso* plus the vast army of Gilbert and Sullivan fans that Launder and Gilliat assured him were out there waiting for such a film made him agree to put up the money. His reservations were not allayed when he read the script. He found their life story dull, the only high spot being the collaboration which both despised. 'From this I can't see a film,' Korda remarked.

He was right. The production was lavish, expensive, and, as he suspected, dull. Scripted as a springboard for a succession of musical numbers, it displeased the Gilbert and Sullivan fans who disliked Morley and Evans and wanted more music; it displeased ordinary cinema-goers who thought there was too much music.

Hollywood had better luck with *Tonight We Sing* (1953), the biography of the Russian-born impresario Sol Hurok who did so much to help introduce opera to America with his tours of famous singers. Ezio Pinza played Chaliapin, singing arias from *Boris Godunov* and *Faust*, Roberta Peters played Elsa Valdine singing 'Sempre libera', and Jan Peerce provided the voice for Gregory Lawrence.

Since everyone wanted a biopic of an opera singer, what could be more natural than to make one of the singer who had started the opera boom on sound film back in the thirties, Grace Moore? *So This Is Love* (1953) starred Kathryn Grayson as the small-town girl who gets to sing at the Met, ending the film with an aria from *La Bohème*.

When it came to tenors on which to base a life story who better than Richard Tauber, who had died in 1948? *Du bist die Welt für mich* was an Austrian film starring Rudolf Schock which told of Tauber's rise to fame and his love for a ballerina who had to give up dancing because of heart problems. Schock mimed to Tauber recordings.

11. The Fifties

Lives of composers were also good opportunities for dropping in the odd aria. Tito Gobbi, Mario del Monaco, Orietta Moscucci and Vito de Taranto were among the singers who appeared in *Verdi, King of Melody*. *Eternal Waltz* told the life story of Johann Strauss and included a scene from *Indigo*, his first operetta. Carmine Gallone reshot his 1935 Bellini biopic *Casta Diva* (1954) in Technicolor with Antonella Lualdi in the Marta Eggerth role as Maddalena.

Helen Traubel, noted as the finest American Wagnerian soprano of her time, (and the woman about whom Rudolf Bing, director of the Met, once commented in exasperation, following yet another bust-up between them, 'Nobody knows the Traubels I've seen') appeared in *Deep in My Heart* (1954), a lavish biopic of Sigmund Romberg directed by Stanley Donen with José Ferrer as Romberg, Merle Oberon as his wife, Rosemary Clooney and guest stars that included Gene Kelly, Cyd Charisse, Jane Powell, Ann Miller and Howard Keel. Traubel played the woman running the restaurant where Romberg worked as a waiter while trying to get his first break. She sang some of his songs, some in duet with Ferrer.

The soprano whom Traubel had succeeded in Wagnerian roles at the Met was herself the subject of a moving biopic. *Interrupted Melody* (1955) was the life story of the Australian soprano Marjorie Lawrence, with Eleanor Parker as Lawrence, Glenn Ford and Roger Moore. The director was the man who had sparked off the row between Lanza and MGM, Curtis Bernhardt. Lawrence had studied in Paris and appeared in Monte Carlo and Lille before making her debut at the Paris Opéra as Ortrud in 1933. She was soon singing such roles as Brünnhilde, Salome, Aïda, Rachel in *La Juive* and Donna Anna. The Met became interested in her and made several attempts to lure her to New York (Edward Johnson wanted her to audition; she sent him a message that he could hear her anytime at the Paris Opéra), and in 1936 she finally made her debut there as Brünnhilde. She knocked out the press by leaping onto Grane at the end of *Götterdämmerung* and riding into Siegmund's funeral pyre, the first Wagnerian soprano to be able to accomplish this feat for many a year. In the summer of 1941, however, she contracted polio. She refused to abandon singing and two years later was back at the Met singing, from a couch, the role of Venus in *Tannhäuser*. She also sang other roles seated, including Isolde.

Lawrence recorded nine arias for *Interrupted Melody* (based on her autobiography of the same name) but they were not used. Instead, Eileen Farrell re-recorded them. The film was nominated for two Oscars and won one for its screenplay.

Another soprano, Lina Cavalieri, who had died in an air-raid on Florence in 1944, was remembered in *The Most Beautiful Woman in the World*, with Gina Lollobrigida as Cavalieri. Her co-stars were Vittorio Gassman and Robert Alda, and she herself sang 'Vissi d'arte' from *Tosca*. The tenor Gino Sinimberghi, who had provided the singing voice for several other actors, appeared as Cavalieri's tenor lover with his singing voice provided by Mario del Monaco.

The film, Lollobrigida's last in Italian, was a huge success in Italy and remains her biggest hit there. In Spain, Alfredo Kraus took the lead in *Gayarre*, a biopic of Julián Gayarre, the most famous Spanish tenor of the nineteenth century. Born in Pamplona, Gayarre appeared in the major houses of Europe, creating the role of Enzo in *La Giaconda*. When he was 45, he collapsed on stage in Madrid during a performance of *The Pearl Fishers* and died. His life was the perfect vehicle for the movies. In the American film *The Day I Met Caruso* (1956), about the singer meeting a small girl on the train, the role of Caruso was played by Lotfi Mansouri, later to become an important opera producer. He mimed to Caruso recordings.

In 1954 Carmine Gallone directed one of the most lavish productions of his career when he made *Casa Ricordi*, the story of the Milanese music publishing house. Described by Ken Wlaschin as 'Hollywood meets the Tiber', the film was a romantic and romanticised tribute to nineteenth-century Italian opera with a host of stars both singing and not singing. Tito Gobbi and Giulio Neri sang scenes from *The Barber of Seville* after Rossini had finished both writing it and having a passionate affair; Mario del Monaco played Francesco Tamagno the tenor who created the role of Otello and is seen singing the final scene; Renata Tebaldi sang Mimi's dying aria and there are appearances by Giuletta Simionato, Gianni Poggi and Italo Tajo. The actors taking part include Paolo Stoppa as the original Ricordi, Marcello Mastroianni, who was to become an international Italian heart throb after *La Dolce Vita*, as Donizetti, Maurice Ronet as Bellini and Gabriele Ferzetti as Puccini. The film was a smash hit in Italy and did well overseas.

It wasn't just biopics that were given a new lease of life by *The Great Caruso*. All films with operatic excerpts were suddenly back in fashion. The Italian bass Ezio Pinza had retired from the operatic stage in 1948, the year after making his first feature, *Carnegie Hall*. In 1949 he had made his Broadway debut in *South Pacific*, singing Emile de Becque, the role Rodgers and Hammerstein had written with him in mind. On the lookout for musical talent, MGM had signed him up to appear in *Mr. Imperium* (1951), playing an exiled king in Hollywood in love with movie star Lana Turner and leaving her for the sake of his country. He didn't sing opera but songs by Harold Arlen.

Then came *The Great Caruso* and Pinza was immediately rushed into *Strictly Dishonorable* (1951), playing a rakish opera star who has a whirl with Janet Leigh and decides to marry her in order to save her reputation. During the course of the film Pinza appeared in a scene from an opera written especially for it by Mario Castelnuovo-Tedesco, the composer who had fled from his native Italy in 1939 to escape anti-Semitism and settled in Los Angeles writing music for the cinema. The opera was called *Il Ritorno de Cesare* and Pinza sang an aria of the same name with Leigh as his sword bearer. He also sang 'Le veau d'or' from *Faust*.

On the lookout for potential stars, Paramount offered Robert Merrill, the leading baritone at the Met, the leading role in *Aaron Slick from Punkin Crick*, opposite Dinah Shore. Rudolf Bing ordered him to stay and go on the company tour but Merrill chose Hollywood with the result that Bing fired him. Not until Merrill made a public apology would Bing have him back. *Aaron Slick* was as American as apple pie with some nice songs (no opera), but it did not turn Merrill into a movie star, so he apologised and returned to opera.

Lauritz Melchior, who had not appeared in a film for three years, was brought back for *Stars are Singing* (1953), playing a former star of the Met who befriends a young Polish refugee (Anna Maria Alberghetti), who wants to be an opera singer and has entered the United States illegally. Norman Taurog directed.

Operas, too, found their way onto the screen in increasing numbers. In true Hollywood tradition, a lavish remake of *The Merry Widow* (1952) went into production with Fernando Lamas (replacing first choice Ricardo Montalban), Lana Turner (dubbed by Trudy Erwin) and Una Merkel. The film received Oscar nominations for its costumes and sets but turned out to be exceedingly dull. 'Nothing has been omitted', wrote one critic, 'except the spirit of the original.'

In Europe, film-makers and singers returned to opera and operetta with fervour. Jan Kiepura and Marta Eggerth appeared in Lehár's *The Land of Smiles*, directed by Hans Deppe. While the music came from the Lehár operetta, the story was not entirely the same. Eggerth played a Viennese operetta star who marries a Siamese prince and returns with him to Bangkok where their different cultures impose strains upon their relationship. The Bangkok sequences were shot on location.

Members of the Vienna State Opera including Paul Schoffler, Hilde Gueden, Erich Kunz, Hilde Zadek, Wilma Lipp and Ludwig Weber, performed extracts from *Die Entführung aus dem Serail*, *Don Giovanni* and *The Marriage of Figaro* in the Austrian feature *Unsterblicher Mozart* (Immortal Mozart, 1954), while in Sweden, Jussi Björling was cast as himself in *Resan till dej* (The Journey to You, 1953), directed by Stig Olin, and was seen singing 'Celeste Aïda' and the Swedish song 'Till havs' in a radio concert.

Hollywood may had found its new singing star in Mario Lanza, but the French cinema discovered its own version in the Spanish tenor Luis Mariano. José Carreras has paid tribute to Lanza many times for being the person who inspired him to sing. His other early screen idol was Mariano. It didn't matter that the plots of his films were often formulaic or insipid. They were designed, like so many others, to show off the voice, and Carreras, along with millions of others in France and Spain, was thrilled.

Mariano had fled from Spain in 1936 when he was 22 to escape the Spanish Civil War and settled in France where he made his operatic debut in Paris in 1943 singing Ernesto in *Don Pasquale*. It was as the star of operetta that he became best known, especially those of Francis Lopez, who, like Mariano, had been born in Spain but worked in France. Trained as a dentist, Lopez had had his first hit in 1945 with *La Belle de Cadix*, starring Mariano. It ran for two years in Paris and had the same effect on the French musical as *Oklahoma!* had on the American musical.

Mariano had made his first film, *Historie de Chanter*, in 1946, singing the role of the Duke in a performance of *Rigoletto* and Alfredo in *La Traviata*. In 1950, he appeared in a film of Lopez's operetta, *Andalouise*, as the bullfighter Juanito, the role he had created in the theatre. He also recreated the role of Carlos in the film version of *La Belle de Cadix* directed by Raymond Bernard in 1953. Both the Lopez films were enormous box-office successes in France and Spain.

In Italy, Tagliavini, Schipa, Gigli and Gobbi all appeared in further films which included sequences of them singing, and Giuseppe di Stefano made his film debut in *Canto per te* (1953), as a tenor having trouble with a policeman who wants his girl. Gallone made a version of *Cavalleria Rusticana* (1953) starring Anthony Quinn, also entitled *Fatal Desire* (with Tito Gobbi's voice), and Sophia Loren became an international star when she took on the title role in Clemente Fracassi's film of *Aïda* (1953). She didn't sing but mimed to the voice of Renata Tebaldi. Amneris was played by Lois Maxwell and dubbed by Ebe Stignani.

The most important opera film of the early fifties was of Gian Carlo Menotti's *The Medium* (1951). Menotti had written his two-act chamber opera about a bogus clairvoyant who suddenly finds she really is psychic, in 1946. It was first produced at Columbia University, and transferred to Broadway within a year but was far from being a smash hit. It played to empty houses until Menotti invited Toscanini, a friend of his mother, to see it. Toscanini enjoyed the evening and returned to see it twice more. Since Toscanini featured regularly in the gossip columns and was a person to be seen with, everyone who was anyone in New York, decided they, too, had to be seen at the show. *The Medium* became the first contemporary opera to enjoy a run on the Great White Way.

Menotti cast Marie Powers, Anna Maria Alberghetti and Leo Coleman in the principal roles for the film and decided to direct himself. Realising his inexperience, he brought in Alexander Hammid to help him. The result cleverly mixes the interior of the medium's room with the world outside. Inside, wonderful camera movements with superb lighting and framing enhance the claustrophobic atmosphere in which the singing takes place. Outside, only the children playing in the streets sing. The two worlds are never allowed to impinge upon one another and the decision to film this way makes events which happen within the apartment appear even more bizarre. *The Medium* is a powerful film which does not resemble a stage work at which cameras have been pointed. Many consider it to be the best union of opera and cinema ever made. Menotti won an Oscar for the music but did not make any more films, a great loss.

Another major opera film was made in England in the early 1950s by Michael Powell and Emeric Pressburger. Looking for a follow-up to their enormously successful ballet film *The Red Shoes*, they had turned to Offenbach's *The Tales of Hoffmann* (1951).

They had been given the idea by Sir Thomas Beecham while working together on *The Red Shoes* in 1948. Beecham had mentioned that he wanted to be involved with a filmed opera. Powell and Pressburger asked him which one, to which Beecham replied either *La Bohème* or *Carmen*. In 1926 Powell had been a stills cameraman on the Jacques Feyder silent of *Carmen* made in France (starring Raquel Meller and based on the novel rather than the opera). He didn't like the idea of doing it as a film. It would, he objected, simply be a film of an opera. Nor was he that keen on *La Bohème* which he felt was so realistic it would have to be shot in a realistic manner. He wanted to do something different, something that would marry cinema and opera in the same way that *The Red Shoes* had married cinema and dance. Asked for something more suitable for such an approach, Beecham suggested *The Tales of Hoffmann*, the opera with which he had established his reputation as a conductor. Pressburger, who had played the violin for a production in Hungary, thought it perfect, while Powell felt Offenbach's name would guarantee box-office success. In 1949 they announced it as their next production.

Aware there would be the inevitable outcry when they cut passages to get the film to length, they went to see Beecham who sang through the entire score at the piano, suggesting which pieces might be lost. By the end of the session, the opera ran just over two hours. Alexander Korda, who was keen to be seen producing films of distinction as well as popularity, and had been toying with the idea of a life of Caruso with Mario Lanza in the lead, a project that never, for him anyway, materialised, wasn't too sure about a complete opera on film but nevertheless agreed to back them.

It was always their intention to film *The Tales of Hoffmann* not as a stage production with cameras on it, but as a through-composed piece of cinema filmed to playback. This was not for the convenience of the singers but because Powell wanted to free the camera from being subservient to the needs of a sound recordist. He shot it, in fact, as if it were a silent film.

In the title role of Hoffmann, Powell needed a singing actor who would both look good on camera and whose singing would satisfy Beecham. It was Beecham himself who suggested the American tenor Robert Rounseville. Born in Attleboro, Massachusets, Rounseville had started his career under the name of Robert Field, singing in night clubs, vaudeville and on radio. He had made his operatic debut with the New York City Opera as Pelléas opposite the Mélisande of Maggie Teyte, and continued to sing with the company until 1966. In 1951, the year Hoffmann was released, he was chosen by Stravinsky to create the role of Tom Rakewell in *The Rake's Progress* in Venice. After Hoffmann, he appeared on Broadway in Bernstein's *Candide* and made one more film, *Carousel* (1956) in which he sang the role of Mr. Snow opposite Claramae Bell.

Powell was happy to engage Rounseville but discovered that in front of camera he was wooden; 'as pliable as the Eiffel Tower' was his comment. American actress Ann Ayers, who had sung opera, was engaged to play Antonia. She and Rounseville were the only two to appear on screen and sing. Bruce Dargavel, a member of the Welsh National Opera, sang the roles of Coppelius, Dapertutto and Dr. Miracle for Robert Helpmann, Monica Sinclair sang Nicklaus (Pamela Brown), and Dorothy Bond was Olympia (Moira Shearer). Grahame Clifford, Murray Dickie, Margharita Grandi, Jean Alexander and Owen Brannigan provided the other singing voices.

It was originally planned that *The Tales of Hoffmann* would be shot on location in Venice and Munich. Powell eventually settled for the silent stage at Shepperton, then the largest in Europe. The way he intended to shoot to playback meant he did not need a sound stage. He also decided that all the optical tricks would be done in the camera rather than in post-production, so he would shoot with the camera upside down, run the film backwards to make the dolls jump from their boxes, use jump cuts and flash cuts (putting in a few frames of white just as Helpmann was seen to pass through a mirror). The result was a choreographed film of imagination and cohesion which did not cost a fortune, being made for under £300,000.

The Tales of Hoffmann received a charity premiere at the Metropolitan Opera House in New York on 1 April 1951, the first time a film had been shown there. It was well received just as it was two weeks later when shown in London. *The Tales of Hoffmann*, wrote the critic of the *Daily Telegraph*, will be a landmark in the history of the screen. *The Times* concurred: 'It is quite magnificent.' Cecil B. DeMille was moved to write Powell and Pressburger a fan letter for being the first to transfer an opera successfully to the screen.

Despite the plaudits, the film only just broke even. It was, according to Michael Korda's biography of his father, an expensive failure, a fiasco in which the cast was overwhelmed by the sets and costumes and the story vanished beneath the dancing and special effects. Exaggeration this might be, but Korda was certainly unhappy with the result and wanted the third act shortened. Powell and Pressburger refused and the inevitable row followed. In fact *The Tales of Hoffmann* picked up two prizes at Cannes, one a special prize for 'exceptional originality of transposition'. On a limited release, the film eventually managed to recover its costs. It was a ground-breaking film which left many in the audience nonplussed. Was it ballet? Was it opera? It did not conform to people's perceptions of either and was dismissed as a hotchpotch, not worth the celluloid it was printed on. Today it can be seen to be one of the masterpieces of cinematic opera.

The comparative failure of *Hoffmann* at the box-office did not stop Powell and Pressburger from thinking about putting more opera on the screen. For some time they had been wanting to make a film of Richard Strauss's *Salome*. Pressburger's alternative idea was a biographical film of Strauss centred on his favourite opera, *Der Rosenkavalier*. While Pressburger began writing the script, Powell went on a fund-raising trip to the United States. Robert Dowling, a New York millionaire, agreed to put up half the money, subject to script approval. Harry Cohn of Columbia offered to finance the entire project, again subject to script approval.

Pressburger's idea for *The Golden Years*, as he called the project, was that since the man and his music were so much part of each other, there was no need to be distracted by seeing the man. The camera became Strauss, who was only glimpsed occasionally in reflections until the very end of the film when the real Strauss would be seen in some home-shot footage taken at the composer's 85th birthday and given to Powell and Pressburger when they visited the Strauss villa near Munich.

When Dowling received the first draft, he simply didn't understand it and couldn't see how it would make a film. Cohn, too, was not enamoured and had grave reservations about the subject matter. Strauss had enjoyed a high public profile with the Nazis. He was politically doubtful. It was, Cohn felt, still too soon after the Second World War for someone with his background to be the subject of a Hollywood biopic.

The rejection of one Strauss led Powell and Pressburger to think of another. If Richard was unacceptable, said Pressburger, what about Johann? Why not a film of the most popular operetta ever written, *Die Fledermaus*? Powell wasn't too keen on the idea, but the more Pressburger thought about it, the more enthusiastic he became. When they had been setting up *The Tales of Hoffmann*, Korda had been shocked to discover that Powell had never seen *Fledermaus*, so sent them to see it in Vienna. At that time Vienna was divided into four sectors under the control of the United States, Britain, France and Russia. Their plane had been delayed by snow storms and when eventually it put down, it was in the Russian sector. It took them more than an hour to get special passes to cross over into the British zone and they arrived at the opera house just in time to see the final curtain come down.

The comic possibilities of this experience gave Pressburger the idea of updating *Die Fledermaus* to just after the war. So, in *Oh ... Rosalinda!!* (1955), as the film became known because, although neither Powell nor Pressburger liked the title, they couldn't think of a better one, Anthony Quayle's Orlofsky became a Russian general, Mel Ferrer (Alfred) became an American captain, Michael Redgrave (Eisenstein) was a French colonel and Dennis Price (Frank), an English major. The Bat Falke was played by Anton Walbrook, Rosalinda by Ludmilla Tcherina, and Adele by Anneliese Rothenberger.

This was not the exact cast they had wanted. Feelers had been put out to get, amongst others, Clemens Krauss to conduct, Bing Crosby to play Alfred, Maurice Chevalier for Eisenstein and Orson Welles as Orlofsky. Neither

Crosby nor Chevalier was interested but Welles agreed to give them three days filming in return for £30,000. He was, however, trying to raise the finance for one of his own films and as the shooting date drew closer and it became obvious he was not going to show up, they went for Quayle instead.

Having failed to get Crosby, they tried for José Ferrer who had just become a star playing Toulouse Lautrec in *Moulin Rouge*, but he wanted too much money and they ended up with Mel Ferrer (no relation). Michael Redgrave was cast in the part they had wanted Chevalier to play, and he, along with Anneliese Rothenberger, were the only two to sing their own roles. When Hilde Gueden, who was providing the voice for Rosalinda, discovered she would be singing opposite Redgrave, she refused to continue. Her place was taken by Sari Barabas. Alexander Young provided the voice for Mel Ferrer, Denis Dowling for Dennis Price and Walter Berry for Anton Walbrook.

Filming on *Oh … Rosalinda*!! was postponed for over a year and did not begin until early in 1955. Even then the finance was not completely in place and some of the stars, including Walbrook and Ferrer, initially took only part of their fees. On several occasions there was insufficent money in the bank to pay the crew.

Oh … Rosalinda!! was one of the first pictures to be shot in CinemaScope, the big screen format designed as part of the fightback against television. Its opening night in November 1955 was a huge disappointment to Powell and Pressburger. The audience was bored with a film that was seen as a throwback to earlier times, despite its contemporary setting. The critical reaction in the States was more favourable but the film failed to get a general release, a sale to television fell through and neither Powell nor Pressburger would look at the film again.

An interesting operatic curio from this time was Anthony Asquith's semi-documentary about Glyndebourne, *On Such a Night* (1955). An American tourist (David Knight) sees people in evening dress at London's Waterloo Station during the middle of the day and is intrigued. He decides to follow and finds himself at Glyndebourne in Sussex where he bumps into John Christie, founder of the opera festival. Christie just happens to have a spare dinner jacket available so invites him to the evening's performance. This is the peg for Asquith to make a film looking at the workings of Glyndebourne which includes footage of the Festival production of *The Marriage of Figaro* with Sesto Bruscantini as Figaro and Sena Jurinac as the Countess, in rehearsal and in performance. It is a fascinating film but the Christie family came to dislike so much the image of Glyndebourne that it portrayed so much that they managed to get it taken out of circulation for a time.

The opera boom of the Fifties came just at the right time for the revitalised German film industry, which returned to its great love, operetta. Georg Wildhagen followed up his *Marriage of Figaro* and *Merry Wives of Windsor* with Johann Strauss' *One Night in Venice*. *White Horse Inn*, directed by Willi Forst,

The Forester's Daughter, The Rose of Stamboul, Der Vetter aus Dingsda by Edward Kunneke, Carl Zeller's *Der Vogelhändler*, Fred Raymond's *Maske in Bleu, The Last Waltz*, Fall's *Die Frau Geschiedene, Die Blume von Hawaii* by Abraham, *Viktoria und ihr Hussar, The Gypsy Baron*, Lehár's *The Little Tsar* and *The World Is Beautiful, Die Fledermaus, Zar und Zimmermann, The Happy Wanderer* and *The Ball at the Savoy*, all appeared on the screen before 1955.

There were also two versions of *Don Giovanni*, the first a swashbuckling German film complete with duels, dancing and music in which all the actors were dubbed (Gottlob Frick providing the voice of the Commendatore); the other made by a director who had left Germany before the war. Hungarian-born Paul Czinner, had started his film career in Austria in 1919. Many of his early films drew on the traditions of contemporary German theatre but he also directed historical costume dramas. After the Nazis came to power in 1933, he and his wife Elisabeth Bergner, a frequent star of his films, moved to Britain. In the early 1950s he became interested in filming opera and ballet. His first opera film was of Herbert Graf's Salzburg production of *Don Giovanni* (1955) with Furtwängler conducting, Cesare Siepi in the title role, Elisabeth Grümmer (Donna Anna), Erna Berger (Zerlina), Anton Drermota (Ottavio), Otto Edelmann (Leporello) and Walter Berry (Masetto).

During the Salzburg season, Elisabeth Schwarzkopf had sung all six performances of Donna Elvira, and Czinner began shooting on the assumption that she would be playing the part on film. She then withdrew and Lisa Della Casa took over, her scenes having to be shot later and cut in. The reason for Schwarzkopf's late withdrawal was that her husband Walter Legge knew Czinner was planning to film *Der Rosenkavalier* next, and he was determined Schwarzkopf would sing the role of the Marschallin in it. During the season, Della Casa had sung five performances of the Marschallin to Schwarzkopf's one, and would logically have been expected to sing it on film. Although *Der Rosenkavalier* was not filmed for another five years, Legge's ploy worked: Schwarzkopf appeared as the Marschallin.

With both *Don Giovanni* and *Der Rosenkavalier*, Czinner was filming existing stage productions. Traditionally this would have been done with a single camera, altering the lighting after each set-up and repeating the action for any change of camera angle.

Influenced by the multi-camera techniques of television, Czinner decided to do something which now seems terribly obvious but at the time was revolutionary: he shot the performance with three film cameras rolling simultaneously. Czinner's films were not, as is frequently claimed, the first to be made of operas on the stage, but they were the first in which three film cameras were kept rolling throughout.

This was not, however, simply a filmed outside broadcast. There was still the important aspect of the sound, and since Czinner was making a film, he did not record the sound simultaneously with the picture. The usual way of making a musical film was to pre-record the soundtrack and let the singers mime to it during the take. Czinner decided to reverse the process. He got his singers to act the performance using half-voice. When they had to sing out, he got them to mime singing out. That way he ended up with a guide track which helped him in the editing. Once the picture had been cut, he got the singers to record the soundtrack to picture.

Both films, shot in colour, now look like early examples of television outside broadcasts but they were an important stepping stone in trying to answer the question of what opera on film should be. Should it be a simple record of a production? Or should it be something more creative, more cinematic? These were questions that would be asked many times.

Carmine Gallone, who had done so much to establish ways of filming opera, answered the question by making a 'realistic' film of *Madama Butterfly* (1955) which used Japanese actors miming to the voices of Italian singers.

Another hybrid was Roberto Rossellini's curious film of Arthur Honegger's 1938 oratorio *Jeanne d'Arc au Bucher* (Joan of Arc at the Stake) (1954) featuring his mistress Ingrid Bergman in the only non-singing role of Joan. Rossellini had been invited to direct a stage production of this part-oratorio, part-cantata, part-opera, which had once been described as *St Matthew Passion* meets *Tristan und Isolde*. His production had opened in Naples then moved on to La Scala, before touring to Barcelona, Paris and London where Jack Hylton presented it at the Stoll Theatre. A sharp increase in seat prices and the first act of *Giselle* danced as a curtain raiser did nothing to attract the public. *Jeanne d'Arc* did not find favour with British audiences. The production then left for Stockholm. Rossellini, desperately short of money, was determined to give the piece an additional life and, although he found it difficult to raise the finance, eventually filmed it with Bergman and dubbed singing voices. The result was not one of his most distinguished films and failed to find an audience in the high street cinemas or art houses.

It wasn't just in Western Europe that there was a burst of operatic film-making in the fifties. As Europe left the Second World War behind and entered the Cold War, producers and directors throughout Eastern Europe and especially in the Soviet Union tended to ignore everything that was happening in the West and go their own way. But all their film projects had to be approved by the state, and film-makers were fast running out of material considered acceptable. Operas which had been approved in the past, were permitted, while at the same time bringing to the masses an art form perceived by many to be elitist.

Several important operatic films were made in the Soviet Union during this period. Vera Stroyeva began the trend when she made *Bolshoi Koncert* (1951), a film designed to show off the wonders of both the Bolshoi's opera and ballet companies. She filmed extensive excerpts from a production of *Prince Igor* with Alexander Pirogov as Igor, Yevgeniya Smolenskay as his wife Yaroslavna and

Maxim Mikhailov as Khan Konchak. She also included an aria from *Ivan Susanin* sung by Mark Reizen and Lensky's aria from *Eugene Onegin* sung by Ivan Kozlovsky.

Stroyeva, who was married to the director Grigory Roshal, was a veteran of the Soviet film industry. She had started her career in the late 1920s, working as a writer and director. *Bolshoi Koncert* was her first film to include opera, and the problems of putting opera on screen clearly intrigued her for next she decided to make a film of the most Russian of all Russian operas, *Boris Godunov* by Mussorgsky. Her husband had made a film about the composer which had featured scenes from the opera and won a prize at Cannes in 1950.

The Pushkin play on which Mussorgsky had based his opera was the subject of the first Russian feature film, made in 1907. When the opera was first staged in 1874, it had angered both church and government, and was still a touchy subject for the Communist authorities in the 1950s, but eventually Stroyeva got permission to go ahead.

She wrote the screenplay herself, helped by the man who was to become the film's sound editor, Dmitri Shostakovich. Together they shaped the opera to the needs of a film. Most of the shooting took place in a studio, with massive sets, but Stroyeva also used locations in and around Moscow, shooting in city squares, outside the Kremlin and in local monasteries. Finding extras to swell the crowds was no problem. It was a stylish and elaborate production using soloists from the Bolshoi including Alexander Pirogov as Boris and Georgy Nellep as Dmitri.

Four years later, in 1959, Stroyeva made a film of another Mussorgsky opera, the unfinished *Khovanschina*. She again worked with Shostakovich on adapting the opera for the screen, and shot it in widescreen with Mark Reizen as the leader of the Old Dissenters, and a cast of singers from the Bolshoi.

Stroyeva's *Bolshoi Koncert* had inspired other Russian film-makers to look at opera. *Stars of the Ukraine* did for the Shevchenko State Opera in Kiev what her film had done for the Bolshoi. The first part of the two-hour film contained an hour's version of *May Night*, Rimsky-Korsakov's opera written to a text by the Ukrainian writer Gogol and directed by Alexander Rou. Part two, directed by Boris Barnett, featured singers and dancers from the company including Boris Gmirya singing an aria from *Boris Godunov*, scenes from *Taras Bulba* by Nicolai Lysenko, the father of Ukrainian opera, and scenes from Gulak-Artemovsky's *Cossack Beyond the Danube*.

Rimsky's *Sadko* was brought to the screen by Alexander Ptushko in 1952 in a lavish production which emphasises the opera's fantastic elements as Sadko (Serge Stolyarov), the poor minstrel, travels the world searching for a magic bird (a slight change from Rimsky's plot), but still ends up under the ocean where he wins the hand of the Sea King's daughter.

The Kirov's production of Rachmaninoff's *Aleko* was filmed by Grigory Roshal and Serge Sidelev. Unlike Ptushko's *Sadko*, which utilised all the tricks of cinema, this was essentially the filming of a stage production with some exterior shots added. Alexander Ognivtsev sang the role of Aleko and other members of the cast included Mark Reizen.

Rimsky's *The Snow Maiden* also made it to the screen but as an animated feature by the leading Soviet animator, Ivan Ivanov-Vano. Voices were provided by members of the Bolshoi. The Russians were not the only animators to turn to opera. In England, Lotte Reiniger continued the series of delightful operatic silhouette animations she had started back in Germany and Italy in the 1930s (including *Carmen* and *The Magic Flute*), with *Hansel and Gretel*, *La Belle Hélène* and *The Abduction from the Harem*. An electronic puppet film was made of Humperdinck's *Hansel and Gretel*, scored by Giuseppe Becce with the voice of the witch provided by Anna Russell.

Film industries around the world were using any means they could to fight back against the new medium that was draining away their audiences: television. One way Hollywood hoped to combat television's rival attractions was by doing what it knew best, producing blockbusters with new technology. The CinemaScope format was developed especially to emphasise the advantages of colour on the big screen over black-and-white at home. Ironically one of the biggest CinemaScope blockbusters of the early fifties contained two elements usually considered a grave disadvantage at the box-office: opera and a black cast. *Carmen Jones* was Otto Preminger's film of Oscar Hammerstein's reworking of the Bizet opera *Carmen*. This had opened on Broadway in 1943, with Bizet's music but updated lyrics and set in America during the Second World War. The cigarette factory became a parachute factory in the South, Don José a GI Joe in line for his pilot's wings with a loyal girlfriend called Cindy Lou, and Escamillo became the prizefighter, Husky Miller.

Dorothy Dandridge's singing voice as Carmen was provided by Marilyn Horne. Horne was then a twenty-year-old studying in Hollywood with Lotte Lehmann and supplementing her income by making pirate recordings imitating such singers as Peggy Lee. She also sang in choirs performing background music for epics such as *Joan of Arc* and appeared in the chorus of the film version of *The King and I*. It is her voice that can be heard behind the opening titles of *The Rose Tattoo*.

Harry Belafonte, who played Joe, was dubbed by LaVern Hutcheson. Other roles were also dubbed including the Husky Miller of Joe Adams (by Marvin Hayes) and Diahann Carroll (by Bernice Peterson). Even though nominated for two Oscars, the film was not one of Preminger's best, being considered too stagey.

If Hollywood customarily ignored complete operas, there was one particular opera producers had been desperate to get their hands on ever since it was first staged in 1935: Gershwin's *Porgy and Bess*. By coincidence the original Porgy, Todd Duncan, had appeared in the feature *Unchained* in 1955, directed by Hall Bartlett. This was about a new prison governor experimenting with a prison that no longer had bars, and Duncan sang the theme song which received an Oscar nomination and was later to become a great hit for the Righteous Brothers, 'Unchained Melody'.

Before he chose Duncan for Porgy, Gershwin had already auditioned a hundred black singers and was in despair at finding someone suitable. He was even considering asking Lawrence Tibbett to black up, when Duncan, who was appearing in an all-black *Cavalleria Rusticana*, was recommended to him. Duncan considered himself to be an opera singer, not a singer of popular ballads, and had no wish to audition for Gershwin. He sang an aria by Secchi. Gershwin, fed up with hundreds of 'Ol'man Rivers's, immediately offered him the part.

Duncan went on to became the first black member of the New York City Opera, where his Escamillo was highly praised, and in 1942 he made an appearance in the RKO jazz film *Syncopation*, which featured such artists as Jackie Cooper, Adolphe Menjou, Bonita Granville, Benny Goodman, Gene Krupa, Charlie Barnet and Harry James.

Porgy and Bess finally made it to the screen in 1959, 24 years after it had first opened on Broadway. During that time, according to Ira Gershwin, there had been some 90 approaches for the films rights, all of them turned down. Al Jolson had wanted the rights so that he could play Porgy, and it was said that Columbia wanted to do a version with white artists blacking up, including Rita Hayworth as Bess and Fred Astaire as Sportin' Life. Everybody, it seemed, wanted to film *Porgy and Bess* but the Gershwin estate and the various copyright holders (of which there were several) could never agree amongst themselves who would handle a film best.

In May 1957, veteran producer Sam Goldwyn announced that he had acquired the rights for $650,000 plus 10 per cent of the film's earnings. He managed to get them for what turned out to be his final film through some very underhand dealings with Robert Breen, the producer and director of a touring stage production of the opera who had an option on the rights held by Dorothy Heyward. Goldwyn had the backing of most of the trustees and rights owners, especially Ira who felt that he would make a film in keeping with what he and his brother had intended. The rest, including Breen, who had never directed a film but felt he was the most qualified to make one, held out against him. When Goldwyn told him he could direct the film, Breen unwisely signed his rights away without getting Goldwyn's promise in writing. When he went off to prepare a screenplay, Goldwyn quietly dropped him.

Even before Breen had signed over his rights, Goldwyn had approached directors such as King Vidor, Frank Capra and Elia Kazan, before settling on Rouben Mamoulian, who had directed the opera's stage premiere. Goldwyn was confident that his final film would be his greatest. He had no idea what he was walking into.

He engaged a scriptwriter whose screenplay was turned down flat by Ira for being condescending and racist. Harry Belafonte cut himself out of being considered for Porgy by announcing he would not play a part which required him to be on his knees for the entire picture. The project was attacked by various black movements. Sidney Poitier, Goldwyn's choice for Porgy, felt the film would be demeaning to black people but was pressurised into accepting because he was desperate to appear in Stanley Kramer's *The Defiant Ones* and knew if he turned down *Porgy*, Goldwyn would make certain he didn't get the other role.

Once Poitier had signed, Dorothy Dandridge agreed to play Bess and Pearl Bailey, Serena. Sammy Davis Jnr. was engaged for Sportin' Life and Brock Peters, Crown. Goldwyn immediately began constructing the set of Catfish Row on a Hollywood stage and the shoot was scheduled for the summer of 1958. As that date grew nearer, friction mounted between Goldwyn and Mamoulian, who felt it was essential to film on location in and around Charleston. Goldwyn wanted everything shot on the stage and if locations were necessary, he told Mamoulian to use the most suitable he could find close to Hollywood.

On the morning shooting was due to start, the Catfish Row set, which had cost more than $2 million to build, burnt to the ground, apparently because of faulty wiring. All the costumes were destroyed as well. Goldwyn was determined not to let the tragedy affect the film. It would, he announced, still go ahead. Mamoulian thought it would be a good time to get in his location filming in Charleston. Goldwyn still disagreed, and announced that as a result of their disagreement, Mamoulian would no longer be directing. His place would be taken by Otto Preminger.

Poitier's singing voice was provided by Robert McFerrin (father of Bobby), a baritone who had appeared at the Met singing the title role in Rigoletto. He had never sung the role of Porgy before although he was later to sing it on stage. The first singer brought in to dub Bess was fired because it was felt her voice did not match Dorothy Dandridge's looks and Adele Addison, a Bach specialist, was hired instead. Although Porgy and Bess sing duets, McFerrin and Addison never actually met, recording their vocal lines separately for dubbing with the orchestra later.

Porgy and Bess proved to be an unhappy shoot, with Preminger at his most sarcastic and tyrannical. At one stage, Poitier walked off the set and refused to return until Preminger apologised. Most of the director's vitriol was reserved for Dandridge with whom he had been romantically involved during the filming of *Carmen Jones*. He even had a row with Goldwyn, threatening to walk off set himself unless Goldwyn kept away.

Porgy and Bess cost $7 million to make. Columbia, the distributors, were not happy when they saw it. The story was, they felt, too downbeat. Couldn't, one executive suggested, Porgy get up and walk at the end? Critical reaction was mixed, with some finding it a marvellous screen version of the opera, others not being so kind. 'Preminger has directed it as though it were a Bayreuth production of *Götterdämmerung*,' wrote one who found it monotonous. The stereophonic sound also came in for considerable criticism. Despite being nominated for four Oscars (and winning one for the musical arrangements by André Previn and Ken Darby), the film failed at the box-office. And although Ira Gershwin and Dorothy Heyward both expressed their enthusiasm in public, it was loathed by the Gershwin estate. They felt Preminger had turned a serious, albeit popular, work into just another musical by retaining just the songs, and not all of those. There was also disquiet that the film, glossily over-produced by Goldwyn and Preminger, prettified the characters while diluting the anger and punch of the original. To add to the criticism, black communities in the States condemned the film for its stereotyping, and picketed cinemas where it was showing. It was no better received in Europe and lost Goldwyn a lot of money.

Rumours circulated that the Gershwin estate so disliked the film that they bought up all the copies they could lay their hands on to ensure it would never be shown again. This was not strictly accurate. Goldwyn had acquired the rights to show his film for only fifteen years and when that period expired, the trustees simply refused to renew it, effectively taking the film out of circulation.

12

Television

Pickwick, an opera by Albert Coates, holds an important place in the history of screened opera: on 13 November 1936, eleven days after the BBC first started public transmissions, it became the first opera to be televised.

Coates had been born in St Petersburg where his English father had a business (his mother was Russian). At school in England, and then as a student at Liverpool University, he showed such musical promise that his father sent him to Leipzig to study with Artur Nikisch. He worked in several German opera houses before taking up a post at the Kirov in St Petersburg from where he fled at the time of the Russian Revolution. In 1919 he settled in London, earning his living as a conductor and composer.

Pickwick was the fifth of Coates's nine operas, written while he was preparing Shostakovich's *Lady Macbeth of Mtsensk* for its BBC radio premiere. Based on Charles Dickens' *The Pickwick Papers*, it reflects the influence of Shostakovich, especially in its orchestration. It has a large cast and makes considerable stage demands, including the use of film. One week before its official opening at the Royal Opera House, Covent Garden, the entire cast, including William Parsons as Pickwick and Dennis Noble as Sam Weller, moved out to Alexandra Palace in North London and performed 25 minutes of the opera, especially adapted for television by Dallas Bower who had worked with Paul Czinner on such films as *As You Like It*. Coates himself conducted.

What the transmission looked like we do not know, except that it would have been very crude by modern standards. BBC Television had opened its service on 2 November, broadcasting for an hour in the afternoon and an hour in the evening, with nothing on at all on Sundays. Since only four hundred television sets, costing £100 each, the equivalent of a small car, had been sold prior to opening night, and reception was confined to the London area, early programmes, including *Pickwick*, would not have been seen by that many people.

The broadcast did, however, establish the precedent that public service broadcasting would provide the high arts for the viewing public whether they wanted them or not (and there is considerable evidence that early audiences did not want classical concerts and certainly did not want opera). During the first three years of television's life in Britain, before the service closed down for the war, the BBC (and there was only the one channel) broadcast almost 30 operas, or to be more accurate, excerpts from 30 operas because of the restrictions on how much time was given to each transmission.

The choice of 9 operas put on in those first few months is surprising. Hardly any of the big, romantic pieces one might expect to be shown in order to build up audiences were scheduled. Instead there were the sorts of opera that would rarely be considered today. There were 25-minute versions of John Blow's *Venus and Adonis*, Thomas Arne's *Thomas and Sally*, Charles Dibdin's *Lionel and Clarissa*, and a 45-minute version of John Gay's *The Beggar's Opera* and its follow-up piece, *Polly*.

It was not until 1937 that Act 3 of Gounod's *Faust* was shown with Noel Eadie, Parry Jones and Roderick Jones, and Act 3 of *La Traviata*. There was no opera at all during July 1937 when the BBC closed down for three weeks in order to repair the equipment. When the station reopened, the first opera to be shown, in September, was Pergolesi's *La Serva Padrona*, given with dialogue instead of recitative but otherwise the first opera to be shown on television complete. Another rarity from those early days was Mehul's *Le Jeune Sage et Le Vieux Fou*.

Staging opera for television was not an easy task. The standard vision unit in a studio consisted of four cameras linked to a control room where the director would tell his vision mixer which camera shot he required. The cameras were heavy beasts with a fixed lens, and the only way a director could change the size of his shot was to move the camera physically. Two of the cameras had their own wheels, the other two were mounted on rails so they could be pushed backwards and forwards but only when the shot being transmitted came from another camera, taking care that the camera on the move did not get itself into shot. The powerful lights needed to produce an image on screen, even in black and white, made the studio extremely hot and uncomfortable for both artists and technicians.

It was not until 1950 that cameras were introduced with turret lenses containing three lenses of different sizes. If the director then wanted to change the size of his shot, he had to cut to another camera while the cameraman swung his lens. As each camera got its own independent dolly, or set of wheels, the challenge for the director became not to tie the camera cables in knots, especially when all his carefully rehearsed shots had to go out of the window because one of the cameras had gone down, as they almost invariably did. On one occasion, two cameras went down simultaneously. Both were mended on the studio floor but in the process the engineers had to disconnect the camera cables and when they put everything back together, they inadvertently attached the cables to the wrong cameras, so that the pictures received in the gallery were on different monitors. Not such a disaster perhaps, but the programme was going out live.

Every programme in the early days was live. There was no pre-recording of programmes until the sixties. If an actor forgot his lines, the rest of the cast had to ad lib to cover. When Jack Buchanan was cast as Eisenstein in *Die Fledermaus* (given the then innocent title *Gay Rosalinda* to pull in audiences who supposedly wouldn't understand a title in German), he kept forgetting his lines in rehearsals and had to have his entire part written out on idiot cards, large boards that could be held up alongside the camera during the transmission. In the middle of the crucial last scene, as he started to explain why Falke had come home dressed as a bat, he began, 'He was blind ...', then dried. Unable to see the idiot board, he started again. 'He was blind ...' His fellow artists held their breath. Still Buchanan couldn't remember his lines. 'He was blind..' he began for the third time, 'as a bat,' he ended triumphantly and there his explanation finished.

Another major problem in early opera performances on television was where to put the orchestra. Singers need to be able to see the conductor and yet one of the advantages of having cameras is that they can cross over the orchestra, over the footlights, and take the viewer into the action. In 1936, the orchestra was placed at one end of the studio with the singers and cameras at the other, the conductor watching them on a monitor, and an assistant, within the eyeline of the singers, trying both to follow and anticipate his beat. If the opera required a chorus, they had to stand silently in the studio until required and the cameras could cut to them.

It was not until the BBC had been on the air for eighteen months that technicians discovered how to link the main studio at Alexandra Palace with the smaller one next door. Once they had achieved this, it meant that the orchestra could be in a different studio during transmission. The first opera to be done this way was *Hansel and Gretel*, presented at Christmas time with a live repeat shortly afterwards. Most programmes at the time were shown twice and since tape had not then been invented, the entire production simply had to be performed again.

Hansel and Gretel marked another departure from tradition since it was produced as a mime with the actors in a different studio from the musicians. Even at this stage, people were beginning to question the casting of singers who did not look the part. It was felt that mime was the best answer to having adults, no matter how petite, playing the roles of children. Playing the part of Gretel was Muriel Pavlow with her voice provided by Jane Vowles.

The month after *Hansel and Gretel* had been shown, the BBC mounted its most ambitious project to date, Act 2 of *Tristan und Isolde*. This, too, was staged as a mime with Walter Widdop providing the voice of Tristan and Isobel Baillie singing Isolde. It was given two transmissions on the same day and excited a great deal of press comment. While some critics referred to it as an audacious and bold experiment in the presentation of opera on screen (obviously not having seen *Hansel and Gretel* the month before), others felt it was a long drawn-out boy and girl routine, to which mime added little or nothing. The general public was largely bored by an experience they found long, slow and tedious.

The BBC then returned to more popular operatic territory and also abandoned the two performances a day. Among the operas they showed was *Cinderella* by Spike Hughes. This is sometimes claimed to be the first opera commissioned by television. It wasn't. Hughes had written the piece, a children's opera, for radio, and then adapted it for television. It was not a direct commission. The first of those was to come after the war in America.

For two years the BBC was the only television station broadcasting opera. Between 1938 and 1940, the Paul Nipkow Sender station in Berlin, which had begun broadcasting in March 1935, showed a film of Mozart's *The Impresario* nine times, and transmitted studio productions of Mozart's *Bastien and Bastienne* (with Bastienne sung by Elisabeth Schwarzkopf), and Lortzing's *Die Opernprobe*. In the United States, NBC in New York became the first television station to show an opera when it broadcast a shortened version of *Pagliacci* in 1940.

During the Second World War, BBC Television went off the air and did not re-open until 1946. Its reappearance was not met with universal delight, especially by those in the entertainment and sporting worlds who viewed the existence of television as a considerable threat. Theatre managers refused to allow the BBC to take live relays of their productions; permission was refused for the BBC to televise live athletics, league football and the Derby. The cinema withheld old films, and variety agencies threatened to blacklist any artist who dared to appear on television.

Those in charge at the BBC were determined, however, to push ahead with bringing the best of everything directly into people's homes. They were men and women with a mission, and that mission included opera. Broadcasts of opera began again in 1947, and by 1950 it had been decided that operas would be a regular feature in the studios at Alexandra Palace. These were to be sung in English, sometimes cut, sometimes complete, under the musical direction of Eric Robinson who appointed as his assistant, a young conductor from Sadler's Wells, named Charles Mackerras.

The operas were staged as they had been before the war, live, with the orchestra in one studio, the singers in another. One of Mackerras's first jobs involved having to conduct the chorus. Unable to stand anywhere in the studio where he could be seen and not end up in shot, he decided to position himself within the chorus and signal to them by raising his eyebrows and nodding his head. He hoped that if any viewers spotted him, they would simply think that one of the villagers was suffering from St. Vitus' Dance.

Mackerras was eventually to replace Robinson as principal conductor of BBC television's operatic output and over the next twelve or so years he conducted live performances of *Carmen*, *Rigoletto*, *Tosca*, *Faust*, *Pagliacci*,

Gianni Schicchi, Cavalleria Rusticana, The Tales of Hoffmann, The Marriage of Figaro, La Bohème, Castor and Pollux, Otello and *Billy Budd*, some of them more than once. The bass Michael Langdon remembered singing in *Faust* when it was transmitted live from the Playhouse in Northumberland Avenue, twice, once for the initial transmission, two days later for the repeat. It was during the last of London's infamous smogs and Langdon recalled the oily yellow vapour swirling under the doors and filling the theatre. The cast, eyes streaming, held handkerchiefs over their mouths and had to try very hard not to cough when not singing.

Langdon also took part in a televised production of *Billy Budd* in 1965, conducted by Mackerras with a cast that included Peter Pears, Robert Tear, Peter Glossop, Geraint Evans and John Shirley-Quirk. Britten himself took charge of the production and was horrified by the seeming chaos of the studio, though pleased with the end result.

It wasn't just in Britain that television executives felt that opera had an important place in the schedules. The French television service had opened with a gala that included Alfred Piccaver singing arias, and in 1948, the New York station WJZ had relayed a performance of *Otello* from the Met. College productions of *The Barber of Seville* and *The Tales of Hoffmann* were seen on local stations, and in 1949, NBC started a programme of regular opera transmissions with a gala of scenes from favourite operas, followed by complete productions of Menotti's *The Old Maid and the Thief*, and Weill's *Down in the Valley*. NBC's commitment to opera was such that they decided to form the NBC Opera Company with Peter Herman Adler as music director. This unit was to become the first to commission an opera directly for television.

It was, perhaps, inevitable that as television grew up and began to develop a language and grammar of its own, those in charge of the medium would no longer be content simply to show operas but would want to create them. There was, and still is, debate about whether opera and television are compatible, about whether pointing cameras at an opera can possibly capture or reflect faithfully what is happening on stage. Creating work that was written specifically for television was one obvious way to solve this dilemma.

In 1949, NBC invited Gian Carlo Menotti to write an opera for television. Two years later, on Christmas Eve 1951, the station showed live *Amahl and the Night Visitors*, the story of a crippled boy who sits outside his house watching a brilliant star. The Three Kings, with presents for the new baby they are seeking, arrive wanting shelter. During the night, Amahl's mother tries to steal some of their treasure. Eventually Amahl gives the Three Kings his crutch, the only possession he has, as a present for the child. He is miraculously healed and joins the Three Kings in their search. Menotti had got his inspiration for the opera from Bosch's painting, *The Adoration of the Magi*.

No one was prepared for the response this piece got. The public lapped up a good story told in a moving way and NBC was bombarded with requests to show it again. On the front page of the *New York Times*, the critic Olin Downes admitted to being immensely moved. 'Television,' he wrote, 'operatically speaking, has come of age.'

Four months later, on Easter Sunday, the public got its wish when the original production was repeated. *Amahl* subsequently became a Christmas fixture on American television, has been shown in countless other countries and is a popular work on stage with amateur societies. It is not only unique in being the first commissioned television opera but is also the only one of those works generated by television to have found a firm place in the affections of the general public. It is also the only one to have had regular repeats. And yet Menotti admitted that he had not thought of *Amahl* as a television opera while writing it, but as a stage opera that happened to be being shown on television. It was a difference that was to be significant, for the only other television opera to have become part of the repertory was also written with more than one eye on the stage, Britten's *Owen Wingrave*.

The success of *Amahl* led to NBC commissioning further operas. From Martinu came *The Marriage* and *What Men Live By*, both shown in 1953. Lukas Foss wrote *Griffelkin* in 1955, and in 1958 Menotti produced *Maria Golovin* (which was actually given a world premiere on the stage in Brussels, so he clearly didn't think of that in television terms either). Menotti also came up with *Labyrinth* in 1963 but neither that nor *Maria Golovin* was able to repeat the success of *Amahl*.

The challenge thrown down by NBC was picked up by other TV stations. In 1962 CBS commissioned *The Flood* from Igor Stravinsky, while the following year the University of North Carolina commissioned *The Sojourner* and *Mollie Sinclair* from Carlisle Floyd. John Eaton, Hans Werner Henze, Stanley Hollingsworth and Benjamin Lees are among other composers who have received television commissions in the States.

The first BBC commission came in 1956 with Arthur Benjamin's *Manana*, generally considered not to be a particularly successful work by the composer of *Jamaican Rumba*. That same year Malcolm Arnold produced *The Open Window*, a chamber work with a libretto by Sidney Gilliat based on a three-page short story by Saki. Lasting about 22 minutes, this comedy about a repressed bank clerk with bad health who goes to the country to convalesce from the thought of a nervous breakdown would make a perfect stage curtain raiser today.

In subsequent years Arthur Bliss, Richard Arnell, Phyllis Tate, Carl Davis, Gordon Crosse, Norman Kay, Robin Orr and Thomas Eastwood were among those composers commissioned to write television operas in Britain. Most of their offerings have disappeared, even when they subsequently got a stage production, and few can be deemed to have been successful.

One TV opera that has had a life after its initial television showing was Benjamin Britten's *Owen Wingrave*. This was commissioned by the BBC in

1967 and completed in 1971. Britten was reluctant to write the piece. He had never owned a television set and had often commented how much he disliked the medium and what it did to music. He had not enjoyed the experience of working on *Billy Budd*, finding the whole process of making a television programme confusing. So, when the BBC and NBC approached him to write something for them, he turned them both down. It was the appointment of John Culshaw as head of music for BBC Television that made him change his mind. Culshaw had, for many years, been Britten's producer at Decca Records. Britten trusted him and eventually agreed to write something.

The subject he chose was a Henry James ghost story because, he said, he needed a story which 'made use of the intimate subtleties of the medium ... which could be quietly watched at home when the excitement of being part of a large audience in the theatre is not missed too much by the viewer'. Owen Wingrave is the latest member of a long line of distinguished soldiers to have begun his military training. During this training, he has come to realise that his conscience will not permit him to continue as a soldier. He returns to the ancestral home to confront his distraught family with his reasons. His grandfather reacts by disinheriting him and when his friend Kate calls him a coward and challenges him to sleep in the house's haunted room, he has to agree. Locked in for the night, the wickedness in the house overwhelms him and he is found dead on the floor in the morning.

Wingrave's pacifism matched Britten's own views (he had spent the war in America) and it was suggested that he had accepted the television commission simply in order to get his message over to as many people as possible (the first UK transmission was watched by just over a quarter of a million viewers).

Benjamin Luxon played the role of Owen, Peter Pears that of his grandfather, with the rest of the cast being Janet Baker as Kate, John Shirley-Quirk, Nigel Douglas, Sylvia Fisher, Heather Harper and Jennifer Vyvyan. The experienced Colin Graham directed the action, while in the gallery directing the cameras was the man who was to become the doyen of television opera directors, Brian Large.

The opera was recorded at the Snape Maltings in Aldeburgh, the Suffolk town where Britten lived. The concert hall was converted into a television studio containing all the opera's sets including the huge hall at the Wingrave family seat. Although the orchestra was also in the hall, with Britten himself conducting, his beat could not always be seen by the singers and it was the task of Steuart Bedford, Britten's assistant, to make sure they knew where they were. Bedford spent most of the recording crouched on the floor, just out of shot but within the singers' eyelines. Once, during a duet between Douglas and Baker, he had to position himself up on a beam. Douglas recalls devising a roll of his eyes heavenwards so that he could see Bedford at crucial moments, hoping the action looked dramatically appropriate.

The television production of *Owen Wingrave* got respectable reviews but little more. There was undoubted disappointment that Britain's senior operatic composer had not taken the opportunity of using television to produce something that was uniquely for and of the medium. When, two years later, *Owen Wingrave* received its stage premiere with the same cast, it became even more clear that Britten had been thinking stage while writing it. Perhaps because of this, the opera was consigned for many years to the compartment of Britten's output labelled interesting but a failure. It is only recently that it has been accepted as being an important work in its own right.

The arrival of television had sent a shudder through the film industries of many nations as cinema attendances showed a marked decline, people preferring to stay at home to watch rather than make their twice-weekly trek to the local fleapit. Television also affected the way opera was put onto the screen. It took over the role of providing a record of stage productions by showing, live or then taped, productions from the world's opera houses, bringing the best singers into people's living rooms (at the same time later generating an important secondary market in home videos). Outside broadcast cameras had begun to visit opera houses in Britain in the 1950s but at first only extracts were shown. It was the arrival of colour television in 1967 which brought with it the first broadcasts of complete operas. The first colour transmission from Covent Garden was, ironically, of Visconti's famous black and white production of *La Traviata*. The landmark production of outside broadcast operas was the 1980 Bayreuth *Ring* staged by Patrice Chéreau, with Donald McIntyre, Gwyneth Jones and Peter Hofmann, directed for television by Brian Large and shown, despite some cries of protest, an act at a time.

Not all opera shown on television came from the stages of opera houses. Television could mount its own studio productions, and at the BBC during the 1950s and 1960s Rudolf Cartier put on some spectacular productions which included an *Otello* and Rosalind Elias and Raymond Nilsson in *Carmen*.

Far from killing the operatic film, the arrival of television actually encouraged it. Throughout the fifties and most of the sixties, the means for recording on tape did not exist. An operatic transmission had, therefore, to be live or it had to be on film and it did not take film-makers long to realise that television provided an important new outlet for operatic product.

As early as 1950, a New York station began showing a series of half-hour films made specifically for television as an Italian-American co-production. *Opera Cameos*, introduced by the tenor Giovanni Martinelli, told the stories of popular operas such as *Cavalleria Rusticana*, *Rigoletto*, *Carmen* and *La Traviata*, using singers such as Mario del Monaco, Regina Resnik, Paolo Silveri, Beverly Sills and Chloe Elmo. Also in the States, *The Great Waltz* was filmed for television with Patrice Munsel and Jarmila Novotná. Bernard Herrmann wrote *A Christmas Carol*, with Fredric March as Scrooge, as a film for the small screen.

Elsewhere people were equally quick to seize the opportunities offered by television. RAI, the Italian state television service, began filming studio productions with some of Italy's biggest names and rising stars. Rosanna Carteri, Nicola Filacuridi and Carlo Tagliabue appeared in *La Traviata*. Franco Corelli, one of the finest tenors of the century whose career was shortened because he suffered from terrible stage fright, appeared in *Pagliacci* with Gobbi and Micheluzzi. He went on to film *Carmen* (he had made his professional debut in Spoleto singing Don José), *Tosca* with Reneta Heredia Capnist in the title role and Carlo Tagliabue as Scarpia, *Turandot* with Lucille Udovick and *Andrea Chénier* with Casapietra and Cappuccili.

Italo Tajo took the title role in *Don Pasquale* with Sesto Bruscantini. Mario del Monaco appeared as *Andrea Chénier* with Antonietta Stella as Maddelena and Giuseppe Taddei as Gerard, and also sang in *Il Trovatore* with Leyla Gencer as Leonora, and appeared in the role for which he was most famous, *Otello*, with Rosanna Carteri as Desdemona. Paolo Montarsolo and Anna Moffo appeared in Pergolesi's *La Serva Padrona* and Magda Olivero sang *Tosca* with Alvinio Misciano as Cavaradossi and Giulio Fioravanti as Scarpia.

Olivero, a soprano who is not that well known today, was considered by some to have been a finer Tosca than Callas. She hardly had an auspicious beginning to her career. She had been born near Turin in 1910, and unlike the majority of Italian singers, did not come from a humble background. Her father was a judge and she was well-educated. He wanted her to study the piano, she wanted to sing. When, through her father's string-pulling, she auditioned for Italian radio the verdict was unequivocal: she had no voice, she had no musicality, she had no personality, she had nothing. She should, she was told, change profession. A second audition confirmed the verdict. But there was one dissenter, a voice teacher who had heard something that persuaded him to take her on as a student.

Olivero made her debut singing Lauretta in *Gianni Schicchi* when she was 22 and appeared at La Scala the following year singing the minor role of Anna in *Nabucco*. Gradually her roles increased in size to include Gilda in *Rigoletto* and she was engaged by the Rome Opera to sing Elsa in *Lohengrin*. Olivero had been told by Tullio Serafin to expect a contract to sing Philine in *Mignon*. The contract came for a different role, she was convinced, because she had resisted Serafin's advances. Her Elsa was a success and helped establish her as one of Italy's leading dramatic sopranos.

In 1941, she gave up the stage to marry an industralist, appearing only at charity concerts. It was the composer Cilea who persuaded her to return to opera in 1951. She was, he said, his ideal Adriana Lecouvreur. Her career again blossomed. She was 50 by the time she made her filmed version of *Tosca*, the role in which she was eventually to make her Met debut in 1975 when she was 65.

These Italian made-for-television films give us an often unique record of some major singers. But they are hardly films in the cienematic sense. There might be an occasional shot of a storm at the beginning of *Otello*, for example, but these are very straightforward, traditional productions, staged in a studio, which happen to be on film because that was the medium of recording them at the time. Ten years later they would have been recorded on tape. No attempt is made to give the films the visual feel of a movie. The camera is often only pointed at the singers, frequently (sometimes too frequently) utilising the camera's ability to get in close and see expressions lost in an opera house.

A director who bucked the trend in Italy of making everything for television was Carmine Gallone who made a film of *Tosca* in 1956 in which all the acts were shot at the locations in Rome specified in the libretto. Filmed in CinemaScope to be able to take full advantage of the settings, it starred Franco Corelli as Cavaradossi and Afro Poli as Scarpia. Franca Duval played Tosca with her voice dubbed by Maria Caniglia.

One of the first musicians to realise the importance of television and the increase in audiences it would provide for him and his work (not to mention the increased sales of his recordings) was Herbert von Karajan, a man who always had one eye open for ways of controlling his artistic product while at the same time making a fortune.

On 26 July 1960, the new theatre in Salzburg, with Karajan in charge, opened with an opulent Rudolf Hartmann production of *Der Rosenkavalier*. The stage, designed by Clemens Holzmeister, was the largest operatic stage in the world, and one on which Karajan intended to shine. The cast of the production included Elisabeth Schwarzkopf as the Marschallin, Sena Jurinac as Octavian and Anneliese Rothenberger as Sophie. The director was Paul Czinner, who had made the successful film of the festival's production of *Don Giovanni* five years earlier. He proposed shooting in a similar fashion to *Don Giovanni*, with several film cameras running continuously. The end result was a marvellous visual record of the production, with Schwarzkopf in particular outstanding, but the film, despite being given a cinema release two years later, was never quite a film, could never quite get away from being a record of a production filmed off the stage.

Karajan, recognising the enormous potential of film, whether made for the cinema or for television, immediately set up his own production company, Unitel, to film for television the operas and concerts he was conducting. It wasn't only *Der Rosenkavalier* that convinced him this was the way forward. The televised concerts of Leonard Bernstein in the United States in which Bernstein preceded the performance with a chat, had made Bernstein immensely popular amongst young viewers. Karajan wanted a slice of that particular action.

Unitel's first films were of Karajan's orchestral concerts, relying heavily on cut-aways of the conductor in action and recorded black-and-white to playback (colour television did not reach Europe until the late 1960s). Once the technical facility to record live with balanced sound had been developed, Karajan abandoned playback.

165

Unitel's first opera film was *La Bohème*, filmed in 1965 and based on Franco Zeffirelli's La Scala production. It starred Mirella Freni as Mimi, Gianni Raimondi as Rodolfo and Adriana Martino as Musetta. The Bohemians were played by Rolando Panerai, Ivo Vinco and Gianni Maffeo. Wilhelm Semmelroth directed and Karajan conducted the orchestra. The film was shot in Italy both in the studio and on location, but the music was recorded in the Munich Opera House. It was an old-fashioned staging, with no attempt to make the Bohemians look realistic. Raimondi, Panerai and Maffeo looked like Peter Pans in a fantasy Bohemia while Vinco was distinctly middle-aged.

Unitel's early films were directed by professional directors such as Henri Clouzot, but Karajan, being Karajan it was not long before he insisted on doing everything himself including directing the films of productions he had staged and was conducting. Karajan was, as a colleague once wrote, incapable of sharing. It was also important to him that opera on the screen should be a faithful representation of what was happening on the stage. He disapproved strongly of the Joseph Losey approach in *Don Giovanni* where images were selected by the director to convey a personal impression or understanding of the music. 'Some of the images were done wonderfully from a filmic point of view,' he told Losey when he met him, 'but it has nothing to do with the opera.' This was, and is, an argument many people have had since the advent of television opera. Should opera have a separate identity as a film? Or should it be a faithful reproduction of the work as left by the composer – the 'best seat in the house' principle? Karajan certainly plumped for the latter.

Talented though he may have been, Karajan certainly wasn't a film director as he demonstrated with his 1967 Salzburg production of *Carmen*. He had a potentially great cast with Grace Bumbry as Carmen, Jon Vickers as Don José, Justino Diaz as Escamillo and Mirella Freni as Micaela. Georges Wakhevitch's designs and costumes were realistic and colourful. Yet the production never gets off the ground due entirely to Karajan's leaden and old-fashioned stage production in which the chorus moves by numbers and Bumbry, who has the looks and voice to be a magnificent Carmen, is made to appear coy when she should smoulder. Vickers simply looks as if he wishes he was in another opera and although Freni sings divinely, it is never enough to stop one wondering just how long it would have taken a Spanish peasant girl to achieve such a hairdo.

Karajan's camera direction is equally uninspired, being of the point-the-camera-at-the-action kind. He makes some very basic mistakes. Bumbry, at one point, is shown in a wide shot sitting on a bench. The close-up has her lying down, before cutting back wide to her sitting up. The overture, it goes without saying, is spent watching Karajan's face or hands.

Karajan also directed film versions of the La Scala productions of *Cavalleria Rusticana* and *Pagliacci* he had conducted, taking them into the studio. Both are given handsome, realistic productions by Giorgio Strehler (*Cav*) and Paul Hagar (*Pag*). Both were shot to playback. Karajan again proved he had no sense of filmic rhythm or knowledge of how to handle crowd scenes, nor could he coax anything more than a wooden performance from Gianfranco Cecchele as Turiddu. The direction of *Cav* is attributed to Ake Falck, presumably under orders from Karajan as to how it should be shot, because he is no improvement on the conductor.

The film of Karajan's 1970 Salzburg production of *Otello* with Jon Vickers in the title role, Peter Glossop as Iago and Mirella Freni as Desdemona, failed to avoid similar pitfalls. Again shot to playback, the singers too often look as though they are whispering when the sound we hear is at full volume. The cast is heavy with make-up, they wear ill-fitting wigs and the entire production is stage bound. But, and this is a most important but, it is now a revelation to see Vickers in one of his finest roles, singing with such assurance and ease. Whatever the shortcomings of the finished film, the principal singers had all performed their roles together many times on stage, and their teamwork comes across strongly on the screen.

Otello also contains an example of Karajan doing his Hitchcock imperson-ation. During Iago's drinking song there is a cut-away of him sporting a black moustache. He can also be spotted in others of his films.

It wasn't just Salzburg productions which were being filmed for television. Rolf Liebermann, the Intendant at Hamburg, was equally determined that more people should see the work going on in his house, but he didn't film off the stage. Instead, throughout the sixties, most major Hamburg productions were taken into the studio to be filmed. Toni Blankenheim, Sena Jurinac, Richard Cassilly and Hans Sotin starred in Liebermann's own production of *Wozzeck*, directed on film by Joachim Hess, who then directed Liebermann's productions of *Fidelio* with Anja Silja, Lucia Popp, Hans Sotin and Theo Adam, and *Der Freischütz* with Ernst Kozub, Arlene Saunders, Tom Krause, Edith Mathis, Gottlob Frick and Sotin. There were films made of *The Marriage of Figaro, Orpheus in the Underworld, Oberon* with René Kollo, *The Merry Wives of Windsor*, and some more rare operas such as Henze's *Der Junge Lord*, Ernst Krenek's *The Magic Mirror*, and Penderecki's *The Devils of Loudon*. *Die Meistersinger* with Giorgio Tozzi (who had provided Rossano Brazzi's voice in *South Pacific*), was filmed, along with *Zar und Zimmermann* and *Elektra*.

Important productions from the Komische Oper in East Germany also ended up as films destined for television, with Walter Felsenstein directing his productions of *Don Giovanni, The Tales of Hoffmann* and *Otello* for the screen. But not all operatic films made for television were taken from stage productions. Czech television made films of Martinu's *Julietta* and of his lesser known final opera, *Ariane*, with American soprano Celina Lindsay in the title role. Swiss composer Heinrich Sutermeister wrote *The Canterville Ghost* and *The Children's Crusade* as films for Swiss television. In 1964, veteran director Michael Powell was asked by Norman Foster, an American producer based in Germany, to make a film of Bartók's opera, *Bluebeard's Castle*. This was the first film to be made in the new studio in Salzburg. Foster, who came from Boston, was also a singer and took the role of Bluebeard himself. His wife Judith was played by Anna Raquel Sartre. Although it only took Powell eight and a half days to shoot, no sooner had he started than the production ran out of money. South German television stepped in with a rescue package and it became a television film.

Jean-Marie Straub and Danièle Huillet, left-wing French-born directors working in Germany, whose work is seen mainly on the festival circuit, made a film of Schoenberg's *Moses und Aron* for television, aimed deliberately at audiences that would never go to an opera house. Since, in their view, the opera was about the masses (a view not matched, incidentally, by Schoenberg), they felt it should have the greater audience provided by television. This was no faithful adaptation of the opera but a radical countering of what they saw as Schoenberg's anti-Marxist views. Filmed on location in a Roman amphitheatre in southern Italy, it was dedicated to one of the Baader-Meinhoff terrorist gang who had died on hunger strike in prison. The film, in which even the blood was claimed to be authentic, was deliberately low key and unspectacular.

Götz Friedrich's studio film of *Salome* was based on his Vienna State Opera production with Teresa Stratas as Salome (a role she never actually sang on stage), Astrid Varnay, guilty of some wild over-acting, as Herodias, and Bernd Weikl as Jokanaan. The production was given Hollywood-style sets and an aura of decadence, described as traditional horror-comic-strip with modern socialist overtones tacked on. What worked particularly well was the final scene, which Friedrich shot as a love scene in close up. Karl Böhm conducted beautifully. Stratas was also in a Canadian TV film of Puccini's *La Rondine* with Cornelius Opthof, directed by Norman Campbell.

One of the major operatic films of this time was of the 1974 Orange Festival production of *Norma* starring Montserrat Caballé and Jon Vickers. Directed by Pierre Jourdan, this was not a cinematic film but a record of a production staged in the open-air at which film cameras rather than video cameras had been pointed. It could just as easily have been shot electronically and was aimed both at television and a theatrical release in art houses, a pattern that had been established by Karajan with his operatic films.

The annual summer festival in Orange in Southern France takes place in July in a Roman amphitheatre seating 8,000. On the evening when the performance was due to take place, the Mistral was blowing in gusts of up to 60 miles an hour. The festival's director was all for cancelling the performance but Caballé persuaded him at least to start it. Under extremely difficult conditions, with costumes being blown all over the place and the orchestra having to peg their music to their stands, Caballé and the rest of the cast (which included Josephine Veasey as Adalgisa, Agostino Ferrin as Oroveso and Gino Sinimberghi as Flavio) gave superlative performances, Caballé later declaring it to be the performance of her career.

Maria Callas, the Norma of her day, who had not sung on stage for ten years, attended the premiere of the film in Paris early the following year. Some time afterwards Caballé received in the post the earrings Visconti had presented to Callas for her performances at La Scala in 1955, which she has worn at every performance since.

The same year that Caballé's *Norma* was filmed, the Swedish director Ingmar Bergman attended a concert in Stockholm given by the Swedish Radio Orchestra. He there met the head of music for Swedish television. Bergman had long had an interest in opera, having directed stage productions of *The Rake's Progress*, a Swedish folk opera and *The Merry Widow*. In 1970, he had announced he was going to make a film of *The Merry Widow* with Barbra Streisand, although nothing came of it.

He and the head of music chatted during the interval and Bergman mentioned that he had always wanted to make a film of *The Magic Flute*. He had first seen the opera as a twelve-year-old and become obsessed with it, working as an assistant on a production in Stockholm's Royal Opera House in 1940. As a boy he had visited Drottningholm, for 400 years the summer residence of the ladies of the Swedish court. On an island not far from Stockholm, the palace contained (and still does) a remarkable baroque theatre. Young Bergman had entered the deserted building and been entranced by the interior. It was in a building like that that he always saw his perfect *Magic Flute*.

The head of music, on hearing his suggestion, promptly told him to do it, putting up the half-a-million Swedish kroner it cost. Bergman approached his task by accepting that the world of opera is unreal and theatrical, and that *The Magic Flute* inhabits a land of illusion. But instead of shooting it as a fantasy (and *The Magic Flute* probably lends itself to that approach as well as any opera), he decided to emphasise the work's theatricality by basing his film on a performance staged in the theatre at Drottningholm. Built largely of wood and still preserving much of its original stage machinery, the theatre is a listed building. No food is served inside and patrons are asked to take special care upon entering, with no touching of the walls and no high-heeled shoes. Under no circumstances would the authorities let Bergman film in there so he had to reconstruct the interior of the theatre in a studio.

As well as emphasising the work's theatricality, Bergman wanted to demonstrate the opera's universal appeal, and so, during the overture, he used cut-aways of children. To point up the artificiality of the staging, Bergman prefaced each act by showing the cast making up, playing chess, smoking cigarettes or checking their scores. Only when the action began did he take the camera through the proscenium arch and allow it to become involved with the events on stage. Even then, the viewer was not allowed to forget the opera house. The production used basic theatrical effects such as the flute on wires, or baskets on pulleys, and Bergman made no attempt to hide them or use film techniques to accomplish his effects.

It was essential for Bergman's concept that his cast, as well as being able to sing, should look right (although the intimate size of the theatre meant he and conductor Eric Ericson could go for voice quality rather than size). Ericson was Bergman's second choice for conductor. He had asked Hans Schmidt-Isserstedt but had been turned down flat. Even Ericson had not accepted immediately.

Most of the singers they chose were unknown outside Scandinavia with Josef Köstlinger as Tamino, Irma Urrila as Pamina, Ulrik Cold as Sarastro, Birgit Nordin as the Queen of the Night, Ragnar Ulfung as Monostatos and Elisabeth Erikson as Papagena. Papageno was Håkan Hagegård and the film made him an international star. It was, Bergman later said, one of the most enjoyable shoots he had ever experienced.

He clearly did enjoy filming an opera for, when it was over, he announced that he intended to shoot *The Merry Widow*, this time with Liza Minnelli, and *The Tales of Hoffmann* with Domingo, which Seiji Ozawa would conduct. This, he said, would be his final film. He made neither.

13

The Cinema Fights Back

Television may have become the major outlet for operatic films by the end of the sixties, but that did not stop producers from filming for the big screen. The most consistent output of operatic features came from the Soviet Union where such films were seen as both worthy and unlikely to rock any political boats. Or that's what the authorities thought until, in 1966, Mikhail Shapiro made a film of Dmitri Shostakovich's powerful opera, *Katerina Ismailova*. This was the composer's own revision of the opera he had based on a short story by Nicolai Leskov, and had originally called *The Lady Macbeth of the Mtsensk District*. Katerina is a married woman who succumbs to the charms of a worker on the estate, poisons her father-in-law, helps in the murder of her husband and is banished to Siberia where she realises she has only been used and commits suicide, but not before drowning her lover's new girlfriend. The opera was a great success when it opened in January 1934 and was soon being performed throughout the Soviet Union and beyond. Then in December 1935, Stalin went to see it and promptly had it banned for what was described as 'animalistic realism ... chaos instead of music'. The composer was forced to make a grovelling, public apology to the Soviet people for writing such decadant, offensive music.

In 1962 Shostakovich revised the opera to exclude text and details which might offend officialdom, took the opportunity to alter some of the vocal lines and renamed the piece *Katerina Ismailova*. Shapiro, with Shostakovich's full approval, turned the opera into a screenplay which exploited to the full the freedom film gave him. He shot the opera partly in the studio but mostly on location, in appropriate settings. While most of the cast had their singing voices dubbed, the soprano Galina Vishnevskaya gave a towering performance both acting and singing the title role. The result was magnificent but proved hardly more palatable to the Soviet authorities than the opera had been on the stage 30 years earlier. Shapiro's film was banned, too, and was not released until 1990.

Earlier Soviet operatic films had included a production of *Mozart and Salieri* (1962), the chamber opera Rimsky-Korsakov had written from the Pushkin poem which claimed that Salieri had murdered his young rival. Shot in Latvia, it was directed by Vladimir Gorriker with Russian actor Innokenti Smoktunovsky as Mozart and Pyotry Glebov as Salieri. All the singing voices were dubbed.

Gorricker went on to make three more opera films, two of them on location in Latvia and all using actors dubbed by singers from the Bolshoi. They were Tchaikovsky's *Iolanta* (1963), Rimsky's *The Tsar's Bride* (1965) and *The Stone Guest* (1967), an opera by Alexander Dargomizhsky based on a poem Pushkin had written after he had first seen Mozart's *Don Giovanni*. This starred Vladmir Atlantov as Don Giovanni but all other roles were dubbed.

Daisi, by the Georgian composer Zakhary Paliashvili, was, unlike *Lady Macbeth of Mtsenst*, Stalin's favourite opera. Important for its position as one of the earliest Georgian nationalist operas, it remains, however, worthy and often banal. But that didn't stop it being filmed by Nicolai Sanishvili in 1966 with Georgian actors dubbed by Georgian singers.

Alexander Ptusko, who, fourteen years earlier, had made a film of Rimsky-Korsakov's *Sadko*, came up with another Rimsky fantasy, *The Tale of Tsar Sultan*, in which the son of the Tsar is turned into a bumblebee so he can spy on his family (the opera from which the famous 'Flight of the bumblebee' comes).

In 1968 Roman Tikhomirov, who had filmed Tchaikovsky's *The Queen of Spades* in 1960 using actors with voices provided by members of the Bolshoi company, directed *Eugene Onegin* with Tatiana's singing voice provided by Galina Vishnevskaya and Onegin's by Yevgeny Kibkalo. He then turned his attention to Borodin's sprawling masterpiece, *Prince Igor* (1970), and gave it the full epic treatment, shooting it as a widescreen spectacular on location in the steppes. Again, he shot with actors miming to a pre-recorded soundtrack made by Kirov artists who included Yevgeny Nesterenko as Khan Konchak.

Alongside those films made specifically for television, a steady stream of operettas destined for the cinema, along with the occasional opera, continued to appear in both East and West Germany, and in Austria. *The White Horse Inn* was filmed by Werner Jacobs in an updated version made on location at the original inn. Jacobs went on immediately to update *The Merry Widow*, shooting both productions in German and French. Geza von Cziffra directed the veteran musical star Marikka Rökk as Adele in an Austrian film of *Die Fledermaus* set at the turn of the century and Strauss's *Gipsy Baron* returned to the screen in a modern version directed by Kurt Wilhelm. The same operetta was given a lavish production in a 1975 made-for-television film by Arthur Maria Rabenalt, one of the leading postwar directors of operetta films. It starred Siegfried Jerusalem, later to become an eminent Wagnerian tenor, in one of his earliest singing engagements, together with Ellen Shade, Martha Mödl and Janet Perry.

Wolfgang Staudte directed *The Threepenny Opera* with Sammy Davis Jnr. as the Ballad singer, Curt Jurgens as Macheath, Hildegard Neff as Jenny and Gert Frobe as Peachum, shooting in English as well as German in an attempt to break into the international market. *The Forester's Daughter*, *The Makropulos Case*, *The Merry Wives of Windsor* with Lucia Popp, *The Circus Princess*, *One Night in Venice* with Julia Migenes, then a member of the Vienna Volksoper,

Countess Maritza with René Kollo and Ljuba Welitsch, *Orpheus in the Underworld*, all were turned into films.

In Czechoslovakia, Vaclav Kaslik, well known for his television films of such operas as *Rusalka*, made a film of *The Bartered Bride* with Gabriela Benackova providing the voice of Marenka, and in Italy, veteran director Carmine Gallone made an updated version of *Carmen* featuring Giovanna Ralli in which he transfered the action from Spain to Trastevere, a poor area of Rome where Don José became a local policeman and Escamillo a motorcyclist. A lavishly costumed and faithful film of Offenbach's *La Vie Parisienne* was made in France.

In Belgium, Jean Antoine made a quirky film of *Your Faust*, an avant-garde opera written by Henri Pousseur, a graduate of the Darmstadt summer school. For four singers, five actors, tape and audience, this had received its premiere in Milan in 1969. A young composer is commissioned to write an opera about *Faust* but a waitress tries to dissuade him. What his decision will be is decided by the audience, so there are variations for the second half. Antoine, renaming the opera *The Travels of Your Faust*, shot it partly in the studio, partly on location, filming the musical sequences in colour, the spoken sections in black-and-white which he then tinted.

Despite the cool reception given to *The Story of Gilbert and Sullivan*, British producers remained convinced there was an audience for Gilbert and Sullivan. In 1963 Michael Winner directed an updated version of *The Mikado* which he had adapted himself. *The Cool Mikado* was set in postwar Japan with Frankie Howerd as Ko-Ko and Stubby Kaye as Judge Mikado. It was, according to one critic, one of the worst films ever made.

Three years later *The Mikado* again appeared on the screen but in a much more traditional form, directed by Stuart Burge. This was Anthony Besch's 1964 production for the D'Oyly Carte Company filmed on the stage of the Golders Green Hippodrome in 1966, using the traditional costumes dating from 1926, and sets designed in 1964 by Disley Jones. The film featured company stalwarts Donald Adams as the Mikado, John Reed as Ko-Ko and Valerie Masterson as Yum-Yum. Isodore Godfrey conducted the City of Birmingham Symphony Orchestra and the film was released in Britain as part of a double-bill with Halas and Batchelor's animated version of *Ruddigore* (for which D'Oyly Carte singers had provided the soundtrack). It was a faithful rendering of the stage production, unlikely to offend any of the purists, but equally unlikely to interest anyone who was not already a Gilbert and Sullivan fan. Unlike the 1939 *Mikado* with Martyn Green, it had not been considered in filmic terms at all. 'The cameras have captured everything about the company's acting except its magic,' wrote a critic in the *New York Times*.

Two D'Oyly Carte singers, the bass Donald Adams and the tenor Thomas Round, had formed a company called Gilbert and Sullivan for All to tour evenings of Gilbert and Sullivan concerts. In 1974 they engaged producer John Seabourne to help them film eight G&S operas under the series title, *The World of Gilbert and Sullivan.* These were hour-long highlights explaining the stories of *The Pirates of Penzance, The Yeoman of the Guard, Trial by Jury, Ruddigore, The Gondoliers, HMS Pinafore, The Mikado,* and *Iolanthe,* aimed at schools and American television. Very low budget, the series was shot in the Odeon cinema in Slough and the sound track recorded at Denham studios. The singers were almost exclusively members or former members of the D'Oyly Carte, and the series was directed by Trevor Evans.

The year before, John Seabourne's brother Peter had produced and directed four films under the generic title, *Focus on Opera,* intended to be shown as supporting films in the cinema. An hour long, these largely featured singers from the English National Opera, and were shot on location at Knebworth House in Hertfordshire, using the house, a barn (in which sets were erected) and the grounds. *La Traviata* featured Valerie Masterson (who had just joined ENO from the D'Oyly Carte Company and was about to become one of Britain's leading exponents of the French repertoire) as Violetta, Kenneth Woollam as Alfredo and Michael Wakeham as Germont. Wakeham sang Figaro in *The Barber of Seville* with Margaret Eels as Rosina. Masterson and Woollam sang Nedda and Canio in *Pagliacci,* and Antonia and Hoffmann in *The Tales of Hoffmann*; Malcolm Rivers sang the title role in *Rigoletto* with John Brecknock as the Duke and Lillian Watson as Gilda.

Education about opera was obviously in the air at the beginning of the seventies for a children's series with Joan Sutherland called *Who's Afraid of Opera?* was made at Shepperton for American television. Sutherland and the cast sang excerpts from the featured opera which were then linked by two puppets sitting in a box making comments and explaining the story (precursors of two similar characters in the Muppets). The operas were *The Barber of Seville, The Daugher of the Regiment, Faust, Lucia di Lammermoor, La Périchole, Rigoletto, La Traviata* and *Mignon.* Sutherland's husband Richard Bonynge conducted the orchestra. The most vivid memory of one of the crew on the shoot is of Joan Sutherland sitting at the side of the set knitting, putting it down in time to sing wonderfully, then returning to her knitting.

Throughout the sixties and seventies, opera singers continued to appear in films other than operas. The American bass Giorgio Tozzi, who had studied with Rosa Raisa and Giacomo Rimini in his home town of Chicago and appeared on Broadway, at La Scala and at the Met, appeared in non-singing roles in *Shamus* (1972), with Burt Reynolds as a private eye hired to recover some jewels and find a murderer; in *One of Our Own* (1975) with George Peppard; and in *Torn Between Two Lovers* (1979) a made-for-television movie with Peppard and Lee Remick.

Ljuba Welitsch, the flame-haired Bulgarian soprano noted for her interpretation of Salome and a popular member of the Vienna State Opera, was seen on stage singing in the last act of *Salome* in *The Man Between* (1953), a British spy thriller directed by Carol Reed which attempted to imitate Reed's *The*

Third Man. In the scene, James Mason and Claire Bloom were in the audience at the Berlin Staatsoper, plotting their escape to the West.

Welitsch was seen on stage again, this time with Mario Del Monaco in the feature *Final Resolution* (1960), the plot of which revolved around the premiere of an opera in Salzburg. She also appeared in *Julia, Du bist Zauberhaft*, adapted from a novel by Somerset Maugham, and in *Arms and the Man*, a German adaptation of Shaw's play, both in non-singing roles. After her retirement from the operatic stage, Welitsch enjoyed a substantial second career as a film actress and by her own reckoning appeared in well over a hundred films and television dramas.

Helen Traubel didn't get to sing either when she appeared as a former opera singer running a Hollywood boarding house for aspiring actresses in the Jerry Lewis comedy *The Ladies' Man* (1961), which Lewis also directed. In *Gunn* (1967), a feature based on the Peter Gunn TV series, directed by Blake Edwards, she was seen running a nightclub.

Tenor Jan Peerce made an appearance at the wedding in *Goodbye, Columbus* with Ali McGraw and Richard Benjamin, a film directed by his son, Larry, and the Austrian soprano Wilma Lipp, a member of the Vienna State Opera who sang at Glyndebourne, appeared in a scene in *The Cardinal* (1964), Otto Preminger's melodramatic story of a Boston curate who fights the Ku Klux Klan, goes to Rome as a diplomat and ends up a cardinal. While in Vienna he hears Lipp singing the 'Alleluia' from Mozart's *Exultate Jubilate*.

The American soprano Anna Moffo appeared in several feature films as an actress. She had been born in Pennsylvania but studied in Rome and made her debut in Spoleto in 1955. The following year she made her American debut in Chicago and three years later sang Violetta in *La Traviata* at the Met, a role she was later to film in Italy with Franco Bonisoli as Alfredo, Gino Bechi as Germont and Afro Poli as the doctor. The film was directed by her husband, Mario Lanfranchi.

Moffo's first film had been an Italian television film of Pergolesi's *La Serva Padrona*. She then starred opposite René Kollo in a Hungarian-German feature of Kalman's operetta, *Die Csárdásfürstin* (The Gipsy Princess) directed by Miklos Szinetar before Lanfranchi directed her again in *Lucia di Lammermoor*, shot on location in a seventeenth-century Italian castle. She was cast opposite Kollo a second time for a German television film of Offenbach's *La Belle Hélène*.

At the same time as she was appearing in such films because she was an opera singer, Moffo was regularly on the screen in Italian films as an actress. She did sing some songs in *Menage all'Italiana* but that was incidental to her role as a singer married to a man who can't stop chasing other women. There was a similar theme, but minus the songs, in *Il Divorzio*, when Moffo played a wife whose husband leaves her to sow some wild oats only to find he has been supplanted by a younger man when he comes home. She did get to sing 'Sempre libera' as one of the characters in *The Adventurers*, Lewis Gilbert's clichéd film of the sensational Harold Robbins sex-and-violence novel. 'Lovers of rotten movies and close-up violence can revel in it,' remarked one unimpressed critic.

When it came to putting opera on the screen, what intrigued film directors more and more was how it should be done. Just about everything had been tried over the years. Films had been shot with singers singing live; they had been shot to playback; they had been shot with the singers recording the soundtrack to picture; they had been shot with actors miming to singers; they had been shot in the studio; they had been shot on location; they had been shot off the stage using single cameras; they had been shot off the stage using several cameras. Pierre Jourdan had already used the multi-camera technique pioneered by Paul Czinner, when he made his film of the 1974 Orange Festival production of *Norma*. He used it again for the 1977 Orange Festival production of *Fidelio* with Jon Vickers as Florestan, Gundala Janowitz as Leonore and Theo Adam as Pizarro. The only difference this time was that he filmed without an audience. Even though his film was destined for a cinema release, it still remained a visual account of a stage production.

The Italian director Gianfranco de Bosio tried yet another approach. Like Carmine Gallone twenty years earlier, he decided not just to shoot *Tosca* (1976) on location but to film it in the precise Roman locations specified by Puccini in his score. He cast Raina Kabaivanska in the title role, Plácido Domingo as Cavaradossi and Sherrill Milnes as Scarpia. Domingo's son, Placi, then aged ten, was the Shepherd Boy. De Bosio managed to get permission to use the Church of Sant' Andrea della Valle for the first act and the Castel Sant' Angelo for the third, but he could not get into the Palazzo Farnese for the second. The building housed the French Embassy and they simply would not allow a film crew in. De Bosio knew what he wanted for the film: it took him nineteen hours to get the first act duet between Cavaradossi and Tosca in the can.

Tosca was produced by the German company Unitel. Unitel may have been set up for the greater glorification of Herbert von Karajan with films of the maestro both for television and the cinema, but it did not take long for the company to become one of the largest producers of arts programming in the world, including making films of opera. Important though television was as a market, the cinema was seen to be equally important, and even more prestigious. One of the directors invited to make opera films which could span the two was the French designer and director, Jean-Pierre Ponnelle.

Ponnelle directed sixteen operatic films before his untimely death in 1988 at the age of 56, following a fall into the orchestra pit while rehearsing a production of *Carmen* in Tel Aviv. He had started his career in Germany as a designer, and began producing operas on stage in 1962, the year he worked on his first operatic film as a designer. This was a production of *Die Entführung aus dem Serail* for the director Heinz Liesendahl with Anneliese Rothenberger, Peter Pasetti, Judith Blegen, Werner Krenn and Oscar Czerwenka. The conductor was Georg Solti.

In 1972 he made his debut as a film director with *The Barber of Seville*, featuring Hermann Prey as Figaro, the always elegant Luigi Alva as Almaviva, Teresa Berganza as Rosina and Enzo Dara as Bartolo. This was shot in the studio in realistic sets designed by Ponnelle himself. The film looks perfect, perhaps too perfect for a film in that the viewer is constantly aware that the action is based on a stage production, but his camerawork is fluid, the cast is excellent and it is clear that Ponnelle knows exactly what he wants.

Ponnelle's next opera was *Madama Butterfly* (1974) with Mirella Freni in the title role and Plácido Domingo as Pinkerton. As a young singer in Mexico, Domingo had spent two years appearing on Channel 11, the Mexican cultural channel, playing the piano and singing a wide range of music. He had also appeared in a number of televised operettas including *The Merry Widow*, *Frou-Frou del Tabarin*, *Luisa Fernanda* and *The Count of Luxembourg* (in which Marta Ornela, who was to become his wife, and Plácido Snr. also appeared) but this was his first time in a film studio. Others in the cast included Christa Ludwig as Suzuki and Robert Kerns as Sharpless.

Madama Butterfly was filmed in a Berlin studio to a track pre-recorded by Karajan and the Vienna Philharmonic in Vienna, Ponnelle directed the film as a flashback, after Domingo, in slow-motion, had crashed through the wall of the house where he and Butterfly had once lived, pushing aside Goro who is offering him another girl.

Since this was not a filmed record of a stage production but a film which happened to be being shot in a studio, it was necessary to make everything look as realistic as possible. It was easy to make Domingo look like an American sailor out for a good time, but Freni as Butterfly was more difficult. To make her look Japanese, she was given white make-up and had her eyes pulled back so hard, she spent the entire shoot in pain.

Madama Butterfly was a great success and Ponnelle and Domingo worked together again on *Hommage à Sevilla*. The idea for the film came from Domingo who felt that so many operas are set in Seville, they could be used as the basis for a musical guide to the city. He asked Ponnelle to direct, Unitel agreed to put up the money and Domingo was filmed singing not just tenor arias but baritone ones as well, sometimes, thanks to modern technology, dueting with himself. He sang Florestan's aria from *Fidelio* in the ruins of the Roman amphitheatre just outside the city, a *Don Giovanni* aria from the tower of Seville's cathedral, the final duet from *Carmen* (with Victoria Vergera) inside Seville's bullring and, at the same location a duet with Virginia Alonzo, from *El Gato Montes*. He sang a duet from *The Barber of Seville* in which he was both Figaro and Almaviva. Plans for him and Ponnelle to go on and make a film of *Turandot* with Unitel came to nothing.

Ponnelle's next film was *The Marriage of Figaro* with Hermann Prey in the title role, Mirella Freni as Susanna, Maria Ewing as Cherubino and Dietrich Fischer-Dieskau as the Count. This time he did not film in Berlin but at

Shepperton Studios just outside London. When details of the cast were sent to London, the German producers announced grandly that they had managed to get a very good Japanese soprano to sing the role of the Countess. Her name, they said, was Kiri Te Kanawa. Te Kanawa is, of course, a Maori from New Zealand. She had made her first film in New Zealand in 1966 when she was 21, singing in a tourist musical called *Don't Let It Get To You*. Her role was so small she wasn't mentioned in any of the reviews. She had then come to London to study at the London Opera Centre. Colin Davis cast her as the Countess in his 1971 Covent Garden production of *The Marriage of Figaro* and although that was to mark the start of her international career, she was still not that well-known when she accepted to appear in Ponnelle's film.

By the time the film was made, fundamental changes were taking place in television. Video tape had almost completely taken over as the day-to-day medium for recording television programmes whether made in the studio or on location. If tape had a drawback it was that, for colour, it required so much light that scenes could look over-lit and rather flat. There was no sense of richness or depth within the frame. For this reason Ponnelle insisted on shooting *The Marriage of Figaro* (and most of his filmed operas) on 35mm film, but to satisfy the needs of the Unitel salesmen who wanted to sell the production as a video, he also agreed to shoot it on tape as well. For each set-up he had two cameras – one film, the other video. This made the schedule very tight and both crew and artists had to work very long hours. While the orchestral track had been pre-recorded in Germany, the singers sang live on set, which created a problem when Fischer-Dieskau lost his voice.

Unitel were having financial problems at the time of filming *The Marriage of Figaro* due to the changing nature of the television and film industries and it was rumoured on the set that the film only went ahead because Hermann Prey had put money into it. The finished film, while beautiful to look at, can now seem a little heavy-handed and leaden in places, especially when Ponnelle was trying to get away from giving the impression that he was simply filming a stage performance by having voices singing over cutaway shots.

With video having taken over as the medium for recording operatic performances, the reasons for using film had to be clear. In the case of a director like Ponnelle it was because he preferred the picture quality. Towards the end of the seventies, Ponnelle, who continued to produce in the opera house throughout his career (several of his productions ending up on videos directed by other people) got together with the conductor Nikolaus Harnoncourt to stage a cycle of Monteverdi operas in Zurich. Ponnelle decided to film them. Baroque opera posed him a much greater problem than any of the previous operas he had filmed, since early 17th century opera is very much stand-and-sing opera, not at all well suited to quick cutting and many modern film techniques. How should he film them?

Ponnelle's solution was to accept Monteverdi's conventions completely and not attempt to modernise the setting or be clever with the staging. He had dressed his singers in elaborate costumes (over-elaborate some might say), placed them in stylised sets and let the music do the work. His films of the operas are made in a similar fashion. Taking his cue from Bergman, he establishes at the very beginning the theatricality of the performances by showing the proscenium arch. In *Orfeo*, like Bergman, he shows the audience, this time mingling with the cast. As each opera begins, the camera slowly moves in until it has entered the world of the stage. Even then, all his camera movements are slow and deliberate: a zoom in that is imperceptable and lasts many seconds, the holding of a shot for what seems an eternity. It is all very slow but it establishes a rhythm, makes the viewer continue to watch lest one misses something, until the music and the atmosphere he has created, like a drug, take over.

The cast for *Orfeo* included Philippe Huttenlocher, Dietlinde Turban, Trudeliese Schmidt, Roland Hermann and Glenys Linos; that for *Il Ritorno d'Ulisse in Patria*, Werner Hollweg in the title role, Schmidt, Francisco Araiza, Paul Esswood, Huttenlocher and Janet Perry; and in the cast of *L'Incoronazione di Poppea* were Rachael Yakar as Poppea, Eric Tappy as Nero, Schmidt, Esswood and Matti Salminen.

Ponnelle's Monteverdi cycle was a deliberate attempt to find an appropriate style for putting a certain formal kind of opera on the screen. A director who came up with a very different solution was Joseph Losey, whose *Don Giovanni* (1978) was the most radical of the seventies' opera films. Losey had been driven out of Hollywood by the McCarthy witch-hunt of left wingers and had settled in Europe. That he should agree to make such a film was surprising in view of the fact he had no musical ear and no great sympathy with languages.

The proposal to film *Don Giovanni* came from Rolf Liebermann, then Director of the Paris Opéra, and Daniel Toscan du Plantier, president of Gaumont Films in France, who had met by chance and discussed the filming of opera. Liebermann, in his days at the Hamburg Opera, had been involved with several attempts to film opera with which he was not entirely happy. They had been films of stage productions made initially for television and he felt that although they provided a useful record of a production, they did not work as films. A cinema film, on the other hand, would be the perfect way to take opera to the masses without involving any form of state subsidy. Toscan du Plantier, a former advertising and marketing man, felt he could sell a 'real' movie of opera as opposed to a stage production that had had cameras pointed at it, however creatively.

The opera that best fitted their purpose, they decided, was *Don Giovanni*. It was written by a composer of whom people had heard, it contains attractive music, it has a good story which is easy to follow by those who don't know it already. Liebermann proposed filming in and around Vicenza, using as a backdrop the buildings designed by Renaissance architect Andrea Palladio. When it came to the director, Toscan du Plantier was adamant: it had to be someone

179

whose first instinct and love was cinema. He didn't have to be an opera buff. In fact, it would be a distinct advantage if he wasn't because the end result had to be a film of an opera, not an opera that had been put on film. Toscan du Plantier suggested Losey, then living in France and trying to raise the money to make a movie of a Proust novel.

When he met Losey, Liebermann was horrified to discover that not only had the director never seen *Don Giovanni*, he was bored by Verdi and even more bored by Wagner. He took him to the Paris Opéra to see what he was missing. As soon as the house lights dimmed, Losey fell asleep. He did, however, agree to the project because, he later said, of the combination of Mozart, the theme of *Don Giovanni* and the architecure of Palladio. In fact he had not worked for a year and felt that here was an opportunity for him to do something that would out-Bergman Bergman. He was undoubtedly also attracted to the opera since he felt that it mirrored his own life in a remarkable way.

Losey had no say in his cast. Liebermann was staging a new production at the Paris Opéra with Ruggero Raimondi in the title role, Kiri Te Kanawa as Donna Elvira, Edda Moser as Donna Anna, Teresa Berganza as Zerlina and José van Dam as Leporello. He simply engaged the entire company for the film.

In the summer of 1978, they recorded the soundtrack in a Parisian church with Lorin Maazel conducting. Losey, who turned up at the recording, was not entirely happy that he and Maazel had not discussed the music at all. He felt that since this was to be the soundtrack for a feature film, the director's requirements should be considered rather than for the conductor simply to make a clean studio recording suitable for later commercial release on disc. Although he did not interfere, Losey's presence upset most of the cast, apart from Kiri Te Kanawa who continued to knit or eat an apple until two bars before she was required to sing, when she would stand up, deliver her lines, then sit down again.

Two months later, filming began in Vicenza and was immediately brought to a halt when a violent thunderstorm was followed by five days of continuous rain. Filming was impossible, not least because Janine Reiss, the harpsichordist who was playing for the live recitatives, had frozen fingers (only the arias were being shot to playback with the cast singing mezzo-voce, or half-voice). Losey had little option but to cancel the filming. This gave him time to work with his sound engineers on another problem that had arisen: how to match the live sound with the pre-recording.

It was a problem that Losey never entirely resolved and when the film opened in Washington in November 1978 before being released in New York and Europe, one of the principal criticisms was that the post-synchronisation was poor.

Audiences generally reacted favourably to the film, but the reviews were mixed with the European critics liking it much more than their American counterparts. While the film was well sung, wrote one, it was poorly acted. Losey, he continued, had added nothing to the story but only succeeded in confusing it, especially for those who didn't know the opera. The camera, added another, had done nothing for Berganza, who looked too old to play Zerlina (something of which she was acutely aware before filming started), nor for Kenneth Reigel, who played Don Ottavio and was clearly overweight.

Losey's fascination with bisexuality had led him to introduce the Valet in Black (played by Isabelle Adjani's younger brother, Eric), a child who followed Don Giovanni around, handing him his mandolin and waiting upon him. Losey, who claimed in interview that while Giovanni was not a homosexual, he was certainly bisexual, refused to elaborate on the presence of the Valet or what he might signify. Many people felt the film showed Giovanni to be gay. Giulini, asked his opinion, commented that the film was neither Mozart nor Da Ponte.

Despite a mass of publicity, the film did not do that well at the box-office. The shooting period had gone from 28 days to 44, sending the production way over budget (instead of 12 million francs it cost 20 million) and it never even covered its costs, although it did turn Raimondi into an international star and pin-up. Raimondi had first sung the role in 1967 at La Fenice in Venice, three years after making his professional debut as Colline in Spoleto, and it was the role with which he had made his first major international engagement, at Glyndebourne in 1969. It had subsequently taken him round the world, but it was through Losey's film that ordinary people first got to know of him.

Away from the publicity surrounding its shooting and free from the prejudice against opera on film, *Don Giovanni* can be seen as one of the most striking examples of an operatic film that works. While it does have flaws (the synchronisation certainly is not ideal) it is a success because Losey made it as a cinematic creation. Despite his initial antagonism towards opera, Losey was extremely happy working on the film, and talked about doing more.

Another director attracted to Italy for filming an opera was the British director Tony Palmer who decided to shoot Britten's final opera, *Death in Venice* (1981), on location. Palmer, too, went for singers to play the roles rather than getting actors to mime to playback. John Shirley-Quirk and James Bowman were asked to reprise the roles they had created in the opera's original production, with Bowman as the Voice of Apollo and Shirley-Quirk in the seven baritone roles including the Traveller, the Elderly Fop, the Hotel Manager and the Hotel Barber. Robert Gard was cast in the central role of Aschenbach.

Palmer used the Venice locations effectively, capturing the listless heat of the city, the endlessly changing light, and the oppressive nature of the labyrinthine streets which never seem to lead anywhere other than to another canal. Occasionally Palmer overdoes such effects as bleaching out scenes to add to the impression of heat, or filming interiors through filters, but overall the film is a notable achievement.

Palmer was later to shoot an epic ten-hour life of *Wagner* (1984) starring Richard Burton in his last major screen appearance. Although made for television (it was broadcast in ten parts) it was shot as a film with Vittorio Storaro, who had won Oscars for *Apocalypse Now*, *Reds* and *The Last Emperor*, as cameraman. Shirley Russell was the costume designer and Kenneth Carey (*The French Lieutenant's Woman*) the designer. The script was written with the approval of Wolfgang Wagner by Charles Wood (who also wrote *Charge of the Light Brigade* and the Beatles' film *Help!*) and an all-star cast was assembled which included Vanessa Redgrave as Cosima, Gemma Craven as Wagner's first wife, Minna, Laurence Olivier, John Gielgud and Ralph Richardson. Among the opera singers taking part were Gwyneth Jones, Peter Hofmann, Heinz Zednik, Yvonne Kenny, Manfred Jung, Adele Leigh and Jess Thomas. There was even a brief appearance by the composer William Walton as Friedrich August II of Saxony. Palmer filmed in six countries over a seven-month period, and the film included scenes from *The Ring*, *Tristan und Isolde*, *Tannhäuser* and *Lohengrin*. The fiasco of the Paris opening of *Tannhäuser* was brilliantly recreated.

Wagner's opera *Parsifal* was in turn the subject of a quite remarkable film by Hans-Jurgen Syberberg, made to celebrate the hundredth anniversary of the opera's first performance at Bayreuth. At over four hours long, this may not seem the most obvious opera to choose for a feature film but Syberberg turned it into a spellbinding piece of cinema. He made no attempt to shoot it realistically, setting it instead on a barren moon-like landscape which turns out to be a giant death mask of Wagner. The film operates on many levels. It is Wagner's opera, albeit in a rather eccentric production (Amfortas's bleeding wound is carried in on a silver salver; Parsifal is portrayed by both a boy and girl) but it is also a partial examination of the place of *Parsifal* in German culture, with images of concentration camp watchtowers, the Allied bombing of German cities, and a swastika among the banners hanging in the hall.

Syberberg used both singers and actors. Robert Lloyd sings and appears as Gurnemanz, Aage Haugland sings and appears as Klingsor and the conductor Armin Jordan, in an inspired piece of casting, plays Amfortas (with Wolfgang Schone's voice). The voice of Parsifal is provided by Reiner Goldberg, and that of Kundry (Edith Clever) by Yvonne Minton. Kundry, acted mesmerically by Clever, is the central character of the film, seen at the end peering at the Bayreuth opera house under construction.

Shot with enormous style, *Parsifal* is compelling because it is not simply four-and-a-half hours of stage opera but a multi-layered piece of cinema. Robert Lloyd said later that none of the cast really understood what Syberberg was on about, they simply did what he asked.

It is sometimes said that opera and film are incompatible because film is realistic and opera is not. No film demonstrates better than *Parsifal* that it is perfectly possible to have illusion in an operatic film. Syberberg succeeds in turning a static stage work into a piece of thought-provoking cinema.

14

The Eighties

Franco Zeffirelli was already a well-known film director before he made his first screen opera, but that wasn't for want of trying. He had started his career in the theatre and opera house as a designer and director before turning to films and working as Visconti's assistant. He was longing to combine his love of opera with his love of film but it took him more than twenty years before he achieved his ambition.

In 1964 at Covent Garden, he had directed Maria Callas and Tito Gobbi in *Tosca* in a production which, by common consent, was one of the great productions of all time. One of the major regrets for anyone who loves opera must be that Callas, who spent her entire career in a visual age, never sang on film and only very rarely on video. Zeffirelli, aware there was virtually nothing of her on the screen, was determined to capture her Tosca performance for posterity.

He had suggested making a film with her once before, in 1958, when they had worked together in Dallas on *La Traviata* and some local wealthy buisnessmen had offered to back a film of the production. But Callas was nervous of film and pointed out that Zeffirelli had no experience of directing one. The project foundered.

During 1966, Zeffirelli finally managed to direct his first film, the rumbustious *The Taming of the Shrew* with Burton and Taylor. He felt confident that, having worked with those two, he could handle any tantrums Callas might throw and so he contacted her about filming the Covent Garden production of *Tosca*. She would, he declared, become the new Greta Garbo. To his surprise, she agreed to do it. Everything seemed to be falling into place. He raised the money from the German company Beta Films, Tito Gobbi agreed to take part, a studio was booked. All that was required was her signature on the contract.

The final details of the contract were ironed out at a meeting between Zeffirelli, Callas and her agent in Monte Carlo. Callas took the contract to show Aristotle Onassis, and it was then that things began to go wrong. Onassis tore up the contract and announced that they would make the film themselves. Zeffirelli was invited on board Onassis's yacht, *Christina*, to discuss the project. He knew, or thought he did, from what she had already told him, that Callas wanted to make the film. She had a fixation on Audrey Hepburn at the time and saw herself singing Tosca while looking like Hepburn in *Roman Holiday*. Zeffirelli, horrified by the way Onassis treated Callas, was convinced he had no intention of letting her take part, and when Onassis gave him $10,000 for research and pre-production, he realised his suspicions were correct. The amount was barely enough to cover the cost of the telephone calls it would take to set up an international production and yet it looked as though Onassis was giving the project his full backing while in reality he was stalling.

Zeffirelli went away to begin setting up the production. He discovered that the film rights for *Tosca* were held by Karajan who was planning to produce a film himself and would never give permission for the Covent Garden production to be filmed. There was also little chance of Karajan and Callas working together harmoniously. They had worked together at La Scala and made recordings but Karajan had once described her voice as like the sound of a knife scraping across a plate; and when a magazine profile invited him to name the greatest singers with whom he had worked, he did not include her. Callas flatly refused to work with him.

In spite of all the time he had spent on designing costumes, finding locations and preparing a shooting script, Zeffirelli had to admit defeat when, as he suspected, Karajan refused to part with the film rights. He laid the blame for the project's failure squarely on Onassis, but film producer Franco Rossellini later maintained that it was Callas herself who did not want the project to go ahead. She did not, he said, believe opera should be filmed and had only agreed to have so many meetings about *Tosca* because Zeffirelli had pushed and pushed her.

Callas did eventually make a film but not one in which she sang. Producers had been trying to get her as an actress for some time. In 1961 she turned down an offer from Carl Foreman to play opposite Gregory Peck in *The Guns of Navarone*, in the part that went eventually to Irene Papas. She refused to appear in a film of Hans Habe's novel *The Primadonna*, even though Onassis was keen for her to do it, and declined an offer from Visconti to play Maria Jeritza in a life of Puccini. Joseph Losey's attempt to cast her in Tennessee Williams's *Boom!* also failed although she did consider it carefully. Losey wanted her to play an ageing star living amongst her diamonds and memories on a Mediterranean island, a role which may have seemed a little too close to the truth for comfort (Elizabeth Taylor took it). She also declined John Huston's offer to appear as Sarah in *The Bible*, the part played by Ava Gardner. In 1969, however, much to everyone's surprise, she agreed to appear in Pasolini's *Medea*, not the opera by Cherubini but an updating of the Greek myth. Callas, whose singing career was effectively over even though she was looking for ways to resurrect it, saw in the story strong parallels with her own life.

As for Zeffirelli, despite the rebuff from Callas, he continued to try and set up operatic films. In 1967 his plan to film *Aïda* on location in Egypt came to nothing because of the Six Day War. Twelve years later, he revived the idea and travelled to Egypt to look for locations. He invited Leonard Bernstein to conduct and together the two men produced a storyboard. The tenor they wanted for the role of Radamès was Plácido Domingo. Both were keen, however, that the Aïda should be unknown, and although they discussed casting Leona Mitchell they agreed it could be someone from outside opera who would have to be dubbed.

They had gone some way towards getting the production off the ground when Zeffirelli suddenly received his first chance to direct an operatic film. RAI, the Italian state television service, planned to broadcast live, in January 1981, the first night of his productions of *Cavalleria Rusticana* and *Pagliacci* from La Scala. Zeffirelli had directed a previous live broadcast of his production of *Otello* but didn't want this occasion to be the same. He agreed to RAI's request on the condition that he be allowed to do something other than point outside broadcast cameras at the production; he wanted to make a film. RAI agreed and Unitel, seeing the commercial potential of the project, especially with Domingo starring in both operas, came in as co-producer. Zeffirelli made one further stipulation. He wanted Teresa Stratas to sing Nedda in *Cavalleria Rusticana*.

The Canadian-born soprano was not, at that time, particularly well-known in Italy. Born in Canada of Greek parentage, she had made her operatic debut in Toronto in 1958 singing Mimi and the following year had begun her long association with the Met when she appeared there as *Manon*. As one of a new generation of acting singers, she had been signed up to appear in the feature film, *The Canadians* (1961), starring Robert Ryan and directed by Burt Kennedy. Stratas played a member of the Sioux nation fleeing into Canada after Custer's Last Stand, only to be harassed by nasty Canadians until the Mounties came to their rescue. It was a dreary film which, according to one reviewer, set back the Canadian film industry by a couple of years.

Stratas had also made operatic films for television including a Canadian production of Puccini's *La Rondine* (1970) and *Amahl and the Night Visitors* (1979). This visually sumptuous production of Menotti's opera had been shot on location in Israel and in the studio in England by Arvin Brown. Stratas played Amahl's Mother, with Giorgio Tozzi, Willard White and Nico Castel as the three kings. Menotti himself had been the film's music consultant.

Despite such films and her successes on stage in Germany, the management at La Scala were reluctant to engage Stratas in place of the singer who had already been invited to sing Nedda, but Zeffirelli insisted and got his way.

The operas were largely filmed at La Scala without an audience. Zeffirelli had a platform built over the front of the stalls on which he could put his cameras to shoot in ten-minute bursts (the length of a magazine of film) with the orchestra playing live. For the wide shots he had to pull all the cameras back.

He allowed himself two days to film both operas, shooting all day on Monday when the house did not have a performance, and for ten hours on Tuesday, still getting out of the theatre in time for the evening performance to go ahead as scheduled. He completed almost everything within that time, having to go into a studio in Milan for some pick-ups, before going to Vizzini in Sicily, the village in which the events depicted in *Cavalleria Rusticana* are supposed to have taken place, for some location filming.

Domingo played Turiddu in *Cavelleria Rusticana* with Elena Obraztsova as Santuzza, Renato Bruson as Alfio, Axelle Gall as Lola and Fedora Barbieri as Mamma Lucia. In *Pagliacci*, Domingo sang Canio with Stratas as Nedda and Juan Pons as Tonio. Both films betray their theatrical origins. *Pagliacci* is played out by the singers through the proscenium arch even though the arch itself is never seen. But the popularity of the operas, the presence of Domingo, and Zeffirelli's stylish direction with its quick cutting of the crowd shots in particular, while never being afraid to hold a shot when necessary, brought in new audiences when the films were shown on television in Italy. Reaction in the United States was even more enthusiastic, revealing a far larger television audience for well-filmed opera than anyone had before realised.

Pagliacci won an Emmy, and looking to cash in on the success of both productions, Zeffirelli immediately tried to resurrect his *Aïda* project, aiming it, like his *Cav* and *Pag*, at television. Unitel agreed to put up half the budget, British, French and Italian television stations expressed serious interest in being partners in the project. It looked as though the cameras might actually begin to roll at last, but then President Anwar Sadat was gunned down, and with his death, Zeffirelli's dream of filming *Aïda* on location in Egypt died too.

Zeffirelli was determined, however, to make another opera film, and the one he had in mind was *La Traviata*, the opera he had first discussed filming with Callas more than twenty years earlier. He had already spoken to Domingo about making a film based on a new production he had been invited to stage at Covent Garden, but the production never happened. Instead, Zeffirelli began to think in terms not of a film based on a stage production but of a cinematic film made from a carefully prepared screenplay. Domingo's other commitments meant he would not be free to take part and so Zeffirelli approached José Carreras whom he had been directing in a production of *La Bohème* at the Met. Carreras and Stratas, the singer he wanted for Violetta, would, he felt, be perfect casting.

Stratas was reluctant. She warned Zeffirelli that she might be trouble and so did everyone to whom he spoke. Carreras, on the other hand, desperate to be in the film, could not get a release from performances he had already lined up in Paris. Zeffirelli went back to Domingo. He, too, had stage commitments but the Teatro Colon in Buenos Aires was more accommodating and Domingo's chief concern became that he was too old to play a young, ardent lover. Zeffirelli eventually talked him into it.

The film was made in Rome using sets designed by Zeffirelli himself. He had decided to film in a style that would enhance the artificality of opera, shooting the story as a series of flashbacks seen by the dying Violetta. The filming went over schedule and involved several of the singers in having to fly out for performances, then fly back. During the shoot, Domingo completed appearances in Buenos Aires, Vienna, Barcelona and Madrid, but since the filming was done to a pre-recorded soundtrack this did not place any strain on the voice. It only made everyone extremely tired.

Stratas lived up to her promise (or threat) to be difficult. She had only just recovered from bronchitis when she recorded the soundtrack with James Levine. Hearing herself singing time and time again as shots were repeated and camera angles changed, she grew to hate the recording, convinced that the entire film would be a disaster because of her. It didn't help that Domingo was on such good form. Matters came to a head when she was asked to wear a dressing gown in the deathbed scene. She refused and when the designer pointed out that it was similar to one Callas had worn, Stratas exploded. She was not Callas, she screamed, she never had been and never would be.

Zeffirelli, hoping to calm her down by letting her see how good she was on screen, showed her some rushes. The viewing had the opposite effect. She loathed seeing herself and when the time came for her to be on the set again, she was nowhere to be found. Filming had to stop. Eventually she was discovered to be in London and agreed to return to Rome only because she did not want everyone else working on the film thrown out of work.

Even after her return, filming did not proceed smoothly. Stratas and Zeffirelli argued about almost everything, but, towards the end of 1982, the film was finished. It was first shown privately at a party in Los Angeles given by Gregory Peck with such Hollywood luminaries as Fred Astaire, James Stewart and Cary Grant present. Its first public showing was in New York the following April. Stratas refused to have anything to do with publicising the film and even planned an alternative press conference to denounce it, but the favourable critical reaction caused her to keep quiet.

La Traviata is often cited as one of the best examples of filmed opera, but while it has much to recommend it, it also demonstrates some of the shortcomings of opera on film. Zeffirelli has stated that as far as he is concerned there are two rules for filmed opera: the first that the story must be universally understood, the second that the singers must look good, be believable and be able to act for the camera. Teresa Stratas is certainly a meltingly lovely Violetta, and Domingo, in rich, ardent voice as Alfredo, looks ideal. But Zeffirelli, despite his avowed intent to move away from realism and incorporate the artificiality of opera into his approach, never quite manages to avoid being too literal in making the story clear. He introduces scenes and images which are irrelevent, cutting away to vaseline-lensed shots of Alfredo's sister, for example, whenever she is mentioned, a device that becomes faintly irritating. We don't see her on stage, we don't need to see her on film. Indeed, the imaginary pictures of her conjured up by the words Germont sings are more powerful than any realistic image.

The cut-aways of Alfredo's father waiting in the bushes outside for his son to leave are similarly unnecessary. The scene in which Germont (a very wooden Cornell MacNeil) appeals to Violetta to leave Alfredo for the sake of his sister is pivotal to the plot. It goes for little in the film because in order to utilise his cameras in a large room, Zeffirelli has the two singers standing far apart. At the height of his most impassioned appeal, Germont is looking out of a window nowhere near Violetta. There are, as one would expect with Zeffirelli, many beautiful images – a shot of Violetta alone in a vast empty corridor is memorable – and he is the master of detail. But *La Traviata* is an opera that does not need opening out, even on the screen.

Not long after *La Traviata* had been released, Zeffirelli and Domingo worked together again at the Met on a production of *Tosca*. They got to talking about the shoot and Domingo remarked that he would like them to do another film together. He had already been promised financial backing by Menachem Golan and Yoram Globus, two American Israelis who owned Cannon Films. Zeffirelli had been toying with the idea of filming *Carmen* with Stratas in the lead but after their stormy relationship on *La Traviata*, he had no wish to work with her again. Golan and Globus wanted Domingo to appear as Manrico in *Il Trovatore*. It was Domingo himself who suggested that they should film Verdi's *Otello*.

Carlos Kleiber was engaged to conduct the recording, but pulled out and was replaced by Lorin Maazel. The young Italian soprano Katia Ricciarelli was cast as Desdemona. Finding an Iago proved more difficuolt and it was Domingo's suggestion that Zeffirelli should screen test Justino Diaz. As soon as he shot the test in Rome, Zeffirelli offered Diaz the part.

Zeffirelli intended to film his exteriors in Heraklion on the island of Crete, where most of the harbour-side buildings are still Venetian, and at the castle at Barletta, a few miles north of Bari in Southern Italy. Just before filming was about to start, there was a devastating earthquake in Mexico. Domingo, who had been brought up in Mexico, still had relatives there. He cancelled all his engagements including filming and rushed back to help. He was not a singer Zeffirelli could replace. He was the Otello of his generation. The entire project hinged on him. It looked as though the film would have to be cancelled but Domingo sent word not to cancel, he would be there. He used the film, Zeffirelli later said, to help him forget the distressing sights he had seen in Mexico, by throwing himself into his work. The tears he shed on screen were real tears.

Zeffirelli faced other problems. Ricciarelli reproduced her opera house style of acting on camera and it took time and patience to coax a film performance from her. The weather in Crete did not do what it should have done. When it should have been good, it was bad. When they wanted storms, there were clear skies. For the opening storm scene, the skies were blue and gallons of water had to be pumped over the artists and the hundreds of extras bussed in from the surrounding villages (and all made to learn Verdi's music). It was cold and unpleasant and bonfires had to be lit to keep everyone warm. Crew members went down with bronchitis and Zeffirelli himself collapsed with pneumonia and had to be flown to a hospital in Rome.

Shooting had to be postponed but since all the singers had prior engagements at the end of their contracted dates for the film, it looked, for the second time, as though the film would have to be abandoned. Domingo took the lead in rearranging his schedule so that the filming could be completed. The scenes they had not managed to pick up on Crete or at Barletta, were filmed in a Rome studio and *Otello* was finished almost a year after Domingo had first suggested it.

The film did not meet with universal approval. Zeffirelli had cut and adapted Verdi's opera for his screenplay, knowing there would be howls of rage that he had done to Verdi and Boito what they had done to Shakespeare. Even allowing for the fact that he was making a film, no one could understand why he cut Desdemona's Willow Song, the opera's best-known aria. He did it, he later explained, because he found the aria boring in the theatre and felt it would be even more boring in the cinema.

Like *La Traviata*, *Otello* was only partially successful, demonstrating the difficulty of marrying realism and artifice on the screen. The Hollywood-style opening storm sequence did not sit easily with the subsequent singing. Even Domingo in fine voice could not dispel the notion that people do not sing under such circumstances. Zeffirelli's plans to reunite Domingo and Diaz in a film of *The Tales of Hoffmann* never got off the ground.

Another film-maker obsessed with opera is the Czech director Petr Weigl. Born in Brno in 1938 and brought up in Prague, Weigl studied at the FAMU film school and began making films in 1964. His earliest operatic film was of *Faust*, made in 1972. In 1978 he filmed Dvorak's *Rusalka*, followed, in 1982, by Britten's *The Turn of the Screw*. This was shot in a similar style to most of his other operatic films. Unlike Zeffirelli, who used the actual singers on screen and therefore had to cast singers who could not only sing but looked right, Weigl opted instead for beautiful locations peopled with actors chosen for their photogenic looks who could mime to a soundtrack recorded by outstanding singers. In the case of *The Turn of the Screw*, he used a commercially available recording featuring Helen Donath, Heather Harper, Robert Tear and Philip Langridge, conducted by Colin Davis.

This was very much the way operatic films had been made in Eastern Europe and the Soviet Union for some years. Vladimir Gorikker had used actors with the singing voices of members of the Bolshoi company for *Iolanta*. Joachim Herz had used the same technique when filming Wagner's *The Flying Dutchman*, as had Roman Tikhomirov for *Prince Igor*. A Hungarian film of *Hary Janos*, directed by Miklos Szinetar, used dubbed actors, and when *Jutro*, an opera by Tadeusz Baird, based on a Joseph Conrad story, was filmed in Poland, it was with actors miming to the voices of the singers who had taken part in the 1966 Warsaw premiere. This was the tradition in which Weigl was brought up. He saw little reason to change it.

For his next operatic feature, however, he did cast two singers in the leading roles. Peter Dvorsky took the title role and Brigitte Fassbaender was Charlotte in his sumptuous production of Massenet's *Werther*. The remainder of the cast was dubbed. Again shot in the Czech countryside, the pictorial richness sometimes tends to overwhelm the plot, much as it did when Weigl came to film *Eugene Onegin*. This used a recording of the opera made after a production at Covent Garden with Georg Solti conducting Bernd Weikl, Teresa Kubiak, Stuart Burrows, Julia Hamari, Anna Reynolds and Nicolai Ghiaurov. Weigl cast his production entirely with Czech actors and filmed on location in Czechoslovakia.

Not having to worry about the singing meant Weigl could concentrate on coaxing performances from his artists and creating beautiful images. The result with *Onegin* is a film that is ravishingly beautiful to look at, full of memorable and striking images, but there is no doubt it does suffer from the fact that the actors miming the singing are clearly not singing themselves. It is very difficult to abandon oneself entirely to the music when one can never escape the feeling that every emotion is always being manipulated.

Where Weigl's approach did work spectacularly well was in his 1989 film of Delius's *A Village Romeo and Juliet*. This is an opera that is rare enough on the stage; to find it on film is quite a surprise. It was written at the beginning of the century and received its first performance in Berlin in 1907. Set in Switzerland in the mid-nineteenth century, it tells the story of two young children whose farmer parents fall out. Six years later, they meet and fall in love. The Dark Fiddler, a vagabond who has had to sell the strip of land dividing the warring fathers, since he is a bastard and cannot legally own land, tries to get them to become vagabonds with him. Meeting at the local inn, The Paradise Garden, he mocks their respectability. They decide to drift away forever on a hay barge from which the bung has been removed so that it slowly sinks.

For the soundtrack, Welsh soprano Helen Field sang the role of the young girl Vreli (played by Dana Morakova) and Welsh tenor Arthur Davies that of Sali (Michel Dlouhy). The other principal singing roles were performed but not acted by Barry Mora and Stafford Dean. Only the American baritone Thomas Hampson, as the enigmatic Dark Fiddler, both sang and appeared in the film. The oustanding conductor of the ORF Symphony Orchestra was Charles Mackerras.

Musically the performance is superb, catching the lyricism and passion of Delius's heartfelt score. The music's emotion is matched by some wonderful photography. With its pastel shades and moody feel, Weigl's film captures and enhances the atmosphere created by Delius. Transitions from scene to scene, often hard to achieve effectively on stage, are handled seamlessly by the camera. It is a remarkably successful example of its kind, although the basic drawback that the singing voices of the young couple so clearly do not belong to the faces on screen, is never quite overcome.

Weigl's films employ all the techniques of feature films. They are feature films, even if they are most frequently shown on television. The take-over of the basic recording of operas by electronic cameras, meant that when a director decided to use film it was always for a specific purpose, to achieve a certain feel or look to the film. Throughout the eighties and nineties, most significant operatic films were made to be shown on television.

Bluebeard's Castle (1981) with Sylvia Sass as Judith and Kolos Kovacs, an impressively grainy bass, as Bluebeard, was filmed for Hungarian television by Miklós Szinetar. The conductor was Georg Solti. The production was a typical futuristic piece of its time, in sets which could just as easily have been for an episode of Dr. Who, but performed with such power it was hard to understand how such a mesmeric score could have been turned down when Bartók wrote it for a competition in 1911.

Operatic feature films continued to be made, but in far less quantity than in previous years. In 1936, 45 operatic films or films with operatic excerpts in them, had been released. In 1984, that number was down to three: Rosi's *Carmen*, a Czech film of *L'Elisir d'Amore*, and *Amadeus*, Peter Shaffer's account of the relationship between Mozart and Salieri which contained scenes from Mozart's operas performed by Samuel Ramey and Anne Howells, amongst others.

By the seventies the film musical, which had been a mainstay of Hollywood for so long, was dead, out-of-fashion and too expensive to make. If a Broadway musical such as Joseph Papp's *The Pirates of Penzance* was turned into a feature film, it became an event. Despite the cast – Kevin Kline, Linda Ronstadt, Angela Lansbury – the film failed to translate the excitement of Papp's stage show. Wilford Leach directed the film 'with not the slightest trace of imagination' according to the critic of the *Monthly Film Bulletin*. 'Anyone who thinks G&S is indestructable should see this,' commented The Observer.

In what turned out to be a last ditch attempt to recapture the heyday of the Hollywood musical, MGM cast Luciano Pavarotti in *Yes, Giorgio!* (1982). In the intervening years since Lanza and all those other singers had been rushed into witless stories which were simply cues for a song, Hollywood seemed to have learnt nothing. They gave Pavarotti an inept plot and a character supposedly based on the tenor himself who was, according to Pavarotti, totally false. He played an opera singer on a gruelling American tour who falls in love with the throat specialist brought in to sort out his tonsils. He would not, he insisted, ever have thrown food as he was required to do in one scene which was supposed to be funny but could not have been more flat. What humour there was in the film was corny and obvious.

Pavarotti was also overweight, reinforcing the public view that opera singers were fat, foreign and smelt of garlic. The film was murdered critically. One reviewer simply confined himself to the two-word comment: No Giorgio. It was an opinion with which Pavarotti himself concurred. 'It was probably the biggest mistake of my career,' he later wrote. The film cost, it was alleged, $19 million to make and took $2 million at the box-office.

Pavarotti appeared on the screen again on more familiar ground in Jean-Pierre Ponnelle's film of *Rigoletto* (1983), which was made, like most of Ponnelle's opera films, primarily for television but also with a theatrical release in mind. It was filmed entirely in Mantua, at locations the Duke and other characters in the opera might well have known.

As well as Pavarotti as the Duke, the cast included Ingvar Wixell as Rigoletto (doubling as Monterone), Edita Gruberova as Gilda and Ferruccio Furlanetto as Sparafucile. Ponnelle shot to a playback recorded by Riccardo Chailly in Vienna. The realistic scenes such as the opening ball which was staged as a grotesque orgy, worked well, with their quick cutting and sense of time and place. What Ponnelle had still not satisfactorily solved was what to do with the set-piece arias and duets. The first meeting in the opera between Rigoletto, frantic something may have happened to her, and his daughter Gilda, is filmed as one mid-shot with a small pull-back and crane upwards. Ponnelle makes no attempt to create any sort of cinematic tension by using camera movements or cutting. Brave – or boring – depending on your point of view.

One of the best of all operatic films was made at this time, Francesco Rosi's *Carmen* (1984). Rosi had started his career as Visconti's assistant on *La Terra Trema* in 1948, and had also worked with such directors as Antonioni before making his own directorial debut in 1958 with *La Sfida* (The Challenge). His films tended to be investigations of the relationship between individuals, corporations, criminal organisations and the state. He was, felt Gaumont's Daniel Toscan du Plantier, who was trying to repeat the Losey/*Don Giovanni* formula, the perfect, distinguished director to bring a fresh view to the filming of opera.

Carmen was shot on location in Andalucia and succeeds vividly in capturing the heat and atmosphere of the music and of Spain. Rosi was also very clever with the lip-synch problem. He shot to playback but made sure that much of the early singing was in wide or mid-shot. By the time he gets in close, the viewer is so involved with the action that the occasional failure to match lips and voice doesn't really matter.

His camerawork is superb, too. There is one memorable tracking shot which lasts about six minutes. And he's very well served by his cast, with Plácido Domingo as a Don José it would be hard to better, Julia Migenes as a raunchy and sexy Carmen and Ruggero Raimondi an appropriately swaggering Escamillo.

Both Zeffirelli's *Otello* and Rosi's *Carmen* did good business at the box office, and Toscan du Plantier was sufficiently encouraged to invite Luigi Comencini to direct a film of *La Bohème*. Andrzej Wajda was also slated to make a film of *Boris Godunov* with new operatic heart-throb Raimondi in the title role, but the project remained on the drawing-board.

Comencini had been a critic and scriptwriter before making his first feature, *Proibito Rubare*, in 1948. Set in Naples, it dealt with childhood, a theme to which he returned frequently in later films. A very versatile director and accomplished storyteller, he had never before directed opera. For *La Bohème*, he cast the black soprano Barbara Hendricks as Mimi and Spanish tenor José Carreras as Rodolfo. Carreras had just made his film debut playing the Spanish tenor Julián Gayarre in *The Final Romance*, a biopic made for Catalan television in which he sang a scene from Gomes' *Il Guarnay* with Montserrat Caballé.

Having been asked to play Rodolfo, Carreras and the other cast members, including Angela Maria Basi as Musetta, Gino Quilico as Marcello, Richard Cowan as Schaunard and Francesco Ellero D'Artegna as Colline, recorded the soundtrack with James Conlon. Shortly after the actual filming had begun, Carreras complained of feeling unwell. It was the start of the leukemia that very nearly killed him and he was forced to withdraw from the film. His place was taken by Luca Canonici who mimed to Carreras's voice.

Verdi's *Macbeth* was turned into a beautifully crafted, atmospheric film by Claude D'Anna. Although shot in colour, it has about it the feel of a black-and-white Russian classic from the sixties. D'Anna's Scotland, actually filmed in the Ardennes region of Belgium, is a cold, forbidding place matched by the cold, forbidding characters who inhabit it. It's a land without warmth or compassion and certainly without humour. Without the breaks between acts that come in the opera house, D'Anna is able to build a tension that becomes almost unbearable. Leo Nucci is outstanding in the title role and Shirley Verrett is an impressive Lady Macbeth. The roles of Banquo and Macduff, sung by Samuel Ramey and Veriano Luchetti, are played by actors.

Shirley Verrett appeared as herself in *Maggio Musicale* (1990) a comedy about the world of opera which revolved around the staging of a production of *La Bohème* in Florence. The American tenor Chris Merritt partners Verrett and Malcolm McDowell appears as the opera's producer. The film was directed by Ugo Gregoretti.

The world of opera continued to fascinate producers and directors throughout the eighties. The American soprano Wilhelmina Fernandez shot to fame singing the aria 'Ebben ... ne andro lontana', from *La Wally*, in *Diva* (1981), in which she played a prima donna in Paris who accidentally becomes involved with drug smugglers when a pirate tape of her singing becomes mixed up with a tape about a drug baron. This French film, directed by Jean-Jacques Beineix and a strange hybrid of thriller and surrealism, obtained a cult following. *Fitzcarraldo* (1982) was the story of an eccentric Irishman's obsession with Caruso and his determination to build an opera house for him in the Amazon jungle (Fitzcarraldo is the nearest the natives can get to pronouncing his name, Fitzgerald). Directed by Werner Herzog, who has also directed opera on stage, the film is a homage to opera. Caruso's voice is heard, the massive boat they have to haul from river to river and over a mountain is named the Molly Aïda, there are scenes from *I Puritani* with Isabel Jimenez Cisneros as Elvira, and scenes from *Ernani* with actors miming to the voices of Mietta Sighele, Veriano Luchetti and Dimiter Petkov.

The veteran Spanish soprano Imperio Argentina, who had appeared in many films during the 1930s, especially Spanish musicals, and played Tosca in Jean Renoir's film *La Tosca* at the outbreak of World War II, was brought out of retirement at the age of 80 to sing in a Spanish film, *Tata Mia*, directed by José Luis Borau.

For *Aria*, the British film-maker Don Boyd invited ten directors, including Jean-Luc Godard, Nicolas Roeg, Robert Altman, Derek Jarman, Bruce Beresford and Ken Russell, to make a short film using any operatic aria they wished. The choices were interesting and eclectic, ranging from Beresford's selection of an aria from *Die tote Stadt* by Korngold, to one from *Pagliacci* chosen by Bill Bryden. None of the films used singers in them and they were all very personal interpretations of the chosen recordings. Russell's film used Jussi Björling singing 'Nessun dorma', as a young woman has fantasies while on the operating table following an accident. *Aria* confused the critics who were not sure how to take it.

The changing nature of cinemagoing in the eighties (it was no longer the most important leisure activity) and the decline in importance of the studios, meant that when opera films were made, it was as a result of the enthusiasm of one person rather than because it fitted in with a pattern of studio production. Those individuals who wanted to film opera, or include arias in their work, were rarely interested in the standard repertoire. If they were, then something fascinating like Peter Brook's *The Tragedy of Carmen* (1983) would appear. Brook, once the *enfant terrible* of British theatre, had made his debut as a film director in 1953 with *The Beggar's Opera*. Its distinguished cast had included Laurence Olivier as Macheath, Stanley Holloway and Dorothy Tutin. All the actors, with the exception of Olivier and Holloway, were dubbed in a score arranged and conducted by Arthur Bliss. Despite being entertaining, the film was never too certain what it was trying to achieve, and received a critical pasting for looking like an animated advertisement for perfume.

In the early eighties, Brook staged *Carmen* in Paris in a version that cut the opera to the bone, his intention being to reveal the inner depths of the piece by stripping away the lavish set pieces everyone expected. The production took place in a circus ring with four singers, two actors and a small band playing the score reduced by Marius Constant. It was also multiple-cast with Hélène Delevault, Eva Saurova and Zehava Gal taking on the role of Carmen, Howard Hensel and Laurence Dale as Don José, Jake Gardner and John Rath as Escamillo, and Agnes Host and Veronique Dietschy as Micaela, portrayed not as a simpering, shy friend from back home but a hard-hitting, knife-toting country girl.

14. The Eighties

The Tragedy of Carmen, as Brook called it to let people know it was not the full Bizet opera, became the hottest ticket in Paris, and Brook decided to film it not once but three times, since he had three Carmens. The films were shown on television.

Another film made for television of a rarely seen piece was Kurt Weill's *Down in the Valley* (1988), directed by Frank Cvitanovich to celebrate the first five years of Channel 4. Weill's one-act folk opera was written in 1948, originally for radio, but before it had been performed, Weill revised it for colleges and amateur groups. It was given its premiere at Indiana University and immediately became very popular, largely because of its use of the folk-song which opens the opera and is repeated throughout. Brack Weaver, a wholesome American boy, is in prison, sentenced to death for killing a drunken, knife-wielding man in a fight at a hoe-down. The cause of the fight was one Jennie Parsons. The evening before his execution Brack escapes to spend the night with Jennie and relives their story. At dawn he returns to his cell. Linda Lou Allen appeared as Jennie, Hutton Cobb as Weaver and Van Hinman as the Narrator, Carl Davis was the musical director and Cvitanovich shot the film on location in the Hambledon valley in Hampshire.

The biopic of classical musicians had generally had its day by the eighties but there were still a few remnants being made. Zeffirelli directed *The Young Toscanini* in which Elizabeth Taylor, playing operatic diva Nadina Bulicoff, appeared in one scene on stage as Aïda, a sight which reduced the audience to laughter when it was first shown at the Venice Film Festival. Carlo Bergonzi was also in the film, which was not amongst its director's most distinguished. In the Soviet Union, Oleg Fialko directed *The Return of the Butterfly*, the story of the Ukranian soprano Salomea Krushelnytska who had sung the title role in *Madama Butterfly* after Puccini had revised the opera following its disastrous opening in Milan.

Where biographies did have a ready market was on television. A mini-series about Melba, using the voice of Yvonne Kenny, was made in Australia, while for the 300th anniversary of the birth of Handel, two films were made in Britain in 1985, one by Anna Ambrose with Simon Callow as Handel (containing an authentically staged scene from *Rinaldo*, amongst other operas); the other by Tony Palmer, who also made a dramatised biography of Puccini which included scenes from Palmer's own production of *Turandot* for Scottish Opera.

The British actor Oliver Tobias played the Viennese Waltz King in *Johann Strauss – the King without a Crown* (1987), a glossy West German/ Austrian/French biopic, with Mary Crosby as one of his loves and Zsa Zsa Gabor as his Aunt Amalia. The script was banal, the acting wooden and despite some spirited excerpts from *Die Fledermaus,* the film did nothing for the genre or little to advance the cause of opera on film.

195

15

The Nineties

In 1986 Glyndebourne staged Gershwin's *Porgy and Bess* with Willard White as Porgy, Cynthia Haymon as Bess and a cast of black singers second to none. Conducted by Simon Rattle and produced by Trevor Nunn, it was a sell-out, eventually moving to Covent Garden where the demand for tickets was so high extra performances had to be put on – ironic, in the sense that few of the cast would have been offered roles at Covent Garden in their own right.

While working on the Glyndebourne production, Nunn began thinking seriously about making a film of *Porgy and Bess*. Although he wanted to use the same cast, he had no intention of filming his production since he knew that the Gershwin estate was against pointing cameras at stage versions of the opera and had no reason to believe they would change their minds for him. He also knew it wouldn't be easy to get them to agree to a film. The trustees had so disliked Otto Preminger's 1959 film with Sidney Poitier and Dorothy Dandridge, that they had vetted every subsequent application extremely carefully, and turned them all down.

Nunn's plan was to shoot the opera on location in South Carolina so he attempted to raise most of the finance in the States. The sixth American producer to turn him down flat explained his decision by saying that because Porgy is about black people, white audiences would stay away, because it was written by a white man, black audiences would stay away; and because it is an opera, everyone would stay away.

Nunn and his producer, Greg Smith (who had produced Nunn's film of his Royal Shakespeare Company production of Shakespeare's *Othello*, also with Willard White) were determined not to give up. The cast album of the Glyndebourne production had already sold 300,000 copies, and they were convinced there was a market for a film. The usual money sources for this kind of production were sceptical and there was the expected hostility towards a film from the Gershwin estate, but Nunn and Smith refused to give up.

Their perseverance paid off, but just when it looked as though they had raised the finance, the stock market crashed, the cost of filming escalated and their backers pulled out. Nunn had gained an important ally, however. Ira

Gershwin's widow had been to see the Glyndebourne production, thought it was the best she had ever seen and agreed that some way had to be found to preserve it. And so the Gershwin family objection to filming a stage show was partially lifted.

Nunn, having accepted he could not raise the money to make a feature film, went to see Richard Price of Primetime, a television programme distribution company which had co-produced his RSC films of *Othello* and *Nicholas Nickleby*. Price was confident he could raise the £2.2 million needed to film the Glyndebourne production for television, and put together a package that included the BBC, which had long wanted to acquire the television rights to the opera, and American Playhouse, in their first joint deal. Such are the finances of television today that no production of this sort stands a chance of being made unless several co-producers are involved. Advance sales to Germany, France and Portugal helped Price creep towards his target but as the day of proposed shooting approached, he was still short. Then, another stroke of luck happened. The London Stock Exchange nose-dived and overnight the value of Price's overseas funding increased dramatically enough for him to give Nunn the go-ahead.

Studio space at Shepperton had been booked for the end of the Covent Garden run, two years before the production moved there, and all the artists engaged. Even so, final permission from the Gershwin estate did not come through until a month before shooting was due to start, and the 60-page document was not actually signed until after shooting had finished.

Nunn took fifteen days to shoot *Porgy and Bess*, filming to playback of the Simon Rattle recording made with the original Glyndebourne cast. This involved some recasting for the film since Bruce Hubbard, who played Jake, had subsequently died. Some cast members found it difficult trying to recreate a five-year-old performance. 'A lot of things had happened to all of us since we made the recording,' recalled Willard White. 'There were things about which we felt differently and would like to have done differently, but couldn't.'

Jamaican-born White had made his name singing the role of Porgy on the first complete recording of the opera, made in 1976 by Lorin Maazel. It had been intended that Sherrill Milnes should sing the part with White contracted to sing the minor role of Jim, but the moment the record producers heard him, they knew he was perfect for Porgy. Although offers to repeat the role on stage then began to arrive, White turned them down, aware that William Warfield had become so saddled with the role that he was never asked to do anything else. By the time he was offered the part at Glyndebourne, White had an international reputation and felt he had sung enough other roles for Porgy not to be a millstone.

Nunn wanted to shoot *Porgy* in the style of an old MGM musical, a genre with which he felt most television viewers would be comfortable. The singing is superb, the cast uniformly excellent – there is a real feel of ensemble playing

– but the film is very nearly sunk by poor lip synchronisation. It is remarkable that the more technically advanced film equipment and techniques have become, the less we seem to be able to match the achievements of the film-makers of fifty years ago.

Porgy and Bess may have been a conscious attempt to look like a cinema musical, but the majority of films in the nineties have been aimed squarely at television and it has been almost incidental whether they were shot on film or on video. The occasion of the Mozart bicentenary in 1991 allowed the BBC to commission a *Not Mozart* series, the brainchild of the founder of the Arts Council's Contemporary Music Network, Annette Morreau. She invited five composers to write an original half-hour opera which would in some way pay tribute to Mozart. One of those composers was Louis Andriessen who wrote the score for *M is for Man, Music and Mozart*, directed by Peter Greenaway. While most of the directors used video, Greenaway insisted he be allowed to film on 35mm. Shot largely in a seventeenth-century Theatre of Anatomy, the film opened with singer Astrid Seriese running through the alphabet, with most of the letters being associated with bodily functions. The letter M stands for Man. Having created Man, it was necessary to give him Movement for which he needed Music which led naturally to Mozart so that there might be perfect music.

A semi-opera commissioned by the BBC from Mark-Anthony Turnage was also made on film, unlike his opera *Greek* which was on tape. *Killing Time* was Turnage's first opera since he had burst onto the international stage with *Greek* and the opera was proving to be a millstone. He had started and abandoned one, feeling he could not live up to expectations, before Dennis Marks, then BBC's Head of Music, put him with director Rob Walker and asked them to produce an opera for television.

At the time Turnage was helping to give musical workshops in Wormwood Scrubs prison in London. This gave him the idea of writing something based on prison life. The opera, which had the working title of *The Prisoner* until the wardrobe lady came up with *Killing Time* on the last day of the shoot, was a half-hour piece about a man serving a life sentence. Turnage and Walker selected a number of poems written by prisoners ranging from Albie Sachs and Ho Chi Minh to a convicted murder, and Turnage then set them, not knowing how they would be used. The actual shape of the film was left to Walker who was probably the only person on the set with any idea of what the finished film would look like.

The role of the prisoner was played by Mike Henry, with Cathy Tyson as his girl-friend. Henry was a contemporary of Turnage at music college, and the composer wrote the part with him in mind. The audience never discovers why he is in prison. Instead, *Killing Time* is about his state of mind, asking how a man can survive life imprisonment, how he fills his day and the memories he recalls.

Many performance documentaries, a new name for what would once have been called biopics, also feature opera. Welsh tenor Dennis O'Neill appeared in a two-part documentary about Caruso, singing his arias in costume but not trying to impersonate him. He also appeared in a documentary directed by Chris Hunt on the life of Adelina Patti filmed in the theatre of Craig-y-Nos, her home in South Wales. June Anderson was Patti, O'Neill her husband. Hunt intended this to be the first of a series of performance documentaries with eminent singers of today playing their heroes, a series which, to date, has not been made.

A lot of thought has gone into the question of how to interest television audiences in opera. As seat prices in the opera house rise, often, in houses like Covent Garden, beyond the reach of ordinary operagoers, the screen is seen as an important way to show that opera is not elitist. There are regular transmissions of operas from the major houses of the world, and producers are always on the lookout for ways to help people understand and enjoy opera.

In 1992, the Welsh channel S4C became partners with the BBC and Christmas Films (a joint US-Russian venture) in a £3 million project to produce six half-hour animated operas for television. The scores were specially adapted by John Stein, leader of the orchestra of Welsh National Opera, and WNO singers were used to record soundtracks for *The Barber of Seville*, *The Magic Flute*, *Carmen*, *Das Rheingold*, *Rigoletto* and *Turandot*. The finished films, using a variety of animation techniques, were charming and excellent introductions to the operas, especially popular with children.

Another attempt to harness animation techniques to the service of educating the public about opera was made with *Opera Imaginaire* (1993), a twelve-part series in which eleven of Europe's top young animators were given free range to interpret any aria they liked as they felt fit, using any animation technique they wished. They responded to the sound of Enrico Caruso singing 'Vesti la giubba', to Nicolai Gedda singing 'La donna e mobile', to choruses and other arias with a wide variety of techniques that included cell animation, a mixture of live action with coloured pencil animation, and 3D computer animation. All opted to tell the story of the aria or opera in their films, and while they demonstrated enormous technical accomplishment, the results showed just how difficult it is to come up with something truly inspired and original. The undoubted highlights of the series were Jonathan Hill's aria from *Madama Butterfly* in which a butterfly is eventually pinned to a board, a chorus from *Carmen* illustrated by ever-increasing playing cards (director Christophe Vallaux) and the duet from *Lakmé*, animated by Pascal Roulion with superb technical accomplishment and imagination. He produced images that both helped an understanding of the music and had a life of their own. A hand that turns into a variety of animals is breathtakingly inventive. The finance for this international co-production came from ten television stations and half-a-dozen other sources.

Opera was the background to Istvan Szabo's feature film, *Meeting Venus* (1991) which is set in the Paris Opera house during rehearsals for a multi-national production of *Tannhäuser* due to be beamed live by satellite to 27 countries. Glenn Close (with singing voice provided by Kiri Te Kanawa and coached for two months by tenor Kenneth Woollam) stars as the Swedish diva whose relationship with a Hungarian conductor (Niels Arestrup) is at the centre of a wonderfully observed and entertaining film. As opening night approaches, the management is locked in a power struggle, the dancers' union has called a strike, the singers are fighting one another, the opera house is being picketed by an environmental action group, the Glenn Close character ignores the conductor, he can't get his money, and people don't turn up for rehearsals. The denouement, incorporating the performance of *Tannhäuser*, is brilliant. The lip-synch is better than in many films in which singers are miming to their own voices, and there remains the intriguing question of which living singers those in the film are modelled on.

Singing lies at the heart of another brilliant feature film, Gérard Corbiau's *The Music Teacher* (1989). Set just before World War I, this tells the story of a world-famous baritone in his prime (played by José van Dam) who mysteri-ously decides to abandon his career and instead coach two young singers for a competition run by his arch rival, Prince Scotti. The singing voices of the two young people were dubbed by Dinah Bryant and Jerome Pruett. It is a magical, multi-layered romance with more than enough suspense, which gets close to the heart of what singing means to us and deservedly won fifteen international awards. It was a notable debut as a feature director by Corbiau, a music docu-mentary maker for Belgian television, who had spent a long time trying to work out a suitable way of marrying music and images so that the sound became as important as the pictures. Included in the film were snatches from *Rigoletto*, *La Traviata*, *Tosca*, *Don Giovanni*, *The Tales of Hoffmann* and Bellini's *Bianca e Fernando* as well as Mahler's Fourth Symphony and *Song of the Earth*, Schubert and Schumann. 'Cinema has become so voyeuristic,' Corbiau commented, 'neglecting all other sensual possibilities, though it's obvious that films need to be heard as much as seen.'

Corbiau's next musical feature was *Farinelli – Il Castrato,* the story of the most famous of all the eighteenth-century castrati singers, focusing on his rela-tionship with his brother, Riccardo Broschi (Farinelli's real name was Carlo Broschi). Of course the question of Could he? or Couldn't he? runs throughout the film, as Farinelli and his brother share women as well as their lives, but the figure of Handel, for whom Farinelli always refused to work, looms large as the singer begins to wonder if it was all worth it. It is a sumptuous film which was nominated for an Oscar as best foreign film and contains some fascinating recreations of baroque operas, in particular an aria by Handel's great German rival, Hesse. The voice of Farinelli (played by Stefano Dionisi) was obtained by mixing the voices of soprano Ewe Mallas-Godlewska and counter-tenor Derek

Lee Ragin. The result shows the range of a castrato voice but probably not the power and warmth of a genuine castrato.

In 1995, Joan Sutherland, having retired from the operatic stage, was cast as Mother Rudd opposite Leo McKern in the Australian feature film, *On Our Selection*, an adaptation of the popular stories of life in the outback by Steele Rudd. The Rudd stories, which had started as newspaper sketches in 1895, were accounts of a family's struggle to survive on land granted to them under Australia's nineteenth-century homesteading laws (their 'selection'). They had already inspired three silent and four sound films as well as several plays and a radio serial. Director George Whaley had adapted the stories for the stage (with Mel Gibson in the cast) and was promised by actor Leo McKern that as soon as he could find the finance for a film, McKern would appear as Dad Rudd. Mel Gibson's production company became one of the film's backers along with the Australian Film Finance Corporation. Who to cast opposite McKern who could match his screen presence? Whaley had once attempted to set up a documentary on Sutherland, which had never been made, and when her name was suggested, he jumped at the idea.

Sutherland wasn't nearly so sure. She had never been noted as a great actress on the stage, and despite the urging of her husband Richard Bonynge, was reluctant to commit herself. For twelve months she refused. Then she had lunch with McKern and expressed her fears. 'Woman,' McKern told her, 'you don't have to act, just be yourself.' She finally agreed.

And still people continue to try to put opera on the screen, whether in the cinema or on television. The rewards, in terms of exposure at least, are high. When Trevor Nunn's production of *Porgy and Bess* was first shown on American television, it attracted almost seven million viewers. To have been seen by that many people at the Met, a production would have to play more than 1,700 performances. Composers, too, remain anxious to see their work on the screen. When Avril MacCrory, then head of music for Channel 4 Television, let it be known in 1989 that she was thinking of commissioning some original television operas, 300 proposals promptly landed on her desk. Eventually she chose six to go into production. The interesting thing about her commissions was that she did not go the conventional route of asking composers to come up with ideas of what they would like to write. Instead MacCrory asked film-makers to submit story-lines appropriate for a one-hour opera (in practice, 52 minutes, with no licence to exceed that time) which could only be for television. She did not want an opera like *Owen Wingrave* that was written with one eye firmly on a stage production. In the case of *Horse Opera*, it was director Bob Baldwin who had his idea accepted before composer Stewart Copeland, son of CIA chief Myles Copeland and former drummer with The Police, was invited to write the music.

Not all six operas were made on film, but *Horse Opera* was. Jonathan Moore's libretto was based on the play *Cowboys* by Anne Caulfield. George

(Phillip Guy-Bromley) is a clerk in the Midlands who dresses up as a cowboy in his spare time and whose home is a recreation of a Wild West ranch house. His wife (Gina Bellman) has had enough and his attempts to write the great Western novel are interrupted by a row with his Bengali neighbour. A blow on the head from a cooking pot knocks him unconscious and when he wakes up he finds himself back in the Wild West where he meets his hero, Wyatt Earp (Rick Mayall). When Earp confesses a fondness for women's cosmetics and a desire to go to Hollywood, George becomes sheriff and stands up to Billy the Kid and Jesse James (played by librettist Moore and composer Copeland) who turn out to be two very ordinary men who can't read or write. One by one George's illusions about the Wild West are shattered.

Horse Opera worked on many levels – as narrative, as comedy, as an expose of bigotry and as an examination of the nature of myth – but it was hardly experimental and kept firmly within the long screen tradition of casting actors rather than opera singers on screen (Guy-Bromley was the only professional singer in the cast)

Christopher Rawlence, who wrote and directed *King of Hearts* (not to be confused with the 1966 anti-war de Broca film), also chose to shoot on film. Rawlence had once noticed a playing card lying face down on the pavement in London and picked it up. It was the King of Hearts. A few months later he was in Leeds and the same thing happened. When it happened a third time, he went into a Ladbroke's betting shop to find out the odds against such a thing happening and was quoted eight million to one. This experience became the starting point for his opera about Antoine, a lonely physics teacher who scavenges in the streets of London for the discarded traces of other people's lives through which he lives his own. Charles is the therapist treating Antoine. Charles's mistress Helen teaches French in Antoine's school. Is it coincidence or fate that a dangerous triangle begins to emerge?

Rawlence had earlier written the libretto for Michael Nyman's opera, *The Man Who Mistook His Wife For A Hat*, and made a film of it with Emile Belcourt, Patricia Hooper and Frederick Westcott. He was hoping to work on the Channel 4 commission with Nyman, but Nyman was too busy to be able to commit to the project and American composer Michael Torke was invited to write his first opera.

Frank Cvitanovich filmed *Good Friday 1663* on location in Suffolk. Mike and Kate Westbrook's opera was based on a short story by Helen Simpson about Belinda who sits in church, heavily pregnant, thinking back over her life while the parson preaches hell fire. All the cast, with the exception of the parson, had singing voices provided by Kate Westbrook – even the bass – a move justified by the fact that the events about which Belinda was musing were all in her head.

The series was interesting but patchy, and not watched by very many viewers, a fact seized upon by commentators to prove that opera on television does not work. But how many people go to see new operas in the opera house, even when the composer is well-known? If 200,000 people had been to see these chamber works in the theatre, would they then be considered a failure?

The saddest reflection on the Channel 4 season was not that the resulting films did not mark any really radical departure in ways of showing opera on television, but that after their initial showing they have not been seen again. At least in the theatre a new work gets a second performance.

Television continues to be the major outlet for experimental operatic films, although in the case of Tony Palmer's study of *Parsifal*, examining the nature of the work and its anti-Semitism, British television has so far refused to show it despite the presence of Domingo singing Parsifal, Violeta Urmana singing Kundry, Nikolai Putilin as Klingsor and Matti Salminen as Gurnemanz. The production seen in the film is the Kirov production staged by Palmer himself, with Valery Gergiev conducting.

One film that was transmitted, at the time the Tour de France was taking place, was *5K Pursuit Opera* (1991), a work commissioned by the sports department of Channel 4 from Leicester composer Pip Greasley. The film featured cyclists racing around a track, their speed and the tempo of the race being fed into a computer which in turn influenced the speed and tempo of the singers. The outcome of the plot was controlled by the cyclists on the track. It was an interesting experiment but hardly likely to produce a work that could be performed in any other medium.

Another young film-maker obsessed with opera is Dominik Scherrer. A former rock musician, born in Zurich, he was always fascinated by the possibilities of combining film and music. Studying film-making in London, he wrote, composed and directed a twenty-minute short entitled *Queen of Fruit*. Lene Lovich is Millicent, wife of a fruiterer (Simon Packham) who fights a duel with her lover, the local taxidermist (Martin Turner). Their weapons are fruit and dead birds. It's a film rich in imagery and symbolism, and extremely accomplished. Scherrer did not follow standard practice and shoot to playback, because he wanted to give himself the freedom to make alterations and change the pace of the film in cutting afterwards. He, therefore, shot the artists singing live, even though they were being filmed on a windswept clifftop in Southern England, rewriting the story as he went along whenever he felt it necessary. That recording then became the guidetrack for re-recording in a studio afterwards, attempting to recreate the atmosphere of the location to match the pictures.

The wind was not the only problem with which Scherrer had to contend. On the first day on location, Lene Lovich fell and broke her arm. Being low budget, Scherrer was unable to reschedule her scenes, so she had to play them with her arm in plaster which meant that earlier scenes filmed in London without the plaster had to be reshot.

Being a student when he made the film, Scherrer could not afford more than a piano accompaniment. Channel 4 stepped in and gave him the money to complete the film and record a sound track with an orchestra. *Queen of Fruit* was shown on Channel 4 and then became a regular on the festival circuit.

It took Scherrer five years to get his second film off the ground and even then he began shooting without having all the money in place. *Hell For Leather* is the story of the fall of Satan and his banishment to Hell, updated to the present time. Satan (sung by José Manuel de Sousa), the leader of a group of bikers, is sent to earth to punish sinners, but the sinners are having such a good time being punished it rather defeats the object. Throughout the film a heavenly voice (counter tenor, Christopher Robson) appears like the voice of God. Eventually The Barefoot Man, as he is called, appears on earth to rescue them but he's considered boring. Satan decides that earth is even more boring than heaven and goes off to hell which is much more fun.

The story was taken from medieval sources and inspired by the paintings of Hieronymous Bosch (one person left the crew on religious grounds). It was shot in three weeks on location in London's East End, on the South Bank and at an army barracks in Woolwich. Apart from the opening and closing sequences, it was filmed in black-and-white to give it a dream-like quality, and Scherrer again shot a live guidetrack to re-record after editing. He is already working on ideas for another operatic film in an attempt to develop the medium. His films are not aimed at the traditional opera audience and if there was a word other than opera to describe what he is doing, he says he would use it.

Another film doing well on the festival circuit is Kevin Lucas's *Black River*. Andrew Schultz's opera had received its first staging in Sydney in 1989. Set in the Australian outback, *Black River* examines the fears and prejudices of a group of five Australians who find themselves sheltering from a storm in a gaol where an Aboriginal boy was recently found hanged. They include the judge investigating the hanging, the local policeman and the town drunk. Singing the pivotal role of Miriam, mother of the dead boy, was the Aboriginal mezzo-soprano, Maroochy Barambah, who had created the role on stage. Lucas had gone to see the opera, been riveted by it, and recognised immediately its potential for a film.

Recent television opera has not been limited solely to experimental films, excerpts in performance documentaries, or relays from the opera house. In 1992, the kind of spectacular for which television is well suited was mounted by the Italian producer Andrea Andermann. He decided to stage *Tosca* in real time on the actual locations in Rome, beaming the results around the world. Plácido Domingo was to sing Cavaradossi, Catherine Malfitano was to be Tosca (her first time in the role) and Ruggero Raimondi, Baron Scarpia. It was the kind of project that could only be done by outside broadcast cameras.

The idea of shooting on the locations specified by Puccini was not new. Domingo had himself appeared in a film partially shot in the actual locations in 1976. What was to make Andermann's production so special and different was that the acts would be taking place on Saturday afternoon, Saturday evening and early on Sunday morning, and that it was going to be transmitted live to 45 countries giving opera its biggest-ever audience.

It was a massive logistical operation which took two years to set up. The orchestra, conducted by Zubin Mehta, was in a studio some three kilometres from the locations. The singers had to wear radio microphones in their hair and be able, on discreetly placed monitors, to see Mehta. Each location had eight cameras, together with all the technical paraphernalia needed for a live transmission. 400 technicians were involved. Twenty hours separated the first act from the last, during which time the singers had to keep their voices in trim and snatch whatever rest or food they could. In between shooting the second act in the Palazzo Farnese and being up on the roof of the Castel Sant' Angelo at dawn, Catherine Malfitano sat up all night exercising her voice while Domingo watched television, worried that if he fell asleep, his voice would not be very good when he woke up. Television director Brian Large (the production on the floor was directed by Giuseppe Patroni Griffi) had recorded a rehearsal and so had a back-up tape if anything went radically wrong. This was live television with no chance for a second go.

It began rather tentatively in the church of Sant' Andrea della Valle on Saturday lunchtime, 11 July, with a series of close-ups which rather negated being on the actual site. But then Large began to open up the shots, giving the viewer an atmospheric sense of place. The mishap that had been allowed for very nearly happened. Halfway through the first act, Domingo ran down a ramp from his painting platform, fell and rolled out of shot. Millions of people worldwide held their breath. Was this the end of the transmission? No. Domingo limped back into shot and began his next scene without missing a beat.

As the opera progressed, Large's camera direction became not only as assured as one would expect from arguably the best director of television opera then working, but positively inspired. It would have been easy to have played safe and worked on a master shot/close-up format, but Large went for broke. The cameras were constantly on the move, tracking, panning, turning, in movements that would have demanded half-a-dozen retakes if they had been recording in a studio. Here they had to be right first time, and invariably they were. The entire production relied not just on the cameramen doing their job but on the singers and chorus hitting their marks, on the lines between the orchestra and the location staying open, on microphone transmitters working. 'The singers were putting themselves on the line, why shouldn't I?' said Large afterwards.

There was so much that could have gone wrong, it was surprising so little did. There was a momentary camera reflection in a glass door in Act 2, caused, according to Large, because Malfitano fell a different way on the night from the way she had fallen in rehearsals, and a chorister briefly masked Scarpia during the Te Deum, but any such mishap (later edited out of the home video) was more than made up for by the thrill of the camerawork and the adrenalin the performers brought to their performances. Cameraman Vittorio Storaro had to light each location to allow for complete coverage, and so there were pools of light and shadows as the artists moved about the locations, adding to the realism. And who of those watching will ever forget the long track down the aisle with Scarpia during the Act 1 Te Deum?

If the telly *Tosca* marked one way of attracting huge audiences to opera, coming as it did on the back of the enormously popular Three Tenor concerts, the BBC's next attempt was to mark another. The phrase 'soap opera' is common currency in television and everyday conversation, coming from the fact that many early dramatic serials on television were sponsored by soap powder manufacturers. Two people, Janet Street-Porter, then head of the BBC's Youth and Entertainment Features department, and director Nigel Finch, were discussing ways of attracting young people to opera. Television opera, they both agreed, was too stage-bound, being either a multi-camera look at a stage performance or something similar staged in a studio. Why not, they wondered, do it as a filmed soap opera?

For the idea to work, they needed an opera with good tunes, one of which there were then no recordings so that purists would have nothing with which to compare it, and one that could be happily updated with cliff-hanging breaks at the appropriate moments. It must also be a work that could translate comfortably into the language of modern television thrillers and drama. They concluded they did not want a modern, commissioned piece but a conventional opera which conformed to public perceptions of what an opera should be. The piece they chose was *Der Vampyr*, an obscure work by the equally obscure German Romantic composer Heinrich Marschner, which had been incredibly popular in its day (it was written in 1828) but had not been staged for many years (although, coincidentally, the Wexford Festival was to stage it in 1992). Few people in the early nineties had even heard of it.

Charles Hart, lyricist for Andrew Lloyd Webber's *The Phantom of the Opera* and *Aspects of Love*, was invited to update the story and provide new words. He set *The Vampire* in London's East End where the tomb of Riley is disturbed during the demolition of a Victorian warehouse. After a 200-year sleep, Riley returns to life and becomes a successful yuppie businessman. But, within three days, he has to kill three women or die. The members of the cast, led by Omar Ebrahim as Riley, Richard Van Allan and Fiona O'Neill, were chosen for their looks as well as their voices.

Finch soon discovered one of the principal problems with filmed opera: how to match the performance on screen with the way a composer demands a vocal line should be sung. The pre-recorded track contained a duet which was written so that, in an opera house, every word would carry to the back row of the gods. Finch wanted it performed across a candle-lit dinner table as an intimate conversation. The singers found it difficult to create the intimacy he wanted without resorting to mannerisms, and even when they did achieve it, the visual impression was at odds with the vocal delivery. His other consideration was that the music dictated the pace of cutting rather than the action.

Finch was aware that the project could fall flat on its face, alienating those who enjoy opera whilst being considered too highbrow, obscure and elitist by a wider audience. But the finished film, shown over five consecutive nights together with an omnibus edition, with its realistic killings, lots of nudity, and fast, punchy, soap-inspired direction, more than achieved its aims, attracting large audiences as well as picking up several awards.

By the nineties, television had completely taken over the task of recording operas for posterity with transmissions of the leading artists of the day in productions from the major houses of the world. Just as we look back to the films of the thirties to see what Tito Schipa, Jan Kiepura or Conchita Supervia looked like, so future generations will look back on today's video recordings to see what Domingo, Carreras, Pavarotti, Alagna, Te Kanawa, José Cura and all, were like when they were on stage.

Most opera shown on television today is invariably of a stage production recorded with electronic cameras, not a specially made film. Film is now the preserve of the director trying to do something special, something different, although many interesting film directors such as the American Peter Sellars and the Australian Baz Luhrmann, have chosen to shoot their operas on tape.

When Sellars does use film, as for example, the opening sequence of *Cosi Fan Tutte*, taken from a car and shot hand-held by Sellars himself with an 8mm camera, he does it for a very deliberate effect, in that case to establish that he has updated the action and make more sense of setting the rest of the opera in the studio set of Despina's roadside diner.

Film was the medium chosen for *Dido and Aeneas*, commissioned by the BBC to celebrate the tercentenary of Henry Purcell's death in 1995. The original director was to have been Nigel Finch, director of the BBC's soap opera, *The Vampire*, but he died just before filming was due to start and Peter Maniura, now head of BBC TV's classical music, took over. Like most television opera of the last fifteen or so years, including those taped from the stage of an opera house, *Dido and Aeneas* could not have happened without co-production money. In addition to the BBC, television stations in Germany, the United States and other countries took a stake in the production.

It had been decided from the outset that the entire production should be shot on location to get away from a studio atmosphere. Hampton Court House, a rundown eighteenth-century building in its own grounds just across the road from Hampton Court Palace, was chosen. Built originally by the Earl of Halifax for his mistress and previously used as an old folks' home, the house contained everything that was required, from an interior that could be dressed as Dido's throne room to a lake from which (on a freezing night, as it transpired) Mercury could emerge.

Visually the film was sumptuous and beautifully lit, and the singing was outstanding with Maria Ewing as Dido, Karl Daymond as Aeneas and a cast that included Sally Burgess, James Bowman and Rebecca Evans. The film, however, lacked ambient sound which gave the soundtrack a distant feel, like watching a film in a shop window while listening to a radio broadcast outside.

Following in the tradition of Bergman's *Magic Flute*, Swedish television produced another remarkable operatic film in 1995 when Inger Åby directed Stravinsky's *The Rake's Progress* with American tenor Greg Fedderly as Tom Rakewell and Barbara Hendricks as Anne Truelove. Håkan Hagegård (who had made his name in the Bergman film) played Nick Shadow and the American-Japanese countertenor Brian Asawa was Baba the Turk.

Åby shot on location and in the studio, giving the film a typically Swedish look, with beautiful framing, pastel colours, and a rhythm of editing which made it seem as if Stravinsky had written the opera for the screen in the first place. Conducted by Esa-Pekka Salonen, this is one of the best screen operas ever filmed.

While *The Rake's Progress* was made for television, it is, without any doubt, a feature film in all but name. There is nothing small scale or limited about the way it was conceived for the screen. But the operatic feature film made for the cinema alone has become more and more rare. The cost of making features has increased so much that opera, never likely to be a box-office smash hit, requires too great an outlay for too little return for opera production ever again to reach the levels of even the sixties.

By coincidence, the year Åby was making her film for Swedish television, Daniel Toscan du Plantier, who had helped produce Losey's *Don Giovanni*, Rosi's *Carmen* and Comencini's *La Bohème*, managed to raise the finance to make a feature of *Madama Butterfly*. To direct it, he again invited a film-maker with no previous experience of opera, Frédéric Mitterand. This French-Japanese-German-British co-production was filmed entirely on location in Tunisia, where a replica of turn-of-the-century Nagasaki was built on a hilltop. Clearly no one would accept a film Butterfly, purporting to be Japanese, who did not at least look Oriental, and so the Chinese soprano Ying Huang was cast in the title role with Richard Troxell, a young American tenor, as Pinkerton, Ning Liang as Suzuki and Richard Cowan as Sharpless.

Madame Butterfly was a throwback to an old style of film-making but none the worse for that. It was shot to playback and was a totally faithful adaptation of the opera, relying on beautiful photography and the fluidity of the camera to sustain visual interest. Mitterand used the sliding doors of Butterfly's house as his motivation to keep the camera constantly on the move, drawing the viewer into her enclosed world. Because there were no jarring images, Mitterand allowed the power of the music (conducted by James Conlon) to weave its magic. Several critics did not like the film because, used to watching transmissions from the opera house, they found it difficult to come to terms with people on screen singing when they were clearly not singing live. Viewers today are so used to video performances in which the singers clearly are singing and their tonsils can be seen whenever they hit a high note that any form of subtlety on the screen inevitably looks artificial if the sound heard is big enough to get over an orchestra. That is just one of the challenges facing film directors who want to put opera on film, and it's a challenge many are still keen to accept.

During 1999, Mike Leigh, director of the Oscar-winning *Secrets and Lies*, has been shooting *Topsy Turvy*, a feature about the first production of Gilbert and Sullivan's *The Mikado*. A performance documentary is being set up about a staging of Mozart's *Die Entführung aus dem Serail* which is to be shot on location in Istanbul's Topkapi Palace. Don Boyd has completed *Lucia*, a film which parallels a performance of *Lucia di Lammermoor* at a Scottish stately home with events taking place in the house (themselves drawn from the Scott novel on which Donizetti based his opera). Boyd, who produced *Aria*, has shot his film using grainy sepia images, with often hand-held cameras. Playing Kate Ashton, joint owner of the ancestral home with her brother, and also the soprano who sings Lucia, is Boyd's daughter, Amanda, who trained as a singer at the Guildhall. Her brother is played by Mark Holland, Richard Coxon plays Ravenswood and young American tenor John Osborn, a winner of the Plácido Domingo Award, plays the American singer whose millions are going to restore the house – when he has married Kate.

Opera North's acclaimed production of Britten's *Gloriana* has been filmed by its producer Phyllida Lloyd for showing on BBC Television. Lloyd does not like direct relays of opera from the stage, and it was the image of Josephine Barstow, who sings Queen Elizabeth, coming off stage and remaining in character while surrounded by stagehands and backstage clutter that gave her the idea of making a film showing the similarities between what happens backstage when putting on an opera with what is happening on-stage. The result is a parallel film of the kind so popular in the thirties and forties, even though shot and cut with the pace expected of a TV drama made at the end of the twentieth century. A hundred years after the first operatic aria hit the screen, the film-maker's fascination with opera continues.

Opera Singers in the Movies

Below is a list of all major opera singers (and some minor) who have made film appearances. Not all of these have involved singing and where artists have appeared in non-singing roles, these are marked with a *.

The list does not include those films for which a singer has provided only his or her voice, nor does it include documentaries. For a full list of appearances on video, I would refer readers to Ken Wlaschin's *Opera on Screen*. His book has been invaluable in helping to compile this list.

Dating films can be a nightmare. *Maria Rosa*, Geraldine Farrar's first film, was not released until the year after her third had been premiered. Does that make it her first film? Or her third? And what date do you give it? The year it was completed or the year it was released? As a general rule, I have tended to follow most reference books by going for the year of release. However, with films made in, for example, the Soviet Union which were banned for twenty years, I have given the year of completion. There can also be confusion with films which were made in two or three language versions, not always simultaneously. These were invariably released at different times and the release date for one language version sometimes gets ascribed to the wrong title.

The original titles of films are given in the following list, with the exception of operas which are better known by their English title. Where there are two or more titles given, it is because two or more language versions of the film were shot.

ADAMS, Donald (1928-1996) English bass
  The Mikado (GB 1966) with Valerie Masterson, John Reed. Dir: Stuart Burge
  The Mikado (GB 1974) with Masterson, Thomas Round, John Cartier, Helen Landis. Dir: Trevor Evans
  The Pirates of Penzance (GB 1974) with Masterson, Round, Landis. Dir: Evans
  The Yeoman of the Guard (GB 1974) with Masterson, Round, Cartier, Landis. Dir: Evans
  HMS Pinafore (GB 1974) with Cartier, Round, Masterson, Landis. Dir: Evans
  Ruddigore (GB 1974) with Round, Cartier, Humphreys, Landis, Ann Hood. Dir: Evans
  The Gondoliers (GB 1974) with Round, Humphreys, Landis, Hood. Dir: Evans
  Iolanthe (GB 1974) with Round, Landis. Dir: Evans

AHLERSMEYER, Mathieu (1896-1979) German baritone
Figaros Hochzeit (Ger 1949). Dir: Georg Wildhagen
ALBANESE, Licia (1913–) Italian-American soprano
Serenade (US 1955) with Mario Lanza, Sarita Montiel, Joan Fontaine, Vincent Price
ALPAR, Gitta (1903–) Hungarian coloratura soprano
Die – oder Keine (Ger 1932) with Max Hansen, Ferdinand von Alten, Paul Otto, Fritz Fischer. Dir: Gustav Fröhlich
Gitta entdeckt ihr Herz (Ger 1932) with Gustav Fröhlich, Paul Kemp. Dir: Gustav Fröhlich
Bal a Savoyban (Hun 1935) with Hans Jaray, Rosi Barsony. Dir: Istvan Szekely
I Give My Heart (GB 1935) with Owen Nares, Arthur Margetson Dir: Marcel Varnay
Guilty Melody (GB 1936) with Nils Asther, John Loder. Dir: Richard Potter
Le Disque 413 (GB 1936) French version of *Guilty Melody* with Jules Barry, Jean Galland. Dir: Richard Potter
The Flame of New Orleans (US 1941) with Anthony Marlowe, Marlene Dietrich. Dir: René Clair
ALVA, Luigi (1927–) Peruvian tenor
Cosi Fan Tutte (Ger 1970) with Hermann Prey, Gundala Janowitz, Christa Ludwig. Dir: Vaclav Kaslik
Don Pasquale (Ger 1972) with Oskar Czerwenka, Reri Grist, Hermann Prey. TV film
The Barber of Seville (Ger 1972). Dir: Jean-Pierre Ponnelle
AMARA, Lucine (1927–) American-Armenian soprano
The Great Caruso (US 1951) with Mario Lanza
AMATO, Pasquale (1878-1942) Italian baritone
A Neapolitan Romance (US 1928) Vitaphone short
Glorious Betsy (US 1928)*. Dir: Alan Crosland
ANDERSON, June (1952–) American soprano
Adelina Patti, Queen of Song (GB 1993) with Dennis O'Neill. Dir: Chris Hunt
ARGENTINA, Imperio (1906-1996) Spanish soprano
Morena Clara (Sp 1936)
Carmen della Triana (Sp 1938). Dir: Florian Rey
La Tosca (It 1941) with Rossano Brazzi. Dir: Jean Renoir and Carlo Koch (her voice dubbed)
Goyescas (Sp 1942). Dir: Benito Perojo
Tata Mia (Sp 1986). Dir: José Luis Borau
BACCALONI, Salvatore (1900-1969) Italian bass
Full of Life (US 1956)* with Judy Holliday
Rock-a-Bye Baby (US 1958)* with Jerry Lewis
Merry Andrew (US 1958)* with Danny Kaye
Fanny (US 1960)*
The Pigeon That Took Rome (US 1962)* with Elsa Martinelli
BACQUIER, Gabriel (1924–) French baritone
Falstaff (Ger 1980) with Karan Armstrong, Marta Szirmay, Max-René Cosotti, Richard Stilwell. Dir: Gotz Friedrich
BARBIERI, Fedora (1920–) Italian mezzo
Il Trovatore (It 1957) with Mario del Monaco, Leyla Gencer, Ettore Bastianini. Dir: Claudio Fino. TV film
Cavalleria Rusticana (It 1982) with Plácido Domingo. Dir: Franco Zeffirelli
Rigoletto (Ger 1983) with Luciano Pavarotti. Dir: Jean-Pierre Ponnelle
BARCLAY, John (1899–) English baritone

2 Vitaphone sound films (US 1927)
The Mikado (GB 1939). Dir: Victor Schertzinger
BARSTOW, Josephine (1940–) English soprano
Gloriana (GB 1999). Dir: Phyllida Lloyd
BARTLETT, Michael (1901– ?) American tenor
Love Me Forever (US 1935) with Grace Moore
She Married Her Boss (US 1935) with Claudette Colbert
The Music Goes Round (US 1936)
Follow Your Heart (US 1936) with Marion Talley
The Lilac Domino (US 1937) with June Knight
BECHI, Gino (1913-1993) Italian baritone
Fuga a Due Voce (It 1943)
Pronto, Chi Parla? (It 1945) with Annette Bach
Torna a Sorrento (It 1945) with Adriana Benetti
Il Segreto di Don Giovanni (It 1947). Dir: Mario Costa
Amanti in Fuga (It 1947) with Annette Bach. Dir: Giacomo Gentilomo
Arrivederci, Papa! (It 1948). Dir: Camillo Mastrocinque
Follie per l'Opera (It 1948) with Gina Lollobrigida. Dir: Mario Costa
Signorinella (It 1949) with Antonella Lualdi
Una Voce nel Tuo Cuore (It 1950) with Gigli, Vittorio Gassman
Soho Conspiracy (GB 1950) remake of *Follie per l'Opera* with scenes lifted from earlier film
Canzoni a Due Voci (It 1954) with Tito Gobbi
Sinfonia d'Amore (It 1955) biopic of Schubert with Claude Laydu as the composer
La Chiamavan Capinera (It 1957) with Irene Galter
La Traviata (It 1966) with Anna Moffo, Franco Bonisoli
Bechi provided the voice for Amonasro in *Aïda* (It 1953) starring Sophia Loren
BELCOURT, Emile (1934–) Canadian tenor
The Man Who Mistook His Wife For a Hat (GB 1987) with Patricia Hooper, Frederick Westcott. Dir: Christopher Rawlence
BERGANZA, Teresa (1935–) Spanish mezzo
L'Italiana in Algeri (It 1957). Dir: Mario Lanfranchi
The Barber of Seville (Ger 1972). Dir: Jean-Pierre Ponnelle
Don Giovanni (Fr 1978). Dir: Joseph Losey
BERGER, Erna (1900-1990) German soprano
Ave Maria (Ger 1936) with Gigli, Käthe von Nagy. Dir: Johannes Riemann
Falstaff in Wien (Ger 1939) with Hans Nielsen, Paul Otto. Dir: Leopold Heinisch
Wen di Gotter lieben (Aus 1942) with Hans Holt. Dir: Karl Hartl
Don Giovanni (GB 1954) with Cesare Siepi, Otto Edelmann. Dir: Paul Czinner
BERGONZI, Carlo (1924–) Italian tenor
Young Toscanini (It 1988) with Elizabeth Taylor. Dir: Franco Zeffirelli
BETTONI, Vincenzo (1881-1954) Italian bass
Pergolesi (It 1932) biog of composer. Dir: Guido Brigone
La Serva Padrona (It 1934) with Bruna Dragoni. Dir: Giorgio Mannini
BJÖRLING, Jussi (1911-1960) Swedish tenor
Fram för Framgang (Sw 1938). Dir: Gunnar Skoglund
En Svensk Tiger (Sw 1948)
Resan till Dej (Sw 1953)
BOHNEN, Michael (1887-1965) German bass-baritone
Tiefland (Ger 1922) with Lil Dagover
Der Rosenkavalier (Ger 1926)

212

Der Zigeunerbaron (Ger 1927) with Lya Mara
Sajenko the Soviet (Ger 1929) with Suzy Vernen
Zwei Kravaten (Ger 1930) with Olga Tschechowa
Viktoria und ihr Hussar (Ger 1931). Dir: Richard Oswald
Wiener Blut (Ger 1932). Dir: Conrad Weine
Gold (Ger 1934) with Brigitte Helm
Der Gefangene des Königs (Ger 1935)
Liselotte von der Pfalz (Ger 1935) with Renate Muller
August der Starke (Ger 1936) with Lil Dagover
Solo Per Te/Mutterlied/Only for You (Ger 1937) with Maria Cebotari, Beniamino
    Gigli. Dir: Carmine Gallone
Das unsterbliche Herz (Ger 1939)
Achtung Feind hört mit! (Ger 1940). Dir: Arthur Maria Rabenalt
Der liebe Augustin (Aus 1940). Dir: E.W. Emo
Die Rothschilds (Ger 1940)
Baron Münchhausen (Ger 1943) with Hans Albers. Dir: Josef von Backy
Meine Herren Söhne (Ger 1945) with Monika Burg
BONANOVA, Fortunio (1896-1969) Spanish baritone
  Don Juan Tenorio (Sp 1922)*
  A Successful Calamity (US 1932)* with Mary Astor
  Tropic Holiday (US 1938)*
  Citizen Kane (US 1941) played Susan Alexander's vocal coach
  Blood and Sand (US 1941)*. Dir: Rouben Mamoulian
  The Black Swan (US 1942)*
  For Whom the Bell Tolls (US 1943)*
  Five Graves to Cairo (US 1943)*
  Double Indemnity (US 1944)*
  The Red Dragon (US 1946)*
  The Moon is Blue (US 1953)* with David Niven, William Holden. Dir: Otto Preminger
  September Affair (US 1951)*
  An Affair to Remember (US 1957)*
  Thunder in the Sun (US 1959)*
  The Running Man (US 1963)*
  The Million Dollar Collar (US 1967)*
BONELLI, Richard (1887-1980) American baritone
  Movietone Numbers (US 1928) – Fox shorts; Bonelli was in two
  Enter Madame (US 1933) with Nina Koshetz, Cary Grant, Elissa Landi. Dir: Elliott
    Nugent
  The Hard-boiled Canary (US 1941) with Susanna Foster. Dir: Andrew L. Stone
BONISOLI, Franco (1938–) Italian tenor
  La Traviata (It 1966) with Anna Moffo. TV film
BOOTH, Webster (1902-1984) English tenor
  Waltz Time (GB 1933) with Richard Tauber. Dir: Paul Stein
  Faust (GB 1936) with Anne Ziegler. Dir: Albert Hopkins
  The Laughing Lady (GB 1946) with Anne Ziegler, Peter Graves. Dir: Stein
  The Story of Gilbert and Sullivan (GB 1953) with Elsie Morison, Martyn Green,
    Owen Brannigan, Marjorie Thomas
BRUSCANTINI, Sesto (1919–) Italian bass-baritone
  On Such a Night (GB 1955). Dir: Anthony Asquith
BRUSON, Renato (1936–) Italian baritone
  Cavalleria Rusticana (It 1982) with Plácido Domingo. Dir: Franco Zeffirelli

BUMBRY, Grace (1937–) American soprano
  Carmen (Ger 1967) with Jon Vickers, Mirella Freni, Justino Diaz. Dir: Herbert von Karajan
  Aïda (Fr 1976) Orange Festival production. Dir: Pierre Jourdan
CABALLÉ, Montserrat (1933–) Spanish soprano
  Norma (Fr 1974) Orange Festival production with Jon Vickers. Dir: Pierre Jourdan
  Romanca final (Sp 1986) with José Carreras
CALLAS, Maria (1923-1977) Greek/American soprano
  Medea (It 1969)*. Dir: Pier Paolo Pasolini
CAMPANARI, Giuseppe (1855-1927) Italian baritone
  Carmen (1917) early sound film
CANIGLIA, Maria (1905-1979) Italian soprano
  Il Vento mi ha Cantato una Canzone (It 1947). Dir: Camillo Mastrocinque
  Follie per l'Opera (It 1948). Dir: Mario Costa
  Soho Conspiracy (GB 1950) remake of *Follie per l'Opera* with scenes lifted
CARRERAS, José (1946–) Spanish tenor
  Romanca Final (Sp 1986) with Montserrat Caballé
CARUSO, Enrico (1873-1921) Italian tenor
  My Cousin (US 1918) with Carolina White. Dir: Edward José
  A Splendid Romance (US 1918). Dir: Edward José
CASE, Anna (1889-1984) American soprano
  The Hidden Truth (US 1918)*. Dir: Julius Steger
  Vitaphone shorts (US 1926/27) made two
CAVALIERI, Lina (1874-1944) Italian soprano
  Manon Lescaut (US 1914) with Lucien Muratore
  La Sposa della Morte (It 1915) with Muratore
  La Rosa di Granata (It 1916) with Muratore
  The Eternal Temptress (US 1917). Dir: Emile Chautard
  Love's Conquest (US 1918). Dir: José
  A Woman of Impulse (US 1918). Dir: Edward José
  The Two Brides (US 1919). Dir: José
  Amore che Ritorna (It 1921)
CEBOTARI, Maria (1911-1949) Bessarabian soprano
  Mädchen in Weiss (Ger 1936) with Norberto Ardelli, Ivan Petrovich. Dir: Viktor Janson
  Starke Herzen im Sturm (Ger 1937) with Gustav Diessl. Dir: Herbert Maisch
  Solo Per Te (It 1937) with Beniamino Gigli
  Drei Frau um Verdi (It 1938) with Folco Giachetti, Gigli. Dir: Carmine Gallone
  Ueber Alles die Treue (Ger 1939)
  Premiere der Butterfly/Il Sogno di Butterfly (It 1939) with Tito Gobbi, Fosco Giachetti, Lucie Englisch. Dir: Carmine Gallone
  Amami, Alfredo!/Melodie der Liebe (It 1940) with Lucie Englisch, Claudio Gora, Paolo Stoppa. Dir: Carmine Gallone
  Odessa in Fiamme (It-Rom 1942). Dir: Carmine Gallone
  Maria Malibran (It 1943) with Rossano Brazzi. Dir: Guido Brignone
CHALIAPIN, Feodor (1873-1938) Russian bass
  Tsar Ivan Vasilyevich Grozny (Rus 1915). Dir: A. Ivanov-Gai
  Don Quixote (Fr 1933) Dir: G.W. Pabst
CONNER, Nadine (1913–) American soprano
  Of Men and Music (US 1950) with Jan Peerce

CORELLI, Franco (1921–) Italian tenor
  Pagliacci (It 1954) with Gobbi. TV film
  Tosca (It 1955) with Renata Heredia Capnist. TV film
  Tosca (It 1956) with Franca Duval. Dir: Carmine Gallone
  Turandot (It 1958) with Lucilla Udovich. Dir: Mario Lanfranchi TV film
  Carmen – made for TV film now lost
  Andrea Chénier (It 1973). TV film
COSSIRA, Emile (1854-1923) French tenor
  Roméo et Juliette (Fr 1900) pioneering sound film
COSTA, Mary (1934–) American soprano
  Marry Me Again (US 1953)* with Robert Cummings
  The Big Caper (US 1957)* with Rory Calhoun
  The Great Waltz (US 1972) with Horst Buchholz, Nigel Patrick. Dir: Andrew
    Stone
  (Costa was also the voice of the Princess in Disney's *Sleeping Beauty*, 1959)
COWAN, Richard (1957–) American baritone
  La Bohème (Fr 1988) with Barbara Hendricks. Dir: Luigi Commencini
  Madame Butterfly (Fr 1995). Dir: Frédéric Mitterand
DAL MONTE, Toti (1899-1975) Italian soprano
  Il Carnevale di Venezia (It 1940). Dir: Giacomo Gentilomo and Giuseppe Adami
  Fiori d'Arancio (It 1944)
  Il Vedovo Allegro (It 1949). Dir: Mario Mattoli
  Cuore di Mamma (It 1954). Dir: Luigi Capuano
DAYMOND, Karl (1965–) English baritone, now tenor
  Dido and Aeneas (GB 1995) with Maria Ewing, Sally Burgess, James Bowman. Dir:
    Peter Maniura
DE CORDOBA, Pedro (1881-1950) American bass
  Carmen (US 1915)* with Geraldine Farrar
  Temptation (US 1915)* with Farrar
  Maria Rosa (US 1916)* with Farrar
  Runaway Romany (US 1920)*
  The Mark of Zorro (US 1920)* with Douglas Fairbanks
  Captain Blood (US 1935)*
  Blood and Sand (US 1941)* Dir: Rouben Mamoulian
  Saboteur (US 1942)*. Dir: Alfred Hitchcock
  The Song of Bernadette (US 1943)*
  For Whom the Bell Tolls (US 1943)*
DELLA CASA, Lisa (1919–) Swiss soprano
  Don Giovanni (GB 1954). Dir: Paul Czinner
  Arabella (Ger 1963) with Dietrich Fischer-Dieskau, Anneliese Rothenberger
DEL MONACO, Mario (1915-1982) Italian tenor
  L'uomo dal Guanto Grigio (It 1948) with Annette Bach
  Mascagni (It 1952) with Pierre Cressoy. Dir: Giacomo Gentilomo
  Cavalleria Rusticana (It-US 1953) with Rina Telli. Made for TV
  Andrea Chénier (It 1955) with Antonietta Stella. TV film
  Casa Ricordi (It 1956) with Marcello Mastroianni, Tito Gobbo, Guilio Neri. Dir:
    Carmine Gallone
  Guai ai Vinti (It 1955)
  Il Trovatore (It 1957) with Leyla Gencer, Fedora Barbieri. TV film
  Otello (It 1958) with Rosanna Carteri. TV film
  Primo Amore (It 1978) with Ornella Muti, Ugo Tognazzi

DE LUCA, Giuseppe (1876-1950) Italian baritone
Three Vitaphone shorts (US 1927-1929)
DE PAOLIS, Alessio (1893-1964) Italian tenor
La Cantante dell'Opera (It 1932) with Laura Pasini
DESTINN, Emmy (1878-1930) Czech soprano
The Lion's Bride (1913)
DIAZ, Justino (1940–) Puerto Rican/American baritone
Carmen (Ger 1967) with Grace Bumbry, Jon Vickers. Dir: Herbert von Karajan
Otello (It 1986) with Plácido Domingo. Dir: Franco Zeffirelli
DIDUR, Adam (1874-1946) Polish bass
Aïda (US 1927) Vitaphone short with Martinelli
DI STEFANO, Giuseppe (1921–) Italian tenor
Canto Per Te (It 1953) with Hélène Remy
DOMGRAF-FASSBAENDER, Willi (1897-1978) German baritone,
The Bartered Bride (Ger 1932) with Jarmila Novotná. Dir: Max Ophuls
Der Weg Carl Maria von Weber (Ger 1934). Dir: Rudolf van der Noss
Figaros Hochzeit (Ger 1949). Dir: Georg Wildhagen
DOMINGO, Plácido (1941–) Spanish tenor
Madama Butterfly (Ger 1974) with Mirella Freni. Dir: Jean-Pierre Ponnelle
Tosca (It 1976) with Raina Kabaivanska, Sherrill Milnes. Dir: Gianfranco de Bosio
Cavalleria Rusticana (It 1982) with Elena Obraztsova. Dir: Franco Zeffirelli
Pagliacci (It 1982) with Teresa Stratas, Juan Pons. Dir: Zeffirelli
La Traviata (It 1982) with Teresa Stratas. Dir: Zeffirelli
Hommage à Sevilla (Ger 1982). Dir: Ponnelle
Carmen (It 1984) with Julia Migenes, Ruggero Raimondi. Dir: Francesco Rosi
Otello (It/US 1986) with Katia Ricciarelli. Dir: Zeffirelli
Parsifal (GB 1998). Dir: Tony Palmer
DRAGONI, Bruna (1896-1962) Italian soprano
La Serva Padrona (It 1934) with Vincenzo Bettoni
DUNCAN, Todd (1903-1998) American baritone
Syncopation (US 1942)
Unchained (US 1955) with Chester Morris. Dir: Hall Bartlett
DVORSKY, Peter (1951–) Czech tenor
The Bartered Bride (Cz 1981) with Gabriela Benackova. TV film
The Love of Destiny (Cz 1983) with Emilia Asaryova. Dir: Petr Weigl
L'Elisir d'Amore (Cz 1984) with Melanie Holliday
Werther (Cz 1985) with Brigitte Fassbaender. Dir: Weigl
EBRAHIM, Omar (1956–) British baritone
The Vampire (GB 1993) with Richard Van Allan, Fiona O'Neill. Dir: Nigel Finch
EDDY, Nelson (1901-1967) American baritone/tenor
Broadway to Hollywood (US 1933)
Dancing Lady (US 1934)
Student Tour (US 1934)
Naughty Marietta (US 1935) with Jeanette MacDonald
Rose Marie (US 1936) with MacDonald
Maytime (US 1937) with MacDonald
Rosalie (US 1937) with Ilona Massey
The Girl of the Golden West (US 1938) with MacDonald
Sweethearts (US 1938) with MacDonald
Let Freedom Ring! (US 1939) with Virginia Bruce
Balalaika (US 1939) with Ilona Massey

Bitter Sweet (US 1940) with MacDonald
New Moon (US 1940) with MacDonald
The Chocolate Soldier (US 1941) with Risë Stevens
I Married an Angel (US 1942) with MacDonald
The Phantom of the Opera (US 1942)
Knickerbocker Glory (US 1944)
Make Mine Music (US 1946) dubbed all voices for Willie the Whale
Northwest Outpost (US 1947) with Ilona Massey

EDELMANN, Otto (1917–) Austrian baritone
Don Giovanni (Ger 1954). Dir: Paul Czinner

EGGERTH, Marta (1912–) Hungarian soprano
Die Brautigamswitwe/The Bridegroom's Widow (Ger/GB 1931) with Georg Alexander, Fritz Kampers. Dir: Richard Eichberg
Trara um Liche (Ger 1931) with Georg Alexander. Dir: Richard Eichberg
Der Draufganger (Ger 1931) with Hans Albers. Dir: Richard Eichberg
Eine Nacht im Grand Hotel (Ger 1931). Dir: Max Neufeld
Ein Lied, ein Kuss, ein Madel (Ger 1932) with Gustav Fröhlich. Dir: Geza von Bolvary
Das Blaue vom Himmel (Ger 1932) with Hermann Thimig, Fritz Kampers. Dir: Viktor Janson. Script by Billy Wilder. Also called *Eine Frau unter Jausend*
Der Frauendiplomat (Ger 1932) with Leo Slezak. Dir: EW Emo
Moderne Mitgift (Ger 1932) with Georg Alexander, Leo Slezak. Dir: EW Emo
Der Traum von Schonbrunn (Aus 1932) with Hermann Thimig. Dir: Johannes Meyer
Where Is This Lady/Es war einmal ein Walzer (Ger 1932). Dir: Viktor Janson. English version Dir: Lazlo Vajda and W. Victor Hanbury
Kaiserwalzer (Ger 1932)
Die Blume von Hawaii (Ger 1933). Dir: Richard Oswald
Leise flehen meine Lieder (Aus 1933) with Hans Jaray. Dir: Willy Forst
Der Zarewitsch (Ger 1933) with Georg Alexander. Dir: Viktor Janson
Audienz in Ischl (Aus 1933) with Willy Eichberger. Dir: Friedrich Zelnik
Mein Herz ruft nach (Ger 1934) with Jan Kiepura. Dir: Carmine Gallone
Die Csárdásfürstin (Ger 1934) with Hans Sohnker, Paul Hörbiger. Dir: Georg Jacoby
Therese Krones or *Ihr grosster Erfolg* (Ger 1934) with Leo Slezak. Dir: Johannes Meyer
The Unfinished Symphony (GB-Aus 1934). Dir: Willi Forst. English version of *Leise flehen meine Lieder*
The Divine Spark/Casta Diva/Bezaubernde Augen (It 1935). Dir: Carmine Gallone
My Heart Is Calling (Ger/GB 1935) with Jan Kiepura, Sonnie Hale. Dir: Carmine Gallone. English version of *Mein Herz ruft nach*
Liebesmelodie (Aust 1935) with Leo Slezak, Hans Moser. Dir: Viktor Tourjansky
Die Blonde Carmen (Ger 1935) with Leo Slezak. Dir: Viktor Janson
Die ganze Welt dreht sich um Liebe (Aus 1935) with Leo Slezak. Dir: Viktor Tourjansky
Das Schloss in Flandern (Ger 1936) with Paul Hartmann, Georg Alexander. Dir: Geza von Bolvary
Wo die Lerche singt (Hung 1936) with Hans Sohnker. Dir: Carl Lamac
Das Hofkonzert (Ger 1936). Dir: Detlef Sierck
The Charm of La Bohème/Zauber der Bohème (Aus 1937) with Jan Kiepura. Dir: Geza von Bolvary
Immer wenn Ich glücklich bin (Aus 1937). Dir: Carl Lamac
For Me and My Girl (US 1942) with Judy Garland, Gene Kelly
Presenting Lily Mars (US 1943) with Judy Garland. Dir: Norman Taurog

Her Wonderful Lie (It 1947) with Jan Kiepura. Dir: Carmine Gallone. Remake of the 1937 *Charm of La Bohème*
La Valse Brillante (Fr 1949) with Jan Kiepura
Das Land des Lächelns (Ger 1952) with Jan Kiepura. Dir: Hans Deppe
Frühling in Berlin (Ger 1957)
EISINGER, Irene (1903-1994) German soprano
Zwei Herzen in Dreivierteltakt (Ger 1930) with Willi Forst. Dir: Geza von Bolvary
Die lustigen Weiber von Wien (Ger 1931) with Willi Forst. Dir: Geza von Bolvary
Die Försterchristl (Ger 1931) with Paul Richter. Dir: Friedrich Zelnick
ELLIS, Mary (1900–) American soprano
Bella Donna (GB 1934)*. Dir: Robert Milton
All the King's Horses (US 1935) with Carl Brisson
Fatal Lady (US 1936) with Walter Pidgeon. Dir: Edward Ludwig
Paris in Spring (US 1936) with Tullio Carminati. Dir: Lewis Milestone
Glamorous Night (GB 1937) with Barry McKay. Dir: Brian Desmond Hurst
The Three Worlds of Gulliver (GB 1960)* with Kerwin Matthews
ELMO, Cloe (1910-1962) Italian mezzo
The Marriage of Figaro (It 1948) with Piero Brasini
Carmen (It 1951) highlights
EWING, Maria (1950–) American mezzo
The Marriage of Figaro (Ger 1976) with Hermann Prey. Dir: Jean-Pierre Ponnelle
Dido and Aeneas (GB 1995) with Karl Daymond. Dir: Peter Maniura
FARRAR, Geraldine (1882-1967) American soprano
Carmen (US 1915)*. Dir: Cecil B. DeMille
Temptation (US 1916)*. Dir: DeMille
Maria Rosa (US 1916)*. Dir: DeMille
Joan, the Woman (US 1917)*. Dir: DeMille
The Woman God Forgot (US 1917)*. Dir: DeMille
The Devil Stone (US 1917)*. Dir: DeMille
The Hell Cat (US 1918)*. Dir: Reginald Barker
The Turn of the Wheel (US 1918)*. Dir: Barker
Flame of the Desert (US 1919)* with Lou Tellegren. Dir: Barker
The Stronger Vow (US 1919)* with Milton Sills. Dir: Barker
Shadows (US 1919)* with Sills. Dir: Barker
The World and Its Women (US 1919)* with Tellegren. Dir: Frank Lloyd
The Woman and the Puppet (US 1920)*. Dir: Barker
The Riddle Woman (US 1921)*. Dir: Edward José
FASSBAENDER, Brigitte (1939–) German mezzo
Das Rheingold (Ger 1978) with Thomas Stewart, Peter Schreier. Dir: Ernst Wild
Hansel and Gretel (Ger 1981) with Edita Gruberova. Dir: August Everding
Werther (Cz 1985) with Peter Dvorsky. Dir: Petr Weigl
FEDDERLEY, Greg (1962–) American tenor
The Rake's Progress (Sw 1995) with Barbara Hendricks, Håkan Hagegård. Dir: Inger Åby
FERNANDEZ, Wilhemena (1955–) American soprano
Diva (Fr 1981). Dir: Jean-Jacques Beineix
FISCHER-DIESKAU, Dietrich (1925–) German baritone
The Marriage of Figaro (Ger 1976) with Hermann Prey. Dir: Jean-Pierre Ponnelle
Elektra (Aus 1981) with Astrid Varnay. Dir: Götz Friedrich TV film
FLAGSTAD, Kirsten (1895-1962) Norwegian soprano
The Big Broadcast of 1938 (US 1938) with Bob Hope

FRANCHI, Sergio. Italian tenor
  The Secret of Santa Vittoria (US 1969) with Anthony Quinn. Dir: Stanley Kramer
FRENI, Mirella (1935–) Italian soprano
  La Bohème (Ger 1965) with Gianni Raimondi. Dir: Wilhelm Semmelroth
  Carmen (Ger 1967) with Grace Bumbry. Dir: Herbert von Karajan
  Madama Butterfly (Ger 1974) with Plácido Domingo. Dir: Jean-Pierre Ponnelle
  Otello (Ger 1974) with Jon Vickers. Dir: Roger Benamou
  The Marriage of Figaro (Ger 1976) with Hermann Prey. Dir: Ponnelle
FRICK, Gottlob (1906-1997) German bass
  Der Freischütz (1968) Dir: Joachim Hess
GARDEN, Mary (1874-1967) Scottish-born American soprano
  Thaïs (US 1918)
  The Splendid Sinner (US 1918)
GASPARIAN, Gohar (1924–) Armenian soprano
  Gohar Gasparian (USSR-Armenia 1971)
  Garine (Armenia 1979)
GATTI, Gabriella (1908–) Italian soprano
  Giuseppi Verdi: Divine Armonie (It 1938). Dir: Carmine Gallone
  Rossini (It 1943)
GENTLE, Alice (1889-1958) American mezzo
  Song of the Flame (US 1930). Dir: Alan Crosland
  Golden Dawn (US 1930) with Noah Beery, Vivienne Segal
  Flying Down To Rio (US 1933) with Fred Astaire and Ginger Rogers
GIGLI, Beniamino (1890-1957) Italian tenor
  Vitaphone shorts: scenes from *Cavalleria Rusticana*; quartet from *Rigoletto; Bergere Legere*; scenes from *Lucia di Lammermoor* with Marion Talley; *La Gioconda* (US 1927); *The Pearl Fishers* duet with Giuseppe de Luca (US 1928)
  Vergiss mein nicht/Non Ti Scordar di Me (Ger 1935). Dir: Augusto Genina
  Forget Me Not (GB 1935) with Joan Gardner. Dir: Zoltan Korda
  Ave Maria (Ger 1936) with Käthe von Nagy, Erna Berger. Dir: Johannes Riemann
  Du bist mein Glück/Sinfonia di Cuori (Ger 1936) with Isa Miranda. Dir: Karl Heinz Martin
  Die Stimme des Herzens (Ger 1937) with Geraldine Katt. Dir: Karl Heinz Martin
  Solo Per Te/Mutterlied/Only For You (Ger 1938) with Maria Cebotari, Michael Bohnen. Dir: Carmine Gallone
  Dein gehört mein Herz/Marionette (It 1938) with Carla Rust. Dir: Carmine Gallone
  Giuseppe Verdi: Divine Armonie (It 1938)
  Casa Lontana/Der Singende Tor/Legittima Difesa (It 1939) with Liva Caloni. Dir: Johannes Meyer
  Ritorno/Traummusik (It 1940) with Marte Harell, Rossano Brazzi. Dir: Geza Von Bolvary
  Mamma/Mutter (It 1940) with Emma Gramatica. Dir: Guido Brignone
  Drei Frau um Verdi (It 1940) with Maria Cebotari, Tito Gobbi, Pia Tassinari, Gabriella Gatti, Apollo Granforte. Dir: Carmine Gallone
  Vertigine/Tragödie einer Liebe (It 1942) with Tito Gobbi, Liva Caloni, Tatiana Menotti. Dir: Guido Brigone
  I Pagliacci/Lache Bajazzo (Ger 1942) with Paul Horbiger, Monika Burg
  Silenzio: Si Gira!/Achtung! Aufnahme! (It 1943) with Rossano Brazzi
  Voglio bene soltanto a Te (It 1946). Dir: Giuseppe Fatigati
  Follie per l'Opera (It 1948) with Gina Lollobrigida, Gobbi, Bechi, Schipa, Caniglia. Dir: Mario Costa

Opera on Film

Taxi di Notte (It 1950). Dir: Carmine Gallone
Una Voce nel Tuo Cuore (It 1950) with Gino Bechi
Soho Conspiracy (GB 1951) remake of *Follie per l'Opera*
GILBERT, Olive (d. 1981) English contralto
  Glamorous Night (GB 1937) with Mary Ellis
  The Dancing Years (GB 1950) with Dennis Price, Gisèle Preville
GLOSSOP, Peter (1928–) English baritone
  Pagliacci (Ger 1968) with Jon Vickers, Raina Kabaivanska. Dir: Herbert von Karajan
  Otello (Ger 1974) with Jon Vickers, Mirella Freni. Dir: Roger Benamou
GOBBI, Tito (1913-1984) Italian baritone
  I Condottieri (It 1937) with Luis Trenker (who also directed)
  Giuseppe Verdi: Divine Armonie (It 1938) with Gigli, Maria Cebotari. Dir: Carmine Gallone
  Il Sogno di Butterfly (It 1939) with Maria Cebotari
  Musica Proibita (It 1943). Dir: Carlo Campogalliani
  O Sole Mio (It 1945) with Gigli. Dir: Giacomo Gentiluomo
  The Barber of Seville (It 1946) with Tagliavini, Italo Tajo. Dir: Mario Costa
  Davanti a lui Tremava Tutta Roma (It 1946) with Anna Magnani, Gino Sinimberghi. Dir: Carmine Gallone
  L'Ecio della Gloria/Les Beaux Jours du Roi Murat (Fr-It 1946) Dir: Theophile Pathé
  Souriez, Sire (It 1946)
  Rigoletto (It 1947) with Mario Filippeschi, Guilio Neri. Dir: Carmine Gallone
  L'Elisir d'Amore (It 1947) with Nelly Corradi, Sinimberghi, Tajo. Dir: Mario Costa
  Follie per l'Opera (It 1948) with Lollobrigida, Gigli, Bechi, Caniglia, Schipa. Dir: Mario Costa
  Pagliacci (It 1948) with Gina Lollobrigida. Dir: Mario Costa
  William Tell (It 1948) Prod: George Richfield
  Lucia di Lammermoor (It 1948). Prod: George Richfield
  Carmen (It 1948) Prod: George Richfield
  The Barber of Seville (It 1948) Prod: George Richfield
  The Glass Mountain (GB 1948) with Michael Denison, Dulcie Gray, Valentina Cortesa. Dir: Henry Cass
  Don Pasquale (It 1949). Prod: George Richfield
  La Forza del Destino (It 1949) with Nelly Corradi. Dir: Carmine Gallone
  Soho Conspiracy (GB 1951) remake of *Follie per l'Opera*
  The Firebird (Sw-It 1952) with Ellen Rasch. Dir: Hasse Ekman
  Verdi, King of Melody (It 1953) with Mario del Monaco. Dir: Raffaello Matarazzo
  Canzone a Due Voci (It 1954) with Gino Bechi
  Casa Ricordi (It 1954). Dir: Carmine Gallone
  The Barber of Seville (It 1956). Dir: Camillo Mastrocinque
GORIN, Igor (1908-1982) Ukranian-American baritone
  Broadway Melody of 1938 (US 1937) with Eleanor Powell, Buddy Ebsen, Robert Taylor. Dir: Roy del Ruth
  The Merry Wives of Windsor (Yug-Aus 1966) with Norman Foster, Lucia Popp. Dir: George Tressler
GRANFORTE, Apollo (1886-1975) Italian baritone
  The Barber of Seville (Australia 1928) scene as Figaro made when on tour with Melba
  Drei Frau um Verdi (It 1938) with Gigli, Maria Cebotari. Dir: Carmine Gallone
GRAYSON, Kathryn (1922–) American soprano
  Andy Hardy's Private Secretary (US 1941) with Mickey Rooney
  The Vanishing Virginian (US 1941)

220

Rio Rita (US 1942) with Abbott and Costello
Seven Sweethearts (US 1942). Dir: Frank Borzage
Thousands Cheer (US 1943) with Gene Kelly
Anchors Aweigh (US 1946)
Ziegfeld Follies (US 1946)
Two Sisters from Boston (US 1946) with June Allyson
Till The Clouds Roll By (US 1946)
It Happened In Brooklyn (US 1947) with Frank Sinatra
The Kissing Bandit (US 1948) with Sinatra
That Midnight Kiss (US 1949) with Mario Lanza
The Toast of New Orleans (US 1950) with Lanza
Grounds for Marriage (US 1950) with Van Johnson
Show Boat (US 1951) with Howard Keel
Lovely To Look At (US 1952) with Keel
The Desert Song (US 1953) with Gordon MacRae
So This Is Love (US 1953) Grace Moore biopic
Kiss Me Kate (US 1953) with Keel
The Vagabond King (US 1956) with Oreste Kirkup
GRUBEROVA, Edita (1946–) Czech soprano
Hansel and Gretel (Ger 1981) with Brigitte Fassbaender. Dir: August Everding
Rigoletto (Ger 1983) with Luciano Pavarotti. Dir: Jean-Pierre Ponnelle
Cosi Fan Tutte (Ger 1988) with Teresa Stratas, Luis Lima. Dir: Jean-Pierre Ponnelle
GRÜMMER, Elisabeth (1911-1986) German soprano
Don Giovanni (Ger 1954). Dir: Paul Czinner
HACKETT, Charles (1889-1942) American tenor
Seven Vitaphone films (US 1927-29)
HAGEGÅRD, Håkan (1945–) Swedish baritone
The Magic Flute (Sw 1974). Dir: Ingmar Bergman
The Rake's Progress (Sw 1995). Dir: Inger Åby
HAMPSON, Thomas (1955–) American baritone
A Village Romeo and Juliet (Cz 1989). Dir: Petr Weigl
HAMPTON, Hope (1899-1982) American soprano
The Bait (US 1920)*
A Modern Salome (US 1920)*
Star Dust (US 1921)*
The Gold Diggers (US 1923)*
Hollywood (US 1923)*
The Truth About Women (US 1924)*
Lover's Island (US 1925)*
The Unfair Sex (US 1926)*
Manon (US 1929) Vitaphone sound test
The Road to Reno (US 1938) with Randolph Scott
HAUGLAND, Aage (1944–) Danish bass
Parsifal (Ger 1982). Dir: Hans-Jurgen Syberberg
HAYMON, Cynthia (1956–)American soprano
Porgy and Bess (GB 1989) with Willard White. Dir: Trevor Nunn
HENDRICKS, Barbara (1948–) American soprano
La Bohème (Fr-It 1988). Dir: Louis Comencini
The Rake's Progress (Sw 1995). Dir: Inger Åby
HOTTER, Hans (1909–) German bass-baritone

Mutterliebe (Aus 1939) with Käthe Dorsch
Bruderlein fein (Aus 1942) with Marte Harrell
Seine beste Rolle (Ger 1943). Dir: Otto Pittermann
I Pagliacci (Ger 1943) with Gigli
Grosstadnacht (Aus 1950). Dir: Hans Wolff
Sehnsucht des Herzens (Ger 1950)

HOUSTON, George (1900-1944) American baritone
The Melody Lingers On (US 1935) with Josephine Hutchinson
Let's Sing Again (US 1935) with Bobby Breen
Conquest (US 1937)* with Greta Garbo
The Great Waltz (US 1938) with Miliza Korjus
The Howards of Virginia (US 1940)* with Cary Grant

HOWARD, Kathleen (1880-1956) Canadian mezzo
Death Takes a Holiday (US 1934)* with Fredric March
You're Telling Me (US 1934)* with W.C. Fields
The Man on the Flying Trapeze (US 1935)* with W.C.Fields
It's a Gift (US 1935)* with W.C. Fields
Ball of Fire (US 1942)* with Gary Cooper. Dir: Howard Hawks
Laura (US 1944)* with Dana Andrews. Dir: Otto Preminger
Centennial Summer (US 1946)*. Dir: Preminger
The Late George Apley (US 1946)* with Ronald Colman
The Petty Girl (US 1950)* with Robert Cummings

HUANG, Ying (1968–) Chinese soprano
Madame Butterfly (Fr 1995) with Richard Troxell. Dir: Frédéric Mitterand

JANOWITZ, Gundala (1937–) German soprano
Cosi Fan Tutte (Ger 1969) with Luigi Alva. Dir: Vaclav Kaslik
Die Fledermaus (Ger 1971) with Renate Holm, Eberhard Wechter, Erich Kunz. Dir: Otto Schenk. TV film
Fidelio (Fr 1977) with Jon Vickers. Dir: Pierre Jourdan

JEPSON, Helen (1904-1997) American soprano
The Goldwyn Follies (US 1938). Dir: George Marshall

JERITZA, Maria (1887-1982) Czech soprano
Grand Duchess Alexandra (Aus 1933) with Paul Hartmann, Leo Slezak

JERUSALEM, Siegfried (1940–) German tenor
Der Zigeunerbaron (Ger 1975) with Ellen Shade. Dir: Arthur Maria Rabenalt. TV film

JURINAC, Sena (1921–) Yugoslav soprano
On Such a Night (GB 1955). Dir: Anthony Asquith
Der Rosenkavalier (GB 1960). Dir: Paul Czinner
Wozzeck (Ger 1967) with Richard Cassilly. Dir: Joachim Hess
Hansel and Gretel (Aus 1981) with Brigitte Fassbaender. Dir: August Everding

KABAIVANSKA, Raina (1934–) Bulgarian soprano
Pagliacci (Ger 1968) with Jon Vickers
Tosca (It 1976) with Plácido Domingo, Sherrill Milnes. Dir: Gianfranco de Bosio

KALICH, Bertha (1874-1939) Romanian soprano
Marta of the Lowlands (US 1914)*
Slander (US 1916)*
Ambition (US 1916)*
Love and Hate (US 1916)*

KIEPURA, Jan (1902-1966) Polish tenor
Die singende Stadt/City of Song (Ger 1930). Dir: Carmine Gallone

Ein Lied für Dich/A Song For You (Ger 1932)
Das Leid einer Nacht/Tell Me Tonight (Ger-GB 1932). Dir: Anatole Litvak.
Mein Herz ruft nach dir/My Heart is Calling You (Ger-GB 1934) with Marta Eggerth.
　　Dir: Carmine Gallone
Ich liebe alle Frauen (Ger 1935). Dir: Carl Lamac
Give Us This Night (US 1936) with Gladys Swarthout
Opernring (Aus 1936). Dir: Carmine Gallone
Zauber der Bohème/The Charm of La Bohème (Aus 1937) with Eggerth. Dir: Geza
　　von Bolvary
Her Wonderful Lie (It 1947) with Eggerth. Dir: Carmine Gallone
La Valse Brillante (Fr 1949) with Eggerth
Das Land des Lächelns (Ger 1952) with Eggerth
KIRKOP, Oreste (1926–) Maltese tenor
　　The Vagabond King (US 1956) with Kathryn Grayson
KIRSTEN, Dorothy (1917-1992) American soprano
　　Mr Music (US 1950) with Bing Crosby. Dir: Richard Haydn
　　The Great Caruso (US 1951) with Mario Lanza
KNIGHT, Felix (1913–) American tenor
　　Babes in Toyland (US 1934) with Laurel and Hardy
　　The Bohemian Girl (US 1936) with Laurel and Hardy
KOLLO, René (1937–) German tenor
　　Oberon (Ger 1968). TV film
　　Wiener Blut (Ger 1971). TV film
　　The Gypsy Princess (Hun-Ger 1971) with Anna Moffo. Dir: Miklos Szinetar
　　Oedipus Rex (US 1973) with Tatiana Troyanos, Tom Krause
　　The Land of Smiles (Ger 1973). Dir: Arthur Maria Rabenalt. TV film
　　Countess Maritza (Ger 1973) with Ljuba Welitsch. TV film
　　La Belle Hélène (Ger 1974) with Anna Moffo. TV film
　　The Bartered Bride (Ger 1975) with Teresa Stratas. TV film
KORJUS, Miliza (1902-1980) Polish soprano
　　The Great Waltz (US 1938). Dir: Julien Duvivier
　　Caballeria del Imperio (Mexico 1942) with Pedro Vargas. Dir: Miguel Contreras
　　Torres
KOSHETZ, Nina (1894-1965) Russian soprano
　　Casanova (Fr 1926)*. Dir: Alexandre Volkoff
　　Algiers (US 1938)* with Hedy Lamarr, Charles Boyer
　　Our Hearts Were Young and Gay (US 1944). Dir: Lewis Allen
　　Summer Storm (US 1944) with George Sanders. Dir: Douglas Sirk
　　The Chase (US 1947) with Robert Cummings and Michele Morgan
　　It's a Small World (US 1950)
　　Captain Pirate (US 1952)
　　Hot Blood (US 1955) with Cornel Wilde, Jane Russell. Dir: Nicholas Ray
KOZLOVSKY, Ivan (1900-1993) Russian tenor
　　Bolshoi Koncert (USSR 1951). Dir: Vera Stroyeva
KRAUS, Alfredo (1927-1999) Spanish tenor
　　The Vagabond and the Star (Sp 1958)
　　Gayarre (Sp 1959)
KRAUSE, Tom (1934–) Finnish baritone
　　The Marriage of Figaro (Ger 1967). Dir: Joachim Hertz. TV film
　　Der Freischütz (Ger 1968). Dir: Joachim Hertz. TV film
　　Oedipus Rex (US 1973) with René Kollo, Tatyana Troyanos

KULLMAN, Charles (1903-1993) American tenor
  The Goldwyn Follies (US 1938). Dir: George Marshall
  Song of Scheherazade (US 1947) with Yvonne De Carlo, Jean Pierre Aumont
LANZA, Mario (1921-1959) American tenor
  Winged Victory (US 1944)
  That Midnight Kiss (US 1949) with Kathryn Grayson
  The Toast of New Orleans (US 1950) with Grayson
  The Great Caruso (US 1951). Dir: Richard Thorpe
  Because You're Mine (US 1952). Dir: Alexander Hall
  Serenade (US 1956) with Joan Fontaine, Licia Albanese. Dir: Anthony Mann
  The Seven Hills of Rome (It 1958). Dir: Roy Rowland
  For the First Time (US-WGer 1959). Dir: Rudolph Maté
LAURI-VOLPI, Giacomo (1892-1979) Italian tenor
  La Canzone del Sole (It 1933) with Vittorio De Sica
  Il Caimano del Piave (It 1950)
LEHMANN, Lotte (1888-1976) German soprano
  Big City (US 1948) with Margaret O'Brien. Dir: Norman Taurog
LEIGH, Adele (1928–) English soprano
  Davy (GB 1957) with Harry Secombe, Joan Sims, Bill Pertwee. Dir: Michael Relph
  Wagner (GB 1983) with Richard Burton. Dir: Tony Palmer
LEMESHEV, Sergei (1902-1977) Russian tenor
  A Musical Story (USSR 1940)
  Russian Salad/Kino-Concert 41 (USSR 1941)
LEMNITZ, Tiana (1897-1994) German soprano
  Altes Herz wird wieder Jung (Ger 1939) with Emil Jannings, Max Lorenz. Dir: Erich
    Engel
LEWIS, Mary (1897-1941) American soprano
  Two Vitaphone films (US 1927)
LIPP, Wilma (1925–) Austrian soprano
  Unsterblicher Mozart (Aus 1954)
  The Cardinal (US 1963) with Tom Tryon. Dir: Otto Preminger
LLOYD, Robert (1940–) British bass
  Parsifal (Ger 1982). Dir: Hans-Jurgen Syberberg
LORENZ, Max (1901-1975)
  Altes Herz wird wieder Jung (Ger 1939) with Emil Jannings, Tiana Lemnitz. Dir:
    Erich Engel
LUGO, Giuseppe (1898-1980) Italian tenor
  La Mia Canzone al Vento (It 1939). Dir: Guido Brignone
  Cantante Con Me (It 1940). Dir: Brignone
  Miliardi, Che Follia! (It 1942). Dir: Brignone
  Senza una Donna (It 1943). Dir: Alfredo Guarini
  Il Tiranno del Garda (It 1956). Dir: Ignazio Ferronetti
McCORMACK, John (1884-1945) Irish tenor
  Song O' My Heart (US 1930) with Maureen O'Sullivan. Dir: Frank Borzage.
  Wings of the Morning (GB 1937) with Henry Fonda, Annabella. Dir: Harold Schuster
MACDONALD, Jeanette (1903-1965) American soprano
  The Love Parade (US 1929) with Maurice Chevalier. Dir: Ernst Lubitsch
  The Vagabond King (US 1930) with Dennis King
  Monte Carlo (US 1930) with Jack Buchanan
  Let's Go Native (US 1930)
  The Lottery Bride (US 1930)

Oh, For a Man (US 1930)
Don't Bet on a Woman (US 1931)
Anabelle's Affairs (US 1931)
One Hour With You (US 1932) with Chevalier
Love Me Tonight (1932) with Chevalier
The Cat and the Fiddle (1934) with Ramon Navarro
The Merry Widow (US 1934) with Chevalier
Naughty Marietta (US 1935) with Nelson Eddy
Rose Marie (US 1936) with Eddy
San Francisco (US 1936) with Clark Gable
Maytime (US 1937) with Eddy
The Firefly (US 1937) with Allan Jones
The Girl of the Golden West (US 1938) with Eddy
Sweethearts (US 1938) with Eddy
Broadway Serenade (US 1939) with Lew Ayres
New Moon (US 1940) with Eddy
Bitter Sweet (US 1940) with Eddy
Smilin' Through (US 1941) with Brian Aherne and Gene Raymond
I Married An Angel (US 1942) with Eddy
Cairo (US 1942) with Robert Young
Follow the Boys (US 1944)
The Birds and the Bees (US 1948) with Jose Iturbi
The Sun Comes Up (US 1949) with Lassie
MACNEIL, Cornell (1922–) American baritone
La Traviata (Fr-It 1982). Dir: Franco Zeffirelli
MALFITANO, Catherine (1948–) American soprano
La Clemenza di Tito (Ger 1980). Dir: Jean-Pierre Ponnelle
MARIANO, Luis (1914-1970) Spanish/French tenor
Historie de Chanter (Fr 1946). Dir: Gilles Grangier
Cargaison Clandestine (Fr 1947)
Fandango (Fr 1948)
Je n'aime pas que toi (Fr 1949)
Pas de Weekend pour Notre Amour (Fr 1949)
Andalousie (Fr 1950). Dir: Robert Vernay
La Belle de Cadix (Fr 1953)
Der Zarewitsch (Ger 1954)
Le Chanteur de Mexique (Fr)
Violettes Imperials (Fr)
Quatre Jours à Paris (Fr)
À la Jamaique (Fr)
MARSHALL, Everett (1901–) American baritone
Dixiana (US 1930) with Bebe Daniels. Dir: Luther Reed
I Live For Love (US 1935) with Dolores del Rio. Dir: Busby Berkeley
MARTINELLI, Giovanni (1885-1969) Italian tenor
Arias and scenes from *Pagliacci, Aïda, Carmen, La Juive, Martha, Il Trovatore, Faust*, and various songs, all for Vitaphone (US 1926-1930)
MARTINI, Nino (1904-1976) Italian tenor
Paramount on Parade (US 1930) with Maurice Chevalier, Gary Cooper, Clara Bow and Paramount stars
Here's to Romance (US 1935) with Genevieve Tobin, Reginald Denny, Ernestine Schumann-Heink. Dir: Alfred E. Green

The Gay Desperado (US 1936) with Ida Lupino, Leo Carrillo. Dir: Rouben Mamoulian.

Music for Madame (US 1937) with Joan Fontaine. Dir: John G Blystone

One Night With You (GB 1948) with Patricia Roc, Bonar Colleano, Stanley Holloway, Irene Worth. Dir: Terence Young

Song of India (US 1949) with Sabu

MASSARY, Fritzi (1882-1969) Austrian soprano

Operetta scene (Ger 1896) with Josef Gianpetro. Early sound film. Dir: Max Skladanowsky.

Duet (Ger 1903) with Josef Gianpetro. Early sound film by Oskar Messter

Die Rose von Stamboul (Ger 1919)*

MASTERSON, Valerie (1937–) English soprano

The Mikado (GB 1966) with Donald Adams, John Reed. Dir: Stuart Burge

La Traviata (GB 1973) with Kenneth Woollam, Michael Wakeham. Dir: Peter Seabourne

The Mikado (GB 1974) with Adams, Thomas Round, John Cartier, Helen Landis. Dir: Trevor Evans

The Pirates of Penzance (GB 1974) with Adams, Round, Landis. Dir: Evans

The Yeoman of the Guard (GB 1974) with Adams, Round, Cartier, Landis. Dir: Evans

Pagliacci (GB 1974) with Woollam, Malcolm Rivers. Dir: Peter Seabourne

HMS Pinafore (GB 1974) with Cartier, Round, Adams, Landis. Dir: Evans

The Tales of Hoffmann (GB 1974) with Woollam, Rivers. Dir: Seabourne

MATORIN, Vladimir (1948–) Russian bass

Boris Godunov (Russia 1991). Dir: Olga Ivanova

MATZENAUER, Margaret (1881-1963) Romanian contralto

Mr Deeds Goes to Town (US 1936)* with Gary Cooper. Dir: Frank Capra

MAUREL, Victor (1848-1923) French baritone

Falstaff (Fr 1900) – sings aria in this pioneering sound film

Don Giovanni (Fr 1900) – sings aria

MELCHIOR, Lauritz (1890-1973) Danish tenor

Thrill of a Romance (US 1945) with Esther Williams. Dir: Richard Thorpe

Two Sisters from Boston (US 1946) with Kathryn Grayson, June Allyson. Dir: Henry Koster

This Time for Keeps (US 1947) with Esther Williams. Dir: Richard Thorpe

Luxury Liner (US 1948) with Jane Powell. Dir: Richard Whorf

The Stars are Singing (US 1953) with Anna Maria Alberghetti, Rosemary Clooney. Dir: Norman Taurog

MELTON, James (1904-1961) American tenor

The Last Dogie (US 1933)

Stars Over Broadway (US 1935) with Pat O'Brien, Jane Froman

Sing Me a Love Song (US 1936) with Patricia Ellis. Dir: Ray Enright

Melody for Two (US 1937) with Patricia Ellis

Ziegfeld Follies (US 1946) with William Powell. Dir: Vincente Minnelli

MERRILL, Robert (1917–) American baritone

Aaron Slick from Punkin Crick (US 1952) with Dinah Shore. Dir: Claude Binyon

MERRITT, Chris (1952–) American tenor

Maggio Musicale (It 1990) with Shirley Verrett, Malcolm McDowell

MICHELENA, Beatriz (1890-1942) Spanish/American soprano

Salomy Jane (US 1914)*

Mrs. Wiggs of the Cabbage Patch (US 1914)*

Mignon (US 1915)*

MIGENES, Julia (1945–) American soprano
One Night in Venice (Ger 1973) with Trudeleise Schmidt, Erich Kunz. TV film
Carmen (Fr-Sp 1984) with Plácido Domingo. Dir: Francesco Rosi
The Threepenny Opera (US 1990) with Raul Julia, Roger Daltrey, Rachel Roberts, Richard Harris. Dir: Menahem Golan
MIKHAILOV, Maxim (1893-1971) Russian bass
Bolshoi Koncert (USSR 1951). Dir: Vera Stroyeva
MILNES, Sherrill (1935–) American baritone
Tosca (It 1976) with Plácido Domingo, Raina Kabaivanska. Dir: Gianfranco de Bosio
MOFFO, Anna (1934–) American soprano
La Serva Padrona (It 1958) with Paolo Montarsolo. TV film
Menage all'Italiana (It 1965) with Ugo Tognazzi
La Traviata (It 1966) with Franco Bonisoli, Gino Bechi. Dir: Mario Lanfranchi
Il Divorzio (It 1969) with Vittorio Gassmann. Dir: Romolo Girolami
Concerto per Pistolo Solista (It 1970) with Eveline Stewart, Lance Percival. Dir: Michele Lupo
The Adventurers (US 1970). Dir: Lewis Gilbert
La Ragazza di Nome Giulio (It 1970). Dir: Tonino Valeri
Lucia di Lammermoor (It 1971) with Giulio Fioravanti, Paulo Washington. Dir: Mario Lanfranchi
Die Csárdásfürstin (Hun-Ger 1971) with René Kollo. Dir: Miklos Szinetar
La Belle Hélène (Ger 1975) with René Kollo. TV film
MOJICA, José (1896-1974) Mexican tenor
One Mad Kiss (US 1930) with Antonio Moreno
Hay que Casar al Principe (US 1933) with Conchita Montenegro
La Ley del Harem (US 1931) with Carmen Larrabeita
Their Mad Moment (US 1931) with Andrès de Segurola
El Caballero de la Noche (US 1932) with Segurola
La Melodia Prohibida (US 1933) with Montenegro
El Rey de los Gitanos (US 1933). Dir: Frank Strayer
Un Capitan de Cosacos (US 1934) with Segurola
La Cruz y la Espada (US 1934). Dir: Strayer
Las Fronteras del Amor (US 1934). Dir: Strayer
El Capitan Aventurero (Mex 1938) with Manolita Saval
Melodias de las Americas (Arg 1942)
Sequire tus Pasos (Mex 1943)
El Portico de la Gloria (Mex 1952)
Yo Pecador (Mex 1965) Mojica's life story, using his voice.
MONTARSOLO, Paolo (1925–) Italian bass
La Serva Padrona (It 1958) with Anna Moffo. TV film
The Barber of Seville (Ger 1972) with Hermann Prey, Luigi Alva, Teresa Berganza. Dir: Jean-Pierre Ponnelle
The Marriage of Figaro (Ger 1976) with Hermann Prey, Mirella Freni, Kiri Te Kanawa. Dir: Ponnelle
Cosi Fan Tutte (Ger 1988) Dir: Ponnelle
Cenerentola (Ger 1981) with Frederica von Stade. Dir: Ponnelle
MOORE, Grace (1901-1947) American soprano
A Lady's Morals (US 1930) with Reginald Denny, Wallace Beery. Dir: Sidney Franklin
New Moon (US 1930) with Lawrence Tibbett
One Night of Love (US 1934) with Tullio Carminati. Dir: Victor Schertzinger

Love Me Forever (US 1935) with Leo Carrillo, Michael Bartlett, Luis Alberni. Dir: Victor Schertzinger

The King Steps Out (US 1936) with Franchot Tone, Herman Bing. Dir: Josef von Sternberg

When You're in Love (US 1937) with Cary Grant. Dir: Robert Riskin

I'll Take Romance (US 1937) with Melvyn Douglas. Dir: Edward H. Griffith.

Louise (France 1939) with Georges Thill. Dir: Abel Gance

MORISON, Elsie (1924–) Australian soprano

The Story of Gilbert and Sullivan (GB 1953) with Robert Morley, Maurice Evans, Peter Finch, Eileen Herlie, Dinah Sheridan, Isabel Dean, Wilfrid Hyde White. Dir: Sidney Gilliat.

MOSCONA, Nicola (1907-1975) Italian bass

The Great Caruso (US 1951) with Mario Lanza

La Forza del Destino (US 1951). Opera cameos TV series

MUMMERY, Browning (1888-1974) Australian tenor

Evensong (GB) with Conchita Supervia, Evelyn Laye, Fritz Kortner, Alice Delysia, Emlyn Williams. Dir: Victor Saville

MUNSEL, Patrice (1925–) American soprano

Melba (GB 1953) with Robert Morley, Alec Clunes, Martita Hunt, Sybil Thorndike, John McCallum. Dir: Lewis Milestone

NAMARA, Marguerite (1888-1974) American soprano

Stolen Moments (US 1920)* with Rudolph Valentino

Gypsy Blood (GB 1931) with Thomas Burke, Lance Fairfax. Dir: Cecil Lewis

Thirty Day Princess (US 1934)* with Cary Grant, Sylvia Sidney

Peter Ibbetson (US 1935)* with Gary Cooper. Dir: Henry Hathaway

NERI, Giulio (1909-1958) Italian bass

Rigoletto (It 1947) with Tito Gobbi

Casa Ricordi (It 1954) with Gobbi, Marcello Mastroianni Dir: Carmine Gallone

The Barber of Seville (It 1956) with Gobbi. Dir: Camillo Mastrocinque

NESTERENKO, Yvgeny (1938–) Russian bass

Aleko (USSR 1989). Dir: Victor Okunzov. TV film

NILSSON, Birgit (1918–) Swedish soprano

Turandot (It 1969) with Gianfranco Cecchele. Dir: Margarita Wallman. TV film

NOVOTNÁ, Jarmila (1907-1994) Czech soprano

Novotná made films in Prague while still a teenager. Below are those she made after arriving in Germany.

Brand in der Oper/Barcarolle (Ger 1930). Dir: Carl Froelich/Henry Roussell

Der Bettelstudent (Ger 1931) with Hans Heinz Bollmann. Dir: Viktor Janson; *The Beggar Student*, made simultaneously with Lance Fairfax. Dir: Victor Hansbury

Die verkaufte Braut (Ger 1932) with Willi Domgraf-Fassbänder. Dir: Max Ophuls

Die Nacht der grossen Lieben (Ger 1933) with Gustav Frölich. Dir: Geza von Bolvary

Frasquita (Aus 1934) with Bollmann. Dir: Carl Lemac

Der Kosak und die Nachtigall (Ger 1935) with Ivan Petrovich. Dir: Phil Jutzi

The Last Waltz/La Dernière Valse (Fr-GB 1936) with Harry Welchman. Dir: Gerald Barry; French version. Dir: Leo Mittler

Song of the Lark (Cz 1937) with Adolf Horalek

The Search (US 1948)* with Montgomery Clift. Dir: Fred Zinnemann

The Great Caruso (US 1951)* with Mario Lanza

NUCCI, Leo (1942–) Italian baritone

Macbeth (Fr 1987) with Shirley Verrett. Dir: Claude D'Anna

OBRAZTSOVA, Elena (1937–) Russian mezzo
Cavalleria Rusticana (It 1982) with Plácido Domingo. Dir: Franco Zeffirelli
OLIVERO, Magda (1912–) Italian soprano
Tosca (It 1960) with Alvinio Misciano, Giulio Fioravanti. TV film
O'NEILL, Dennis (1948–) Welsh tenor
Adelina Patti, Queen of Song (GB 1993) with June Anderson. Dir: Chris Hunt
PAGLIUGHI, Lina (1907-1980) Italian soprano
Rigoletto (Ger 1931) with Carlo Galeffi, Primo Montanari, Maria Castagna-Fullin
PAINTER, Eleanor (1886-1947) American soprano
Eleanor Painter, The Lyric Soprano (US 1929) Vitaphone short
PASERO, Tancredi (1892-1983) Italian bass
Rossini (It 1943). Dir: Mario Bonnard
PASINI, Laura (1894-1942) Italian soprano
Pergolesi (It 1932) with Vincenzo Bettoni. Dir: Guido Brigone
La Cantante dell'Opera (It 1932) with Alessio De Paolis. Dir: Nunzio Malasomma
PAVAROTTI, Luciano (1935–) Italian tenor
Yes, Giorgio (US 1982) with Kathryn Harrold, Eddie Albert, Paolo Borboni. Dir: Franklin J. Schaffner
Rigoletto (Ger 1983) with Edita Gruberova, Ingvar Wixell. Dir: Jean-Pierre Ponnelle
PEDERZINI, Gianna (1900-1988) Italian mezzo
Rossini (It 1943). Dir: Mario Bonnard
Il Trovatore (It 1949) with Gino Sinimberghi, Enzo Mascherini. Dir: Carmine Gallone
PEERCE, Jan (1904-1984) American tenor
Keep 'Em Rolling (US 1943)
Hymn of Nations (US 1946). Dir: Alexander Hammid
Something in the Wind (US 1947) with Deanna Durbin, Donald O'Connor
Of Men and Music (US 1950) with Nadine Conner. Dir: Irving Reis
Tonight We Sing (US 1953) with David Wayne, Anne Bancroft, Ezio Pinza, Roberta Peters, Tamara Toumanova, Isaac Stern. Dir: Mitchell Leisen
Goodbye, Columbus (US 1969)* with Richard Benjamin, Ali MacGraw. Dir: Larry Peerce, Jan's son
PERNET, André (1894-1996) French bass
Louise (Fr 1939) with Grace Moore, Georges Thill. Dir: Abel Gance
PETERS, Roberta (1930–) American soprano
Tonight We Sing (US 1953 109 mins) with David Wayne, Anne Bancroft, Ezio Pinza, Tamara Toumanova, Isaac Stern, Jan Peerce. Dir: Mitchell Leisen
PICCAVER, Alfred (1884-1958) English tenor
Abenteuer a Lido (Aus 1933) with Nora Gregor, Szoke Szakall
It would appear Piccaver made another film in 1932, now lost
PINZA, Ezio (1892-1957) Italian bass
Carnegie Hall (US 1947) with Risë Stevens, Lily Pons. Dir: Edgar G. Ulmer
Mr Imperium (US 1951) with Lana Turner. Dir: Don Hartman
Strictly Dishonourable (US 1951) with Janet Leigh. Dir: Melvin Frank and Norman Panama
Tonight We Sing (US 1953) with David Wayne, Anne Bancroft, Roberta Peters, Jan Peerce. Dir: Mitchell Leisen
PIROGOV, Alexander (1899-1964) Russian bass
Appeared in Russian feature (1949) singing Serenade from *Faust*.
Bolshoi Koncert (USSR 1951). Dir: Vera Stroyeva
Boris Godunov (USSR 1954). Dir: Vera Stroyeva

PONS, Juan (1946–) Spanish baritone
Pagliacci (It 1982) with Plácido Domingo, Teresa Stratas. Dir: Franco Zeffirelli
PONS, Lily (1898-1976) French soprano
I Dream Too Much (US 1935) with Henry Fonda, Osgood Perkins, Lucille Ball. Dir: John Cromwell
That Girl From Paris (US 1936) with Gene Raymond, Jack Oakie, Herman Bing, Lucille Ball. Dir: Leigh Jason
Hitting a New High (US 1937). Dir: Raoul Walsh
Carnegie Hall (US 1947) with Ezio Pinza, Risë Stevens
PONSELLE, Rosa (1897-1981) American soprano
Carmen (US 1936) screen tests – she didn't get the part
POPP, Lucia (1939-1993) Czech-Austrian soprano
The Merry Wives of Windsor (Aus 1965) with Norman Foster. Dir: George Tressler
Fidelio (Ger 1968) with Hans Sotin, Theo Adam, Anja Silja. Dir: Joachim Hess. TV film
Zar und Zimmermann (Ger 1969) with Raymond Wolansky. Dir: Joachim Hess. TV film
Zar und Zimmermann (Ger 1976) with Hermann Prey, Karl Riddersbusch. Dir: Axel Corti. TV film
Carmina Burana (Ger 1976) with Hermann Prey. Dir: Jean-Pierre Ponnelle
POWERS, Marie (1910-1973) American contralto
Give Us Our Dream (US 1950). TV drama
The Medium (US-It 1951). Dir: Gian Carlo Menotti and Alexander Hammid
PREY, Hermann (1929-1999) German baritone
Cosi Fan Tutte (Ger 1970) with Luigi Alva, Gundala Janowitz, Christa Ludwig. Dir: Vaclav Kaslik
Eugene Onegin (Ger 1971) with Teresa Stratas, Julia Hamari. TV film
Don Pasquale (Ger 1972) with Reri Grist, Luigi Alva. Dir: Axel Corti. TV film
The Barber of Seville (Ger 1972) with Luigi Alva, Teresa Berganza, Enzo Dara. Dir: Jean-Pierre Ponnelle
The Marriage of Figaro (Ger 1976) with Mirella Freni, Kiri Te Kanawa. Dir: Ponnelle
Zar und Zimmermann (Ger 1976) with Lucia Popp, Karl Riddersbusch. Dir: Axel Corti. TV film
Carmina Burana (Ger 1976) with Lucia Popp. Dir: Jean-Pierre Ponnelle
Hansel and Gretel (Aus 1981) with Brigitte Fassbaender, Edita Gruberova, Sena Jurinac. Dir: August Everding
RAIMONDI, Ruggero (1941–) Italian bass-baritone
Don Giovanni (Fr-It 1978). Dir: Joseph Losey
Carmen (Fr-It 1980) with Plácido Domingo, Julia Migenes. Dir: Francesco Rosi
Boris Godunov (Pol 1989). Dir: Andrzej Zulawski
RAISA, Rosa (1893-1963) Polish-American soprano
Three Vitaphone sound shorts (US 1927-1928)
REIZEN, Mark (1895-1992) Russian bass
Bolshoi Koncert (USSR 1951). Dir: Vera Stroyeva
Aleko (USSR 1954). Dir: Grigory Roshal/Serge Sidelaw
Khovanshchina (USSR 1959). Dir: Vera Stroyeva
RICCIARELLI, Katia (1946–) Italian soprano
Otello (It 1986) with Plácido Domingo, Justino Diaz. Dir: Franco Zeffirelli
RIEGEL, Kenneth (1938–) American tenor
Don Giovanni (Fr 1978) with Ruggero Raimondi, Kiri Te Kanawa, Edda Moser. Dir: Joseph Losey
Boris Godunov (Pol 1989) with Ruggero Raimondi. Dir: Andrzej Zulawski

RIMINI, Giacomo (1887-1952) Italian baritone
  Il Trovatore (US 1927) Vitaphone short with his wife Rosa Raisa
RITCHIE, Margaret (1903-1969) English soprano
  Pink String and Sealing Wax (GB 1945) with Googie Withers. Dir: Robert Hamer
ROSWAENGE, Helge (1897-1972) Danish tenor
  Martha or The Last Rose (Ger 1936). Dir: Karl Anton
ROTHENBERGER, Annelise (1924-) German soprano
  Der Rosenkavalier (GB 1960) with Elizabeth Schwarzkopf. Dir: Paul Czinner
  Die Entführung aus dem Serail (Ger 1962) with Peter Pasetti, Judith Blegen, Werner
    Krenn, Oscar Czerwenka. Dir: Heinz Liesendahl. TV film
  Oh Rosalinda! (GB 1964). Dir: Michael Powell
ROUND, Thomas (1918-) English tenor
  The Mikado (GB 1974) with Donald Adams, Valerie Masterson, John Cartier, Helen
    Landis. Dir: Trevor Evans
  The Pirates of Penzance (GB 1974) with Adams, Masterson, Landis. Dir: Evans
  The Yeoman of the Guard (GB 1974) with Adams, Masterson, Cartier, Landis. Dir:
    Evans
  Trial By Jury (GB 1974) with Gillian Humphreys, Michael Wakeham. Dir: Evans
  HMS Pinafore (GB 1974) with Cartier, Masterson, Adams, Landis. Dir: Evans
  Ruddigore (GB 1974) with Cartier, Humphreys, Landis, Ann Hood, Adams. Dir:
    Evans
  The Gondoliers (GB 1974) with Adams, Humphreys, Landis, Hood. Dir: Evans
  Iolanthe (GB 1974) with Adams, Landis. Dir: Evans
ROUNSEVILLE, Robert (1914-1971) American tenor
  The Tales of Hoffmann (GB 1951). Dir: Michael Powell
  Carousel (US 1956) with Claramae Turner. Dir: Henry King
RUFFO, Tito (1877-1953) Italian baritone
  Three sound shorts for MGM (US 1929/30)
RUSSELL, Lillian (1861-1922) American soprano
  Lillian Russell (US 1906)* 2 mins. Dir: F.A. Dobson
  Wildfire (US 1915)* with Lionel Barrymore, Glen Moore. Dir: Edward Middleton
SACK, Erna (1898-1972) German soprano
  Blumen aus Nizza (Ger 1936). Dir: Augusto Genina
  Nanon (Ger 1938). Dir: Herbert Maisch
SCHEFF, Fritzi (1879-1954) American soprano
  Pretty Mrs Smith (US 1915)*. Dir: Hobart Bosworth
SCHIPA, Tito (1889?-1965) Italian tenor
  Two shorts made for Paramount (1929/30)
  Tre Uomini in frac (It 1932). Dir: Mario Bonnard. English version: *I Sing For You
    Alone*; French: *Trois Hommes en Habit*
  Vivere (It 1937) with Caterina Borrato. Dir: Guido Brignone
  Chi e piu felice di me! (It 1937) with Borrato. Dir: Guido Brignone
  Terra di Fuoco/Terre de Feu (It 1938)
  In Cerca di Felicità (It 1943). Dir: Giacomo Gentilomo
  Rosalba (It 1944)
  Vivere Ancora (It 1944)
  Il Cavalieri del Sogna (It 1946) with Amedeo Nazzari. Dir: Camillo Mastrocinque
  Follie per l'Opera (It 1948). Dir: Mario Costa
  Una Voce nel tuo Core (It 1950) with Gigli, Bechi. Dir: Alberto D'Aversa
  I Misteri di Venezia (It 1951)
  Soho Conspiracy (GB 1951) remake of *Follie per l'Opera*

SCHMIDT, Josef (1904-1942) Romanian tenor
Der Liebesexpress (Ger 1931). Dir: Robert Wiene
Gehetzte Menschen (Ger 1932). Dir: Friedrich Feher
Ein Lied geht um die Welt/My Song Goes Around the World (Ger 1933). Dir: Richard
   Oswald
A Star Fell From Heaven/Ein Stern fellt von Himmel (GB/Aus 1936)
SCHMIDT, Trudeliese (1934–) German mezzo
One Night in Venice (Ger 1973) with Julia Migenes. Dir: Václav Kaslík. TV film
Orfeo (Ger 1978). Dir: Jean-Pierre Ponnelle
L'Incoronazione di Poppea (Ger 1979). Dir: Jean-Pierre Ponnelle
Il Ritorno d'Ulisse in Patria (1980). Dir: Jean-Pierre Ponnelle
Mignon (Ger 1982). TV film
SCHOCK, Rudolf (1915-1986) German tenor
Du bist die Welt für mich (Aus 1953). Dir: Ernst Marischka
Schön ist die Welt (Ger 1954) with Renate Holm. Dir: Geza von Bolvary
Der fröhliche Wanderer (Ger 1955)
Die Stimme der Sehnsucht (Ger 1956)
Die Csárdáskönig (Ger 1958). Biopic of Kalman
Countess Maritza (Ger 1958)
Das Dreimaderlhaus (Ger 1958). Dir: Marischka
Die Zirkusprinzessin (Ger 1969) with Ingebord Hallstein
Giuditta (Ger 1970) with Teresa Stratas. Dir: Gunther Hassert
SCHUMANN-HEINK, Ernestine (1861-1936) Czech, later American, contralto
Three Vitaphone sound films (US 1927)
Here's to Romance (US 1935) with Nino Martini. Dir: Alfred E. Green
SCHWARZKOPF, Elisabeth (1915–) German soprano
Die Drei Unteroffizieren (Ger 1939). Dir: Werner Hochbaum
Nacht ohne Abschied (Ger 1943) with Peter Anders. Dir: Erich Waschneck
Der Verteidiger hat das Wort (Ger 1944). Dir: Werner Klingler
Der Rosenkavalier (GB 1960). Dir: Paul Czinner
SEGUROLA, Andrès de (1875-1953) Spanish Bass
The Love of Sunya (US 1927)* with Gloria Swanson. Dir: Albert Parker
Glorious Betsy (US 1928) with Dolores Costello, Pasquale Amato
Song O' My Heart (US 1930) with John McCormack
Their Mad Moment (US 1931) with José Mohica
El Caballero de la Noche (US 1932) with Mohica
Un Capitan de Cosacos (US 1934) with Mohica
One Night of Love (US 1934) with Grace Moore
Public Opinion (US 1935) with Lois Wilson. Dir: Frank Strayer
SIEPI, Cesare (1923–) Italian bass
Don Giovanni (Ger 1954). Dir: Paul Czinner
SILLS, Beverley (1929–) American soprano
Uncle Sol Solves It (US 1936)
La Traviata (US 1954) with John Druary, Frank Valentino. TV film
SINCLAIR, Monica (1926–) English mezzo
Daughter of the Regiment (Can-GB 1972) with Joan Sutherland, Ramon Remedios,
   Spiro Milas. Dir: Ted Kotcheff. TV series, 'Who's Afraid of Opera?'
La Périchole (Can-GB 1972) with Sutherland, Pieter van der Stolk, Francis Egerton,
   John Fryatt. Dir: Piers Haggard. TV series, 'Who's Afraid of Opera?'
La Traviata (Can-GB 1973) with Sutherland, Ian Caley. Dir: Kotcheff. TV series,
   'Who's Afraid of Opera?'

SINIMBERGHI, Gino (1913–) Italian tenor
 Davanti a lui Tremava Tutta Roma (It 1946) with Tito Gobbi, Anna Mascagni. Dir:
  Carmine Gallone
 L'Elisir d'Amore (It 1947) with Gobbi, Nelly Corradi, Italo Tajo. Dir: Mario Costa
 La Forza del Destino (It 1949) with Gobbi. Dir: Gallone (Sinimberghi was dubbed
  by Galliano Masini)
 Puccini (It 1952) with Nelly Corradi. Dir: Gallone
 La Favorita (It 1952) with Sophia Loren. His voice was dubbed by Piero Sardelli
 La Donna piu Bella del Mondo (It 1955) with Gina Lollobrigida. His voice dubbed
  by Mario del Monaco
SLEZAK, Leo (1873-1946) Austrian tenor
 appeared in 44 films after his retirement from operatic stage, including:
 Die Frauendiplomat (Ger 1932) with Marta Eggerth
 Grand Duchess Alexandra (Aus 1933) with Maria Jeritza
 Rendezvous in Wien (Aus 1934). Dir: Viktor Janson
 G'schichten aus dem Wienerwald (Aus 1934) with Magda Schneider, Georg
  Alexander. Dir: Georg Jacoby
 Die Lustigen Weiber (Ger 1935). Dir: Carl Hoffmann
 Liebesmelodie (Aus 1935) with Eggerth. Dir: Viktor Tourjansky
 Die Blonde Carmen (Ger 1935) with Eggerth. Dir: Janson
 Die ganze Welt dreht sich um Liebe (Aus 1935) with Eggerth, Rolf Wanka. Dir:
  Tourjansky
 Die Frauenparadies (Aus 1936). Dir: Arthur Maria Rabenalt
 Liebe im Dreivierteltak (Aus 1937). Dir: Hubert Marischka
 Gasparone (Aus 1937) with Marika Rokk. Dir: Georg Jacoby
 Die vier Gesellen (Ger 1937) with Ingrid Bergman
 Rosen in Tirol (Ger 1940) with Marte Harell. Dir: Geza von Bolvary
 Operette (Ger 1940) with Willi Forst, Curt Jurgens. Dir: Forst
 Baron Münchhausen (Ger 1943). Dir: Josef von Baky
SOBINOV, Leonard (1872-1934) Russian tenor
 Peter the Great (Rus 1918?)
SÖDERSTRÖM, Elisabeth (1927–) Swedish soprano
 Den Svenske Ryttaren (Sw 1947)*
SOTIN, Hans (1939–) German bass
 Wozzeck (Ger 1967) with Toni Blankenheim, Sena Jurinac, Richard Cassilly. Dir:
  Joachim Hess
 Fidelio (Ger 1968) with Anja Silja, Lucia Popp, Theo Adam. Dir: Joachim Hess
 Der Freischütz (Ger 1968) with Ernst Kozub, Arlene Saunders, Tom Krause. Dir:
  Joachim Hess
 Zar und Zimmermann (Ger 1969) with Raymond Wolansky, Lucia Popp. Dir:
  Joachim Hess
 Elektra (Ger 1969) with Gladys Kuchta, Regina Resnik
 The Magic Flute (Ger 1971) with Nicolai Gedda, William Workman, Edith Mathis.
  Dir: Joachim Hess
STABILE, Mariano (1888-1968) Italian baritone
 Rossini (It 1943). Dir: Mario Bonnard
STEVENS, Risë (1913–) American mezzo
 The Chocolate Soldier (US 1941) with Nelson Eddy. Dir: Roy del Ruth
 Going My Way (US 1944) with Bing Crosby. Dir: Leo McCarey
 Carnegie Hall (US 1947) with Lily Pons, Ezio Pinza
STRATAS, Teresa (1938–) Canadian/Greek soprano

The Canadians (Canada/GB 1960)* with Robert Ryan. Dir: Burt Kennedy
La Rondine (Can 1970) with Cornelius Opthof. TV film
Giudetta (Ger 1970) with Rudolf Schock. TV film
Eugene Onegin (Ger 1971) with Hermann Prey. Dir: Václav Káslik/Gerhard Reutter. TV film
Paganini (Ger 1972) with Antonio Theba. Dir: Eugen York. TV film
Der Zarewitsch (Ger 1973). Dir: Arthur Maria Rabenalt. TV film
Salome (Ger 1974) with Bernd Weikl, Astrid Varnay. Dir: Gotz Friedrich. TV film
The Bartered Bride (Ger 1975) with Rene Kollo, Walter Berry. TV film
Amahl and the Night Visitors (US 1979) with Willard White, Giorgio Tozzi
Pagliacci (It 1982) with Plácido Domingo, Juan Pons. Dir: Franco Zeffirelli
La Traviata (It 1982) with Domingo. Dir: Zeffirelli
Cosi Fan Tutte (Ger 1988). Dir: Jean-Pierre Ponnelle
SUPERVIA, Conchita (1895-1936) Spanish mezzo
Evensong (GB 1934) with Evelyn Laye, Alice Delysia, Emlyn Williams, Browning Mummery. Dir: Victor Saville
SUTHERLAND, Joan (1926–) Australian soprano
Daughter of the Regiment (Can-GB 1972) with Ramon Remedios, Monica Sinclair, Spiro Milas. Dir: Ted Kotcheff. TV series, 'Who's Afraid of Opera?'
La Périchole (Can-GB 1972) with Pieter van der Stolk, Francis Egerton, John Fryatt, Sinclair. Dir: Piers Haggard. TV series, 'Who's Afraid of Opera?'
The Barber of Seville (Can-GB 1972) with Remedios, Tom McDonnell, Milas, Clifford Grant. Dir: Kotcheff. TV series, 'Who's Afraid of Opera?'
Rigoletto (Can-GB 1973) with Andre Turp, van der Stolk, Huguette Turangeau. Dir: Herbert Wise. TV series, 'Who's Afraid of Opera?'
La Traviata (Can-GB 1973) with Ian Caley, Sinclair. Dir: Kotcheff. TV series, 'Who's Afraid of Opera?'
Mignon (Can-GB 1973) with Turangeau, Caley, van der Stolk. Dir: Wise. TV series, 'Who's Afraid of Opera?'
Faust (Can-GB 1973) with Caley, van der Stolk. Margreta Elkins. Dir: Kotcheff. TV series, 'Who's Afraid of Opera?'
On Our Selection (Australia 1995)* with Leo McKern. Dir: George Whaley
SWARTHOUT, Gladys (1904-1969) American mezzo
Rose of the Rancho (US 1935) with John Boles. Dir: Marion Gering
Give Us This Night (US 1936) with Jan Kiepura. Dir: Alexander Hall
Champagne Waltz (US 1937) with Fred MacMurray
Romance in the Dark (US 1938) with John Boles. Dir: H.C. Potter
Ambush (US 1938)* with Lloyd Nolan
SYLVA, Marguerita (1875-1957) Belgian/American soprano
Carmen (It 1916) with Andre Habay
The Honey Bee (US 1920)*. Dir: Rupert Julian
The Seventh Victim (US 1943)*. Dir: Mark Robson
The Gay Senorita (US 1946). Dir: Arthur Dreifuss
TADDEI, Giuseppe (1916–) Italian baritone
Andrea Chénier (It 1955) with Mario del Monaco. Dir: Mario Landi. TV film
TAGLIAVINI, Ferruccio (1913-1995) Italian tenor
Voglio Vivere Cosi (It 1941). Dir: Mario Mattoli
La Donna e Mobile (It 1942). Dir: Mattoli
Ho Tanta Voglia di Cantare! (It 1944). Dir: Mario Monicelli
The Barber of Seville (It 1946) with Tito Gobbi. Dir: Mario Costa
Al Diavolo la Celebrità (It 1949). Dir: Monicelli

I Cadetti di Guascogna (It 1950) with Ugo Tognazzi. Dir: Mattoli

Anema e Core (It 1951) Dir: Mattoli

Vento di Primavera/Vergiss mein nicht (Ger-It 1959). Dir: Giulio del Torre (Italian version); Arthur Maria Rabenalt (German version)

TAJO, Italo (1915-1993) Italian bass-baritone

The Barber of Seville (It 1946) with Tito Gobbi. Dir: Mario Costa

Lucia di Lammermoor (It 1946) with Nelly Corradi, Mario Filippeschi. Dir: Piero Ballerini

L'Elisir d'Amore (It 1947) with Tito Gobbi. Dir: Costa

Faust (It 1949) with Gina Mattera. Dir: Carmine Gallone

Casa Ricordi (It 1954). Dir: Gallone

Don Pasquale (It 1955) with Sesto Bruscantini. TV film

TALLEY, Marion (1907-1983) American soprano

Three Vitaphone shorts (US 1926/27)

Follow Your Heart (US 1936) with Luis Alberni, Michael Bartlett. Dir: Aubrey Scotto

TAPPY, Eric (1931–) Swiss tenor

L'Incoronazione di Poppea (Ger 1979) with Rachael Yakar, Paul Esswood, Matti Salminen. Dir: Jean-Pierre Ponnelle

La Clemenza di Tito (Ger 1980) with Catherine Malfitano, Tatiana Troyanos, Carol Neblett. Dir: Jean-Pierre Ponnelle

Orfeo (Swiss 1985) with Gino Quilico. Dir: Claude Goretta

TAUBER, Richard (1892-1948) Austrian tenor

Achtung! Aufname! (Ger 1923)

Ich glaub' nie mehr an eine Frau (*Das Dirnenlied*)(Ger 1930) with Maria Solveig

Das Land des Lächlens (Ger 1930) with Mary Losseff. Dir: Max Reichmann

Die grosse Attraktion (Ger 1931). Dir: Max Reichmann

Melodie der Liebe (Ger 1932). Dir: George Jacoby

Das Lockende Zeil/The End of the Rainbow (Ger 1933) with Lucie Englisch. Dir: Reichmann

Wie werde ich reich und glücklich (Ger 1933). Dir: Paul Stein

Blossom Time (GB 1934) with Jane Baxter, Carl Esmond, Athene Sayler. Dir: Stein.

Heart's Desire (GB 1935) with Diana Napier, Leonora Corbett. Dir: Stein

Land Without Music (GB 1935) with Diana Napier, Jimmy Durante. Dir: Walter Forde

Pagliacci (GB 1936) with Steffi Duna. Dir: Karl Grune

Waltz Time (GB 1945) with Anne Ziegler, Webster Booth, Patricia Medina, Peter Graves. Dir: Stein

The Lisbon Story (GB 1946) with Patricia Burke, David Farrar. Dir: Stein

TEBALDI, Renata (1922–) Italian soprano

Casa Ricordi (It 1954) with Marcello Mastroianni, Tito Gobbi, Mario del Monaco. Dir: Carmine Gallone

TE KANAWA, Kiri (1944–) New Zealand soprano

Don't Let It Get to You (NZ 1966). Dir: John O'Shea

The Marriage of Figaro (Ger 1976) with Hermann Prey, Mirella Freni, Dietrich Fischer-Dieskau. Dir: Jean-Pierre Ponnelle

Don Giovanni (Fr 1978). Dir: Joseph Losey

TETRAZZINI, Luisa (1871-1940) Italian soprano

Roméo et Juliette (Ger 1909). Early sound film, now lost

THEBOM, Blanche (1918–) American mezzo

Irish Eyes are Smiling (US 1944) with Leonard Warren, Dick Haymes

The Great Caruso (US 1951) with Mario Lanza

THILL, Georges (1897-1984) French tenor
Louise (US-Fr 1939) with Grace Moore. Dir: Abel Gance
THOMAS, John Charles (1887-1960) American tenor
Under the Red Robe (US 1923)*. Dir: Alan Crosland
Three Vitaphone shorts (US 1927)
TIBBETT, Lawrence (1896-1960) American baritone
The Rogue Song (US 1930) with Catherine Dale Owen, Laurel and Hardy. Dir:
Lionel Barrymore
New Moon (US 1930) with Grace Moore. Dir: Jack Conway
The Prodigal/The Southerner (US 1931) with Esther Ralston, Roland Young, Cliff
Edwards, Hedda Hopper. Dir: Harry Pollard
Cuban Love Song (US 1932) with Lupe Velez, Ernest Torrence, Jimmy Durante. Dir:
W.S. Van Dyke
Metropolitan (US 1935) with Virginia Bruce, Alice Brady, Cesar Romero. Dir:
Richard Boleslawski
Under Your Spell (US 1937). Dir: Otto Preminger
TROXELL, Richard American tenor
Madame Butterfly (Fr 1995) with Ying Huang, Ning Liang, Richard Cowan. Dir:
Frédéric Mitterand
TOZZI, Giorgio (1923–) American bass
Die Meistersinger (Ger 1969) with Arlene Saunders, Richard Cassilly. Dir: Leopold
Lintberg. TV film
Shamus (US 1973)* with Burt Reynolds
One of Your Own (US 1975)* with George Peppard
Amahl and the Night Visitors (US-Isr 1978) with Teresa Stratas
Torn Between Two Lovers (US 1979)* with George Peppard. TV film
TRAUBEL, Helen (1899-1972) American soprano
Deep in My Heart (1954) with Merle Oberon and José Ferrer
The Ladies' Man (US 1961)* with Jerry Lewis
Gunn (US 1967)*. Dir: Blake Edwards
TROYANOS, Tatiana (1938-1993) American mezzo
The Devils of Loudun (Ger 1969). Dir: Joachim Hess. TV film
Oedipus Rex (US 1973) with René Kollo, Tom Krause
La Clemenza di Tito (Ger 1980) with Catherine Malfitano. Dir: Jean-Pierre Ponnelle
TURNER, Claramae (1920–) American contralto
Carousel (US 1956) with Robert Rounseville
VALDENGO, Guiseppe (1914–) Italian baritone
The Great Caruso (1951) with Mario Lanza
VAN DAM, José (1940–) Belgian bass-baritone
Otello (Ger 1974) with Jon Vickers, Mirella Freni. Dir: Roger Benamou
Don Giovanni (Fr 1978). Dir: Joseph Losey
The Music Teacher (Belg 1989). Dir: Gerard Corbiau
VARNAY, Astrid (1918–) Swedish soprano/mezzo
Salome (Ger 1974) with Teresa Stratas, Bernd Weikl. Dir: Götz Friedrich
Elektra (Aus 1981) with Dietrich Fischer-Dieskau, Leonie Rysanek
VERRETT, Shirley (1931–) American soprano
Macbeth (Fr 1987) with Leo Nucci. Dir: Claude D'Anna
Maggio Musicale (It 1990) with Chris Merritt, Malcolm McDowell
VICKERS, Jon (1926–) Canadian tenor
Carmen (Ger 1966) with Grace Bumbry. Dir: Herbert von Karajan
Pagliacci (Ger 1968) with Raina Kabaivanska, Peter Glossop. Dir: Karajan

Otello (Ger 1974) with Mirella Freni, Glossop, José van Dam. Dir: Roger Benamou
Fidelio (Fr 1977) with Gundala Janowitz, Theo Adam. Dir: Pierre Jourdan
VISHNEVSKAYA, Galina (1926–) Russian soprano
Katerina Ismailova (USSR 1967). Dir: Mikhail Shapiro
VON STADE, Frederica (1945–) American mezzo
La Cenerentola (Ger 1981) with Francisco Araiza. Dir: Jean-Pierre Ponnelle
WALSKA, Ganne (1891-1984) Polish soprano
Child of Destiny (US 1916)*. Dir: William Nigh
WARREN, Leonard (1911-1960) American baritone
Irish Eyes are Smiling (US 1944) with Blanche Thebom
WELITSCH, Ljuba (1913-1996) Bulgarian soprano
Appeared in more than 75 films as a character actress after her retirement from opera.
The Man Between (GB 1953) with James Mason, Claire Bloom. Dir: Carol Reed
Final Resolution (Ger/It 1960) with Mario del Monaco
Adorable Julia (Fr/Aust 1961)* with Lilli Palmer, Charles Boyer
Arms and the Man (Ger 1962)* with Liselotte Pulver
Countess Maritza (Ger 1973) with René Kollo. TV film
WHITE, Willard (1946–) Jamaican bass
Amahl and the Night Visitors (US-Is 1979) with Teresa Stratas
Porgy and Bess (GB 1989). Dir: Trevor Nunn
WIXELL, Ingvar (1931–) Swedish baritone
Rigoletto (Ger 1983) with Luciano Pavarotti. Dir: Jean-Pierre Ponnelle

Select Bibliography

As well as consulting the books listed below, I have drawn on many sources including my own articles, interviews and reviews written for *Opera Now*, *BBC Music Magazine* and *Classical Music*. Video and record sleeves have provided useful information, as have magazines and newspapers. Of particular use have been the British Film Institute's *Monthly Film Bulletin* and programme booklets for the National Film Theatre, *Sight and Sound*, *Variety*, *Photoplay* and *Opera* magazine.

Alpert, H., *The Life and Times of Porgy and Bess* (Nick Hern Books 1990)
Bachmann, R., *Karajan: Notes on a Career* (Quartet 1990)
Bakshian Jr, A., *The Barbed Wire Waltz* (Robert Stolz Publishing Co. 1983)
Barrios, R., *A Song in the Dark* (OUP 1995)
Bassette, R.L., *Mario Lanza: Tenor in Exile* (Amadeus 1999)
Berg, A.S., *Goldwyn: A Biography* (Hamish Hamilton 1989)
Bergman, I., *Images: My Life in Film* (Bloomsbury 1994)
Björling, A. and Farkas, A., *Jussi* (Amadeus 1996)
Carreras, J: *Singing from the Soul* (Souvenir Press 1991)
Carroll, B.G., *The Last Prodigy* (Amadeus 1997)
Castanza, P., *The Films of Jeanette MacDonald and Nelson Eddy* (Citadel 1978)
Castle, C., *Noel* (W.H. Allen 1972)
Castle, C., *This Was Richard Tauber* (W.H. Allen 1971)
Daniels, O., *Stokowski: A Counterpoint of View* (New York 1982)
De Rham, E., *Joseph Losey* (Andre Deutsch 1991)
DeMille, C.B., *Autobiography* (W.H. Allen 1960)
Domingo, P., *My First Forty Years* (Wiedenfeld & Nicolson 1983)
Douglas, N., *Legendary Voices* (Andre Deutsch 1992)
Douglas, N., *More Legendary Voices* (Andre Deutsch 1994)
Douglas, N., *The Joy of Opera* (Andre Deutsch 1996)
Drew, D., *Kurt Weill, A Handbook* (Faber & Faber 1987)
Duchen, J: *Erich Wolfgang Korngold* (Phaidon 1996)
Eyman, S., *Ernst Lubitsch, Laughter in Paradise* (Simon & Schuster 1993)
Eyman, S., *The Speed of Sound* (Simon & Schuster 1997)
Farkas, A. (ed), *Lawrence Tibbett, Singing Actor* (Amadeus 1989)
Farrar, G., *Such Sweet Compulsion* (Greystone Press 1938)
Feuer, J., *The Hollywood Musical* (Indiana University Press 1982)
Freedland, M., *The Warner Brothers* (Harrap 1983)
Ganzl, K., *The Encyclopedia of the Musical Theatre* (Blackwell 1994)
Garden, M. and Biancolli, L., *Mary Garden's Story* (Simon and Schuster 1951)
Gifford, D., *The British Film Catalogue 1895-1970* (David & Charles 1973)
Gobbi, T., *My Life* (Macdonald and Jane's 1979)
Greene, G., *The Pleasure Dome* (Secker & Warburg 1972)
Halliwell, L., *Halliwell's Film Guide* (Grafton Books 1989)
Halliwell, L., *The Filmgoer's Companion* (HarperCollins 1995)
Harding, J., *Ivor Novello* (W.H. Allen 1987)

Select Bibliography

Higham, C., *Cecil B.DeMille* (Dell 1976)

Holden, A. (ed), *The Viking Opera Guide* (Viking 1993)

Hughes, S., *Glyndebourne* (David and Charles 1981)

Jackson, P., *Saturday Afternoons at the Old Met* (Duckworth/Amadeus 1992)

Jefferson, A., *Elisabeth Schwarzkopf* (Gollancz 1996)

Jefferson, A., *Lotte Lehmann* (Julia MacRae 1988)

Korda, M., *Charmed Lives: A Family Romance* (Allen Lane 1980)

Larkin, C. (ed), *The Guinness Who's Who of Film Musicals* (Guinness 1994)

Leamer, L., *As Time Goes By* (Hamish Hamilton 1986)

Macdonald, K., *Emeric Pressburger: The Life and Death of a Screenwriter* (Faber & Faber 1994)

Mannering, D., *Mario Lanza* (Robert Hale 1991)

McNab G., *J. Arthur Rank and the British Film Industry* (Routledge 1993)

Moore, G., *You're Only Human Once* (Garden City Publishing Co 1944)

Norman, B., *Talking Pictures* (BBC Books/Hodder & Stoughton 1987)

Nowell-Smith, G.(ed), *The Oxford History of World Cinema* (OUP 1996)

Oliver, R.W., *Ingmar Bergman: An Artist's Journey - on stage, on screen, in print* (Arcade 1995)

Orrey, L. (ed), *The Encyclopedia of Opera* (Pitman 1976)

Pasternak, J., *Easy the Hard Way* (W.H. Allen 1956)

Pavarotti, L. and Wright, W., *My World* (Chatto & Windus 1995)

Perry, G., *The Great British Picture Show* (Pavilion 1974)

Phelan, N., *Charles Mackerras: A Musician's Musician* (Gollancz 1987)

Ponzi, M., *The Films of Gina Lollobrigida* (Citadel 1992)

Powell, M., *A Life in the Movies* (Heinemann 1986)

Powell, M., *Million Dollar Movie* (Random House 1992)

Pullen, R. and Taylor, S., *Montserrat Caballé* (Gollancz 1994)

Ringgold, G. and Bodeen, D., *The Complete Films of Cecil B.DeMille* (Citadel 1969)

Rodgers, R., *Musical Stages* (W.H. Allen 1976)

Sadie, S. (ed)., *New Grove Dictionary of Opera* (Macmillan 1992)

Salkeld, A., *A Portrait of Leni Riefenstahl* (Jonathan Cape 1996)

Salter, L., 'The Birth of TV Opera', *Opera*, March 1977

Salter, L., 'The Infancy of TV Opera', *Opera*, April 1977

Schnauber, C., *Placido Domingo* (Robson 1997)

Scott, M., *The Great Caruso* (Hamish Hamilton 1988)

Shipman, D., *The Great Movie Stars: The Golden Years* (Hamlyn 1970)

Shipman, D., *The Great Movie Stars: The Silver Years* (Angus & Robertson 1972)

Shipman, D., *The Story of Cinema*, Vol. 1 (Hodder & Stoughton 1982)

Shipman. D., *The Story of Cinema*, Vol. 2 (Hodder & Stoughton 1984)

Sills, B. and Linderman, L., *Beverly: An Autobiography* (Bantam 1987)

Sklar, R., *Film: An International History of the Medium* (Thames & Hudson 1993)

Steane, J., *Singers of the Century* (Duckworth 1996)

Tambling, J. (ed), *A Night In at the Opera* (John Libbey 1994)

Tauber, D.N., *My Heart and I* (Evans 1959)

Taylor, R., *Kurt Weill, Composer in a Divided World* (Simon & Schuster 1991)

Thomas, T., *The Complete Films of Henry Fonda* (Citadel 1983)

Tuggle, R., *The Golden Age of Opera* (Holt, Rinehart & Winston 1983)

Turing, P., *Hans Hotter: Man and Artist* (John Calder 1983)

Vincendeau, G. (ed), *Encyclopedia of European Cinema* (Cassell/BFI 1995)

Wlaschin, K., *Opera on Screen* (Beachwood Press 1997)

Zeffirelli, F., *The Autobiography* (Wiedenfeld & Nicolson 1986)

Index

This index includes all those people mentioned in the text, although composers appear only when featured as themselves. The operas listed do not include stage productions but only those that have been filmed or provided arias for films, and, as with most film titles, are generally given in English.

Index

241

Index

Index